CAMBRIDGE LATIN AMERICAN STUDIES

EDITORS

MALCOLM DEAS   CLIFFORD T. SMITH
JOHN STREET

21

Chilean Rural Society
from the Spanish Conquest to 1930

THE SERIES

Chilean Rural Society
from the Spanish Conquest to 1930

ARNOLD J. BAUER

Department of History, University of California, Davis

CAMBRIDGE UNIVERSITY PRESS

Cambridge

London · New York · Melbourne

Published by the Syndics of the Cambridge University Press
The Pitt Building, Trumpington Street, Cambridge CB2 1RP
Bentley House, 200 Euston Road, London NW1 2DB
32 East 57th Street, New York, NY 1002, USA
296 Beaconsfield Parade, Middle Park, Melbourne 3206, Australia

© Cambridge University Press 1975

Library of Congress Catalogue Card Number: 75-2724

ISBN: 0 521 20727 4

First published 1975

Composition by Linocomp Ltd, Marcham, Oxfordshire

Printed in the United States of America
by Vail-Ballou Press, Inc., Binghamton, N.Y.

. . . did you lift
stone upon stone on a groundwork of rags?

Pablo Neruda, *The Heights of Macchu-Picchu*

For
Alvaro Jara
and
my daughter
Rebecca

CONTENTS

TABLES

Tables

Tables

FIGURES

MAPS

PLATES

ACKNOWLEDGEMENTS

Several people in Chile kindly gave me advice and assistance. The most helpful were Silvia Hernández, Carlos Hurtado Ruiz-Tagle, and Gonzalo Izquierdo. To the staff of the Centro de Investigaciones de Historia Americana, University of Chile, and especially to Professors Alvaro Jara and Rolando Mellafe, I am grateful for hospitality and encouragement. Marcello Carmagnani, now of the University of Turin, took the time and interest to write over the past seven years long letters of suggestion and critique. Private papers and estate account books were generously lent by Professors Horacio Aránguiz Donoso and Javier González Echenique, don José Manuel Larraín Echeverría, don Antonio Tagle, and don Sergio de Toro, all of Santiago.

Professors William McGreevey and Thomas Wright, and Mr Arnold Kessler read the manuscript and suggested a number of salutary changes; Mr Thomas Meierding and Silvia Hernández made Map 1 in the Berkeley Geography Department; and Mr Brooks C. Sackett and Jorge Hidalgo helped with bibliography and quantitative material. Ilia Howard helped with the Index.

I am indebted to the Latin American Teaching Fellowship Program (LATF) and its directors, Mr William Barnes and Mr G. Glenn; the Chile–Californian *Convenio*, and especially to its Santiago coordinator, Mr T. E. Menzie; the Latin American Center at Berkeley, the Mabelle McLeod Lewis Memorial Fund and the University of California at Davis, for financial assistance.

PREFACE

To be understood is to be found out.
Oscar Wilde

It is never clear for whom this kind of book is written. 'For the professionals,' my professional friends say, arguing that it should be aimed, as studies about mating bees or a rare disease are, at seven or eight people in the world who are interested (or perhaps apprehensive) about what one has to say. Besides, unless they are eliminated through fulsome praise in the Acknowledgements, these are the same people who review the book. 'For the university student,' others say, for although one's colleagues may want to read it, they of course won't have time. But they will inevitably pass it on to their students who, not yet aware of the impossibly huge mountain of scholarly literature before them, may actually read a chapter or two. In my wildest reverie, I imagine two lively and inquisitive friends, one a printer, the other an architect, settling down with pipe and rug for a winter's evening of reading. Alas, my own rereading of the manuscript has jarred that fancy from my head. But I have tried, with the help of my editors, to make the book readable and to appeal not only to Latin Americanists but to others who may find in the experience of Chile a useful contrast in the larger pattern of modern history.

The main concern in this book is the response made by Chileans to the onrush of liberal capitalism in the years after 1860. During that time many parts of the world were pulled into the orbit of the North Atlantic economy. Some regions or states remained on the periphery and were barely touched; others – the Amazon basin, Bolivia – were used up and discarded; still others such as the United States locked step with Great Britain and Western Europe and moved on to the affluence and horror of industrial society. When one takes such a broad and perhaps cavalier view of historical experience in the West over the past century, it is apparent that different regions involved in the Atlantic economy were changing at different rates; moreover, when we look more closely, it turns out that change was often in opposite directions.

In England and Western Europe, economic development was accompanied by a shift of population and political power to the cities. Greater markets and intense competition led to effective and more diversified agriculture. In the United States, the industrial North crushed the agrarian society of the South; and in the new lands of the Great Plains, in Canada and Australia, where there were no archaic farming practices to overcome, where the indigenous occupants could not be induced to work, agricultural expansion brought into existence wholly new rural societies, up to date from the start. The impact of Western economic expansion was also strongly felt in Chile: first through the European demand for grain and then through nitrates and copper. But because of the peculiar nature of Chilean society and the way the new wealth percolated through it, the resulting change was along very different lines from those we are familiar with in Western Europe or the former British colonies.

Not many people who write about Spanish America have been concerned with rural society in the nineteenth or earlier twentieth century. There are fine studies of the colonial era and a lot of work has appeared on the subject of recent agrarian reform and revolt. But even in Mexico, which has attracted hundreds of scholars and where the countryside has played such an important part in modern history, the nineteenth is a silent century when it comes to rural society. And just now a few studies, mainly by French scholars, are beginning to appear on Peru. In Chile there are the occasional accounts of individual estates, the insightful and experienced observations of Francisco Encina and Carlos Keller, two or three technical manuals on farming, and hagiological discussion of landowners. On either side of our period, two studies were done by foreigners: Claudio Gay's two volumes on agriculture in the 1830s and George McBride's book published in 1936. Both of these are better described as contemporary observation and comment – this is especially true of McBride's work, which for all its perception and insight, does not explain very much. My book, then, is a belated exploration into the field of Spanish American rural society and it has, I believe, the interest and weakness of such a pioneering effort. I hope that my rasher hypotheses will be challenged or clarified by the work of others.

In the following pages I have attempted first to summarise the recent work of Chilean scholars on the colonial centuries, and then present a descriptive chapter on town and country *ca* 1850. My aim here is to point out the peculiarities of Chilean agrarian evolution within a broader Spanish American framework and typology and to draw attention to those features that were particularly affected by later developments. The subsequent five chapters treat topics that are central to rural structure: markets, credit, land, labor, and landowners. Each of these topics is carried through the entire period of 1850–1920, and then in Chapter 8 the various threads are gathered together again and the story is brought forward to the 1920s.

Since my earlier research, I have gradually shifted my emphasis from statistics to people and ideas and accordingly most of the cows and kilograms have been banished to the Appendix. Quite a few, however, seem to have crept back into the chapters on markets and credit. I think they are necessary but the reader may find these sections tedious. If it is any consolation, many of the figures are new or newly assembled. The other central chapters are based mainly on unpublished or obscure material and I believe the sections on rural workers and landowners are especially interesting.

Unless otherwise mentioned, the book deals with the Chilean *nucleo central* or the entire central region from Aconcagua to Concepción. This was essentially the limit of colonial settlement and today it is the heartland of modern Chile. The Araucanía and the far south and the northern desert regions are excluded from direct analysis; but of course what happens there is often important and is referred to when appropriate. Throughout the study, I try to keep before the reader a general picture of Chilean development and to point out connection or contrast with other rural societies if doing so helps clarify the subject at hand. I try to demonstrate the use of history in social analysis by pointing out the stubborn persistence of certain forms: the habits and institutions that resist change or seemingly change only to reappear in different guise. Rural settlement patterns, the relationship between resident and seasonal laborers, and the long-established deference of service tenants to landowners, are only a few examples of the *longue durée* that are important in understanding modern Chile.

If I could have made this a better book it would deal with things that are left out. It would say something, for example, about the elaborate strands of informal kinship (*compradazgo*) that weave the various levels of rural society into a network of affection and obligation that immensely complicates any simple notion of social class. My discussion of landlords and workers should not dilate so much on *what* they did but rather *why* they did it or – better still – why they thought they did it. It is probably true that such a history of men's ideas and emotions can only be undertaken by a person of the country itself, someone steeped in the popular culture with keen sensitivity to philological subtleties. In any case, although I admire more than any other the work of Lucien Febvre and Marc Bloch, my sources and perhaps my own *outillage mental* are not adequate to treat these questions properly. Finally, if this were a better book it would make clear the delightful qualities of the country and the people. The reader will not sense the tranquility of willows on the Estero Zamorano, see the sea birds glitter on the beach at Santo Domingo, or ride on a thick Chilean saddle in the woods along the Maule. I would not presume to say of Chile, as the great Frenchman does about his Mediterranean, that 'I have passionately loved' the region I study because my *affaire* is not nearly so intense or profound; but I admit to an enduring affection for this pleasant land and a sense of gratitude at being always so warmly encouraged and so gently admonished in my work.

A.J.B.

March 1975

ABBREVIATIONS

ARCHIVAL COLLECTIONS

ACM   *Archivo de la Contaduría Mayor.* National Archive, Santiago

AMH   *Archivo del Ministerio de la Hacienda.* National Archive, Santiago

AMI   *Archivo del Ministerio del Interior.* National Archive, Santiago

CJ   *Collección Judicial* – by major city. National Archive, Santiago
- *CJ* (Linares)
- *CJ* (Rancagua)
- *CJ* (Rengo)
- *CJ* (San Fernando)
- *CJ* (Santiago)
- *CJ* (Talca)
- *CJ* (Valparaíso)

CN   *Colección Notarial* – by major city. National Archive, Santiago
- *CN* (Concepción)
- *CN* (Linares)
- *CN* (Rancagua)
- *CN* (Rengo)
- *CN* (San Fernando)
- *CN* (Santiago)
- *CN* (Talca)
- *CN* (Tomé)
- *CN* (Valparaíso)

CMR   *Colección Notarial Municipal* (Municipal Archive, Rengo)

PRIVATE RECORDS

Aculeo   Account book of the hacienda of Aculeo

Cunaco   Account book of the hacienda of Cunaco

Huique   Account book of the hacienda El Huique

Ñuble   Account book and letter file of the hacienda de Ñuble

Pichidegua   Account book of the hacienda of Pichidegua

Vichiculén   Account book of the hacienda of Vichiculén

xvii

Abbreviations

PERIODICALS AND JOURNALS

Anales	*Annals of the University of Chile*
BLEY	*Bulletin of the Laws and Decrees of Chile*
BSNA	*Bulletin of the National Society of Agriculture*
HAHR	*Hispanic American Historical Review*
RCHG	*Revista Chilena de Historia y Geografía*

CENSUSES AND STATISTICAL YEARBOOKS

Censo (year)	Population census
AE (year)	Anuario estadístico
EC (year)	*Estadística comercial*

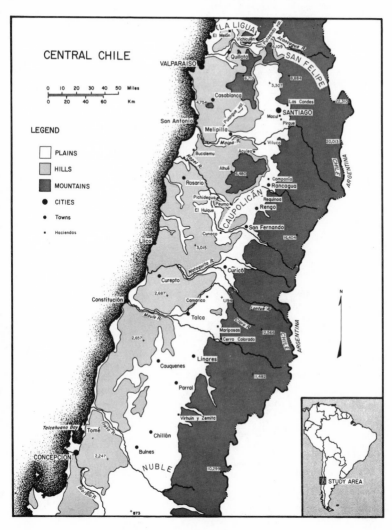

Map 1 Central Chile

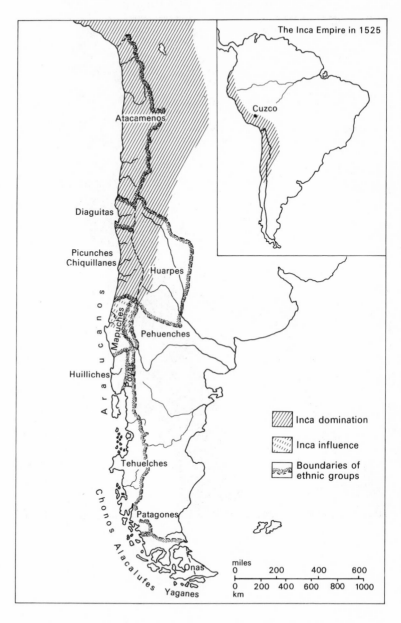

The Inca Empire in 1525

Cuzco

Atacamenos

Diaguitas

Picunches
Chiquillanes

Huarpes

Pehuenches

Araucanos

Mapuches

Huilliches

Poyas

Tehuelches

Chonos

Patagones

Alacalufes

Onas

Yaganes

Inca domination

Inca influence

Boundaries of
ethnic groups

miles
0   200   400   600

0   200   400   600   800   1000
km

Map 2   The indigenous population of Chile at the time of the Spanish
Conquest

2

Rural settlement and agrarian society to the early nineteenth century

'Chile, fértil provincia . . .'
Alonso de Ercilla, 1569

When the first Europeans moved onto the American mainland in the sixteenth century, they were scarcely prepared for the dramatic variety or harsh conditions in the new lands they found. 'This land of Peru', wrote Cieza de León, 'consists of three ranges of barren stretches unfit for human habitation.'[1] And in a well-known story, when Hernán Cortés was asked by his king to describe the landscape of New Spain, the conqueror simply crumpled in his hand a piece of paper to demonstrate the extremes of broken terrain. At lower elevations in these latitudes the Europeans were usually faced with fog-bound deserts or the unfamiliar luxuriance of the tropics. With this in mind, we can better understand the delight expressed by the first settlers in Central Chile. After five years in the country, Pedro de Valdivia wrote to Charles V that he had found a happy land, 'level and healthy,' with a mild winter, a summer of 'pleasant breezes' and soil and climate where the plants and animals of Spain would flourish. For Valdiva and his fellow settlers, a land admirably suited to the vine, olives and wheat, together with an abundant indigenous population must indeed have seemed as if 'it had been deliberately created by God in order to have everything close at hand.'[2] This early impression was only slightly overstated: Chile alone among Spanish colonies produced an agricultural surplus for export and the extraordinary attractiveness of the central valley led to the creation of a rural society that has been both a distinctive feature and a persistent burden in Chilean life.[3]

From the sixteenth-century Spaniard's point of view, two things – land and Indians – were necessary for settlement; but the way these two factors were obtained and combined varied a great deal in this enormous empire that stretched out north and south from Mexico and Peru.[4] Recent Chilean scholarship has focused on the sixteenth and seventeenth centuries and we are now able to see more clearly the early formation of Chile's peculiar agrarian society.[5] In Chile as in other colonies, the newly formed town councils (*cabildos*), made up in large

[1] Notes appear at the end of chapters.

3

part of the most important conquerors, were initially given the responsibility of assigning the surface of America – which the Spanish Crown claimed through conquest – to worthy settlers, mainly themselves. The instruments used for this purpose were land grants (*merced*) of several types. There were urban plots (*solar*) which in the beginning were one-fourth of a city block for the town house. The Spanish settlers, apart from their clear need to live together in a potentially hostile environment, were naturally inclined to live in town. Sixteenth-century Spaniards were 'men from the plaza mayor', and if some built houses among their Indians in the countryside, their principal dwelling was always around the central square of Santiago.[6] Close by the main towns, grants were awarded for *chácaras* (plots for horticulture) and in 'the vast spaces beyond', the most powerful and influential settlers were given large areas for farming and ranching.

All of these grants carried in theory certain restrictions and obligations. The rights of native settlers were not to be infringed, land could not be sold to ecclesiastics, and there was normally a requirement that settlers personally occupy the property and build on it. But in most cases such regulations could be cheerfully ignored or systematically violated if necessary.[7] In colonies like Mexico or Peru where royal authority could be brought to bear more effectively, the Crown attempted to limit the concentration of property and protect native lands by depriving the town councils of their land-granting capacity and giving this right to the King's direct representatives: the Viceroy, Audiencias or Governors. But in Chile, this measure did not arrive until 1575, and by that time the process of land grabbing was well along. In any case it made little difference: in Chile, according to Mario Góngora, the governors as well as the town councils handed out land to the settlers with the utmost generosity. The local Crown officials continued to award new grants and enlarged old ones in the face of royal legislation to the contrary.

Nor was there a coherent policy to protect Indian property. Land grants were given to Spaniards in the very center of native communities and the inhabitants were scattered or resettled and eventually organised into work gangs.[8] Under the circumstances, native culture was shattered, and Indian lands were almost totally absorbed by the new settlers. This fact should be underlined and contrasted with experience elsewhere. In Meso–America many freeholding Indian communities managed to survive alongside the European haciendas; and in Peru, however brutally carried out, the Toledan reforms at least permitted the existence of Indian towns. But in Chile, the European settlers, virtually unrestrained by distant authority, came quickly to dominate the countryside

4

and draw the uprooted native population within the boundaries of the large estates. The Council of the Indies was fully aware of the peculiarity of Chilean development but chose only to request additional information, to await the impression of local officials, and in the end it was unable to impose a coherent policy.

The native population itself was the other main element in the system of prizes awarded to the conquerors by the Spanish Crown. In the north of Chile, in fishing communities, along the narrow transversal valleys that run down to the sea, and on the margin of the imposing desert, there were a series of pre-hispanic cultures including the Atacameño and Diaguita. These people had domesticated llamas and alpacas, cultivated a wide range of nourishing plants, and traded their silver and gold work with distant regions.[9] When the men in Valdivia's colonising expedition moved through this region in 1540, they found a harsh terrain and uncooperative people who had not forgotten Almagro's brutal *entrada* a few years earlier. Not until the Europeans reached the fertile plain formed by the Maipo and Mapocho rivers in central Chile did they attempt to form a permanent settlement.[10] The native people of this region are widely known – in large part because of Alonso de Ercilla's epic poem that praised their qualities – as Araucanos. But this term technically refers to a wider, heterogeneous population extending from the present *norte chico*, into the southern rain forests (see Map 2).

In the sixteenth century the inhabitants of this central region called themselves *picunche* (*picun*, north; *che*, people), and to the south, below the river Maule, they were known as *mapuche* (*mapu*, land).[11] These were all farming people who cultivated maize, beans, potatoes and other plants and lived in loose clusters of households. Not much is known about the political and social organisation of these indigenous people, partly because central Chile was not the scene of extensive missionary work by the regular clergy, nor were inquisitive Crown officials present in the early years of this frontier area. Consequently, we have no Sahagún or Polo de Ondegardo to rely on. Nor has the kind of demographic research done in Mexico and Peru been carried out in Chile. We are still left with Rolando Mellafe's informed guess of 1 000 000, plus or minus twenty per cent, for the entire region of present-day Chile.[12]

Within a month of the foundation of Santiago (12 February 1541), Valdivia was busy distributing the native population among his European followers, through the device of *encomienda*. In doing so, he had before him the model of rural organisation that he knew as a young man: the great seignorial holdings of the military orders in Extremadura.

This meant that Valdivia did not envision, as did the Crown, a pattern of rural settlement where European farms would exist alongside villages of free-holding Indians. Rather, there undoubtedly 'floated before him a seignorial image' in which the two main prizes of the Indies would be juridically mixed: native workers would be subordinated to the eminent domaine of a powerful lord and they would reside within the legal boundaries of the great estate. This seignorial aim, according to Mario Góngora, was always present among the early conquerors. It was attempted, for example, by Cortés in Mexico; but only in a region like Chile, which was considerably removed from the centers of imperial power, could the desire to have dominion (*señorío*) over both men and lands together be satisfied.[13]

Valdivia's 'seignoral vision' gave Chilean society its initial form and the early outline was maintained despite the mild efforts of later officials to change it. No doubt the indigenous inhabitants of central Chile, less organised than those of Mexico or Peru, offered less resistance to Spanish efforts to dispossess them. And the fact that Chile was on the outskirts of the empire, thousands of miles and months by sea from Lima or Spain, meant that the Crown's control was slack; moreover, it had to rely primarily on the Spanish settlers themselves for military service against the Araucanians on the southern frontier. Under these circumstances it is no surprise that a layer of powerful men arose – the very 'nerve' of the new society, as they describe themselves – who were able to deal with the natives with very nearly a free hand.[14]

During the first decades of European occupation in central Chile, the *encomienda* adequately supplied the requirements for labor, first in the gold washings, and then for agriculture. But in Chile as in other regions touched by European expansion, new disease and exploitation took their toll.[15] Added to the undisputed fact of steady demographic decline in Chile was the violent 1599 Araucanian insurrection in the south which cost the Spanish their control of all territory below the Bío-Bío. With the normal caveats that must apply to data of this sort, Rolando Mellafe has put together a wide range of material to produce the figures in Table 1. According to these estimates, the Indian population from which workers could be drawn (those 'in *encomiendas* and other') declined from 450 000 to 230 000 between 1570 and 1600. This decrease was only slightly offset by a slow rise in the number of mixed bloods while the labor demands of the dominant groups represented by the Spanish, European and Creole settlers and probably a good number of the 'white *mestizos*,' steadily increased. Labor was required in the rudimentary textile industry, and on the estancias where animal products and food were produced for the military garrison in the south and the Peruvian market.[16]

The reduction in the population of central Chile led to a search for new workers and increased pressure on the ones at hand. Beginning in 1550, slaves were imported from Africa but high prices kept the traffic

Table 1   Population of Chile from 1540 to 1620

Years	Spanish European and Creole settlers	White *mestizos*	Negroes and coloured *mestizos*	Peaceful Indians (*encomienda* and others)	Unconquered Indians	Totals
1540	154	—	10	—	1 000 000	1 000 164
1570	7000	10 000	7000	450 000	150 000	624 000
1590	9000	17 000	16 000	420 000	120 000	582 000
1600	10 000	20 000	19 000	230 000	270 000	549 000
1620	15 000	40 000	22 000	230 000	250 000	557 000

Source: Mellafe, *Introducción de la escavitud*, p. 226.

thin.[17] Less expensive than Africans were Indians captured in the Araucanian wars and enslaved. This was a thriving practice even before the 1608 Royal Decree that made Indian slavery legal and it continued for nearly a hundred years, down to the end of the seventeenth century. Very close to slavery was the forced draft of Huarpe Indians from the transandine region of Cuyo, an area that included the towns of Mendoza, San Juan and San Luis of present-day Argentina. These Indians were brought in chains through the Andean passes and assigned to various agricultural tasks around Santiago. Often the *indios huarpes* were rented by their *encomenderos* to other Spaniards; in other cases landowners let their land with a certain number of laborers attached to it and thus obtained a higher rent.[18]

All of these new laborers, the black and mulatto slaves, the captured Indians, the Huarpes from the 'mita de Cuyo,' worked and lived next to the ordinary Indians in *encomiendas*. The difference between enslaved and other Indians was not cultural or ethnic but juridical. As we move into the seventeenth century, under the constant pressure of the need for labor, the slender rights of 'free' Indians were eroded and there was a natural tendency to blur the distinction between them and those legally enslaved. This could do nothing but deteriorate the already low social status of Indians and strongly reinforce the original ties of a seignorial society. Here we can recognise the nucleus of the future *campesinado,* 'subjected from the beginning to the lowest possible social conditions'.[19] In Chile, the conquest swept away native culture and values and the Indian was forced into a foreign system he could not comprehend. It was a system against which he had no defense, no tradition of resistance to draw upon, no understanding of his own rights. The combination of 'vast, open spaces,' a conquered mass of potential workers, together with the exigencies of empire, created within a century in Chile a seignorial society that has been one of the 'most powerfully determinant structural elements in the formation of the country.'[20]

By the 1650s, landownership and *encomienda* were fully integrated; or put another way, 'the *encomienda* was absorbed by the land.'[21] This does not mean that *encomenderos* with the greatest number of Indians were necessarily the largest landowners; or that the greatest landowners necessarily had large numbers of Indians. Economic power was determined by the combination of resources: the number of Indians together with the size, quality, and location of land (that is, its nearness to Santiago or the export route to Valparaíso). Obviously, there were cases of *encomenderos* with many Indians but poor land, and great *estancieros* with well-situated land which was worked with non-*encomienda* labor. In Mario Góngora's picture of mid-century society the most important *encomenderos* are still surrounded by a certain aura of feudal prestige – some, in fact, refer to themselves in their wills and other legal decuments as *'vecinos feudatarios'* – but several others are only minor figures. The 'aristocracy is now a landholding class' and its labor supply comes only in part from the *encomienda,* the rest through slavery – black and Indian – and other forms of coercion.[22]

We know more about the mid-seventeenth-century *encomenderos* than we do about the pattern of landownership. In 1655, the Governor called on the *vecinos encomenderos* of Santiago to assist in putting down a general Araucanian uprising in the south. Based on a list made at that time, Góngora has put together a description of 164 *encomenderos.* All of these lived in Santiago, even though their *encomiendas* may have been in Cuyo or as far away as Serena or Chillán, and each held at least six Indians. A count made by the Audiencia shows that in 1657 Santiago had 516 established households (*vecinos con casa poblada*) and a total population of nearly 5000 inhabitants. This means that at least a third of the *vecinos* (164 of 516) held an *encomienda* among their possessions.

Fifty-nine of the *encomenderos* in the 1655 list were descended either from important sixteenth-century *encomenderos* or from Crown officials. Some of these men and women who along with their *encomiendas* held vast tracts of good land, were at the top of Santiago society. Don Josephe de Riberos y Figueroa, for example, owned 3600 cuadras (5650 hectares) in Colchagua, herds of livestock, and seven slaves together with his Indians. He was, besides, engaged in commerce, and was elected *regidor* and *alcalde* of Santiago. Another such magnate was don Francisco Bravo de Saravia with fifty-nine Indian households, who owned the great *estancia* of Pullalli complete with livestock, chapel, forge etc., and other land in Illapel and Pama. He was also a captain of infantry, *regidor and alcalde* of Santiago.[23]

The remaining 105 *encomenderos* in the 1655 list came from families that either arrived in Chile in the seventeenth century, from earlier settlers who had not managed to obtain *encomiendas* in the previous century, or from families that had moved to Santiago from other Chilean towns.[24] Several of these were merchants or military officers who managed to obtain through influence, service or money, a few Indians. Some newcomers married into wealth, others obtained official positions, probably all acquired land. At the top this was a fluid society in which the market, chance and ability caused one to rise or fall, often quite suddenly.

If the *encomenderos* have become visible through recent research, there unfortunately is not yet a general study of rural property or land-owners in the colonial era. But from detailed studies of certain regions, the accounts of individual estates, and from scattered data generated by recent studies, a fairly reliable impression of landownership is at least possible. There was a tendency in the mid-seventeenth century toward larger units and from then until the late nineteenth century, and even beyond in many cases, the large properties were remarkably stable. In the valley of Putaendo some ninety kilometers north of Santiago, twelve original land grants were combined in the second half of the seventeenth century into eight large *estancias* each holding between 600 and 5500 hectares, not counting the large areas of hills and scrub land then still used as common pasture among the estate owners. Through purchase or inheritance these *estancias* evolved into four huge haciendas that remained intact down to 1960. One of these had 2400 hectares of level, irrigated land and over 90 000 of hills and cordillera.[25] The Borde and Góngora study of another valley about the same distance west of Santiago reveals a similar pattern. In this larger area of some twenty by forty kilometers, there were thirty-two large estates in 1690 and after rearrangement of boundaries as some estates enlarged and one or two split into several fragments, the surface of the Puangue valley was still dominated by only thirty-six haciendas a century later.[26] Throughout central Chile the large – and enlarging – estate was the rule. In the environs of Santiago there were *chacras* and some smaller estates, but as one moved south in Rancangua and Colchagua the typical *estancia* contained several thousand hectares of potentially arable land, which during these years was largely natural pasture, and often thousands more of hills and scrub land.[27]

There is no comprehensive list until the nineteenth-century *catastros* so it is not possible to tell who the landowners were nor even how many there were. It appears that all of the 164 *encomenderos* discussed above held some type of rural property and probably the same could be said of many of the 516 principal residents (*vecinos con casa poblada*) in Santiago. Often various properties were owned by different members of the same family. Almost all of the important landowners in what today is called the 'central nucleus' (Aconcagua through Ñuble) maintained a *casa principal* in Santiago. They participated in the town council either through election or purchase of office; they commanded local militias; supplied the clergy with sons and daughters; and were linked economically to the Church through contracts of *censos* and *capellanías*.[28] Lawyers were recruited from the main landholding group, or if they came from other sectors had the easiest access to it. The entrance of merchants into the landed elite took time and often depended upon a title or the prior purchase of, or election to, office. I can offer no better summary of upper seventeenth-century society than that of Mario Góngora on whom I have relied so heavily for this section: 'The *estancieros*, because of landownership alone, did not have special prestige since land was still worth very little compared to the value it acquired in the following centuries. The aristocracy was, in summary, a more or less open landowning and urban-dwelling class in which power derived from the combination of several factors, never one alone. These included the possession of the Santiago *casa principal*, *chacras*, vineyards, important *estancias*, large herds of livestock, Indians in *encomienda* and slaves, all of which were helped along by a prestigious marriage, public officeholding and the governor's blessings.'[29]

Was this a system that is directly comparable to European experience? A minor historical squall has blown up recently over proper labels. A number of writers have objected to the shorthand expression of 'feudalism' often used to describe Spanish colonial society and have sought instead to characterise the system – and identify the villain – as 'capitalist.'[30] In fact, there were elements of both, or better said, elements of several kinds of feudalism and capitalism.[31] The *encomi-*

enda established reciprocal obligations among King, *encomendero*, and Indian, but the imperial Spanish bureaucracy, however lax or weak, never relinquished its right to juridical supremacy over all classes in the colonies, and used the award and reassignment of *encomienda* as an administrative tool. *Encomenderos* were not really 'vassals' but simply a privileged group of subjects, and they in turn held no formal jurisdiction over the conquered people 'entrusted' to them. In this sense, one of the essential features of classic European feudalism was missing from colonial society in Chile and elsewhere in the Indies. At the same time the ability of the Crown to enforce its regulations diminished in the seventeenth century and distant settlers came to exercise a *de facto* authority on their own estates. This was certainly and perhaps especially true in Chile as *encomienda* and *estancia* merged into a large seignorial unit. The Chilean '*señor de indios*,' in Alvaro Jara's opinion, was able to reduce his workers to a condition of dependency that far surpassed the aims of a European lord toward his serfs.[32] In this sense, in terms of the real authority wielded over rural workers by the *encomiendero-estanciero*, the Chilean estate was more 'feudal' than the medieval Castillian *señorío*.

In terms of economics and market organisation, the Chilean estate contained elements of both monetary and natural economy. *Estancieros* produced for the market and sold their produce in Santiago and Peru. They received money and credit and were keen to turn a profit. But below the level of the *estanciero* and the handful of his salaried employees we are in the presence of a natural economy. In Chile, the head-tax (*tributo*) imposed on male adult Indians by the Crown was originally paid in personal service and never converted – as it was in other colonies – into cash payment; and neither Indian nor African slaves, of course, were renumerated with a money wage. Even 'free labor' was rarely paid in coin. In a study of some five hundred late-sixteenth-century labor contracts between non-*encomienda* workers and Spaniards, Alvaro Jara found that less than one per cent were paid in money, the rest in food and clothing; consequently the great mass of the population was excluded from the European economy.[33] Here again, we have a structural feature of Chilean rural society – deriving from the concentrated ownership of land and the personal relations between conqueror and conquered – of long duration. In the mid-twentieth century, attempts were still being made to require landowners to pay at least half of the service tenant's salary in money.

It should be clear from this brief summary of recent scholarship that the Chilean estate contained elements of rural systems found in other

Spanish colonies as well as in Europe and Asia. In the end it was a *sui generis* system that can perhaps best be understood through comparison with the great estates beyond the Elbe in Germany and Poland. There is not much point in discussion over terminology; certainly the insistence on either feudal or capitalist is misleading. If a label is needed, the suggestion of values, style, *de facto* jurisdiction and size that is conveyed by the term 'seignorial' makes that word as useful as any.

We have been dealing with the Chilean countryside in a way Fernand Braudel condemned in his magisterial work on the Mediterranean, 'as if the flowers did not come up each spring, as if flocks stopped in their tracks, as if ships did not have to navigate on the waters of a real sea that changes with seasons.'[34] In the seventeenth century the main activity in Chile was ranching and the rhythms of livestock culture together with climate and terrain helped shape the boundaries of estates and formed the nature of rural society. At the ordinary elevations, central Chile has a Mediterranean climate: rain in the winter months of May through August and barely a drop the rest of the year. Higher in the cordillera, between 2000 and 4000 meters, there is more precipitation and adequate pasturage can be found for several months after the valley has dried up. Before the later ninteenth century when little of the valley floor was irrigated, large-scale ranching was almost impossible without access to different ecological niches.[35] In a common pattern of movement, for example, livestock pastured in the coastal range through winter and spring and were then moved across the valley and up into the *veranadas* (summer pastures) of the Andes. There they stayed through the summer, and were brought down in the fall when animals were selected for breeding or slaughter.

The need for such a system of transhumancy helps explain the *estancieros'* interest in additional grants of land in different areas and elevations.[36] And since pasture was nothing except thin natural grasses, bushes and tree leaves, its carrying capacity was slight and several hectares were needed for each animal. Fences were unknown in hill-land until the nineteenth century and in time, as livestock penetrated further into the open stretches of cordillera, the boundaries of the vast *estancias* tended to conform to the natural divisions made by streams or ranges of hills. The main *estancia* house, sheds, and workers' shacks were generally in the level land of the valley floor where there were small sections of land for vines, a few hectares of wheat or alfalfa, and plots of corn and beans. The various parts of such *estancias* formed a unit, were interdependent, and once the pattern was established, there was a natural and logical resistance to change. Subdivision required difficult and expensive surveying, re-routeing of canals, and care that the proper combination of level, hill, and cordillera pasture was maintained. In many cases the original boundaries of colonial *estancias* remained unchanged into the twentieth century. As we shall see, the evolution of level land as it came under irrigation in the nineteenth and twentieth centuries followed a somewhat different pattern: the increasing value of land and the more elaborate management required by cultivation led to more subdivision.

The pastoral year on the great *estancias* turned around the rodeo and autumnal slaughter when the angular *criollo* cattle were converted into lard, leather and jerked beef (*charqui*) and sheep were killed for their pelts (*cordobanes*). Not many workers were needed in this kind of extensive ranching economy. Even on the great *estancias* of thousands of hectares, one has the impression from Góngora's description of the largest estates that thirty or forty *encomendado* families and a few Indian or African slaves were sufficient. Most workers lived all year round on the estates in loose clusters of shacks near the *estancia* buildings and until cereal cultivation and a more diversified production developed in the following centuries, there was little need for seasonal labor. In the seventeenth century, and indeed into recent years, Chilean agriculture retained the duality imposed by the introduction of European plants and animals on native culture. European cereals were produced with the aid of plows and draft animals; the resident workers continued to use the hoe for the native crops of maize, potatoes, beans and squash. European livestock was not integrated with indigenous practice. Maize or turnips were not fed to animals and the manure of livestock was not used in agriculture: *chacra* and ranching remained separate activities.[37]

The large estates were engaged almost from the beginning in the export trade. Animal products were bundled into skins, hauled by muleback to Valparaíso and consigned to a handful of merchants who negotiated their sale. The most lucrative seventeenth-century markets were Lima and (after 1650) the army garrisons of Bío-Bío and Valdivia. The *estancieros* closer by Santiago sold their still very modest quantities of wine and garden crops, flour, candles and lard in the city, converting sections of their own houses into stalls that opened to the main streets.[38]

From the late seventeenth century onwards, the Peruvian demand for wheat and a steadily growing population began slowly to transform the Chilean countryside. Although the beginning of Chilean grain exports is commonly explained by a series of earthquakes in late 1687 that presumably devastated Peruvian fields, recent studies explain the trade – which lasted for over two centuries – in terms of economic geography and comparative advantage.[39] The volume of exports rose in the early eighteenth century to some 180 000 qqm and then leveled off. (One metric quintal is equivalent to 100 kilograms.) Added to the Peruvian demand was a slowly growing internal consumption as mixed races and the surviving indigenous population adopted the dietary habits of Europeans. By mid-eighteenth century it appears that around 400 000 qqm of wheat were produced in Chile, which means that some 45 000 hectares were devoted to that activity.[40] This does not seem today like a vast area of cultivation, and practically it meant then that each of the principal haciendas within reach of Santiago or the export route probably had between 25 and 100 hectares under cultivation and an equal amount in fallow. Although the acreage was still small, the gradual addition of cultivation to a pastoral economy brought a need for a more varied and increased rural labor force. The growing market was accompanied by demographic increase and shifts in the racial composition of the population.[41]

The Indians of central Chile gradually but persistently withered away. Demographic attrition began with the impact of European disease and demands in the first decades of settlement and continued into the eighteenth century. Moreover the indigenous groups were further depleted through interbreeding or assimilation and were no longer considered to be Indians by either their contemporaries or the census takers. They were passing on cultural as well as biological criteria into the categories of 'Spanish' or 'mestizo.' Thus in the 1770s only ten per cent of the total population of central Chile was classified as 'Indian' and twelve per cent as Negro or mulatto. From an estimated 320 000 in 1785, the total population grew to some 500 000 by the early nineteenth century and the white or pseudo-white groups continued to increase: seventy-four per cent of the population was designated 'Spanish' and another ten per cent *'mestizo'* in 1813.[42] By the time Maria Graham visited Chile in 1822, even those described as 'Indians' in central Chile were almost completely assimilated into European culture.[43]

In the eighteenth century the open and fluid society of the earlier years evolved into a system in which the great estates were increasingly dominant. In this more consolidated and stratified society the prospects of the nominally white groups were lower than during the sixteenth and much of the seventeenth century, when land and Indians were abundant. Many of the whites or pseudo-whites – described in contemporary documents as 'poor Spaniards' – were slowly incorporated into agrarian society as *mayordomos* or *vaqueros* and they were often permitted to graze their livestock in unused portions of the vast estates. For such tenancies little or no rent was paid. The squatters occasionally assisted the estate during rodeos, they were expected to keep an eye out for thieves, and they recognisd the personal nature of their tie with the landowner. As the market for agricultural produce – particularly for wheat – grew, the land became more valuable and more hands were needed for cultivation. The landowners stepped up the amount of service required from the families that were allowed to settle on estate land. Instead of occasional labor during roundup or slaughter, each 'renter' was required to supply an able-bodied man to the estate all year round to help with plowing, planting or irrigation. As we move through the eighteenth century, the market forces at work led to increased social stratification: the landowners became gradually wealthier and more clearly set off from the landless tenants; the tenants in turn, faced with the alternative of expulsion, were willing to accept the stepped up service requirement. This meant less time for their own interests and a consequent erosion of their economic position. These service tenants were less and less referred to as 'renters' (*arrendatarios*) which after all could describe men of medium and even substantial means, but rather by the specialised term, still used, of *inquilinos*.[44]

What we see in the course of the eighteenth century is the progressive abolition of legal coercion but a continuation of informal pressure on rural laborers. Very few Indians were enslaved after 1700, while most African slaves were freed in the latter eighteenth century, and the *encomienda* was finally outlawed in 1791.[45] At the same time, the labor required of service tenants was increased and the remuneration given to occasional workers remained exceedingly low. All this implies an increase in the labor to land ratio, a condition that is borne out by contemporary testimony and recent demographic studies. There seems to have been in fact a surplus of hands. Landowners were unwilling to give a permanent plot to more families than they could possibly employ and so a large part of the increasing population could not be absorbed by the estates. Many families pitched their rude shacks along streams, on marginal land in the interstitial niches of the central valley, or simply kept on the move foraging for existence. Some chose banditry and there is one account that mentions twelve thousand 'wretches' infesting the roads of central Chile.[46] The rootless or floating population continued to increase into the nineteenth century. Some settled into the straggling new towns of central Chile such as San Fernando, Melipilla, Curicó and Rancagua, founded for this purpose in the 1740s; others drifted into the mining camps to the north of Santiago. The large estates drew the temporary workers they needed from the landless people who either sought shelter in the *inquilinos'* shacks or simply slept during the season in the open air.[47]

This is a general picture of the free rural work force that grew out of late colonial decades. Neither *inquilino* nor seasonal peon had much incentive to work and no doubt their productivity was low. Scores of landowners and foreign observers have described them over the past two or three centuries as 'idle' and 'lazy.' Their principal spur to activity was the simple urge to exist and this was more likely on the large estates, especially those that offered a small bit of irrigated land. Given their early and enduring control of nearly all cultivable land, the large estate owners did not need the devices of debt or force commonly employed in a labor-scarce economy. For the Catholic and Spanish-speaking rural poor there was no frontier in the Araucanian south and few prospects in the towns or rudimentary mines. Under the circumstances the dispossessed lined up to get a plot on the valley estates and supplied their labor at a minimal price. At the same time the growing agricultural earnings their work made possible and the pleasure and prestige their services provided, made the rural estates an attractive investment for the newly rich of Bourbon Chile.

Between 1701 and 1810, some 24 000 immigrants arrived in Chile from Spain and forty-five per cent of these came from Navarre and the Basque provinces. Everyone agrees on the extraordinary impact these last groups had, including Miguel de Unamuno who called Chile along with the Jesuit order the two great creations of the Basque people.[48] Their road to economic success and social prominence ran from commerce to the countryside to office. The Eyzaguirre, Errázuriz, Echeverría, Urrutia, and above all the Larraín, quickly established themselves in commerce and invested their earnings in the best rural estates. It was their good fortune to arrive in Chile in a period of expanding trade and also at a time – after 1767 – when the extensive holdings of the Jesuits were confiscated and sold at public auction.[49] Many of the great Jesuit haciendas and others that came on the market, put up for sale by older families 'ruined by luxury and idleness,' were purchased by Basques. Besides the energetic Basques, other immigrant families such as the Ovalle, Valdés, Garcia-Huidobro and Cerda also

Rural settlement and agrarian society

made commercial fortunes in the eighteenth century and invested their money in land, entails and noble titles. These together with the Basques and a handful of descendants from the Arauco wars, made up the two-hundred or so landholding families of the late colonial 'vecindario noble.'[50] So completely did these new families displace or absorb the seventeenth-century *encomendero–estanciero* elite that only five sur-

Table 2 Chronological list of titles, entails and major *vínculos* in Santiago society with family names of holders

Date	Creation	Family Name
1684	Marqués de la Pica	Irarrázabal
1685	Conde de Sierra Bella	Mesía
1693	Torres Mayorazgo	Mesía
1702	Marqués de la Cañada Hermosa	Marín de Poveda, Ruiz de Azúa
1703	Cerda Mayorazgo	Cerda
1728	Irarrázabal Mayorazgo	Irarrázabal
1728	Marqués de Villapalma	Calvo de Encalada
1736	Larraín Mayorazgo	Larraín
1744	Aguirre Mayorazgo	Aguirre
1748	Azúa Mayorazgo	Ruiz de Azúa
1752	Toro Mazote Mayorazgo	Caldera
1755	Marqués de Montepío	Aguirre
1755	Marqués de Casa Real	García Huidobro
1756	García Huidobro Mayorazgo	García Huidobro
1763	Conde de Quinta Alegre	Alcalde
1763	Valdés Mayorazgo	Valdés
1768	Lecaros Mayorazgo	Lecaros, Larraín
1770	Conde de la Conquista	Toro Zambrano
1778	Balmaceda Mayorazgo	Fernández de Balmaceda
1779	Rojas Mayorazgo	Rojas
1780	Larraín y Rojas Mayorazgo	Rojas de Larraín, Larraín
1783	Ruiz-Tagle Mayorazgo	Ruiz-Tagle
1785	Prado Mayorazgo	Prado
1787	Marqués de Larraín	Larraín
1789	Toro Zambrano Mayorazgo	Toro Zambrano
1789	Aguila y Rojas Mayorazgo	Herrera
1791	Aecalde vínculo	Alcalde

Source: Barbier, 'Elite and cadres,' p. 419.

names of the 1655 list of 164 principal *encomenderos* are found among the holders of entails and noble titles in the later eighteenth century.[51] The predominance of Basque names can be seen in the chronological list of titles, entails and major *vínculos* in Santiago society.

Several writers have pointed to the qualities of industry, parsimony, common sense and narrow-mindedness displayed by this eighteenth-century elite which Alberto Edwards has artfully called 'bourgeois aristocracy.' 'Bourgeois in its formation due to its spirit of enterprise,' the Chilean elite had none of the 'egalitarian passion' of the European bourgeoisie but finding itself instead in a colonial setting, at the un-disputed head of the social and racial hierarchy, it quickly developed a sense of superiority. There was also, particularly among the Basque element, a highly developed sense of family cohesion. Jacques Barbier's recent study demonstrates how this closely knit Chilean elite was able to marry into the families of Bourbon officials and entice the Spanish cadres to reciprocate.[52] Where the Bourbon reforms of the later eighteenth century forced many of the creole elite from positions of political power in Mexico and Peru, the local Chilean elite and the Spanish overseas bureaucrats became more and more interrelated. Many Chileans attained high administrative offices including positions as *oidores* in the Audiencia, Superintendent of the Mint, Administrator General of the customs house, and in Barbier's view the local elite was even more influential in its ability to co-opt the foreign cadres.[53]

The network of strong creole family alliances became even more closely woven in the years just before independence. Many Spanish officials sent to rend this fabric of local interest were in fact enmeshed within it; and as Spanish power disintegrated in the first decades of the nineteenth century, the cohesive and class-conscious creole elite moved smoothly, compared with other former Spanish colonies, to control the machinery of republican government. The early-nineteenth-century elite shared a compact geographic region and common economic interest. There were squabbles within the elite, most notably between the Larraín and Carrera clans, but in Chile, more so than in the rest of Spanish America, there is a strong social continuity that runs right through the Independence period.[54]

Continuity – the almost undisturbed persistence of structure and habit – was especially true in the countryside. There is no compre-hensive survey of rural estates until the *catastro* of 1834, so there is no way of telling at this point the number or size of eighteenth-century estates.[55] Carmagnani thought that 230 estates shared the export trade and from what we know from the detailed regional studies it is reason-able to suppose that there were in the region between Aconcagua and Concepción some five hundred properties of over 1000 hectares each, perhaps 125 of which contained well over 5000 hectares each.[56] Some of these yielded a good income and others, outside the Santiago or export market areas, were virtually worthless regardless of their size.

Two descriptions may help us visualise the eighteenth-century estate system. The hacienda of Calera de Tango 15 kilometers south of

Rural settlement and agrarian society

Santiago had some 3700 hectares of level land. The 30 to 40 hectares of wheat, 600 to 700 head of livestock, vines, olives, horticulture, and fruit trees were tended by proto-*inquilinos*, and a decreasing number of black slaves.[57] Such an estate was rented for between $2500 and $1500 pesos during 1767 and 1776 and was purchased – including all animals, buildings, and equipment – by Francisco Ruiz-Tagle for $30 000 in 1783: a relationship between income and investment that indicates an annual yield of between eight and five per cent. Another great Jesuit estate, La Compañía near Rancagua, was purchased for $90 000 by don Mateo Toro-Zambrano in 1771. The price included over 10 000 prime hectares and '*inmensas serranías*,' 7600 head of cattle, 4900 sheep, 525 horses, 1250 mares, 104 burros, 540 mules and 38 slaves, together with all buildings and equipment.[58] Such an estate, which was in an excellent location to supply Santiago and the export route, had a tax evaluation of $16 000 annual income in 1834; after irrigation works were extended and the market grew over the next twenty years, La Compañía's official taxable income increased to $89 000 a year. In both surveys, Compañía's yield was the largest in Chile.

A handful of other well-situated haciendas such as Aculeo or Cunaco produced handsome incomes for their owners but this should not lead us to exaggerate the economic importance of rural property before the 1850s or '60s.[59] In the years before the railways and the rise of much stronger foreign and domestic markets, haciendas could be huge in area and employ (or at least give sustenance to) hundreds of people, but they were frequently poor in terms of cash income. A rough notion of the relative importance of agriculture can be obtained from data based on colonial tithe records and the official tax rolls of the nineteenth century. For the 1770s Marcello Carmagnani calculated an average annual figure of 620 000 pesos for the value of all agricultural output. This increased very slightly in the 1820s to $824 000; but by 1874, the tax records give the annual *renta* at $9 693 000, a twelve-fold increase over the fifty years.[60]

Since export data are easier to gather than production figures, a more reliable indication of the relative poverty of colonial agriculture are in the trade statistics showing that export before 1840 never exceeded two per cent of the volume during the years 1871–5.[61] Only under the most fortuitous circumstances could one expect to get rich in agriculture before the mid-nineteenth century. Some did, of course, but the faster road to wealth was through trade, mining and office. From Independence onward, however, and especially as we shall see after the 1870s, the relationship between urban and rural sectors began to shift as foreigners gradually came to dominate commerce and mining while better markets and prices lifted the Chilean estate owners to a stronger relative position in national society and politics.

Although there is no doubt that rural property frequently changed hands, the evidence available shows that the boundaries and internal structure of the large estates remained generally undisturbed through the independence period and into the 1840s. Borde and Góngora's work on Puangue shows a remarkably constant tenure pattern throughout the eighteenth and early nineteenth century; in Putaendo the great haciendas retained their colonial form and the scattered information that exists on individual estates elsewhere tells the same story. Some haciendas were divided, but in as many cases adjoining estates merged through marriage or purchase. Within Spanish law a landowner could will to one heir property that represented a *tercio* and *quinto* of his total wealth. Often such a share might encompass the value of the major rural estate, thus keeping it intact while other children were compensated with money, urban property or *chacras*. The wealthier or the more varied a landowner's holdings, the more likely that the hacienda would be inherited in one piece. Sometimes two heirs would receive the estate but they could work it together, sharing the income and avoiding subdivision.[62] As much as anything, the scale of operations required by a livestock hacienda and the minimum income required to support an elite life-style determined the size of estates. When later in the nineteenth century a shift to cultivation and a more diversified output increased the problems of management and also the yields so that more than one family could be comfortably supported, the great colonial haciendas began to be subdivided.

In regard to questions of land distribution, the much maligned system of *mayorazgos* (entails) seems to have had very little effect. The great entailed haciendas such as La Compañía probably would have remained intact regardless of legal restraints on subdivision because their size was appropriate to a pastoral economy. By the time the Liberals mounted their doctrinaire and somewhat turgid attack against the 'ominous feudal vestige' in the 1820s, most holders of *mayorazgos* were quite ready to accept ex-vinculation. Once the Republic abolished titles of nobility, the principal motive for these cumbersome and expensive displays of wealth was past. The great furor of the 1820s over the *mayorazgos* seems to have been mainly concerned with political idoeologies, not economic issues. A few Liberals held that entails led to sloth and bad agricultural practice ('*Mayorazgos* looked like abandoned property'), but a causal link between entail and low productivity was difficult to maintain when holders of *mayorazgos* simply pointed out that their land was no more slovenly farmed than any other. Undoubtedly the intransigence of the Liberals and the uncertainty of the period stiffened the resolve of the *pelucón* magnates to preserve the entails to as late as the 1850s. Moreover, contesting heirs presented a delicate question as the eldest son (most entails designated male heirs as successors) claimed rights and the rest of the family threatened suits.[63]

A main disadvantage of the entailed estate was that it could not easily be pledged to guarantee loans; and mortgage loans, not noble titles, were the fashion in republican Chile. The law read that entailed property could not be 'alienated, divided, exchanged, traded, mortgaged, obliged to guarantee annuities (*censos*), nor rented for long terms . . .' Nor could parts be sold to pay for improvements on the remaining land or to pay expenses in lean years – an onerous burden in a land of low and irregular agricultural incomes. This was the point of José Toribio Larraín's (the ex-Marqués de Larraín) petition to the State in 1822 that his *mayorazgo*, consisting of the great haciendas of Viluco and Cauquenes, the *chacra* of Ñuñoa, and a Santiago town house, be disentailed. Larraín claimed that the cost of improvements on Viluco had so impoverished him that mortgage loans or partial sale was imperative. The Constitution of 1828 made it possible to disentail estates; the Constitution of 1833 made it possible not to. From then until the 1850s, a few estates were disentailed and sold (the ex-Jesuit hacienda of Bucalemu, a part of the Ibacache *mayorazgo*, for example), but the institution lingered on until the 1852 legislation – a measure that some have called a 'rude blow to the colonial aristocracy' – provided an acceptable recompense for heirs. *Mayorazgos* went without a bang and barely a whimper while the great landowners remained firmly in control of the countryside.[64]

CHAPTER I

[1] *The Incas of Pedro Cieza de León* (ed. Victor von Hagen, trans. Harriet de Onís, Norman, Okla., 1959), p. 17.

[2] Pedro de Valdivia, *Cartas* (Intro. by Jaime Eyzaguirre, Santiago, 1955), p. 36.

[3] This description excludes extraordinary foodstuffs such as cacao or sugar, or hides and fibers. In Chile as in other Spanish colonies, it was the lure of precious metals that first drew men into these distant regions; but here unlike in New Spain or Peru, important silver strikes did not immediately follow

Chilean Rural Society

the early gold washing cycle, and by the end of the sixteenth century the rudimentary mining economy had petered out. See for example Alvaro Jara, 'Salario en una economía caracterizada por las relaciones de dependencia personal,' *RCHG*, no. 133 (1965), p. 44.

4 Magnus Mörner has reviewed the recent literature in 'The Spanish American hacienda: a critical survey of recent research and debate,' *HAHR*, vol. 53, no. 2 (May 1973), pp. 183–216.

5 Especially useful is the work of Mario Góngora, *El estado en el derecho indiano* (Santiago, 1951); (with Jean Borde), *Evolución de la propiedad rural en el valle del Puangue* (2 vols., Santiago, 1956); *Origen de los 'inquilinos' de Chile central* (Santiago, 1960); *Encomenderos y estancieros* (Santiago, 1970); 'Vagabundaje y sociedad fronteriza en Chile (siglos XVII a XIX),' *Cuadernos del Centro de Estudios Socio-económicos*, no. 2 (Santiago, 1966); Marcello Carmagnani, *El salariado minero en Chile colonial* (Santiago, 1963); 'Colonial Latin American demography: growth of Chilean population 1700–1830,' *Journal of Social History*, vol. 1, no. 2, pp. 179–91; 'Formazione di un mercato coloniale: Cile, 1680–1830,' *Rivista Stórica Italiana* (September 1969), pp. 480–500; *Les mécanismes de la vie économique dans une société coloniale: le Chili, 1680–1830* (Paris, 1973); Fernando Silva Vargas, *Tierras y pueblos de indios en el Reino de Chile* (Santiago, 1962); Rolando Mellafe, *La introductión de la esclavitud negra en Chile* (Santiago, 1959); and Alvaro Jara, *Guerre et société au Chili: essai de sociologie coloniale* (Paris, 1961); and, among several fundamental articles by the same author, 'Salario en una economía caracterizada por las relaciones de dependencia personal,' *RCHG*, no. 133 (1965), pp. 40–60; 'Importaciones de trabajadores indígenas en el siglo XVII,' *RCHG*, no. 124, pp. 177–212; 'Lazos de dependencia personal y adscripción de los indios a la tierra en la America española: el caso de Chile,' *Cahiers du monde hispanique et luso-brésilien*, *Caravelle*, no. 20 (1973), pp. 51–67.

6 Fernand Braudel, *El mediterráneo y el mundo mediterráneo en la época de Felipe II* (2 vols., trans. by M. H. Toledo and W. Roces, Mexico City, 1953), I, p. 315. See also Mary Lowenthal Felstiner, 'The Larraín family in the independence of Chile, 1780–1830' (Unpublished Ph.D. diss. in hist., Stanford, 1970), p. 49.

7 Borde and Gongóra, *Puangue*, I, p. 30.

8 The land measurement carried out by Ginés de Lillo in 1604 was part of a feeble Crown effort to protect the remaining Indian lands. See Ernesto Greve, 'Mensuras de Ginés de Lillo,' *Colección de Historiadores de Chile* vol. 48 (Santiago, 1941), pp. ix–xc; and Borde and Góngora, *Puangue*, p. 30–3.

9 Eugenio Pereira Salas, 'El desenvolvimiento histórico–étnico de la población,' *Geografía económica de Chile* (Santiago, 1967), pp. 337–41; see also the pioneering work by Ricardo Latcham, especially, 'Ethnology of the Araucanos,' *Journal of the Royal Anthropological Institute*, vol. 39 (1909), pp. 334–70.

10 Diego Barros Arana, *Historia de Chile* (16 vols., Santiago, 1884–1902), vol. I, pp. 161–255. Valdivia's expedition carried pigs, fowls, European grains, and a collection of farming tools, but only one European woman.

11 Louis Faron, *The Mapuche Indians of Chile* (New York, 1968), pp. 9–10.

12 Mellafe, *Introducción de la esclavitud*, p. 215. Much more is known about the people of the Araucanian frontier through the writings of the Jesuit missionaries than about the Mapuche.

13 Valdivia, *Cartas*, p. 38; Góngora, *Encomenderos*, p. 7–8. There is a longstanding debate over the relationship between land and *encomienda* in Spanish America. Scholars early in this century confused the rights of the

22

Rural settlement and agrarian society

encomendero (the holder of an *encomienda*) with land possession, but this overly vague notion was put right in a series of publications in the 1930s by Silvio Zavala and Lesley B. Simpson who demonstrated that in Mexico at least, the *encomienda* had no juridical connection with land. Now modern writers looking at different regions and beyond the legislation to social and economic practice, tend to agree that there is 'some sort of equivalence' between *encomienda* and the large estate. In the Chilean case, however, the two were combined not only in practice but juridically as well. Valdivia gave himself and his followers land and with it Indians who were bound to work on the estate. In fact, both men and land could be granted together in the same decree. See James Lockhart, 'Encomienda and Hacienda: the Evolution of the Great Estate in the Spanish Indies,' *HAHR*, vol. 49, no. 3 (August, 1969), pp. 411–29, for a general discussion of the literature; and Góngora, *Encomenderos*, pp. 6–8.

14 Góngora, *Encomenderos*, p. 16. The Araucanians, of course, put up fierce resistance to the southward advance of the Europeans and before them to the Incas; but the absence of a strong, well-rooted village community meant that their position in central Chile was rapidly eroded after the early fighting died down.

15 Mellafe, *Introducción de la esclavitud*, pp. 212–26.

16 Three terms are used in Chile to designate a landed estate. *Estancia* was used from the beginning of European settlement to mean a large livestock ranch. It was generally replaced in the eighteenth century by *hacienda* which also implies large size but carries the further connotation of some cultivated land. By the nineteenth century, *fundo* was often used interchangeably with hacienda but gradually came to mean a smaller, usually irrigated farm, while hacienda was reserved for the larger (over 5000 hectares) dry-land estate. *Chacras* were smaller still: plots devoted to horticulture.

17 Mellafe, *Introducción de la esclavitud*, p. 196, estimated that between 1550 and 1615, some 3000 blacks were sold in Chile; but (since some were sold several times) the actual number introduced was probably lower. Philip Curtin, *The Atlantic Slave Trade* (Madison, 1969), p. 45, attributes a figure of 2000 to Mellafe and then inexplicably revises that figure upward to 6000.

18 Jara, *Guerre et société*, 165; 'Salario,' p. 52–5; 'Importaciones,' pp. 177–212.

19 Jara, 'Lazos de dependencia,' p. 66. The Spanish, *campesinado*, is retained because I hesitate to use even in its ordinary sense the English 'peasantry' to describe these rural workers.

20 Jara, 'Lazos de dependencia,' pp. 55–9.

21 Góngora, *Encomenderos*, p. 107.

22 Góngora, *Encomenderos*, p. 112.

23 Góngora, *Encomenderos*, pp. 102, 153.

24 Góngora, *Encomenderos*, p. 104.

25 Rafael Baraona, *et al.*, *Valle de Putaendo* (Santiago, 1960), pp. 145–52.

26 Borde and Góngora, *Puangue*, II, maps 2 and 3.

27 There are a number of studies of individual haciendas. See, for example, Carlos J. Larraín, *Las Condes* (Santiago, 1952); and *El Huique* (Buenos Aires, 1944).

28 See discussion in Chapter 5.

29 Góngora, *Encomenderos*, p. 126.

30 Luis Vitale, *Interpretación marxista de la historia de Chile*, (2nd ed., 3 vols., Santiago, 1967–71), vol. 2, pp. 15–26, provides the most thoughtful discussion of the anti-feudal point of view; see also Marcelo Segall, *Desarrollo del capitalismo en Chile* (Santiago, 1953), and Andrew Gunder Frank, *Capitalism and Underdevelopment in Latin America* (New York, 1967),

and the scathing review of Frank's 'thesis' by Ruggiero Romano in *Desarrollo económico*, vol. 10, no. 38 (July-September 1970), pp. 285–92.

31 Góngora, *Encomenderos*, pp. 117–29.

32 Jara, 'Lazos de dependencia,' p. 59.

33 Góngora, *Encomenderos*, p. 120; Jara, 'Salario,' pp. 50–1.

34 Braudel, *Mediterráneo*, v. 1, p. XVIII.

35 I have profited on these points from discussion with Drs Juan Gastó and Sergio Lailhacar of the University of Chile, and Dr Floyd Carroll, of the Department of Animal Science, University of California at Davis, California.

36 Baraona *et al.*, *Putaendo*, p. 108. Livestock yield was low. The *criollo* steer weighed no more than 300 kilograms and was kept for six to eight years. This may be compared with modern animals that weigh 4–500 kilos and are sold after three or four years.

37 *Chácara*, shortened to *chacra*, is of Quéchua origin and refers to horticulture. For a perceptive and often poetic description of farming practice in central Chile see Baraona *et al.*, *Putaendo*, especially pp. 105–7.

38 Góngora, *Encomenderos*, p. 108.

39 Sergio Sepúlveda, *El trigo chileno en el mercado mundial* (Santiago, 1956), pp. 17–19; Demetrio Ramos, *Trigo chileno, navieros del Callao y hacendados limeños entre la crisis agrícola del siglo XVII y la comercial de la primera mitad del XVIII* (Madrid, 1967), pp. 21–31.

40 Sepúlveda, *Trigo chileno*, pp. 22, 23, 30.

41 Carmagnani, *Mecanismes*, p. 220 says that some 230 haciendas participated in the export trade. Horacio Aránguiz Donoso, 'Notas para el estudio de la hacienda de la Calera de Tango,' *Historia* (Catholic University of Chile) no. 6 (1967), p. 240, indicates that some twenty to thirty hectares of this well-located estate were planted to wheat. A great hacienda such as La Compañía undoubtedly produced much more.

42 Carmagnani, 'Colonial Latin American demography,' pp. 187–8, who cites the *Censo de 1813* (directed by Juan Egaña, first published, Santiago, 1953).

43 Maria Graham, *Journal of a residence in Chile during the year 1822* (London, 1824), p. 266.

44 Góngora, *Origen de los 'Inquilinos,'* esp. pp. 113–17.

45 Barros Arana, *Historia*, VI, p. 250, tells of slaves confiscated from the Society taken to Lima for sale; María Isabel González Pomés, 'La encomienda indígena en Chile durante el siglo XVIII,' *Historia* (Catholic University of Chile), no. 5 (1966), p. 77, says there were less than 1000 Indians still in *encomienda* in 1791.

46 Luis Galdames, *A History of Chile* (I. J. Cox, trans. and ed. Chapel Hill, N.C., 1941), p. 138; see Góngora, 'Vagabundaje,' pp. 8–9.

47 Barros Arana, *Historia*, VI, pp. 141–8; Góngora, 'Vagabundaje,' p. 81.

48 Felstiner, 'Larraín family,' p. 21, relies on Luis Thayer Ojeda, *Navarros and vascongados en Chile* (Santiago, 1904), and *Elementos étnicos que han intervenido en la población de Chile* (Santiago, 1919). Thayer Ojeda, one of the most accomplished of many Chilean genealogies, thought that 'three-fourths of the distinguished personages of nineteenth-century Chile were of Basque descent.'

49 Ricardo Donoso, *Las ideas políticas en Chile*, 2nd ed. (Santiago, 1967), p. 89. On the Jesuit estates, see Barros Arana, *Historia*, VI, pp. 248–50, who lists thirty-five large rural properties the Society owned in central Chile and fifty-nine in the entire country.

50 Alberto Edwards Vives, *La fronda aristocrática*, 6th ed. (Santiago, 1966), p. 16; Donoso, *Las ideas*, p. 89.

51 Domingo Amunátegui, *Mayorazgos i títulos de Castilla* (3 vols., Santiago, 1901–4); Góngora, *Encomenderos*, pp. 141–72. A close genealogical study is

needed to determine lines of descent but the lack of coincidence bears out the intuitive work of Alberto Edwards Vives, Donoso and others. The five surnames that do appear in both the 1655 *encomendero* and the *mayorazgo* and titles lists are Irarrázabal, Toro, Cerda, Fernández, and Herrera.

52 Edwards Vives, *Fronda*, pp. 16–17; Felstiner, 'Larraín family,' p. 21; Jacques Barbier, 'Elite and cadres in Bourbon Chile,' *HAHR*, vol. 52, no. 3 (August 1972), p. 434.

53 Barbier, 'Elite and cadres,' pp. 417, 434.

54 Felstiner, 'Larraín family', p. 55. There were occasional but feeble regional movements centered on La Serena and Concepción.

55 *ACM*, 2nd series, no vol. no., 'catastro' (1834). Unfortunately the entire province of Colchagua is missing from the archival copy.

56 This estimate is based on the Borde and Góngora, *Puangue*; Baraona *et al.*, *Putaendo*; and fragments of the manuscript worksheets for the 1854 tax rolls in *AMH*, vols. 304–6. In Caupolicán, which had about six per cent of all large estates in central Chile, there were thirty *fundos* over 1000 hectares. The income data from this tax roll, published as *Estado que manifiesta la renta agrícola . . .* (Valparaíso, 1855), lists 145 estates with annual *renta*, or income, of $6000 pesos or more. Income would probably not coincide very closely with acreage.

57 Aránguiz Donoso, 'Notas para el estudio,' pp. 221–62. The Jesuits and other religious orders did not have access to encomienda labor and tended to favor the use of black slaves. In Calera de Tango there were 125 and in all the Jesuit estates there were 1200 at the time of expulsion. Barros Arana, *Historia*, VI, p. 250.

58 Jaime Eyzaguirre, *El conde de la conquista* (Santiago, 1966), pp. 70–2.

59 For tax evaluation, see *Catastro* (1834) and *Renta agrícola*. For individual haciendas, the account books in *Cunaco* and *Aculeo*, no p. no. The private accounting records show Aculeo with an annual income of $39 000 pesos of which one-fifth was from interest on loans.

60 Carmagnani, *Les mécanismes*, Part III, ch. 2. Data include plant and animal production. The 1874 tax data are in *Impuesto agrícola: rol de contribuyentes* (Santiago, 1874). The $9 693 000 is for Central Chile.

61 Peak exports in 1770s were worth $275 000 pesos; in 1871–6 their value rose to over $13 000 000. *EC* (1871–6). The stagnation of the Chilean economy in the late eighteenth and early nineteenth century based on a study of prices is discussed in Ruggiero Romano, *Una economia colonial: Chile en el siglo XVIII* (Buenos Aires, 1965), especially pp. 41–7.

62 Borde and Góngora, *Puangue*, I, p. 54; also *Aculeo*, no p. no.

63 Francisco Encina, *Historia de Chile*, 4th ed. (20 vols., Santiago, 1955), vol. 9, pp. 298–300, scorns Liberal rhetoric as inflated and unnecessary since [the institution of *mayorazgo*] 'was already spiritually dead' in the 1820s. For debate over exvinculation, see the *Sesiones de los cuerpos lejislativos de la República de Chile 1811 a 1845*, compiled by Valetín Letelier (Santiago, 1891), especially vols. 10, p. 364 and 14, pp. 120–40. Also the discussion in Donoso, *Las ideas*, ch. vi. Writers dealing with the *mayorazgos* have generally fallen into two groups. Those who have seen a 'new and powerful bourgeoisie' emerge in the nineteenth century pushing aside 'the land-holding aristocracy' assign more importance to the *mayorazgos*. See, e.g., Julio César Jobet, *Ensayo crítico del desarrollo económico y social de Chile* (Santiago, 1955), pp. 40–52; and Julio Heise González, 'La constitución de 1925 y las nuevas tendencias políticos-sociales,' *Anales*, no. 80 (1950), p. 129. Others such as Alberto Edwards Vives, in *Fronda aristocrática*, argue that 'aristocracy' and 'bourgeoisie' actually merged in the eighteenth century and no conflict developed in the nineteenth. In this view, the question of the *mayorazgos* is played down.

64 The legal restriction on *mayorazgos* can be seen in Amunátegui, *Mayorazgos*, I, p. 225; for fuller discussion see José María Ots Capdequí, *Manual de historia del derecho español en las Indias y el derecho propiamente indiano* (2 vols., Buenos Aires), I, 161. For a copy of the ex-Marqués de Larraín's petition, I am endebted to Mary Felstiner. The original is in the private archive of don Sergio Fernández Larraín in Santiago. For presentation and discussion of the petition, see *Sesiones de los cuerpos lejislativos*, vol. 8, p. 146. See also the debates recorded in *Sesiones de la cámara de Senadores* (ord., 1852), pp. 124–5; *Sessiones de la cámara de Diputados* (ord., 1857), pp. 10–13, 26–30. Frederick Pike, 'Aspects of class relations in Chile, 1850–1960,' *Latin America: Reform or Revolution*, ed. by James Petras and Maurice Zeitlin (New York, 1968), p. 204, follows Heise Gonzáles.

CHAPTER 2

Town and country in 1850

> The day is not far off when an
> intelligent and Christian reform will
> complete the rescue of our rural
> classes from the abject servitude to
> which they were reduced by
> conquest and colonialism.
>
> *Benjamín Vicuña Mackenna, 1856*

Although by 1850 most colonial restrictions had been abolished, the limitations to growth remained; and if Chileans had a new flag and national hymn, their economy had merely reached a new level of stagnation. The excitement and activity provoked by the 1832 Chañarcillo silver strike had died down while the great deposits of nitrate and copper lay still unexplored in the northern desert. Peru, the once opulent viceroyalty and now chaotic republic was still the main, if somewhat reduced, foreign market for agriculture while domestic demand was barely changed from the eighteenth century. A few sacks of grain moved by muleback or ox-cart for export to Lima; except for the area immediately surrounding Santiago, the large estates lay in isolated neglect populated by droves of cattle and casual workers. Despite the formal end of one imperial attachment and the informal beginning of another, regardless of new proclamations and constitutions, little occurred to disturb the languor of provincial life.

A flurry of new building and a series of urban improvements were just beginning to change the face of Santiago into what a later visitor would describe as the 'Paris of South America,' but in 1850 the capital still retained its colonial appearance. The scarcity of timber and fear of earthquakes suggested the propriety of low houses and only the churches and a handful of private buildings rose above one storey. 'The approach from the westward,' wrote Lt Gilliss in 1852, 'is not of the most interesting character . . . with wretched hovels inhabited by a slovenly and unwashed population . . . suburban streets in many places deep in mire from negligence of the *acequias* (irrigation ditches).'[1] The capital of Chile covered some seven square miles but the better houses were concentrated within a few blocks of the colonial Plaza de Armas, along the streets of Santo Domingo and Compañía. Each morning these

27

streets filled with crowds of vendors from the nearby farms giving the city an unmistakably rural air. There were 'peons from the country with panniers and baskets of fowl, fruit and vegetables; bakers and milk-women, droves of water-vendors selling their daily supplies from the turbid fountains, men enveloped to their nostrils in bundles of alfalfa . . . every material and variety of food and clothing may be bought in the streets.' At night long lines of lanterns marked the course of the streets and the principal bridges and at regular intervals men of the public watch called out the hour and condition of the weather ('las dos han dado y sereno'). These *serenos* alternated with the daytime *vijilantes* to maintain firm and somewhat arbitrary order in the city.[2]

The 'smells and bells' of the Church were the most obvious reminders that a colonial culture continued. In this low flat city the stone piles of the Church as well as its spiritual weight seemed much greater then than now when the plaster and glass boxes of bureaucracy and business dwarf the colonial buildings. There were six parishes in Santiago and these together with the rest of the secular church employed 232 ordained priests and a host of lay brothers. The regular clergy, led by the Augustinians and Dominicans, were the more imposing and wealthy; there were eight convents holding 527 nuns and lay sisters and 529 religious in the city's seven monasteries.[3] Most foreign visitors were impressed – and several of the Protestants among them outraged – by the heavy clerical atmosphere. Unlike Valparaíso where the bustle of trade and foreign contact created a somewhat more irreverent attitude, in Santiago the entire population 'dropped to their knees and beat their breasts . . . at the moment the tinkle of the bell (announcing the passage of the Archbishop's carriage) first struck their ears.' Although the ratio of clerics to total population – about 1 to 75 – does not seem exceptionally high, the religious were concentrated around the city center. 'The town is full of priests,' sniffed Francis Head, and 'the people are consequently indolent and immoral.'[4] And as elsewhere in Spanish America the Church was almost wholly responsible for health, education and welfare. San Juan de Dios and San Francisco de Borja (the two largest hospitals), the orphanage and an alms house were all under the direction of the Church.

Although the '*huaso* on his daring steed . . . the man of business and the modest *donzella* alike acknowledge the power of the priest,' the Church from the metropolitan cathedral to the rural hacienda was most closely identified with the upper class. This relationship was underscored in the city during Quasimodo when the high dignitaries of the Church were driven about by the gentlemen of Santiago, and in the countryside where the resident priest dined and gamed with the *hacendado*.[5] The Church had less influence on the rural lower classes in Chile than in other Spanish American countries, in large part because there was no village or community focus for the parish or mission. The imposing church towering over the countryside, a common scene in Mexico or the Andean countries, is absent in Chile. The best rural chapels were on the hacienda; the straggling towns and scattered population were virtually ignored.

Santiago at mid-century, and in fact up to the 1940s, was essentially a bureaucratic–commercial center. After the early attempts to form a federal republic collapsed and Concepción's mild challenge to Santiago was definitely crushed shortly after Independence, political power came to be concentrated in Santiago; and then a deliberate policy was undertaken to make the city into the banking and social center as well. In the 1840s and early '50s better roads and bridges were built to tie the nearby provinces to the capital and this trend was reinforced with the coming of railroads. All lines were routed through Santiago even though Concepción–Talcahuano had the best natural port on the central coast. The longitudinal railroad that logically should have been built from Concepción inland to service the central valley was begun in Santiago in 1858 and driven south even before the link from Valparaíso was completed (in 1863). This made it necessary for rails, construction equipment and disassembled rolling stock to be brought overland by ox-cart but it also meant that the rich central valley would be tributary to Santiago.[6]

With its concentration of political and economic power Santiago began to grow out of proportion to other cities. Although it may have seemed on 'the outskirts of civilisation' to Europeans and even to some North American visitors, Santiago was already in 1850 a sophisticated and somewhat snobbish and aloof capital from a *provincianos*'s perspective. Martín Rivas, the provincial hero of Blest Gana's novel, is made to feel the inadequacy of his dress and origins by a Santiago doorman, and José Joaquin Vallejo's short account of 'el provinciano en Santiago' shows the considerable gap that separated the *Santiaguino* from the rustic. Outside the capital no proper education, no adequate medical care could be obtained; even the scant comfort and amenities that Santiago offered were vastly superior to what was available in the straggling towns of the provinces.[7]

It is small wonder that anyone who could afford it built a house in Santiago and by 1850 this included most of the larger surrounding landowners. Together with the handful of prosperous merchants and miners they dominated Chilean society. They lived within easy walking distance of each other around the Plaza de Armas, met in *tertulias* or salons, and attended the same Mass and schools. Their business interests frequently overlapped as miners bought land, *hacendados* became interested in commerce, and merchants financed miners; and all this was reinforced and confused as their children intermarried.[8]

A list of the 145 wealthiest landowners that was compiled from the 1854 tax rolls by the National Society of Agriculture designates the core of the mid-century elite. At the risk of excessive clutter, they are all included in Table 3. Besides the names of the owners, the table shows the name of the estate, its location by province and its assessed annual income. Although we do not have the Santiago addresses of these landowners, it would be difficult to find one who did not live at least a few months of the year in the capital.

A glance confirms what anyone familiar with Chile knows, that the 'Castilian–Basque' elite is much in evidence. Especially around Santiago but also in neighboring Aconcagua and Valparaíso province, one finds the rasping names of Errázuriz, Larraín, Undurraga, Irarrázabal or Izquierdo that so tax the Anglo-Saxon's feeble capacity for foreign tongues. As much as this group liked to trace its ancestry to the captains of the conquest or even to celebrated families of medieval Spain, most in fact owed their position to a handful of enterprising Basque merchants and Spanish veterans of the war with Arauco who in the later eighteenth century invested their earnings in rural property. This *vecindario noble* of some 200 families was further distilled through the foundation of entails.[9] As we have seen, seventeen entails were formed in all (only one in the late seventeenth century; the rest between 1703 and 1789) and twelve of these were the basis for a noble title of Castille. Although in the 1850s entails were just being abolished and noble titles had disappeared some thirty years before, several haciendas and landowning families on the 1854 tax roll derived from these foundations. The most widespread and powerful of these was the enormous Larraín clan; great landowners themselves, they were related to at least seven of the principal *mayorazgo* holders.[10]

Actually, in 1850, this landed elite was less impressive close up. Some of the magnates, such as the Marqués de Larraín who so impressed Maria Graham, did affect a princely style and a handful of others had a certain pretension to this manner. Yet theirs was a distinctly provincial way of life, and even though an estate held thousands of hectares and a score of softly padding servants to attend to every wish and supported a comfortable house in the city, in the absence of adequate

Table 3 Landowners in central Chile in 1854

Name of estate	Name of owner	Annual income $	Name of estate	Name of owner	Annual income $
[Santiago Province]					
La Compañía	Juan de Dios Correa	89 000	—	R. Muñoz Bazanilla	8000
La Calera	Fco. Ruiz-Tagle	50 000	—	José Santos Cifuentes	8000
Pirque	R. Subercaseaux	34 000	—	Test. J. M. Matte	8000
Bucalemu	Manuel Fernández	26 700	Mayorauco	Mayorazo de Sierra Bella	8000
El Peral	Test. Rafael Correa	25 950	—	Patrico Larraín	8000
Codao	Fco. Ignacio Ossa	21 950	—	Pedro Errázuriz	8000
—	Mariano E. Sánchez	18 000	Naltagua	J. I. Alcalde	8000
Aculeo	Fco. de Borja Larraín	18 000	Quiyayes	Dolores Ovalle	7812
Lo Herrera	Fco. Arriagada	17 000	Popeta	Ramón Errázuriz	7700
Huechún	Melchor de S. Concha	15 000	El Cármen	Cármen Núñez	7650
San José	José Anjel Ortúzar	15 000	Bellavista	Fco. Cuadra Muñoz	7650
—	Test. J. V. Izquierdo	14 000	Campusano	José M. Larraín	7500
—	Bernardo Solar	14 000	Viluco	Rafael Larraín	7500
—	Santiago Pérez Matta	14 000	Hospital	Enrique Campino	7500
Punta de Cortez	Ambrosio Sánchez	13 500	—	V. Valdievieso	7500
—	Ignacio Ortúzar	12 000	Mercedes	Manuel Montt	7500
Angostura	Pedro José Luco	12 000	Marco	Matías Cousiño	7500
Chiñihue	José A. Alcalde	11 500	Cocauquen	Pablo Alvárez	7400
Cocalán	Vicente Subercaseaux	11 400	La Boca	Fernando Luco	7304
—	Test. V. Vargas	11 000	Aguila	Domingo Toro	7200
—	Recoleta Dominica	11 000	Pudagüel	J. Domingo Dávila	7000
Cabras	Juan José Gandarillas	10 400	—	Vicente Cifuentes	7000
—	Manuel Balmaceda	10 000	—	Juan Vargas	7000

Continues

31

Table 3 *(cont.)* Landowners in central Chile in 1854

Name of estate	Name of owner	Annual income $	Name of estate	Name of owner	Annual income $
[Santiago Province] *cont.*					
Cabras	José María Solar	10 000	—	Mercedes Gandarillas	7000
El Principal	Huidobro	10 000	Ibacache	Domingo Matte	7000
Esmeralda	José A. Lecaros	9500	Pico	M. Covarrubias	7000
San Miguel	Javiera Carrera	9500	Guindos	Domingo Matte	7000
Puangue	José María Hurtado	9500	San Diego	Pedro N. Barros	6800
Peldehue	Recoleta Dominica	9500	Salinas	Eujenio Matta	6800
Alhué	Santiago Toro	9200	Sta Filomena	Santiago Larraín	6750
—	Santiago Varas	9500	Parral	Diego Carvallo	6600
Tres Hijuelas	Maria de la Luz Mascayano	9000	—	J. Gandarillas	6500
Santa Cruz	Cesáreo Valdéz	9000	Esperanza	Manuel Elizalde	6500
Hijuela del Medio	José A. Valdéz	8400	—	Jose Gregorio Castro	6440
Rinconado	Juan de D. Gandarillas	8300	Quinta	Matias Cousiño	6300
Arañas	Rafael Dávila	6200	—	Miguel Prado	6000
—	Ant. Larraín	6000	—	Domingo Velasco	6000
—	Concepción Echeverría	6000	Palmas	Matilde Cisternas	6000
—	José N. Larraín i Rojas	6000	Paine	J. A. Garcia Huidobro	6000
[Curicó Province]					
La Puerta	Justo Vergara	7236	Quinahue	M. A. Barahona	6207
Guaico	Lucas del Rio	7000	Teno	Marcos Castillo	6000
Nilahue	Test. Carmen Herrera	7000			

Continues

Table 3 (*cont.*) Landowners in central Chile in 1854

Name of estate	Name of owner	Annual income $	Name of estate	Name of owner	Annual income $
[Aconcagua Province]					
—	Fco. Videla	17 500	Peña Blanca	Mayorazgo de la Cerda	8485
San Lorenzo	Mayorazgo de la Cerda	15 000	Toro	Gabriel Vicuña	8085
Catapilco	Fco. Javier Ovalle	15 000	Alicahue	Amador Cerda	8000
San Felipe	M. J. Hurtado	13 000	Tartan	Juan E. Rosas	7860
Penquehüe	Máximo Caldera	13 000	Huahue	P. Ovalle Errázuriz	7500
Pullalli	J M. Irarrázabal	12 500	San José	Luis Ovalle	6860
Longotoma	Fco. Javier Ovalle	11 000	Sobrante	Manuel Silva Ugarte	6500
Catemu	Borja Garcia Huidobro	10 825	Quebradilla	Santiago Vargas	6000
Higuera	Mayorazgo de la Cerda	10 743	Marquis	José Vicente Sanchez	6000
[Colchagua Province]					
Tagua-Tagua	Fco. Javier Errázuriz	18 000	Cauquenes	Rafael Larraín Moxó	10 000
Callenque	Fco. Ign. Ossa	15 000	Cunaco	Ign. Valdéz Carrera	9350
Chimbarongo	Padres de Merced	12 000	San José	P. E. Iñiguez	9000
Armahue	Dolores Ramírez	12 000	Colchagua	Federico Errázuriz	9000
San Antonio	Vicente Ortízar	11 300	Huemul	J. de Dios Correa	8700
Huique	Test. Miguel Echenique	11 000	San José del Carmen	Juan José Echenique	8000
Pataguas	Fco. de Borja Eguiguren	7 600	—	Jose M. Ureta	6500
Chuchui	José M. Guzmán	7000	—	Borja Valdéz	6500
Tambo	Fernando Plata	7000	San Jose de Chimbarongo	Pedro Valdéz	6400
Barriales	Test. J. M. Ugarte	7000	San José del Toro	Fco. J. Valdés	6000
Sierra	Test. J de D. Vial	6800		Carmen Calvo.	6000

Continues

33

Table 3 (*cont.*) Landowners in central Chile in 1854

Name of estate	Name of owner	Annual income $	Name of estate	Name of owner	Annual income $
[Valparaíso Province]					
Purutún i Melon	F. Cortéz i Azúa	60 000	Calera	Ildefonso Huici	8342
Palmas	Diego Ovalle	13 200	Ocóa	Fco. Echeverría	8150
San Pedro	Josué Waddington	13 000	Ocóa	Manuel Echevarría	7900
—	Ramón de la Cerda	11 700	Colmo	Ramón Subercaseaux	7012
Concón Alto	Ramón Subercaseaux	11 200	Romeral	Juan Morandé	6309
—	Micaela Errázuriz	10 075	Hijuela	Paula Recabárren	6000
Las Tablas	J. M. Ramírez	10 000	Santa Teresa	J. V. Sánchez	6000
Quinteros	Ramón Undurraga	9000	San Fermín	Fermín Solar	6000
La Hijuela	Enrique Cazotte	8921			
Ocoa	Jose Manuel Guzmán	8900			
[Talca Province]					
Quechereguas	Nemecio Antunez	12 000			
[Maule Province]					
Rinconada	Fco. Vargas Bascuñan	10 000			
Calivero	Zenón Manzanos	6340			
Huemitil	Rafael Benavente	6081			

Source: *Renta agrícola* (1854).

markets agriculture provided few of the amenities associated with landed society elsewhere. We may best appreciate the quality of life from the perspective of foreign travelers, less impressionable than successive generations of writers who sought to claim a landed aristocracy in their background or to condemn the 'feudal latifundists.' W. S. W. Ruschenberger, who had occasion to make extended trips into the countryside, found the landowners hospitable and charmingly rustic. One 'don Vicente,' a 'short, corpulent, good humored' owner of 50 square miles was a 'facsimilie of Sancho Panza in person, whom he admires with all his heart.'[11] The inventories and property appraisals of these mid-century estates bear out the travelers' impressions. The fine hacienda El Huique valued at $330 000 in land and livestock had less than $3500 in all household furnishings and only $19 worth of books; the sprawling adobe house of Aculeo, one of the great haciendas of Chile in 1850, was decidedly rustic. Others were 'no better than a barn.' Even the town houses, where more attention was paid to furniture and decoration, were still generally of one storey, badly lighted, and several blocks away from the nearest baths appropriate for 'people of quality.'[12]

If life in Santiago was not overly elegant or exciting by the standards of London or Paris, it was, at least for the fortunate few, comfortable. The records of one such family, the Echenique, permit a glimpse into this way of life at mid-century.[13] The family's income was drawn almost entirely from the hacienda El Huique some 200 km to the south. This estate, rented to two sons, produced for the widow of the owner (Sra Antonia Tagle de Echenique) about $15 700 a year during the period 1853–9. This is somewhat higher but reasonably close to the $11 000 given in the 1854 tax roll as El Huique's 'renta anual.' Just what $15 000 annual income meant is difficult to say. The highest ranking general then was paid $4500 and the President $18 000. The tax rolls that we have seen above show 145 estates in central Chile that produced $6000 or more (the highest was $89 000). Out of Huique's $15 700 a large house – one of the few of two storeys in 1853 in Santiago – was maintained along with the not inexpensive tastes. The four young childrens' allowances amounted to $1000 a year ($20.00 a month to each), a tutor for $500, piano lessons were 'una onza' ($17.25) a month for a daughter, dental care cost $86.25 for one sitting, a 'tailor for Nicolás' was $83.00. These and several other miscellaneous expenses nibbled away at income. The house was one of the first to have gas lighting ($11.00 a month), and the municipal tax for street lighting and night watchman was another $10.00 a month. There were two full-time servants living in at $10.00 a month salary and others hired for special tasks. The 'household expenses' averaged around $200.00 a month expect for January, February and March, when the entire family lived on the hacienda. The furnishings do not appear extravagant: they were appraised at around $7000 and improved with only a small shipment of furniture from Paris ($312 plus $188 freight). The Church was another expense. Two *capellanías* cost $300 a year; there was one donation to the Capuchines and fees for ceremony. Beggars, who were not by municipal law allowed on the streets but were permitted to plead for 'una limosnita por el amor de Dios' on certain days, got $20.00 from the Echenique on one such occasion. All this would have been manageable but the family had gone into debt during the previous decade building the Santiago house. Servicing loans that had been obtained from friends and relatives was a considerable drain and even though the hacienda's earnings were growing through the 1850s (partly as a result of the California and Australian markets that had recently opened) additional loans – of $12 000 at twelve per cent in 1858; $20 000 from the government at nine per cent in 1859 – were needed to survive the lean years.

For such a family as the Echenique, Santiago in 1850 actually offered little diversion. There were three fairly shabby theatres and they were poorly attended. The elegant clubs of La Unión or Club Hípico were not yet established and the Sunday strolls in the Alameda, now a smoggy and tasteless ravine of cars and trash but then a tranquil path lined with twin rows of poplars, was the center of public life. Every proper family had at least one carriage for a weekly spin and the young dandies spent hours at public billiard tables, 'a game as necessary to the happiness of a Chilean . . . as eating or smoking cigars.' Santiago social life turned around Mass and the visits to the parlors of relatives and friends, marathon sessions of smoking, gossip, flirtations, the occasional light piece on the piano, and food. Among the respectable classes the *yerba mate* infusion, another colonial vestige, was being replaced by the more fashionable tea brought in by the British.[14]

Added to the early republican land-holding elite was a steady and welcome intrusion of new faces and money. Although the former *mayorazgo* and titled families made up the core of the Chilean upper class, this was by no means a closed society. One critic claimed that mid-century Chileans practically made a 'religious cult' of the aristocratic, often Basque, family names but money and distinguished military service permitted entry into the best circles.[15] Trade began to flourish after independence as foreign and local merchants moved into the vacuum created by the break with Spain, and by 1850, maritime traffic suddenly increased as sailing ships round the Horn and bound for the goldfields of California called at Valparaíso for repair and provisions.

It is easy, however, to overstate the importance of the new commercial activity especially since two groups of writers – nationalists praising the salutary effects of independence, and modern critics scourging the onset of a new imperialism – tend to exaggerate the volume of business.[16] As Christopher Platt has pointed out, there were actually two levels of trade: high-priced imports and the truck of daily needs and local produce. At the upper level, goods such as porcelain, cutlery, high-quality cloth, silks, were imported for the small upper class. Much of this trade was brought in by the large commercial houses in Valparaíso and funneled through the better retail stores in Santiago. In the first half of the century neither the port, the trade nor the merchants were very imposing. Valparaíso had only 3000 inhabitants in 1820 and less than 50 000 by mid-century; the city was a hastily assembled collection of warehouses and wooden buildings, distinctly inferior to Santiago. A great many fortunes grew out of Valparaíso over the course of the century, but before 1850 the trade was too insignificant to allow the traders to make much of a dent in Chilean society. The small market for European manufactures was easily glutted and the country drained of precious metals – the only export available to balance international payments. By mid-century this was beginning to change with grain shipments to California and Australia, and the export of copper.[17]

The British were the single most important foreign commercial group in Valparaíso and although their number fluctuated with the arrival and sailing ships, a reliable observer in the 1820s thought that about four hundred people including sailors was a good estimate of the total, with only a few 'respectable' families in permanent residence. Besides the British, the Germans and French were also well represented, and in both Valparaíso and the capital about sixty per cent of the principal merchants in 1850 were foreigners.[18] Table 4 shows this more clearly.

A word should be said about the social position of foreigners and recent immigrants just then in the process of obtaining Chilean citizenship. In 1850 these new merchant groups were still unaccepted by the Santiago elite. A few merchants built comfortable *quintas* in the hills behind Valparaíso and one or two such as Josué Waddington acquired rural estates; but for the most part, this was a 'very civil, vulgar people' and if they found solace 'twirling in the waltz with the fair Chilenas' their partners were rarely from the best families. In these early years of the republic, the foreign merchant families generally intermarried or mixed with Chileans of the same middling commercial class. Not until the export economy got fully underway after 1850 did the soaring fortunes of the Cox, Edwards, or Lyon families enable them to enter the best social circles. They were accepted to the extent that their incomes grew, and by the last half of the century the more established Chilean elite families sought to marry their children to the new merchants, just as the Spanish immigrants were courted a century before.[19]

Table 4 Nationality of the principal wholesale merchants in Santiago and Valparaíso in 1849

Nationality	Number in Santiago	Number in Valparíso	Totals	%
Chilean	14	22	36	37%
British	7	17	24	
German	2	9	11	
French	2	8	10	
North American	—	7	7	63%
Spanish	—	3	3	
Other	—	7	7	
Totals	25	73	98	100

Source: *Repertorio nacional*, 'Matricula del comercio de Santiago según el rejistro de las patentes tomadas en 1849'; 'Matricula del comercio de Valparaíso . . . en 1849' (Santiago, 1850), vol. 2, no p. nos. The data are for '*casas de consignación*' and '*almacenes*,' the most important of the commercial houses.

Many Chileans of older but unprominent families followed the same track as the immigrants. Although foreigners dominated the main wholesale business in Valparaíso, there was still room there for several energetic Chileans; and in Santiago local merchants were by far the most important group. One of these was José Besa, owner of the business house founded in 1838 that dealt in copper exports, who obtained a monopoly for the distribution of a local beet sugar mill and provided a principal support for the Bank of Chile. Matías Cousiño, Chile's most outstanding capitalist of the era, got rich in trade as did Domingo Matte, the son of a Spanish immigrant, whose merchant house on Compañia Street was the base for a large fortune later invested in banking and rural property.[20] In time such Chilean merchant families intermarried with the landed elite, took on sons of landowners as partners or managers in the business, and often themselves bought rural estates. There is not yet a study of the nineteenth-century merchants that would permit an evaluation of their social position. Obviously some rose from obscure beginnings to wealth and social prominence but it is also clear from even a cursory reading of the tax rolls where merchants are listed that the Larraín, Echevarría, Gandarillas – names usually associated with the eighteenth-century elite – continued to be active in trade. It is not just that merchants made money in trade and moved into elite circles; many stayed in business after attaining social prominence; and in other cases, important landowners or their sons branched out from agriculture into commerce. There is no evidence that Chile's 'bourgeois aristocracy' ever saw trade as demanding.

The better retail merchant houses were along the two or three main waterfront streets in Valparaíso. Of the 142 that paid the *patente* tax in 1849, 96 were Chilean owned. In Santiago, the merchants occasionally rented space in the houses of the elite, or in large stalls in the *portal* around the Plaza de Armas; but the retail commercial district was slightly to the south of the most fashionable residential district, on the wrong end of Compañía, Estado, Huerfanos, and Ahumado streets. In 1849, nearly all of these stores – 88 out of a total of 101 – were owned by Chileans. Table 5 shows the nationality of retail merchant houses in Valparaíso and Santiago.

Table 5   Nationality of retail merchants in Santiago and Valparaíso in 1849

Nationality	Number in Santiago	Number in Valparaíso	Totals	%
Chilean	88	96	184	76%
British	—	10	10	
German	—	4	4	
French	8	12	20	
North American	—	—	—	24%
Spanish	4	11	15	
Other	1	9	10	
Totals	101	142	243	100%

Source: *Repertorio nacional*, 'Matrícula del comercio.' The data are for *'tiendas'* and *'bodegas.'*

These stores distributed imported cloth, sugar and tea and a wide range of merchandise to the inhabitants of Santiago including the urban based landowners who purchased a handful of items here – things that could not be made or grown on the estates – for the hacienda store. It is difficult to estimate the importance in volume or income of these retail merchants. They were required to pay an annual tax of 50 pesos which may suggest an average income of $500 to $750 pesos.[21]

Below this level of trade circulated the local produce: the output of local artisans and cottage industry, and the cheap drink and food from outlying farms. All this was sold in Santiago through the thoroughly Chilean *baratillos* and *pulperías* in the local marketplace along the Mapocho river and also throughout the countryside. Much of the rustic clothing, sandals, hats, and shirts were made by women in rural or village households; and even after British cottons were imported, seamstresses used the foreign cloth but still made their own shirts and dresses. The local industry most affected by Lancashire cottons was that of spinners and weavers, but even here, high transportation costs protected the provincial cottage industry until later in the century when railways and better roads lowered costs and put most *hilanderas* and *tejedoras* out of business.[22]

Mining offered the fastest road to wealth and social prominence. Francisco Ignacio Ossa, for example, struck it rich in Copiapó, bought the haciendas of Codao and Callouque and moved easily into the Santiago upper class and a seat in the Senate. The lives of Ramón and Vicente Subercaseaux, sons of a French immigrant, demonstrate the common progression from mining to landowning. The first, born in 1790, was by 1830 a millionaire, the son-in-law of the President, and owner of three great haciendas. Vicente, somewhat less enterprising in society or politics than his brother, also invested a mining fortune in land. Military service or high civil office provided another avenue to wealth, status, power, and usually to landownership. Such families as the Lazcano or Blanco Encalada who had served in the Spanish administration in Rio de la Plata, or Manual Bulnes, the famed general from Concepción (and in 1850, Chile's President) moved easily in the best society of Santiago. By mid-century, there were eleven Army generals on active duty, one vice-admiral in the Navy, some 340 Army and 49 Navy lesser officers.[23]

Among the professionals, lawyers were held in the highest esteem. The 1849 *Repertorio Nacional* records the names of over 300 degree-holding *licenciados* and *doctores* in law and perhaps seventy-five per cent of these lived in Santiago. There is no study of the social origins of nineteenth-century lawyers but a brief examination suggests what contemporaries claimed, that most came from the upper classes. Many lawyers were themselves landowners or relatives of landowners for the study of law was the sign of cultivation and erudition, and usually a prerequisite for election to Congress or a good position in the bureaucracy.[24] Almost all lawyers were Chileans and as the export economy developed in the course of the nineteenth century, many found employment with the new corporations, often hired perhaps as much for their influential political connections as for their legal competence. Many lawyers served in the top positions of the public administration, but below the Ministers and important judgeships there was a wide range of over 1000 public employees throughout the ministries, postal service, customs, the intendancies and courts. The best-paid positions conferred status on their holders, and as with so many of the top positions in Chilean society, these men too were usually recruited from among the wealthy landowning families.[25]

Members of the liberal and technical professions such as professors and engineers were concentrated in the capital and Valparaíso. Santiago apparently had nearly half of the total engineers, university teachers, and dentists. But all these together totaled less than half the number of lawyers. Engineers and medical doctors occupied a somewhat ambiguous position in mid-century society. The figures are open to question but probably half of all engineers – they came in with the imported engines, railway and mining equipment – were foreigners. Later in the century, even after degrees could be obtained more easily in the country, about a third of such technical people were foreigners. Like the immigrant merchants, their acceptance depended on income; and by the later nineteenth century, the descendants of such families as the Lambert or Bunster were firmly within the elite circles.[26]

The few local doctors and dentists were untrusted and scorned until the mid-nineteenth century. Public opinion held that such a profession was 'worthy only of mulattoes'; doctors were treated 'with less consideration than an artisan' in the better houses. Foreign physicians, undoubtedly because of their better training, enjoyed a higher status. Until 1834, according to Tornero, the best doctors of Chile were all Spaniards, Englishmen, French, or Peruvians from the University of San Marcos. Foreign doctors treated the wealthy of Santiago – the Echenique family we have seen had an English doctor and dentist – and sat on the Junta Examinadora that certified local practitioners. As medical training improved, treatment became more reliable and doctors' fees larger, Chilean physicians rose in esteem and later in the century medicine became a springboard to status and frequently to a political career.[27]

Although salaries as stipulated in the official regulations of the Public Administration do not tell the entire story of a person's income, Table 6 gives some indication of how much a number of positions were worth in 1844–5 and these can be compared with the income of merchants, the annual yields of rural estates or the wages of peons. Some positions such as those in the Church or military provided substantial perquisites such as housing, rations and expenses.

Table 6   Representative annual salaries of the Military, Church, and Public Administration: 1844–5 (in pesos)

Military	Annual salary $	Church and Public Administration	Annual salary $
		President	12 000
		Archbishop of Santiago	6000
		Minister of Treasury	4500
		Chief, Valparaíso customs	4000
General of Division (top army rank)	3500		
Vice-Admiral (top naval rank)	3500[1]		
Colonel in army	2640		
		Judge [*juez de letras*] of Talca or Colchagua	2400
		Civil Engineer in State corps	1500
		Rector of the University	1500
		Dean of the Faculty of Philosophy and Humanities	1000
Captain in army	840		
Second Lieutant	600[1]		
Sub-Lieutant	480		
		Doorman in Ministry	150
		Ordinary janitor	125
Common soldier	96		

Source: Anguita, *Leyes*, vol. I, pp. 441-62 and 497.
[1]Data from 1849.

Unless otherwise stated, monetary values throughout this book are expressed in the Chilean peso, and in centavo fractions (cents) of the peso. Until the mid-1870s the peso was worth approximately 44*d* of the £ sterling, or around 90 cents of the American dollar. For the changing value of the peso in terms of the £ sterling, see Appendix 4.

In the same social group as middling professionals were the smaller landowners, the class of 'mechanics,' retail merchants, and the owners of the larger artisanal industries. The same weak market that restricted agricultural development also limited manufacturing. Incentives and exclusive privileges were offered to foreigners and Chileans but no manufacturing as we understand the term today developed. The most likely single item would have been textiles; but most common woolens were provided by cottage industry and the British cotton imports dominated the urban market.

Most local needs were satisfied by artisanal industry and although Chilean craftsmen were greater in number, it appears that the better combination of technical knowledge and entrepreneurship was supplied by foreigners, especially the French, 'whose mechanical productions as well as personnel, are more numerously represented than those of any other foreign nation.' Above all, the French shaped the local fashions as they were the best hatters, *modistes*, and hairdressers. Other foreigners prospered as tanners, smiths, and carpenters. Several of the larger shops were fairly large businesses and the owners were true entrepreneurs employing capital and several workmen. In several cases, not only the top craftsmen but also the materials such as lumber and dressed stone were brought by sail around the Horn. There is no easy way to estimate the earnings of such petty capitalists but Gilliss tells us that there were several such foreigners in 1850 who were 'worth more than $50 000 each.'[28]

Since it is difficult to find a middle class capable of creating its own set of cultural values and prestige symbols as late as 1965, we should not expect to find one a century earlier.[29] A great many diffuse and misleading terms have been applied to nineteenth-century society, from 'middle sectors,' 'middle class,' 'aristocracy,' to the more inventive, 'bourgeois aristocracy' or even hyperbolic, 'tremendous bourgeoisie' (*burguesía tremenda*); but one hesitates to apply any of these labels to the amorphous group of people we have just seen.[30] There is some argument for drawing a single social line just below the respectable professions, better retail merchants and petty entrepreneurial groups and above the mass of individual shopkeepers, common artisans, peddlars and day laborers as shown in Table 7. Above this line, people considered themselves and each other to be white and respectable (*decente*), and there were only ordinary obstacles to greater wealth, intermarriage and social mobility. The mass of people (*el pueblo*) below this line were described as European to foreign visitors but were really seen by their social superiors as 'people of color' (*gente de color*); they worked with their hands and had little hope of improving their lot.[31]

There were important differences of income and status within the upper group. The values, manners, and morals of the conglomerate of wealthy miners and merchants, but most especially of the large landowners, were considered desirable; everyone strove to emulate them and hopefully to adopt their life style. The energetic attempts on the part of the less fortunate to imitate their social superiors gave rise to an enduring Chilean term, *siútico*, which designates such a social climber. The term itself was first used in the 1860s but the attitude was clearly perceived by the observant Gilliss. Writing in the early 1850s, he described the 'mechanics and retail merchants' in terms that remind one of the impoverished Spanish nobleman in *Lazarillo de Tormes*: 'they will

Table 7   Chilean and foreign urban society *ca* 1850

Chileans	Foreigners and recent immigrants
[I]	
Large landowners	
Miners	
Wholesale merchants	
Upper clergy	
Military officers	
Lawyers	
Upper level of cadres	Miners
Liberal professionals; engineers,	Wholesale merchants
professors	Engineers, doctors, dentists
Retail merchants	Retail merchants, shopkeepers
Entrepreneurs	Entrepreneurs
[II]	
Shopkeepers (*pulperos, baratilleros*)	
Artisans, peddlers,	
Skilled laborers	
Day laborers	
Domestic servants	
Vagrants	

go to any lengths to obtain fine cloth and fine furniture or to attend the theatre on holidays; yet (they) constantly live in the utmost discomfort.' In the course of the nineteenth century the disdain for manual labor and a persistent striving for upper-class status on the part of these groups was reinforced by liberal university education and the willingness of foreigners to replace them not only in industry but in retail commerce as well.[32]

Within the groups of landowners, miners, merchants, and professionals, there was little conflict. The political leadership of mid-century Chile grew out of a tradition that reached back to the last decades of the colony. Unlike the case of Mexico or Peru where more aggressive Bourbon leaders attempted to roll back the political gains made by creoles and to impose Spanish rule, in Chile the families of local elite and the imperial cadres intermarried and collaborated in running this distant colony. When independence forced many Spaniards from their administrative posts and disrupted imperial trade and bureaucracy, the cohesive and class-conscious creole group whose vital center was the large landholders, stood ready to move into the new positions of republican government.[33] Because colonial Chile was geographically compact – almost all of the population lived between Serena and Concepción – few regional differences arose and those that did could be easily put down. Moreover, a large part of the commercial or nascent industrial sectors that in other ex-colonies – one thinks, for example, of the merchant class in the early-nineteenth-century United States – competed for political leadership, were in Chile in the hands of foreigners who had moved into the vacuum created by the departing imperial merchants. The class interests of the landowners – foreign markets, credit, a source for luxury imports and manufactures – led them unhesitatingly into an alliance with the commercial emissaries and investors of the new foreign metropoli, while their status aspirations could be satisfied by the exercise of public office. Moreover, this small, stable and geographically compact society had intermingled: blood and informal kinship ties extended throughout the clergy, upper bureaucracy and liberal professions. A definition made of Chile's elite around the final days of the colonial epoch still largely held: 'some are powerful landowners, others clerics and lawyers of outstanding talent and enlightenment – all of them with interminable family relationships and ramifications which extend from one end of the kingdom to the other.'[34]

By 1850, the Correa, Errázuriz, Subercaseaux, Ossa, Larraín and Lazcano together with the 'sword of Penco' (i.e., the military families from Concepción) were firmly in control. In Congress and the presidency itself, the landowners were the single most important group. Fourteen of the twenty-nine Senators and twenty of the fifty-four Deputies of the tenth legislative session (1852–5) appear in our list of large landowners and several others were related to or undoubtedly shared the interests of the landowning class. The President then in office, Manuel Montt; one to come, Federico Errázuriz; and the father of another, Manuel Balmaceda, were all owners of large estates. The leaders of this 'autocratic republic' insisted on sober and effective administration and a firm hand with the *plebe*. Most got their degree in law from the University of Chile and had 'learned to command in the school of the hacienda.'[35]

Except for the squabbles of 1851, there was barely a challenge to the government, and one may obtain a credible picture of this ruling system – whose conservative and almost effortless influence was described as the 'weight of the night' – through the eyes of foreign visitors. The landowner visited by Ruschenberger, lord of 50 square miles and one of the best houses in Santiago, rarely saw the need to occupy his seat in the Senate. 'Para que amigo? Why should I, friend? There are enough there without me.' And finally Lt Gilliss again, who provides such an excellent account of mid-century Chile, described this decidedly un-hysterical scene: 'There is scarcely more life among the speakers (of Congress) than moderate Quaker meeting offers.' Speakers never rose to address the chamber but simply turned to the president and spoke, 'until his "*he dicho*" notifies you that he will drop back to apathy again . . . once seen, there is nothing to induce the repetition of a stranger's visit.'

We must not gain the false impression that the country was run by landowners alone because development in the late colonial and early republican decades produced overlap and intermingling of economic interests and one finds in the ministries and public administration men whose primary experience had been in trade and mining. But this was a society in which the landowners were dominant; this is clear not only from their political positions but from the tax records of their income and through contemporaries' appreciation of their status and prestige.[36] Let us now move out from Santiago into the surrounding countryside in order to examine the social and economic base that underlay the landowners' influence in mid-nineteenth-century Chile.

In 1854, according to the tax records, there were 862 landowners who received some two-thirds of all agricultural income in central Chile. The most important of these – the 145 whose names are listed below – received between $6000 and $89 000 apiece. They alone

Table 8

Annual income of rural properties in central Chile: 1854

Category in pesos	No. of properties	Percentage	Total income	Percentage
$25–99	12 403	64.9%	143 712	2.5%
$100–99	3130	16.4%	469 500	8.1%
$200–499	1957	10.2%	733 875	12.7%
$500–99	748	3.9%	561 000	9.7%
$1000–5999	717	3.8%	2 324 000	40.2%
$6000 up	145	0.8%	1 552 643	26.8%
Total $	19 100	100%	5 784 730	100%

Source: *BSNA*, vol. I (1869), Table I. Data are compiled from *Renta agricola* (1854).

account for nearly twenty-seven per cent of all income. The rest of the 18 000 landowners listed in the rolls, and an indeterminate number of tiny 'minifundists' too small to be taxed, shared the remaining agricultural yield.[37] Estates with the largest annual incomes were found close by the market centers of Santiago and Valparaíso. As one moves out from Santiago, the commercial value of land rapidly decreased. In 1854, over half the highest-yielding estates were in the province of Santiago alone, while the vast haciendas to the south, although often holding thousands of hectares, were worth very little. [38]

The peculiar historical development outlined in Chapter 1 helps explain the nature of rural Chile by 1850. Unlike Middle America or the Andean highlands, there were here only a handful of 'Indian' communities and these were Indian in name only for the inhabitants were indistinguishable from other *mestizos* and their land was simply agglomerations of small properties. Travelers noticed the small *comunidad* of Pomaire near Melipilla which then as now was busy making a chocolate brown pottery. In nearby Talagante, Maria Graham saw that there was 'no difference whatever between the language, habits or dress of these Indians and other Chileans.' In the northern desert, remnants of the Atacameño and Diaguita cultures survived and below the Bío-Bío, of course, the Araucanos although much reduced since Ercilla's epic praise still held tenaciously to their lands. But throughout central Chile where an insufficiently rooted culture could not withstand the Spanish settlement, native tenure forms were obliterated while the indigenous plants and techniques were absorbed into a hybrid agriculture.

Nor – again unlike the richer and more heavily populated areas of Spanish America – were corporate landholding forms very important. The eighteenth-century expulsion of the Jesuits and the subsequent sale of their estates placed the most important ecclesiastical lands in private hands. By the middle of the nineteenth century the *catastro* shows only three large clerical estates, two owned by the Recollect Dominicans and the other by La Merced.[39] In regard to privately entailed land – that held in *mayorazgos* – its importance as we have seen has been habitually exaggerated, and in any case by 1857 nearly all had been exvinculated. Corporate land companies, unlike those in neighboring Argentina, were not important in central Chile even at the end of the nineteenth century. The decisions to vary production, to increase acreage under cultivation, or to retrench, were in the hands of the thirty or forty large landowners or their leaseholders in each Department. Their decisions, passed down to the men who worked the estates, affected about eighty per cent of the land of central Chile and affected nearly all the commercial agriculture.

Income as reflected in the *catastro* was a function of markets and in 1850 the lack of transportation sharply reduced the possibilities for gain outside the market districts of the capital and main ports. Deep in the provinces a large tract was required to provide upper-class standing. In 1840, for example, don Miguel Echenique explained that he divided his estate of some 11 000 hectares (of excellent land) into only three *hijuelas* (i.e., of 3800 each) because 'the hacienda did not contain enough land to satisfy all my heirs . . . further subdivision would reduce them to scant fortune.'[40] If the estates could support a number of sons they were more likely to be subdivided and this is the pattern of the later nineteenth century as the great sprawling colonial *estancias* were broken up into still large *fundos*. But there was more than meets the casual eye in subdividing an estate. By 1850, most farms functioned as units with buildings, fences and irrigation canals arranged for a single operation. To create new farms out of the larger estates it was necessary to change boundaries, build new buildings, reroute canals and endure the cost and bother of surveying and legal fees. Then, too, central Chile contains a number of micro-climates and a varied terrain that produce a very uneven resource base. Ten hectares of irrigated vineyard can be more valuable than five hundred of arid hillside.[41]

Up to now we have been mainly concerned with the distribution of income among the larger properties. These are some of the data that help explain rural Chile; but the more interesting questions about the substance of life itself – what people were faced with, how they perceived their situation and how they attempted to cope with it – are more elusive, difficult to recreate and can be generalised only at great risk. There were differences in regions, especially between Santiago and the hinterland, but also between one estate and the next.

For those families with a place in the country like the Echenique's, the major occasion of the year was the festive if dusty journey to the family *fundo*. More than one traveler, fortunate to be asked along, left a vivid picture of this progression. Wives, daughters and maids were bundled into a great squeaking ox-cart which, surrounded by sons and swains on prancing horses, rolled past the squatter settlements already forming on the city's outskirts and then lurched down dusty roads into a pastel-colored countryside that was an important part of the creole life style. January and February, when the heat can be oppressive in Santiago, were the favorite months in the countryside.[42] This coincided with the wheat harvest, one of the busiest times of the agricultural year. But for the owners these were still unhurried years with time for picnics and horse races, the entire rural scene of tranquil and carefree days on the *fundo*. 'Up at nine, breakfast at ten, a saunter in a small flower garden with a cigar . . . an occasional ride or a game of chess with the curate, a sly joke or *bon mot* with some of the ladies, [the landowner] manages to get through the day till three o'clock when he dines. After dinner which occupies about two hours, when alone he smokes and dozes away the afternoon and evening at which time he sups heartily and retires to bed about twelve.' The *misión* provided another occasion for visits to the estate and to promote solidarity among workers and *empleados*. Displays of horsemanship, fiestas and frolic were combined with religion, decoration and repair of the chapel and the exhortation to good works. Ramón Subercaseaux left in his memoirs a nostalgic picture of these days in the country without which it is difficult to comprehend either the ties of affection and respect that bound together owner and workers or the important non-economic pleasures and advantages that made estate ownership desirable.[43]

Deeper in the provinces conditions were more primitive. In Curicó, Talca and below the Maule, even a huge estate was insufficient to support anything beyond a modestly respectable style to say nothing of a Santiago town house. In the 1850s many provincial landowners lived all year round on the *fundo* or maintained a modest place in the local towns like San Fernando or Talca. In such places local oligarchies grew up to control the municipality, courts, and police.[44]

Up to 1860 at least much of the country shared the common fate of oscillation between feast and famine. The result of the first was often low prices and bankruptcy for the landowner; of the second, misery and occasionally starvation for the rural poor. The problem of large harvests may be seen from an anonymous article in the landowners' *El Agricultor* that complained that a high yield of wheat 'brought sadness instead of joy' because of even further price drops. On the eve of the California gold rush, a Talca paper described the mood in a common lament: 'the present epoch has been fatal for mercantile transactions in the province; no demand and overproduction. Wheat production has been twice the consumption.'[45]

The social structure inherited from the previous centuries provided only a tiny market for agriculture. Much of the population either grew its own food or received food rations in exchange for services performed on the estates. Others scrounged for their meagre subsistence, living on the barest minimum of caloric intake. Only the cities of Santiago and Valparaíso, the northern mining districts and people in road or bridge construction gangs offered any outlet, and because the cities were still small (Santiago had about 90 000; Valparaíso 52 000 in 1855) and the Atacama coast was still sparsely populated, landowners knew that the possibilities of growing rich by supplying this market were obviously limited to those farms on the outskirts of Santiago. The export market was hardly more attractive. The first formal trade statistics show that about twenty-five per cent less wheat was exported to Peru in the 1840s than during the late eighteenth century. Except for a short period during the Independence struggles, the Peruvian trade fluctuated around 135 000 qqm a year. At an average yield of 10 qqm only 15 000 hectares were needed to grow the entire Peruvian export. Presented in this light it is easy to understand that wheat could hardly have made the great impact on the countryside that has often been suggested. More than anything else, it was the simple lack of markets that perpetuated a backward agriculture.[46] A common and entirely understandable landowner attitude was pointed out in 1856: 'Do we not have empty fields everywhere on our haciendas? When we need them, we'll plow; if not, we'll let them lie.' Under the circumstances there was little need to make improvements or develop new techniques: land and labor were both readily at hand.[47]

If high yields brought fear of low profits to some, crop failure was an unmitigated disaster to a great many. The kind of research recently done in Mexico on pre-1860 agricultural crises, famine and disease has not yet been undertaken in Chile; but there is no doubt that before an easier mobility of people and resources permitted some escape or relief, the specter of famine was never far off. Crop failure in 1839 caused 'centenares de infelices' to perish from hunger and the local government could respond only with good intentions. Again in 1857, a local paper reported that a small steamer carrying relief supplies was lost and that 'los pobres de la provincia de Maule jimen en una espantosa miseria.' Such for a great many people was life in the countryside. Time was marked by the seasons – something the railroad timetable, posted everywhere, would soon begin to change: 'work dragged along languidly, there was no fixed plan for plowing or sowing, no need to keep books.'[48]

Labor on mid-century estates was supplied by two main kinds of workers: the *inquilinos*, or service tenants, and the peons, or seasonal day laborers. As we have seen, the institution of *inquilinaje* grew out of a century-long process in which men were gradually transformed into permanent residents on the large estates. Between the late seventeenth and the early nineteenth centuries agricultural land increased in value. This was accomplished by social stratification between landholders on one side and the landless 'poor Spaniard' (usually *mestizos*) on the other. As this took place the latter's prerequisites and duties as residents became more specific. The older designation of 'renter,' which after all could be applied to men of high rank, gradually gave way to the term *inquilino*. The new usage reflected not only a change in function but the stricter eighteenth-century social stratification as well.[49]

By the time Claudio Gay carried out his investigation of Chilean agriculture in the 1830s *inquilinaje* was a common if still incompletely formed labor system. *Inquilinos* were settled on large estates throughout Chile but they were mainly concentrated in those areas that produced for the small export wheat market. Cultivation obviously required more resident laborers than did livestock and so there were more families on the arable estates of the central valley than anywhere else. Until grain cultivation spread south, *inquilinaje* below the Maule River barely existed.[50]

Service tenancy was not, of course, limited to Chile. In Middle America and the Andean highlands, the terms *peón acasillado, huasipunguero,* and *yanacona* all describe men who exchanged labor for the privilege of cultivating a tiny plot of estate land. In times of labor scarcity or where well-established indigenous communities provided an alternative means of subsistence, landowners occasionally used the additional device of debt to bind workers more closely to the estate. This as we shall see, was rarely needed in Chile. But everywhere in Spanish America the system was weighted heavily in favor of the landlords. They had a near monopoly of the land, they were virtually politically autonomous, and in effect they always enjoyed a free hand in the administration of their estates.

Service tenancy developed in Europe as well and may have reached its greatest extension in the late eighteenth and in the nineteenth centuries. There are many terms, including *statartorpare* (Swedish), *robota* (Czech), and *Instleute* (German), that describe this practice. Just how rural labor systems arose and the conditions under which they were modified is a complex subject; indeed, it has been suggested as one of the keys to understanding modern society.[51] Close analogy with Europe is difficult, however, since few Latin American rural societies were put under the same kind of pressure at the same time. If Chilean *inquilinaje* in the first half of the nineteenth century seemed casual and mild in comparison, it was because it had not yet felt the stepped-up demand common in an industrialising Europe. In general, because of the lack of strong local markets and the autonomy of the landlord class, Latin American service tenancy was probably most akin to that of Eastern Europe – especially to the system of 'robot' labor.[52]

Although similar to the robot and to labor systems in other parts of the Western Hemisphere, *inquilinaje* was a peculiar institution. From Claudio Gay and a number of other contemporary accounts, a description of the *inquilinos* in the first half of the century may be pieced together with some confidence. Unlike medieval manorial labor the *inquilnos* were not bound legally to the land nor by custom or practice to the community. They settled in loose groups on the estates. Usually their dwellings lined the hacienda access roads, but at times they were placed in the extremities of the large properties to help keep the cattle in and the thieves out. There was no village into which they fitted, no fixed farming system that required their participation – they were not bound by 'submission to common agricultural practices.'[53] Although credit or supplies may have been advanced to the *inquilinos*, central valley estates had little need to bind labor to land through debt. A hacienda with good land to let had no difficulty attracting resident labor and we may be certain that there were always men willing to accept the limited plots available on the estates. Gay's major criticism of *inquilinaje* was the lack of suitable leases between owner and tenant. Seeing nothing 'contrary to justice' or unusual in paying one's rent in labor, Gay went so far as to suggest that many families in France 'would subscribe with pleasure' to a similar arrangement.[54]

In the absence of regulation or formal contracts, arrangements varied from district to district and even from one estate to the next. In the 1840s an 'average' *inquilino* received a *cerco* (garden plot) of from 2 to 6 hectares of watered land, grazing rights for ten to twenty animals, a modest shack (or the materials to build one), often a few hectares of land for sharecropping on the estate, and a daily food ration. Many observers during this period comment on the ability of *inquilinos* to accumulate wealth, and although these cases may have been exceptions it was at least possible through good management to make money and move into the ranks of the small, or even medium-sized, landholders. Some *inquilinos* were 'permitted up to five hundred cows . . . or have produced more than 1000 *fanegas* of wheat.' The later descriptions that stress the upward mobility of *inquilinos* draw their examples from the early period.[55]

Just as the *inquilinos*' perquisites varied widely so also did the amount of labor required of them. Obviously they went together. In return for the perquisites described above, the 'average' *inquilino* in the first half of the nineteenth century was required as a matter of course to assist in all rodeos and in the grain and grape harvests. Besides this he worked two or three days each week for the estate in a variety of agricultural labors and odd jobs. Those *inquilinos* with access to more land or the right to graze more animals correspondingly had greater obligations. The *grado más alto* of *inquilinos* during Gay's time was required to make available to the estate one full-time laborer. Often this *peón obligado* (the man who fulfilled the *inquilino's* labor responsibility) could be drawn from among the adults who lived in his house or from among the nearby small-holders or ambulatory peons. It was the *inquilino's* strict responsibility to see that the worker presented himself for work and to remunerate him (the estate only supplied food). In this system the more favored *inquilinos* ('the better class' of *inquilinos* as foreign consular officials called them) became a kind of labor broker who recruited workers, provided their maintenance, and insured that they were on the job on time. If the *peón obligado* did not turn up, the *inquilino* was required to work in his place.

Female members of the *inquilino* household also found work on the estates. Servants, cooks, and milkmaids were usually wives or relatives of the *inquilinos*. The women were also important economically, however, in another way. Rural women produced most of the cloth and the finished garments, hats, shoes, and other items of household manufacture. Although the effect of cheap British cottons was felt by the 1840s in the northern mining districts and in the larger cities, most of the rural area of central Chile still produced its own clothing. 'The Chilean *campesino*,' Gay noted, 'isolated in the countryside and far removed from society sees the necessity of being at once his own weaver, tailor, carpenter, mason, etc.' Urízar Garfias was struck by the extent of household industry in Maule, where, although there were no formally established textile industries there was 'considerable activity in making *bayeta* [a coarse woollen cloth], wool socks, *mantas*, and ponchos.' On a trip to the province of Talca in 1852 Gilliss found that 'a large proportion of the ponchos, blankets, church carpets and rugs and coarse cloth are . . . of domestic manufacture, showing that the poorer classes of women are not idle beside their spinning wheels and hand-looms.' The Talca newspaper in a rare statistic estimated that 36 000 yards of cloth, 12 000 ponchos, and a variety of boots and shoes were made annually in that province.[56]

There is a good description of household industry and a hint of the coming change in Gay:

The women [of the *inquilinos*] occupy themselves while waiting to prepare meals by spinning wool that they themselves have previously dyed yellow, blue, red, and green. Their dresses consisted before of a kind of loose wool spun and woven by these same women and dyed most always blue with the indigo obtained from Central America.[57] Today, they prefer to sell the wool and cover themselves with the cotton cloth the foreigners – and above all the English – bring in at low prices.[58]

The beginning of the change from homespun to imports that Gay noticed was very likely the difference between what he observed during his first stay in Chile from 1829 to 1842 and the information he later received in Paris from Chileans on tour.[59] During the interval increased British trade permitted country people to substitute cooler material for coarse and scratchy woolens; but at the same time Lancashire cloth drained the country of specie and began to wipe out the spinners and weavers, an important segment of the household industry. The effect of cheaper imports was not felt, however, by those who made garments from this cloth or other manufactured items. Rural people continued to make their own clothing, sandals, hats, and ponchos with little change throughout the nineteenth century.[60]

The bare data and scant sources we have seen reveal how little is really known about the rural worker in the nineteenth century. The few travelers who undertook to describe rural life rarely strayed from the beaten track through central Chile and confined their comments to those model haciendas where the generosity and charm of the owner undoubtedly helped dull the edge of the visitor's critical faculties.[61] Nor do the public documents provide much light. The contracts between owner and laborer were verbal, the arrangements informally agreed upon as new owners or lessees took possession of the estate. The rural worker's complaints, or even his crimes, were usually too insignificant to be recorded in the provincial court. The countless pages of litigation useful for information on the lower classes in the colonial epoch are here in the Republic nearly non-existent. The landowner himself – or his administrator – summarily dispensed justice, distributed the workers' land in the absence of surviving heirs, and settled most accounts without recourse to the troublesome and lengthy process that was common in the lawyer-filled upper levels of society.[62] Even in the private accounting records of haciendas the *inquilinos* are inconspicuous. Occasional entries tell of rations for *inquilinos* and others note an advance of a *fanega* of corn or merchandise against his account.[63]

We are left with little information about *inquilinaje* before 1850 partly because the system worked and imposed no excessive burdens. Later in the century, when the economy required greater output, the rural labor system was examined and discussed. Before that time the *inquilinos* lived and worked virtually unnoticed. On the great haciendas of central Chile where good land was abundant *inquilinos* formed a stable, permanent labor force. An eyewitness of the 1850s noted that

> there is not a hacienda that does not have its ancient families of
> *inquilinos* . . . and just as Santiago has its great landowning families
> of Larraín, Errázuriz, Vicuña, Cerda, and Toro; Talca its Cruces,
> Vergaras, and Donosos . . . so also each hacienda has its notable
> families of Ponces, Carranzas, Carocas, Aguilas, Montesinos,
> Pobletes, etc.[64]

Residents on the large estates had little notion of the larger society; and as the following complaint demonstrates, even the provincial functionaries did not have a clear idea of the meaning of 'nationality.' 'Upon filling the space [in the 1854 census] to express their nationality,' the local official noted, 'many people have not designated the name of the Province (!) but rather the name of the Department, hacienda, etc.'[65] In fact the hacienda was the *inquilino*'s only *patria* as the following contemporary observation makes clear:

> The *huaso* (*inquilino*) knows there are Englishmen, Frenchmen, and
> Spaniards because now and then he has seen people from these
> countries or has heard them mentioned at least. But he has no idea
> where England or France or Spain might be. He has heard of *godos*
> and *patriotas* and knows that both made war but who they were or
> why they fought he has not the slightest idea or interest . . . The
> *inquilino* believes himself to be indigenous to his hacienda . . . and
> if he were transported to Paris or London and interrogated there as
> to the country of his birth . . . he would not answer 'Chile', but
> Peldehue, Chacabuco, Huechún or Chocalán. He has no idea if his
> ancestors are Spaniards, Englishmen, Russians, or Chinese . . . He
> has heard people talk of Spaniards and Indians, but he does not
> imagine that he has had contact with those races or that their blood
> circulates through his veins.[66]

This description by an anonymous eye-witness can probably be accepted for a great many large estates in the early nineteenth century. Most writers agree that conditions were different on newer or smaller haciendas. This is suggested but rarely observed, since most visitors from Santiago or abroad passed their time on the traditional estates easily accessible from the capital. Most of Gay's description, for example, is based on the great hacienda of La Compañía, a favorite of many travelers. Darwin was an exception to most foreign visitors. His scientific interests led him into more out of the way places, which perhaps explains why he found the *inquilinos'* situation to be worse than others did.[67]

Whether the smaller haciendas actually exacted more from workers or whether the comments reflect a prevailing prejudice in favor of the rural oligarchy is difficult to say. Gay thought the *inquilinos* suffered when they 'fell into the hands of a *pequeño hacendado*' or 'one of those "hacendados ávaros" who do not hesitate to take advantage of their position to exploit and at times even to oppress them.' A few years later, Horace Rumbold, British consul in Santiago, noted the same difference: '[The *inquilino*] certainly fares better in every way on the broad domains of the Correa or Larraín families or on the Vicuña estates . . . than he does on many smaller properties that shall be nameless.'[68]

Whatever differences there may have been among the estates we are still left with the impression that *inquilinaje* was – at least compared with what followed – not oppressive, that it was still an easy going labor system. If inefficient it nevertheless provided suitable workers in a society where obedience and loyalty were valued over productivity. Numerically few, the *inquilinos* were the cream of rural labor. 'Since the *hacendado* is concerned that the people on his hacienda be honorable . . . the body of *inquilinos* is always composed of the healthiest part of the lower class (*bajo pueblo*) that lives in the country.' This selectivity was made possible by the limited need for estate labor and the lack of alternatives open to the numerous rural families. The good fortune of being accepted on the hacienda was repaid by the *inquilinos* with service and loyalty.[69]

Rural settlement in central Chile contrasted with that of countries that had a more advanced indigenous population, or, for that matter, with the urban tradition of Mediterranean Europe. Before 1850 there were few villages and hardly any rudimentary settlements. Except for the agglomerations of residents on the haciendas and a handful of provincial towns, the population was widely scattered. Gay wrote about the rural Chileans that 'their love of isolation . . . so opposed to the spirit of the Latin race, which is always quick to group its dwellings in small hamlets [was proof that] European blood had mixed very little in this class of society.' The Crown had made repeated efforts in the eighteenth century to establish a few towns as provincial capitals, but by 1850 (except for Talca) even these consisted of little more than a single long dusty street. The large number of rural inhabitants who lived outside the system of large estates were called a 'floating' or 'ambulatory' mass by the mid-century census takers, and if they stayed put long enough to be counted, entered the statistics as *gañanes* or *peones* – people who had 'no residence or fixed destiny.'[70]

The impact of economic expansion on Chilean agriculture as well as the changes brought about in the rural labor force is the subject of a later chapter; my aim here has been to provide a description of rural society at a time when local or foreign demand had not yet altered an essentially colonial pattern. By the time Lt Gilliss and his scientific team left Chile in 1852, the steel rails that would tie the entire country to the flourishing economy of the North Atlantic basin were being laid inland from Valparaíso. The growth during the following decades took place within a rural economy already staked out in large privately owned estates; where an abundant and underemployed mass of men and women could easily be set to work; and where a traditional landowning elite was the principal social and political force.

CHAPTER 2

1 Lieut. J. M. Gilliss, *The U.S. Naval Astronomical Expedition to the Southern Hemisphere during the Years 1849–'50–'51–'52* (Washington, 1855), vol. I (Chile), p. 125.

2 Several British, North American, French, and German travelers wrote down their impressions of early nineteenth-century Chile. The best of these are: Maria Graham, *Journal*; Wm S. W. Ruschenberger, *Three Years in the Pacific (1831–34)* (Philadelphia, 1834); Alexander Caldcleugh, *Travels in South America During the Years 1819, 1820, 1821* (London, 1825); John Miers, *Travels in Chile and La Plata (1819–35)* (2 vols., London, 1826); Gabriel Lafond de Lurcy, *Viaje a Chile* (first pub. 1844) (Santiago, 1970); Eduard Pöeppig, *Un testigo en la alborada de Chile (1826–29)*, (trans. Carlos Keller, Santiago, 1960); and Francis Head, *Rough Notes Taken During Some Rapid Journeys Across the Pampas and Among the Andes (1825–6)* (London, 1826). This literature is discussed by Guillermo Feliú Cruz, *Notas para una bibliografía sobre viajeros relativos a Chile* (Santiago, 1965), and the same author has compiled two useful anthologies, *Imágenes de Chile* (Santiago, 1937) and *Santiago a comienzos del siglo XIX: crónicas de los viajeros* (Santiago, 1970). For the material cited, see Feliú Cruz, *Santiago a comienzos*, pp. 44–5, 60–1; and Gilliss, *Naval expedition*, p. 177.

3 *Repertorio nacional* (Santiago, 1850), no p. nos. The *Repertorio* lists all clerics, lawyers, and military officers by name and position.

4 Head, *Rough notes*, p. 109; Gilliss, *Naval expedition*, p. 157.

5 Gilliss, *Naval expedition*, p. 158.

6 The policy of centering all transportation on Santiago that at times unnecessarily routed traffic through the capital was opposed in the nineteenth

century and was an issue in the Liberal revolts of the 1850s. One Liberal critic, for example, claimed that Aconcagua should have a better link directly to the port instead of being tied to Santiago. 'The present road,' he pointed out (in the 1850s), 'permits a few dried peaches to be sent down to Santiago, but [it was really designed] to send troops up to the province to stamp out rebellions.' See Diego Barros Arana et al., *Cuadro histórico de la administración Montt* (Santiago, 1861), p. 460. The province of Concepción constantly called for government funds for provincial roads. See, e.g., *Correo del Sur* (Concepción), 27 January 1853; and for later complaints of the same kind, see *BSNA*, vol. 24 (1893), pp. 603–6.

7 Alberto Blest Gana, *Martín Rivas*, published in 1862 but set in 1850, provides a classic description of mid-century Santiago society; José Joaquin Vallejo (Jotabeche) published a series of 'artículos de costumbres,' in *El Mercurio* (Valparaíso) in 1844. 'El provinciano en Santiago,' and others are published in Raúl Silva Castro (ed.), *Artículos de costumbres* (Santiago, 1954.

8 José Zapiola, *Recuerdos de treinta años (1810–1840)*, 8th ed. (Santiago, 1945), shows where the prominent families lived. See also Ramón Subercaseaux, *Memorias de ochenta años*, 2nd ed. (2 vols., Santiago, 1936), I, pp. 13–45.

9 Barros Arana, *Histora*, VII, pp. 431–2, Amunátegui, *Mayorazgos i titulos*

10 Felstiner, 'Larraín family,' p. 47.

11 Ruschenberger, *Three years*, p. 144; Graham, *Diary*, p. 255.

12 *CN* (Santiago), vol. 342, no p. no., *Aculeo*; *CJ* (Santiago), leg. 554, p. 2 (1847); *CJ* (Linares), leg. 97, p. 7; Felstiner, 'Larraín family,' p. 47; Feliú Cruz, *Santiago a comienzos*, p. 60.

13 The discussion of the Echenique family is based on the following evidence: the entire vol. 342 in *CN* (Santiago), which is concerned with the division of property of the Echenique estate and contains the inventory, appraisal and household accounts kept by the owner's widow for the period 1853–61; and the *libro de caja* for the years 1861–7. The account books were kindly lent by the González Echenique family in Santiago. See also my 'The hacienda el Huique in the agrarian structure of nineteenth-century Chile,' *Agricultural History*, vol. XLVI, no. 4 (October 1972), pp. 455–70.

14 Gilliss, *Naval expedition*, p. 196; Ruschenberger, *Three years*, p. 129.

15 Recaredo S. Tornero, *Chile ilustrado, guía descriptivo . . .* (Valparaíso, 1872), p. 449.

16 Aníbal Pinto Santa Cruz, *Chile, un caso de desarrollo frustrado*, 2nd ed. (Santiago, 1962), pp. 14–25; D. C. M. Platt, *Latin America and the British Trade 1806–1914* (London, 1972), pp. 3–4; discusses the tendency to exaggerate the importance of early trade.

17 Platt, *Latin America*, p. 18; and Tulio Halperín-Donghi, *Historia contemporánea de America Latina* (Madrid, 1969), p. 151.

18 Miers, *Travels in Chile*, quoted by Platt, *Latin America*, p. 40.

19 Ruschenberger, *Three Years*, p. 11; Graham, *Journal*, pp. 156, 179.

20 Virgilio Figueroa, *Diccionario histórico y biográfico de Chile* (5 vols. in 4, Santiago, 1925–31), II, p. 193, IV–V, pp. 221–5.

21 Ricardo Anguita and Valerio Quesney, *Leyes promulgadas en Chile desde 1810 hasta 1901 inclusive* (2 vols., Santiago, 1902), I, p. 226.

22 Several travelers noticed the widespread cottage industry in the 1840s (see note 56 below). Platt, *Latin America*, p. 13, points out that even in India where Lancashire piece goods had every advantage in penetrating an overseas market, the local hand-loom industry still supplied twenty-five per cent of all cloth at the beginning of the twentieth century.

23 *Renta agrícola*, Figueroa, *Diccionario*, and *Repertorio nacional*, pp. 10–16.

24 Feliú Cruz, *Viajeros*, p. 64, Vitale, *Intrepretación marxista*, II, p. 90. The

Repertorio nacional differs a great deal from the data on occupations in the 1854 population census which shows only 147 lawyers.
25 Tornero, Chile ilustrado, pp. 448–50.
26 Repertorio nacional; Censo (1854); Figueroa, Diccionario, III, 627.
27 Feliú Cruz, Viajeros, p. 150; Tornero, Chile ilustrado, p. 462.
28 Gilliss, Naval expedition, pp. 180, 214.
29 Claudio Véliz (ed.), Obstacles to Change in Latin America (Oxford, 1965), p. 7.
30 Carlos Suero, 'Tipos chilenos,' Anales, 3rd series (1937), p. 74; Edwards, Fronda, pp. 16–17; cf. Frank Safford, 'Social aspects of politics in nineteenth-century Spanish America,' Journal of Social History (1972), pp. 344–70.
31 Gilliss, Naval expedition, p. 217, has a perceptive discussion of social class; Tornero, Chile ilustrado, p. 464.
32 Gilliss, Naval expedition, p. 219; Edwards, Fronda, pp. 188–9; Francisco Encina, Nuestra inferioridad económica, 2nd ed. (Santiago, 1955), pp. 5–7.
33 See Barbier, 'Elite and cadres,' pp. 416–35; Mark Burkholder, 'From Creole to Peninsular: the transformation of the Audiencia of Lima,' HAHR, vol. 52, no. 3 (August 1972), pp. 395–415; D. A. Brading, Miners and Merchants in Bourbon Mexico 1763–1810 (Cambridge, England, 1971).
34 Quoted in Simon Collier, Ideas and Politics of Chilean Independence, 1808–1833 (Cambridge, England, 1967), p. 362; for interpretation of the independence movement in general, Halperin-Donghi, Historia contemporánea, chs. 2 and 3.
35 Members of Congress from Luis Valencia Avaria, Anales de la república (2 vols., Santiago, 1951), II, pp. 179–86; Guillermo Feliú Cruz, 'Un esquema de la evolución social de Chile en el siglo XIX hasta 1891,' Chile visto a través de Agustín Ross (Santiago, 1950), p. 25.
36 Edwards, Fronda, p. 82; the phrase is that of Diego Portales, the éminence grise of the early Conservative regime; Ruschenberger, Three Years, p. 144; Gilliss, Naval expedition, p. 131.
37 The 1854 renta agrícola (tax roll) listed 19 100 rural properties with an annual income of at least $25 pesos. Table 8 shows the distribution of these haciendas, fundos, and smallholders by income. These records obviously must be read as approximations.
38 Only five estates in Curicó, for example, and one in Talca, produced more than $6000 in annual income. Thus, although the catastro helps identify the people with the largest incomes from land, by itself it tells very little about the distribution of land or the structure of rural society. Indeed, income data alone are misleading and a cursory reading of the material just presented might lead to the conclusion that the largest estates in area were concentrated around Santiago and that outlying districts were either unsettled or contained small farms. But this was not the case; nearly all the territory between Aconcagua and the Ñuble was already legally held in private ownership and the individual units were in fact larger as one moved out from Santiago.
39 Graham, Journal, p. 266; the background on Indian land is in Silva Vargas, Tierras y pueblos de indios; and Domingo Santa Maria, Memoria del intendente de Colchagua (Santiago, 1848), p. 10, discusses the few surviving remnants of Indian properties. A number of Regular holdings were confiscated by the Liberal government of 1827–8. See my 'The Church and Spanish American agrarian structure, 1765–1865,' The Americas, vol. XXVIII, no. 1 (July 1971), pp. 78–98.
40 Larraín, El Huique, p. 62.
41 The great range of land value in Chile was recognised in the 1964 agrarian reform law which attempted to rate all land in terms of 'eighty basic

hectares of the Maipo valley.' Thus, a dry land *fundo* of 10 000 hectares in Coquimbo province could have been equivalent to only 100 hectares of irrigated land close to good transportation. Innumerable tendentious tracts call attention to 'great latifundia' of 60 000 or 80 000 hectares without pointing out that only 70 or 80 of the hectares have agricultural value.

[42] *CN* (Santiago), vol. 342.

[43] Many travelers left their impressions of summers in the countryside; see Graham, *Journal*, pp. 231–55, and Ruschenberger, *Three years*, p. 144. Subercaseaux's account is in *Memorias*, I, pp. 45, 218.

[44] Gustavo Opazo M., *Historia de Talca 1742–1942* (Santiago, 1942), pp. 284–6, 319–20; Tomás Guevara, *Historia de Cúrico* (Santiago, 1890), p. 299.

[45] *El Alfa* (Talca), no. 222 (27 January 1849) and (5 March 1849); *El Agricultor*, vol. I, no. 6 (August 1849); *AMH*, vol. 250.

[46] Romano, *Una economía colonial*, pp. 41–3; Sepúlveda, *El trigo*, p. 34 and *EC* (1844–9) for export data. My estimates include ten per cent for seed.

[47] *Mensajero de la agricultura*, vol. I (1856), p. 348.

[48] *Mensajero*, I, p. 347; for famine, see *Documentos parlamentarios*, vol. I (1840), pp. 113–15; and *El Eco* (Talca), 1857. D. A. Brading and Celia Wu, 'Population growth and crisis: León, 1720–1860,' *Journal of Latin American Studies*, vol. 5, no. 1 (May 1973), pp. 1–36.

[49] Góngora, *El origen*, pp. 113–17.

[50] Claudio Gay, *Historia física y política de Chile: Agricultura* (2 vols., Paris, 1862–5), I, p. 193. Gay, a Frenchman, came to Chile in 1829. He wrote a multivolume work on Chilean history and the best nineteenth-century study of Chilean agriculture.

[51] Magnus Mörner, 'A Comparative study of Tenant Labor in Parts of Europe, Africa, and Latin America 1700–1900: A Preliminary Report of a Research Project in Social History,' *Latin American Research Review*, vol. 5, no. 2 (1970), pp. 3–15; Barrington Moore, Jr, *Social Origins of Dictatorships and Democracy: Lord and Peasant in the Making of the Modern World* (Boston, 1967).

[52] Jerome Blum, *Noble Landowners and Agriculture in Austria, 1815–1848* (Baltimore, 1943), pp. 71–4, 171–87. See also Max Weber, *General Economic History* (New York, 1961), pp. 78–81.

[53] As was, for example, the medieval serf. See Marc Bloch, *Feudal Society*, trans. L. A. Manyon (2 vols., Chicago, 1964), I, p. 242.

[54] As late as 1870, when the need for labor was much greater, *inquilinos* lined up to obtain a position on the estates. Santiago Prado, 'El Inquilinaje en el departamento de Caupolicán,' *BSNA*, 2 (1871), p. 378; Gay, I, pp. 182–5.

[55] Atropos, 'El Inquilino en Chile. Su vida. Un siglo sin variaciones, 1861–1966,' *Mapocho*, 5 (1966), p. 214. This article, by a writer I have not been able to identify, first appeared as 'El inquilino en Chile,' in *Revista del Pacífico*, no. 5 (1861). Luis Correa Vergara, *Agricultura chilena* (2 vols., Santiago, 1939), II, pp. 394–8. Gay, I, pp. 115–21; *BSNA*, II, p. 381; *El mensajero de la agricultura*, II, (1856–7), pp. 204–6; *BSNA*, II, p. 384; *CJ* (Talca), Leg. 359, p. 2.

[56] Gay, *Agricultura*, I, p. 159; Fernando Urízar Garfias, *Estadística de la República de Chile: provincia de Maule* (Santiago, 1845), pp. 92–4; Gilliss, *Naval expedition*, p. 57; *El Alfa* (Talca), 10 January 1849.

[57] The inventory of the Cunaco hacienda store shows 75 pounds of indigo (*añil*) at 1.20 pesos a pound. Account book of the hacienda of Cunaco, in the possession of Manuel Valdés, Santiago.

[58] Gay, *Agricultura*, I, p. 163.

[59] Gay's investigations were carried out from 1829 to 1842, but the first volume of *Agricultura* was not published until 1862 and the second not until 1865.

For background to Gay's work see *Correspondencia de Claudio Gay* (compiled with preface and notes by Guillermo Feliú Cruz and Carlos Stuardo Ortíz; trans. Luis Villablanca, Santiago, 1962).

60 The overall data on professions before 1865 are difficult to deal with. Between then and 1895 the spinners and weavers continued to disappear (from 18 000 in 1865 to 4000 in 1895, for example, in the Maipo–Maule Zone). See the national censuses of 1865 and 1895.

61 There are many travel books that deal with nineteenth-century Chile, but only a few have worthwhile information on rural life. See Guillermo Feliú Cruz, *Notas para una bibliografía sobre viajeros relativos a Chile*.

62 All civil cases involving less than 12 pesos were handled by the political head of the *distrito*, the *inspector*. His decision could not be appealed. For cases of 12 to 40 pesos his decision could be appealed to the *subdelegado*, and cases from 40 to 150 pesos were handled by the *subdelegado*. Effectively, only cases concerning medium or large landowners ever reached the departmental *juez de letras* (and therefore are available in the judicial collection). The *Archivo de Intendencias*, which has not yet been organised, may contain information on the lower rural society. For an idea of how provincial justice was supposed to have been dispensed, see *Manual o instrucción para los subdelegados e inspectores en Chile* (Santiago, 1860). The system described was reorganised in the 1870s.

63 This is how *inquilinos* were remunerated on the haciendas of Cunaco and Pichidegua. Account book of the hacienda of Pichidegua (hereafter *Pichidegua*), in the possession of Sergio de Toro, Santiago. For an interesting discussion of wages on a Mexican hacienda of the same period, see Jan Bazant, 'Peones, arrendatarios y aparceros en México, 1851–1853,' *Historia Mexicana*, vol. XXIII, no. 2 (1973), pp. 330–57.

64 Atropos, 'El Inquilino en Chile,' p. 200.

65 *Censo* (1854), p. 7.

66 Atropos, 'El inquilino,' pp. 200–1.

67 Gay, I, chs. 8, 9, 10; Ramón Domínguez, *Nuestro sistema de inquilinaje* (Santiago, 1867), pp. 33–64; John Miers, 'La agricultura en Chile en 1825,' *Mensajero*, 2 (1856), p. 127, for a description of Ocoa; Charles Darwin, *The Voyage of the Beagle* (Natural History Library ed., Garden City, 1962), p. 339.

68 Gay, *Agricultura*, I, p. 185; Horace Rumbold, *Reports by her Majesty's secretaries . . . on the manufacures, commerce . . .* (London, 1876), p. 396.

69 Atropos, 'El Inquilino,' p. 206.

70 Gay, I, p. 155; *AMH*, vol. 362 (1859), no p. no., has report by the administrator of the *estanco* (State tobacco monopoly) to the intendant: 'The population is very scattered; there are a very few small *aldeas* [hamlets].' This picture is borne out by censuses. The *estanco* administrators often provide worthwhile information about business conditions in the provinces.

Economic expansion: the impact of the Atlantic economy

When in 1866 Stanley Jevons proudly boasted that 'the Chinese grow tea for us . . . Peru sends her silver, Australia contains our sheep farms . . . the several quarters of the globe are our willing tributaries,' he was describing the world market then rapidly forming around Great Britain and Western Europe. From the 1860s on, rail and steam enabled the industrial powers to draw on distant regions for bulky foods and raw materials. Until the entire system collapsed in the world crisis of the 1930s this market, directly and indirectly, was the main stimulus for the Chilean rural economy. Directly, through the demand for cereals which Chile helped supply after the 1860s; and indirectly, through massive investment in mining, transport and banking which helped create a thriving market for agriculture in the northern desert and in the burgeoning cities of Santiago and Valparaíso. The social consequence of economic expansion are conditioned by a great many things, some obvious, others understandable, and a few quite unfathomable. Nebraska, Java, and Jamaica were all pulled into the same orbit as Chile but of course they came out of it quite differently.

The various markets for agriculture cannot be cleanly separated since throughout our period from 1860 to 1930 there was always some export as well as domestic demand; yet there are two natural phases. From mid-century to the 1880s the foreign market was the most dynamic. Chile exported grain and flour to Argentina and England. As massive cereal production from other countries began to eliminate central Chile from the world market (the newly opened Araucanía continued to export for several more decades) a thriving mining sector stimulated an internal demand that more than compensated for the loss of foreign markets. My purpose here is first to set out the nature of the foreign market by piecing together and presenting the scattered but fairly reliable export data; then I will examine the peculiarities of domestic demand and the role of agriculture in the national economy toward the turn of the century.

Actually, we must backtrack a bit to 1850 because it was then that the gold rushes in California and Australia began to change visibly the

1. The Quinta Waddington, *ca* 1860. Foreign merchants moved into the new opportunities created by the break with Spain in the early nineteenth century and dominated overseas trade. One such merchant was Josué Waddington, who built this suburban house in the hills behind Valparaíso.

2. An ordinary *fundo* near Casablanca, *ca* 1860. Notice the scrawny *criollo* cattle, a type common in central Chile.

(Photos: The Oliver Collection, courtesy of the Bancroft Library, Berkeley.)

3. The dwelling of a nineteenth-century service tenant or small proprietor, *ca* 1860. Before cultivation required more resident workers who lived close by the estate house, most tenants lived in rude huts in scattered settlements on the hacienda's land.

(The Oliver Collection, courtesy of the Bancroft Library, Berkeley.)

4. Threshing grain in central Chile, *ca* 1830. Landowners were slow to replace the *trilla a yegua*, which sometimes required as many as 400 mares, with machines. The method shown is still used on a small scale by sharecroppers in the coastal range.

(Reprint of a lithograph from Gay, Atlas, vol. 1, pl. 19.)

5. Air view of a small *fundo*, *ca* 1960. On both sides of the formal estate garden are the rows of service tenants' houses within the small *cerco* or garden plot allotted to them. This is a typical scene in the irrigated valley floor of central Chile.

(*Courtesy, the University of Chile.*)

6. *Estado* street in Santiago, *ca* 1910. The middling well-to-do, including land-owners, lived in houses like these. The mounted man is a *sereno* or watchman. By the time this picture was taken, the fashionable district was shifting to the southwest down the Alameda and along the streets of República and Ejército Libertador.

7. The Palacio Irarrázabal on the Alameda in Santiago. The Irarrázabal family held a title of Castille in the late seventeenth century, and land and important office in the nineteenth and twentieth. Many wealthy Chileans built their Santiago houses in the Second Empire style.

(*Photos: Courtesy, the University of Chile.*)

older market structure. In California, the discovery of gold and the cession of that territory by Mexico to the United States brought a sudden increase in population. These people – particularly in the San Francisco Bay area – were dependent upon imports of food until land in California could be put under cultivation. In Australia another gold strike a few years later drew local labor and transportation from agriculture to the goldfields creating a need for imports.[1]

Chile had a natural advantage in supplying the new markets. Concepción and Valparaíso were the first good ports to welcome ships after the difficult Cape Horn passage, and apart from Oregon, Chile was the only important wheat-producing area on the Pacific coast. The number of ships that called at Chilean ports doubled with the Gold Rush. A wholly new outlet for wheat and flour developed, and during the years 1850–3, some 340 000 quintals were exported annually.[2] By 1855, however, sufficient grain was raised in California to take care of local needs, and except for rare bad harvests, Chilean wheat was not imported again. By the end of the decade California not only became self-sufficient but quickly ended the near monopoly that Chilean growers enjoyed in the Pacific. From 1858 on Chile faced stiff competition from West Coast grains throughout the Pacific, and California flour was even offered for sale in Valparaíso.

The Australian market opened under similar conditions. Although this new colony had imported small amounts of wheat off and on throughout the first forty years of the nineteenth century, it had some 200 000 acres under cultivation by 1850 and was normally able to supply its own needs. Then as in California the gold discovery brought a momentary disruption. Labor and animals were drawn off by the new mines, acreage fell and by 1855 about 700 000 quintals of wheat and flour were imported. This market prolonged the boom of the 1850s for Chile. Australia for a few years was a significant market for wheat and flour. But like the California market before, it was entirely fortuitous and merely demonstrated Chile's weak competitive position. Even under fortunate circumstances Chile was able to supply less than half of Australia's imports in the peak year of 1855. After 1857, Australian export was effectively finished for Chilean producers: not because the market 'closed' but because of Californian competition. In 1860, California shipped over 170 000 quintals compared with Chile's 20 000 to the Australian market.[3]

These brief outlets provided by the Californian and Australian markets occupy what at first seems a disproportionately large space in the historical literature of nineteenth-century Chile. This is partly due to the reports of such figures as Benjamín Vicuna Mackenna and Vicente Pérez Rosales who publicised the fabulous profits that were obtained from the sale of Chilean products during this romantic time, and partly because it was the first major development in the export market since the beginning of the Peruvian wheat trade. For a few years in the 1850s Chile dominated the Pacific grain market. The absence of competition permitted prices to rise higher than ever again in Chilean history.[4] Even though the high prices and sense of adventure produced by the Gold Rush markets have caused many to view the 1850s as a great age of Chilean agriculture, the total of exports (wheat and flour) in any one year never exceeded 600 000 qqm. If a yield of 10 quintals per hectare is used to estimate the area of cultivation, at most only 65 000 additional hectares would have been required to supply the entire Pacific market in the 1850s.[5]

Another development was the rise of the flour market. During the first third of the nineteenth century no outlet appeared for the flour ground in the rudimentary Chilean mills. For seven years (1824–31) flour was not permitted to enter Peru and throughout the 1830s and '40s a heavy duty was placed on Chilean imports. Occasional ship-loads found their way to the Río de la Plata or the Pacific Islands, but the average annual export throughout the decade prior to the Pacific gold rushes was probably not over 45 000 qqm. The northern mining regions in the Atacama did, however, constitute a market of some importance. When to this was added the sudden demand for flour from born.[6]

California and Australia, Chile's modern milling industry was

During the first years of the 1850s, Chile's only competition in the Pacific came from Yankee traders hauling flour from the United States' East Coast around Cape Horn. High California prices made such a trip possible on a limited scale, but it involved crossing the hot and humid equator twice in a voyage that lasted at least three months and often longer. Only with kiln-drying and better handling and storage (barrels in place of bulk or sacks, for example) and the use of clipper ships or the even more effective 'Down Easters' was the United States' penetration into this area possible. That the United States could offer any competition at all was an early sign of Chile's vulnerable position. In addition to East Coast millers, a new and powerful industry quickly grew up in San Francisco.[7] By 1855 California was not only self-sufficient in flour but had captured most of the Australian market as well. A Valparaíso merchant explained the commercial facts of life to a Talca mill administrator in 1860:

There is now loading for that part of the world [Australia] a vessel
in which a German house ships 6000 quintals of flour bought here
[Valparaíso] on speculation . . . of a price rise which not having
taken place they in despair resolved themselves to ship. The excessive
quantities of wheat shipped from San Francisco should be quite
sufficient to frighten the boldest speculator . . . There will be no
chance for a continuation of shipments.[8]

Except for the bad harvest year of 1864 in California when some
Chilean imports were required (at much lower prices than in 1850), the
outer Pacific flour market was lost for good. But Chile continued to
send quantities around the Cape to Río de la Plata and Brazil throughout the 1860s, and the coastal trade with the northern province of
Coquimbo and Atacama (the Atacama desert became Chilean territory
after the War of the Pacific of 1879) was generally retained throughout
the century.

Table 9   Flour exports by port, 1848–85 (annual averages of five-year
periods in '000 of metric quintals)

Years	Tomé	Constitución	Valparaíso	Totals
1846–50[a]	136	20	45	201
1851–5	190	92	4	286
1856–60	101	89	20	210
1861–5	109	156	109	374
1866–70	71	163	262	496
1875[b]	63	148	230	441
1880[b]	6	2	147	155
1885[b]	183	—	84	341[c]

Source: *Estadística comercial.* [a] Average of three years only. [b] Single years.
[c] Export for 1885 does not add up because of shipments from below Tomé.

The breakdown by port in Table 9 indicates the regional development of the industry.[9] Until the late 1860s, the southern millers – those
from Tomé or Talcahuano Bay, and the Talca area – supplied the
largest share of the market. This was because of water transportation.
The port of Tomé was adjacent to the grain fields of Concepción, and
millers around Talca were able to use the fluvial network of the Maule,
Claro, and Loncomilla rivers to reach the sea. In the 1850s several
attempts were made to improve the port of Constitución at the mouth
of the Maule. Local millers, supported by Valparaíso merchants,
formed a corporation to operate steam tugs, but their efforts had limited
success. In the 1870s an increasing number of irrigation canals drew

water from the river, larger launches were forced to lighten their loads, and transportation costs went up. By 1890 Maule river traffic dwindled to an end. When the railroad was finally built from Constitución in 1915, it was to bring in merchandise because as a port for shipping agricultural produce, the once thriving Constitución was dead. Talca's decline as a milling center coincides with the penetration of the railroad from the north. The main line reached Curicó in 1870 and Talca four years later: Valparaíso's share of flour exports rose from less than a quarter in the years 1846–50 to over ninety per cent in 1880.[10]

Despite the advantages that Chile held, however, in shipping to its nearby coast, foreign flour was beginning to reach these mining districts toward the end of the century. Some 30 000 qqm were imported from the United States in 1878. Chile's disastrous harvest of that year may explain the need for foreign imports in 1878, but by the 1890s imports were common and a tarriff was imposed on flour in 1898. If Chile could barely compete on her own coast, obviously there was little hope for foreign markets. By 1890, total flour exports had fallen to 22 000 quintals. The spread of cereal cultivations onto the Argentine pampa and the growth of a powerful milling industry in Montevideo eliminated Chilean flour from the Atlantic coast of South America. At the same time California millers provided increased competition in the traditional market of Peru.[11]

The lack of technological improvements played an important role in the decline of the Chilean milling industry. The mills constructed in Chile in the 1850s as a response to the new Pacific markets were technologically equal to any mills in the world at that time. The equipment was purchased in Europe or in the United States. Generally foreign technicians were brought along to install the new machinery and many stayed on to supervise the mill operations. But beginning in the late 1870s tremendous changes were introduced in the milling industry in the United States and Europe. Greatly improved 'purifiers' were developed by the La Croix brothers in Minneapolis, and in the same decade roller mills – first successfully used in Budapest – replaced stone mills. A major advantage of roller mills rested in their capacity to grind properly the hard winter wheat which produced superior flour. Without the new technology Chile did not develop new strains and continued to produce flour from soft wheats.[12]

The new technology left Chile far behind. Julio Menandier, the National Society of Agriculture's editor, noted that if the mills of the 1850s were among the best in the world, the 'numerous inventions of recent years have rarely been applied' to the national industry. By 1890, when the United States had some 20 000 mills of the new roller type, they were hardly known in Chile. The huge Minneapolis mills, built in the 1870s, cost over 350 000 dollars and could produce upwards of 2000 barrels of flour a day. With this rival Chile was not able nor willing to compete for the export market.[13] At home, however, the newly formed Manufacturers Association (Sociedad de Fomento Fabril) promoted the use of the latest techniques and machinery and under this impulse and some tariff protection, new mills were built and local millers continued to supply the domestic market for flour.[14]

Coinciding with the years of peak flour exports was the grain export to England. This new and important agricultural market opened for Chilean producers about 1865. For the next ten years, prices remained high while good yields on newly cultivated land kept costs down. The peak in grain exports was reached in 1874 and throughout the years between 1865 and 1880 the annual exported volume averaged around one million quintals. A good indication of the value of the export market for Chilean agriculture can be seen in Table 10. The most im-

Table 10   Value of agricultural exports 1844–90 (annual averages of five-year periods in 'ooo pesos)

Years	Current pesos	Pesos of 44*d*
1844–5[a]	872	872
1846–50	1705	1705
1851–5	3756	3756
1856–60	3949	3949
1861–5	5283	5283
1866–70	9244	9244
1871–5	13 241	13 241
1876–80	10 452	9031
1881–5	9845	7157
1886–90	8311	4978

Source: *Resúmen de la hacienda pública* (London, 1917?). [a] Average of two years only.

portant items in these exports throughout the period 1844–90 were grain (wheat and barley) and flour. Before 1850 these amounted to slightly over half the total but with the opening of the California and Australian markets and later with the British grain trade, the share of grain and flour in total agricultural exports grew. In 1851–5 cereals accounted for about eighty-one per cent and in 1866–70, about seventy-four per cent. During the rest of the century, cereal or cereal products accounted for around two-thirds of total agricultural export earnings.[15]

It seems surprising now that central Chile could ever have competed in the world grain trade. After 1900 occasional food imports became necessary, and since 1950 the country has increasingly required basic agricultural imports. How was it possible that Chile was able to sell wheat and barley on the English market? First of all, important changes in transportation were necessary to make the possibility even exist. Before 1850, high freight rates from the Pacific were an effective barrier except in cases of extremely high European prices. The prohibitive rate of about 100 shillings per ton in 1850, however, was cut to 60 in 1870 and to 30 by 1885. These reductions in the Pacific were primarily due to improved sailing vessels and better knowledge of ocean geography. Also, rates were lowered on the North Atlantic and Suez routes (after 1869) because of the use of higher-efficiency steam engines. But steamship rates had little direct effect in the Pacific where bulk cargo continued to be carried in sailing ships until well into the twentieth century. Although reduction in ocean rates cut costs everywhere, the long haul sailing routes benefited the most.[16]

After 1866 – partly because of the influence of tramp steamers and the telegraph – Chilean grain prices were increasingly determined by the London, or world, price. The world price in turn, especially after 1880, was overwhelmingly influenced by North American production. The relationship between London and Santiago prices can be seen in Table 11.

Between 1866 and 1880, high world prices and falling transportation costs were the reasons behind Chile's large grain exports. The development of railroad transportation was the other major improvement in the nineteenth century. Before 1850, large areas of the inland provinces of Chile were cut off from the export market by the high cost of transport. Between 1852 and 1863 the line running from Valparaíso to Santiago was completed. At the same time (in 1858) a second line was begun leading south from Santiago, and by the mid-1860s the interior provinces of Colchagua and Curicó were linked by rail to Valparaíso. But if these improvements in rail and sea transportation helped shrink the distances between Chile and the European market, the sheer number of additional miles that Chilean grain had to travel compared to that of the United States, Russia or Canada still presented a formidable obstacle. In addition, Chile's internal transportation and handling facilities were poor.

Timing was another important factor in Chile's ability to export grain. The peak years of exports from central Chile were between 1865 and 1875, a period in which the extensive producers had not yet

Table 11 Comparative wheat prices in London and Santiago,
1851–1900 (in Chilean pesos per fanega)

Years	London prices Sterling equiv. pesos[a]	Ocean freight pesos/fanega[b]	Santiago prices Sterling equiv. pesos[c]	 Current pesos
1851–5	5.05	[2.00]	2.72	2.72
1856–60	4.85	[1.70]	3.74	3.75
1861–5	4.31	[1.40]	2.36	2.36
1866–70	4.94	[1.15]	2.79	2.79
1871–5	4.92	[1.00]	2.96	2.96
1876–80	4.26	[0.85]	3.38	3.92
1881–5	3.63	[0.60]	2.62	3.60
1886–90	2.83	[0.50]	2.49	4.45
1891–5	2.52	[0.50][d]	1.85	5.05
1896–1900	2.58	[0.50][d]	2.41	6.59

Sources: [a] John Kirkland, *Three Centuries of Prices of Wheat, Bread and Flour* (London, 1917), pp. 33–5. [b] Ocean freight rates from *El Mercurio* (Valparaíso). [c] Santiago prices in appendix; London prices see (a) and (b). [d] Estimated from *El Mercurio*.

Note: Kirkland gives London prices in shillings per quarter. I have converted at rate of three fanegas per quarter and forty-four pence per peso. One fanega = 71.5 kilos = 157 lbs; one quarter = 480 lbs.

entered the market on an overwhelming scale. Chile was able to enter the export market at a time when the brief conjuncture of falling freight rates and the still high world wheat prices made export most favorable. Fortunate timing was combined with another advantage in the early years: Chile was the only exporter in the southern hemisphere. Cereal cultivation in the Río de la Plata did not surpass that of Chile until the 1890s and wheat was not exported from there on a large scale until after the turn of the century. Australia, the other future great exporter in the southern hemisphere, still intermittently imported wheat in the 1860s and did not become a great exporter until just before World War I. Therefore during the peak years of its export, Chile was helped by being a country that harvested grain during the European winter. If wheat harvested in December and January could be placed on the English market by April or May before the northern grain arrived, a price advantage of about ten per cent was obtained.[17]

Bad harvests in Europe and disruptions caused by wars were other factors that enabled Chilean grain to be sold on European markets. The essential point however is that the trade could only exist under unusual and temporary conditions. Chilean producers understood the precariousness of the European market. It was one factor in their unwillingness to invest in agriculture, for under the best of circumstances, Chile was barely able to compete with physically better-endowed regions. Chilean *hacendados* produced for export by merely extending the existing system because it was easy and for a time profitable to do so. To modernise production would have required widespread reorganisation of land and technology. This would have been at best a risky venture in view of developments elsewhere, a theme that was repeated in articles of the National Society of Agriculture's *Boletín*. From 1870 on, this influential journal frequently pointed out the uncertainty of Chile's grain trade.[18]

Wheat prices in Table 12 clearly reveal why the period 1865–80 stands out as an exceptionally fortuitous interlude.[19] During these years

Table 12   Average annual wheat prices in Santiago, 1848–1910 (in current and sterling equivalent pesos per fanega)

| Years | Current pesos | | Sterling equivalent pesos of 44p | |
	Price	Index	Price	Index
1848–50	1.06	34	1.06	35
1851–5	2.72	91	2.72	91
1856–60	3.74	126	3.74	126
1861–5	2.36	79	2.36	79
1866–70	2.79	94	2.79	94
1871–5	2.96	100	2.96	100
1876–80	3.92	132	3.38	114
1881–5	3.60	121	2.62	88
1886–90	4.45	150	2.49	84
1891–5	5.05	170	1.85	62
1896–1900	6.59	222	2.41	81
1901–5	8.01	270	2.91	98
1906–10	12.85	434	3.21	108

Source: Appendices 1 and 4.

the European grain market increased Chilean agricultural export earnings to over three-fourths the value of mining exports (13.2 to 17.5 million of pesos). Agriculture prices remained high throughout the 1870s, while better ships and new railroads sharply reduced transportation costs. Increased agricultural output was obtained by employing additional units of land and labor – both of which were still cheap. For the first time in the history of Chile, big money could be be made in farming.

Very soon, however, the windfall was over. By 1880, massive grain production in North America, Australia, the Russian steppes, and later in Argentina brought a sharp decline in prices.[20] Central Chile could no longer compete on the world market; the amount of grain exported from the traditional heartland of the country dwindled to insignificance.[21] The situation faced by Chilean growers at different periods in the nineteenth century may be more easily seen in Table 13 where

Table 13   Prices and costs of wheat export: selected years (in current pesos per fanega)

	1855–7	1871–3	1885–7
Selling price	7.00–8.00	5.17	2.89
Ocean freight	1.95	1.17	0.58
Handling, insurance, storage, etc.	0.95	0.65	0.30
Price at Valparaíso	4.56	3.35	2.01
Freight charge to port	1.90	0.80	0.60
Price at estate	2.66	2.60	1.40
Production costs	1.46	(a) 1.50	(a) 1.65
		(b) 1.30	(b) 1.35
Gross profit	1.20	1.10	0.10

Source: The data available from the nineteenth century do not, of course, permit very exact calculations. Present data are approximate and intended only to convey a rough idea of the comparative costs through time. Only direct costs are considered; such things as administrative costs, or salaries of household servants, etc., are not included.

For 1855, I have used Gay, *Agricultura*, vol. II, p. 44, who gives a cost of 44 pesos to produce 30 fanegas of wheat (the produce of 1 cuadra, i.e., 1.57 hectare). The figure is a rough average of dry and irrigated types of culture. For 1871–3, I have used the calculations in *BSNA*, vol. V (1873), pp. 9–10. Cost (a) is estimated using no machinery; (b) with mechanical reaper and thresher. Since data on 1885–7 period are more difficult to calculate, I have added ten per cent to the (a) cost (all manual), figuring that this was approximately the increase in wages in constant money; (b) costs were increased five per cent which reflects the increased labor cost. The improved efficiency of the machinery that could have occurred in fifteen years was probably at least offset by lower yields (and thus higher costs) caused by less suitable lands being sowed to wheat in the central valley.

All prices at *fundo* and at port (Valparaíso) were taken from newspapers. The hypothetical *fundo* would be located about on the Cachapoal, i.e., about the same distance below Santiago as Santiago itself was from Valparaíso. 'Price at *fundo*' was obtained by subtracting freight from *fundo* to Santiago from the Santiago prices.

Handling costs, storage, insurance, etc., includes such items as sacks for grain and storage at Valparaíso. The estimates were made from several *BSNA* that carried regular information on the subject. See especially *BSNA*, vol. XXIX (1898), pp. 290–2.

Surface freight was taken from newspapers. For newspapers see, for example, *El Ferrocarril* (Santiago), no. 107, 26 April 1856 and no. 1012, 12 March 1859. These data are for dry season; in the winter the rate could be fifty per cent higher. Data includes tolls on Valparaíso–Santiago road. The railroad rates are taken from the published schedules for third-class freight. The rates are reproduced in newspapers and the *BSNA*. Ocean rates are figured at 100 shillings per ton in 1855–7 to Pacific markets or to England. *El Mercurio*, 29 April 1855, gives rates of 24–8 pesos (nearly 100 shillings). For 1872–3 see *El Mercurio*. There is a *Revista del Vapor* published every fortnight that gives prices of charters, etc. The same source was used for 1885–7. The *BSNA* during these years often has information. The London wheat prices are from Kirkland, *Three Centuries of Prices*.

prices and costs are presented for a hypothetical estate in the central valley.

The selling price of $7.00 to $8.00 per fanega in the 1850s represents the amount received from sales in the Pacific markets of either California or Australia. Much of this price was absorbed by high ocean and land freight costs. London prices in 1855–7 were $5.50 or about $1.00 higher than the price of wheat in Valparaíso. Freight and handling costs of nearly $3.00 between Valparaíso and London amply demonstrate why Chile was excluded in these years from the European market. Because of the small volume of the only outlet available to Chile – the California or Australia markets – total income from grain exports was small.

By 1871–3 transportation and handling costs between central Chile and London dropped from $4.80 (this included land transport from the central valley to port) to $2.60. This reduction meant that wheat sold at the estate for $2.60 could now be placed on the London market at the going price of $5.00 to $5.25 per fanega. At these prices Chilean growers were willing to expand cultivation; by 1874 the all-time peak in grain exports was reached as some 2 000 000 qqm of wheat and barley were shipped abroad.[22]

The third period of 1885–7 shown in the table falls in the midpoint of the 'Great Depression.' London wheat prices dropped to $2.89 which meant that a central Chilean estate could be offered no more than about $1.40. At this price central Chile could not compete with the more favorably endowed and efficient zones elsewhere in the world. The brief and lucrative European grain trade was finished, and only the still undeveloped home market remained. By 1890 the National Society of Agriculture's earlier optimisim was replaced by frequent references to 'nuestra aflijida agricultura.' By 1900 the 'decadence' of cereal production in central Chile was commonly accepted.[23]

After 1880 the effect on Chile of massive production shipments from North America can be seen in wheat prices. From $3.88 in 1876–80, Santiago prices fell to $1.85 in 1891–5. Had there been no devaluation of the peso or if $1.85 represented the true purchasing power of the peso, Chilean wheat could not have been marketed at that price. But along with decline in the world price, there was a devaluation of the peso. Instead of receiving $1.85 the Chilean grower actually got $5.05 delivered at the Santiago railhead. To repeat, until a cost of living index is constructed for the nineteenth century we will not know how much $5.05 represented in purchasing power. But the price apparently was not sufficient to induce growers to export. In 1890, Chilean *hacendados* offered only 290 000 qqm of wheat to the foreign market. More efficient production in the virgin lands of the Araucanian Frontier permitted further exports from the south. But for central Chilean growers, the day of large export earnings was past.[24]

So far we have been concerned only with agricultural exports and mainly with cereals. These provide a better indication of agricultural activity than one might think because although central Chile was capable of producing a wide variety of plants and animals throughout much of the nineteenth century, there was little internal demand for a diversified output. The small high quality market was satisfied by imports from Europe and the mass of the people still provided only a weak incentive to agriculture; thus extra earnings could only come from sales abroad and this is why the export cereal trade looms so large in the Chilean economic literature.[25]

Without a foreign market and until nitrate and copper mining began to transform the Chilean economy the main obstacle for the landowner was the lack of someone to whom his produce might be sold. The great mass of the population was itself rural and if not self-sufficient, as were by and large the resident workers and smallholders, it was incapable of buying much beyond beans and coarse flour. A few regions produced specialities – a good cheese from Chanco, dried fruit from Aconcagua – but these were exceptions of slight significance. For the mass of Chileans, the diet was monotonously constant. Peons on construction gangs were normally alloted a half-pint of toasted wheat mixed with water for one meal and beans cooked with lard and chile peppers for the other. The standard ration prescribed by M. J. Balmaceda in the well-known *Manual del hacendado Chileno* was about one pound of flour in the morning, the same quantity of beans at midday, and for supper another pound of flour. Resident laborers on estates generally enjoyed a better diet than peons, particularly if the plot they were alloted was on irrigated land. If so, maize, potatoes, and other vegetables could be raised to supplement the standard ration of flour, beans, and the occasional chicken or pig cooked for feast days. All this was accompanied, especially on holidays and Sundays, by a great deal of local wine and occasionally with cheap brandy.[26]

The lower rural classes in the countryside rarely ate fresh meat. Until after the 1860s when such forage crops as alfalfa came into wider use, few animals were kept in slaughtering condition all year round; rather, there was an annual roundup when butchered animals were turned into salted, dried beef (*charqui*). This was the common form of meat and still today *charqui* is popular among rural people. Meat in this form as well as lard and hides could be more easily handled for export and certain quantities found their way to mining camps and to the ports for ships' provisions. It was too expensive to give fresh meat to workers and few had the land to raise their own animals; so except for theft, meat for the the rural poor remained a coveted but unattainable luxury. Claudio Gay thought that the national average in the 1840s was not more than 13 kilograms annually and other observers have lower estimates. Nearly a century later there was little improvement in diet and despite the merits of 'the very noble bean' (as the well-fed landowners liked to describe the peons' staple), rural people suffered the effects of protein deficient nourishment.[27]

If the mass of people – over eighty per cent in 1865 – that lived outside the cities offered little encouragement to agriculture, the economic forces at work in the Atlantic world began to have repercussions that considerably brightened prospects in the northern desert and in Santiago. Until European farmers under heavy competitive pressure were willing to pay for fertilisers, and until the efficient 'nitrate clippers' could make the long Cape Horn run at reasonable costs, the Atacama was of little use to anyone. But by the 1880s, the enormous possibilities of nitrates had led Chile into a most successful war and soon a relatively well-off force occupied the newly won provinces of the far north. The number of workers increased rapidly in the later nineteenth century and a stable population grew up around mining camps and port cities in the north. By 1913 there were around 50 000 nitrate workers and population in the Norte Grande alone went from 2000 in 1875 to nearly 300 000 by 1930. Added to nitrate was copper mining. From around 1917, the *gran minería*, centered on Chuquicamata came into production and although the more capital-intensive and concentrated copper sector always employed fewer men – only ten to twelve thousand by 1930 – this activity and the local support it required contributed to growth in the arid north. Nearly all the agricultural supplies for these people had to be brought in from central Chile.[28]

The impact of the Atlantic economy

Public revenue from the export of nitrate and copper increased steadily from the 1880s onward. By the turn of the century an unexpected flow of wealth poured into the centralised national treasury and ultimately into projects such as railways and port construction, urban modernisation and the military. Inevitably a vast and ever-proliferating bureaucracy accompanied the increase in public revenue and Santiago was confirmed as the administrative center of the country. Here besides, financial intermediaries flourished, political patronage and economic concessions were awarded, the first proper factories of light industry appeared. Under the impulse of this fairly sudden and quite accidental activity, there began the extraordinary growth of Santiago that continues to the present. From a modest and still essentially colonial town of some 115 000 in 1865, the capital increased to nearly 700 000 by 1930: an annual rate of over three per cent, double that of the country as a whole. Valparaíso, the second city, lagged behind, growing over the same period from 70 000 to just under 200 000.[29] The bureaucracy, created in part to administer and disburse the new state revenue; the private professionals – lawyers, bankers, accountants – who counseled and counted during these boom years; new merchants, foreign and native; the thriving absentee landlords; and an incipient light industrial sector all confirmed Santiago as the vital center of the country. The opulent and often ostentatious houses of the rich marched south-west, away from the colonial plaza to the newly fashionable streets of Diesiocho, Ejército Libertador, and República. The inhabitants of these districts and a spreading middle layer of employees and managers created a new market for Chilean agriculture, important for the higher quality and diversified nature of the produce it demanded.

The reader has been put on guard that statistics on total output, especially before the agricultural censuses of 1935–6, are a shaky affair. Although exports are fairly easy to count, data on internal production are the most difficult to gather and the least reliable. From 1859 on, the statistical yearbook (*Anuario estadístico*) provides data on the value of agricultural output but these, as the yearbook readily admits, are little more than guesses and inconsistent guesses at that. And even if the figures for production are allowed they do not tell us how much produce was actually marketed or how much income was actually obtained by growers. In 1874, as an example of this, the official data are not only unreliable but absurd. The port records show that some $4 000 000 more was exported than the (official) tax records show as produced in the entire country. The same problem exists for livestock. The 1863

Anuario gives a total of about one million cattle while by 1870, the SNA *Boletín* estimated that the stock had fallen to around 270 000. The disastrous outbreak of hoof and mouth disease (*aftosa*) in the 1870s might have caused such fluctuation and this may have contributed to the price increases in the 1870s. By 1906 there were estimates of 1.6 million and in 1930, around 2.4 million.[30]

Nevertheless it is clear that the first third of this century were excellent years for Chilean agriculture. The area under cultivation greatly increased – the statistics suggest it nearly doubled – between 1900 and 1930, and apart from the years of really rapid adjustment between 1895 and 1910, prices rose more slowly for food than for other items.[31] As the quality of the market steadily improved, several landowners within reach of Santiago consumers installed dairies, others improved their herds, planted orchards, produced honey and poultry. Throughout central Chile – especially between Aconcagua and Talca – the acreage devoted to the vine was greatly increased. The *cepas del país* (called *misión* in Mexico and California; *criollo* in Peru and Argentina) introduced by the Spaniards in the sixteenth century, gave way to improved varieties brought in from France in the 1850s and '60s. From the latter nineteenth century excellent vineyards such as Macul, Tarapacá or Concha y Toro, modeled after Bordeaux châteaux were established and consumption increased from around 81 million liters in 1875 (25 per annum per capita) to 275 million (nearly 90 per capita) in 1903. The consumption of wine leveled off to around 75 liters per capita by 1942. All this indicated a quite impressive elasticity of supply for an agriculture that was increasingly condemned as 'feudal,' 'slovenly,' and 'inefficient.' Yet, as we shall see, increased output and archaic agricultural practices were not necessarily incompatible.[32]

The livestock sector of agriculture was the first to feel the full impact of the almost fierce interest and enormous demand for beef which for decades now has been consumed by the urban mass and middle classes to the near total exclusion of all other meat. Already in 1905, high beef prices provoked riots and there are few *Santiaguinos* today who are not deeply grieved over the scarcity of their favorite viands. Landowners in central Chile responded to the growing demand for beef by planting alfalfa, and attempting to improve and increase herds of cattle. On many *fundos, charqui* and lard were abandoned by 1870 because 'deja mas cuenta' to sell fat animals on the hoof. Still the market was so strong that supply could not keep up. By 1888, each *Santiaguino* managed to consume nearly 150 kilograms of beef annually, twice as much as New Yorkers or Parisians. In England the national average in the years 1900–4 was a robust 130 lbs per capita yet this was only forty per cent of the amount carved up by each person in the Chilean capital, according to my sources.[33]

From around $10 pesos a head for a 'fattened cow' (*vaca gorda*) in 1845 beef prices rose 3.7 per cent annually to around $30.00 in 1876 and then the prices soared. Landowners had been slow to introduce better beef breeds and while the hardy *raza criolla* survived well on thin pastures they were not efficient meat producers. Moreover stockraisers frequently kept animals for six or seven years before selling them. By 1890 prices had risen about $50.00 and for the next three decades cattle prices were well above the average price index.[34] (See Table 14.)

Table 14   Cattle prices in Santiago: 1846–1925 (annual averages of five-year periods in current pesos per head)

Years	Current pesos	
	Price	Index
1846–50	10.12	32
1851–5	12.66	40
1856–60	25.83	82
1861–5	20.40	65
1866–70	23.30	74
1871–5	31.20	100
1876–80	30.50	98
1881–5	43.40	139
1886–90	49.40	158
1891–5	57.00	182
1896–1900	64.75	207
1901–5	104.00	312
1906–10	210.00	673
1911–15	207.00	663
1916–20	282.00	904
1921–5	356.00	1141

Source: See Appendix 1.

It is clear that external stimuli were the driving force in the Chilean economy: first the British demand for grain and later the rapid rise of the export mining sector. As a result of the peculiar development Chile underwent from the 1880s on, a number of distortions appeared that had important implications for agriculture and rural society. The rapid growth of Santiago as a commercial and bureaucratic center meant that the city offered disproportionately better opportunities for women migrants – as domestics, cooks, nursemaids, washerwomen – than it did for men, creating serious sexual imbalance. Because of large investments of public revenue in urban improvements such as better drainage, lighting, and transportation, and because of the cultural amenities, the capital was dramatically set off from the countryside and the straggling provincial towns. Every landowner who could afford it, built a second house in Santiago. *Hacendados* in the nearby districts had always lived in the capital; now – especially as their economic interests multiplied – they tended to spend more time in the city while lesser owners and those deeper in the provinces were also understandably attracted to urban pleasures and possibilities.[35]

There is in fact a double explanation for the widening rural–urban gulf in the *belle époque* years of the early twentieth century. On one hand, the landowners themselves, who had always been the only social group that linked city and countryside, became more and more urban oriented. The agricultural fairs and technical exhibits were held in Santiago; whatever storage facilities and rudimentary packing houses existed were also there along with the main banks and mortgage houses; the only adequate schools or university; the only proper medical or dental care were in the capital or Valparaíso. In short, Santiago – and to a lesser extent the port – monopolised all the services and amenities that the landowners required. Landowners supported the modernisation of Santiago because they lived there; and they were obliged to give way to the rising demands of the urban middle and lower classes, even though their interests were still articulated mainly through suggestion and riot rather than formal parties. Political power was perceptibly shifting to the city. The export economy, then, rapidly accelerated the development of a modern, literate, politically advanced, urban society in which the principal landowners were increasingly involved.

At the same time, very little of the enormous wealth generated in the export sector found its way into the rural areas. The few rude school buildings in existence were put up by the more 'philanthropic' landowners; there was no electricity, rarely a supply of potable water, and modern medicine was virtually unknown. Nor did the political ideas of the mines and cities penetrate the countryside. All through the 1920s the mass of rural inhabitants were outside the new unions and they remained unorganised and politically impotent until recent years. As a result little public spending was applied to the countryside and few social welfare measures reached rural society. An agrarian structure and a set of economic relationships that effectively excluded the mass of rural population from participation in the wider market were perpetuated. In 1917, about seventy per cent of all agricultural land was contained in less than 1000 estates and the owners insisted on a

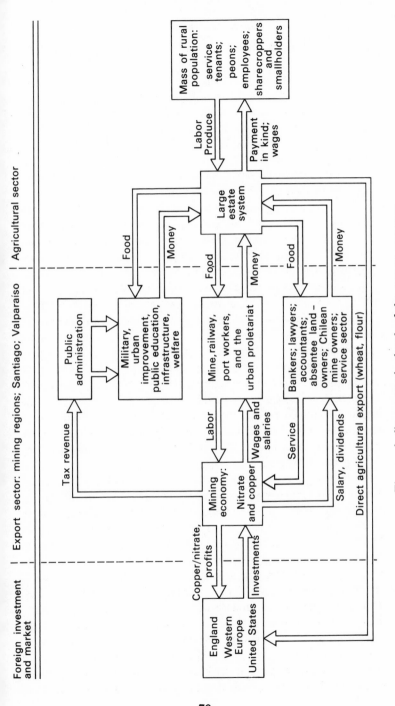

Foreign investment and market | Export sector: mining regions; Santiago; Valparaiso | Agricultural sector

Fig. 1 A diagrammatic sketch of the export economy

79

paternalistic regime that featured many elements of a medieval natural economy.[36]

Perhaps the relationship among the various parts of the Chilean economy can be visualised better in Figure 1 which shows three areas: the 'foreign market and investments'; the 'export sector' consisting of the mining regions and Santiago and Valparaíso; and the traditional 'agricultural sector.' Because Chile had a stable government and a well-organised public administration throughout the period 1830–1925, the country was able to impose a substantial tax on nitrate exports and effectively funnel that revenue into a multitude of urban improvements, port and railway works, and pay the salaries of government and military employees. The mine, railway, and port workers were well-paid wage earners, who, together with the growing number of the urban proletariat, constituted a good market for agriculture.

Production on the large estates in the agricultural sector was directed by the landowner or his delegate, transported by estate-owned mules or carts to the railhead or urban market and sold to merchants. Outside of the area dominated by the larger estates were two groups theoretically able to sell independently their own produce. The owners of farms under 200 hectares were in this category as were sharecroppers. If these producers had the capital – equipment, tools, seed – or access to credit and the means to get their produce to buyers, they could participate in the market economy. In practice, many sharecroppers and the marginal smallholders were drawn into the orbit of the large estate through their need for credit or transport. When this was the case, the estate owners could offer a lower price – often by advancing money before harvest: the practice of buying the unripe grain (*venta en yerba*) – and reap a profit by selling at the higher prices of the free market economy. There is no way of knowing the share of total agricultural output that was sold by the larger estates, but since they controlled some seventy per cent of the land, it is reasonable to suppose that they produced at least that amount of the total grain and livestock. A few independent smallholders and sharecroppers on the outskirts of cities were active in supplying the daily urban market for horticulture, fruit, and an entire range of specialty items of low volume. But when one considers that some of this produce was sold through the larger *fundos*, the picture of an estate-dominated agriculture – and within that the extraordinary share of estate income that went to the landowner alone – is reinforced. The impact of a wider market seems to have created greater inequality of agricultural income in favor of the large estates. It is difficult to arrange the twentieth-century data to make them comparable with the earlier figures, but as far as one can determine from the tax data, estate income became more concentrated between 1854 and 1875, and this trend seems to have continued into the 1930s.[37]

To say that some eighty-five per cent of agricultural produce in the early twentieth century was sold by the large estates means that a very large part of the rural population was excluded from the market economy and, in fact, from even a money economy. Resident workers on the estates (*inquilinos*) exchanged their labor for payment in kind (a subsistence plot, daily ration, shelter); and a part of the outside laborers' (or peons) wage, although often calculated in money, was in fact often paid in merchandise, food or supplies from the hacienda store. Understandably, this regime did not stimulate the growth of provincial cities. Outside of Santiago and Valparaíso, there were only ten towns with more than 10 000 inhabitants throughout central Chile in 1920. Most local towns had a long single unpaved street, a few cheap stores or bars. No doctors, lawyers or important bankers or landowners lived in these backwaters; rural society still turned around the large estates.[38] The countryside remained isolated, and arguably more cut off than before, from an impressive urban culture whose lower classes began to look to Marxism for inspiration while the elite sought its culture and manufactures in France and England.

There are two final observations that should be made here about the relationships between agriculture and the export economy. The availability of an easily accountable source of public revenue – bags of nitrate or bars of copper – meant that any need for the Chilean government to intrude into the affairs of landowners was reduced and consequently the possibilities of conflict was practically eliminated. With the experience of Louis XIV's France or eighteenth-century Russia in mind, one can imagine a number of ways the state and landowners might have clashed over rural tax or 'peasant' produce; but in Chile the more politically vulnerable, largely foreign-owned export sector, paid the national bills and the state kept its political hands off the countryside until the overwhelming urban demands for more food and political support in the 1960s.[39]

There was one last important implication for agriculture in the development of a strong export sector. Although the new wealth led to a much larger market for Chilean landowners, the fact that a rich and nearly unlimited land lay just across the cordillera reduced the pressure for reform or radical modernisation of Chilean agriculture. After the turn of the century more and more influential people felt that given 'the limited horizons of agricultural expansion' that the country should be 'converted into an immense mining camp fed by Argentina and supplied with manufactures from Europe.' Thus, despite an intermittent and fairly modest tax from 1898 to 1935 on Argentine cattle, the deficit in Chilean output was made up by imports through the Andean passes. Between 1874 and 1930, some 432 millions of pesos' worth of Argentine livestock (mostly cattle) were brought in to satisfy the national craving for red meat.[40] Even though the new lands of the Araucanía were added to central Chilean production, the country came to depend more and more on imported food. In recent decades, copper – the present 'wage of Chile' – has been hard pressed to pay the bill.

CHAPTER 3

[1] For Australia, see Edgars Dunsdorfs, *The Australian Wheat-Growing Economy 1788–1948* (New York, 1956); for California, two unpublished theses are useful: E. E. Marten, 'The Development of Wheat Culture in the San Joaquín Valley 1846–1900' (unpublished Master's thesis, History: University of California at Berkeley); and M. H. Saunders, 'California Wheat 1867–1910: Influences of Transportation on the Export Trade and the Location of the Producing Areas' (unpublished Master's thesis, Geography: University of California at Berkeley, 1960).

[2] Claudio Véliz, *Historia de la marina mercante de Chile* (Santiago, 1961), p. 94. The average annual number of ships in 1846–8 was 1374; from 1849 to 1851, 2773; Sepúlveda, *Trigo chileno*, p. 44. The quintal is the metric quintal of 100 kilos.

[3] Horace Davis, 'California Breadstuffs,' *Journal of Political Economy*, vol. II (1893–4), p. 533.

[4] Benjamín Vicuña Mackenna, *Páginas de mi diario durante tres años de viaje. 1853, 1854, 1855* (Santiago, 1856), p. 33; and Vicente Pérez Rosales, *Recuerdos del pasado*, 6th ed. (Santiago, 1958), pp. 277–80. California prices in Davis, 'California Breadstuffs,' p. 610. Chilean prices in *El Mercurio* (Valparaíso), 1850–5.

[5] Sepúlveda, *Trigo chileno*, p. 44–8.

[6] Sepúlveda, *Trigo chileno*, pp. 35–6, 127.

[7] M. H. Saunders, 'California Wheat,' p. 42, discusses types of ships in flour trade. John Storck and Walter D. Teague, *Flour for Man's Bread* (Minneapolis, 1952), pp. 175–95, discuss the changes in US milling and shipping techniques; and Gilliss, *Naval Astronomical*, pp. 234–5, comments on the practice of kiln-drying to combat the effects of equatorial climate in the mid-1850s.

[8] *CJ* (Talca), Leg. 330, p. 2.

[9] The average for the period 1846–50 is based on three years only. Before 1846 flour exports were about 50 000 qqm a year. The figures for 1875, 1880, and 1885 are for single years only. This is because after 1870, the *Estadística comercial*, the source for all these data, is exceedingly difficult to deal with regard-

82

ing coastal trade. Sepúlveda, *Trigo chileno*, pp. 127–8, has national figures for flour export but in compiling these figures I included the coastal trade in order to give a better idea of the regional development of the industry. The coastal trade actually amounted to between half and one third of flour exports. In 1856–60, for example, Sepúlveda's export totals average 117 000 a year whereas my export and coastal are 210 000 qqm. In 1881–5, the total of 341 000 qqm is not the sum of the three ports shown because by that time new ports (Valdivia, Talcahuano) were exporting flour.

10 Claudio Véliz, *Marina mercante*, pp. 170–6; 'Proyecto de un ferrocarril a vapor entre la ciudad de Talca y el puerto de Constitución,' (Valparaíso, 1879), pp. 1–20. Sepúlveda, *Trigo chileno*, p. 103.

11 *Estadística comercial* for appropriate years. Import duties are given for each item in the *Estadística*; 'Causas de la decadencia de la industria molinera en Chile,' *BSNA*, vol. XXI (1890), pp. 678–9.

12 Jules Foster set up the large La Unión mill in Linares and was later put in charge of all operations. Another North American, William White, was also administrator of this mill. Nearly all the Talca mills, whether owned by Chileans or foreigners, had United States technicians. In the case of the large Corinto mill on the Maule, Silas Smith, a North American, was made an equal partner and, lacking capital, was required to supply only his 'industry and service.' *CN* (Talca), vol. 90, f. 604. Wm C. Edgar, *The Story of a Grain of Wheat* (New York, 1903), pp. 149–68, says that, 'the purifier was to milling what the reaper was to agriculture.' For discussion of milling technology of this period, see Storck and Teague, *Flour*, esp. pp. 158–240. The two main varieties of wheat in nineteenth-century Chile were *trigo blanco* (*triticum vulgare*), which accounted for about ninety per cent of the wheat cultivated below Santiago; and *trigo candeal* (*triticum durum*) raised in much smaller quantities in the north.

13 Julio Menandier, 'Aforismos sobre la molinería nacional,' *BSNA* vol. XVIII (1885), p. 464; Storck and Teague, *Flour*, pp. 254–5; *BSNA*, vol. XXI (1890), pp. 678–81; *BSNA*, vol. XI (1880), pp. 49–50. In 1890 a display of the new milling equipment was organised by the Fomento Fabril because of the 'clear decadence' of the industry in Chile. See 'Memoria que la sociedad de fomento fabril presenta sobre el concurso de molinería.' (Santiago, 1892), pp. 35–53.

14 Henry Kirsch, 'The industrialization of Chile, 1880–1930' (Unpub. Ph.D. diss., University of Florida, 1973), pp. 69–70, says that thirty-five of the new roller mills were in operation by 1904; Luis Galdames, *Jeografía económica de Chile* (Santiago, 1911), p. 188, discusses the importance of milling by 1911.

15 The value of exports is conveniently broken down into categories in *BSNA*, vol. XXI (1890), p. 89. After 1875, the declining value of the Chilean peso in terms of foreign currency introduces certain difficulties in the presentation of data. All prices in the tables of this chapter are expressed both in 'current pesos,' and 'sterling equivalent' pesos. The first is the amount of Chilean pesos received for produce in Santiago at the time of sale; the second the value of produce in terms of £ sterling. From 1875 onwards the Chilean peso was steadily declining as shown in Appendix 4.

16 *El Mercurio* (Valparaíso) gives frequent quotations on ocean freight rates. See also Véliz, *Marina mercante*, pp. 233–44. In 1850 one shilling equalled about 25 centavos of the Chilean peso. Carl August Gosselman, *Informes sobre los estados sud-americanos en los años 1837–8*, Intro. by Magnus Mörner, trans. from Swedish by Ernesto Dethorey (Stockholm, 1962), has a good discussion of ocean rates in the period treated. On ocean geography, the work of James Rennell and the later amplification of his work by M. F. Maury, *Explanations and Sailing Directions to Accompany the Wind and*

Current Charts (1850), are valuable; see Véliz, *Marina mercante*, pp. 236–8, for discussion of effects on Chile.

17 Wilfred Malenbaum, *The World Wheat Economy: 1855–1939* (Cambridge, Mass., 1953), pp. 238–9. *BSNA*, vol. III (1872), p. 374.

18 See for example, 'El porvenir del cultivo del trigo en Chile,' *BSNA*, vol. XI (1879), pp. 48–52; 'El porvenir de nuestro cultivo i commercio del trigo,' *BSNA*, vol. XII, pp. 22–6. The excellent report on Chile in 1875; Horace Rumbold, *Reports by Her Majesty's Secretaries . . . on the Manufactures, Commerce, etc.* (London, 1876), pp. 379–81, notes that 'the cultivation of cereals has probably been carried very nearly as far as the cultivable area at present available will permit . . .' But Rumbold thinks that the 'tide of good fortune has been for some years so much in favour of Chilean corn growers that they may well be excused if they have at all over-rated [their] position' (p. 380). The future of Chilean wheat exports became a major concern of the National Society of Agriculture. Julio Menandier, 'El porvenir de nuestro cultivo i comercio de trigo,' *BSNA*, vol. XII (1880), pp. 21–6, recognised the 'peculiar character of the agriculture of the Far West' and notes that from that time on, the London price will be regulated 'not by the European harvest but by the North American.' The *Boletín* urged at this time the use of artificial fertilisers to increase yields 'because the present production costs cannot be reduced in Chile' (p. 22).

19 Since we have no price index for nineteenth-century Chile the purchasing power of the peso cannot be accurately determined. Internal prices were rising but at what rate is not clear. The price of many imports probably increased at about the same rate as the peso devalued. Thus a bottle of Spanish sherry that sold for only £1 (or 5 pesos) in 1850 still cost £1 in 1900, but now the equivalent in Chilean currency was nearly 14 pesos. The £ sterling prices of other imports such as cloth and manufactures and machinery fell during the course of the nineteenth century but until a reliable price index of imports is made we cannot be sure how much more or less could be purchased with a quintal of wheat. It is reasonable to assume that from 1876 to 1895 the terms of trade were slightly less favorable to Chile (i.e., that of quintal of exported wheat paid for slightly less imported goods). Domestically there was a steady but gradual upward pressure on prices from 1875 to 1890 and then a rather more accelerated increase after that time. Some items, notably the cost of rural labor, lagged behind the other rates of increase.

Adolfo Latorre Subercaseaux, 'Relación entre el circulante y los precios en Chile,' (Catholic Univ., Santiago, 1958), contains an index of some agricultural prices taken from newspaper quotations but there is nothing on prices of imported goods, cost of labor, housing, etc. Robert E. Lipsey, *Price and Quantity Trends in the Foreign Trade of the United States* (Princeton, N. J., 1965), p. 146, suggests a slightly falling price for machinery imports between 1879 and 1899.

20 Folke Dovring, 'The Transformation of European Agriculture,' *Cambridge Economic History of Europe* (Cambridge, 1965), VI, Part II, pp. 604–72. A recent survey is Michael Tracy, *Agriculture in Western Europe* (New York, 1964), 19–106. For earlier period see B. H. Slicher Van Bath, *The Agrarian History of Western Europe A.D. 500–1850* (trans. from the Dutch by Olive Ordish, London, 1963).

21 The home market remained low in volume and monotonously unvaried (and unprofitable) in quality until late in the nineteenth century. The export market, except for the brief interval of 1865–80, offered little relief. Even during the quinquenium 1856–60, when prices were extraordinarily high, export earnings from mining were still three times the value of agricultural

exports. When large-scale exploitation of the Atacama nitrate fields got underway toward the end of the century, agricultural exports were further eclipsed. During 1886–90 agricultural earnings averaged $8 311 000 a year while mining exports produced $54 000 000 or nearly seven times as much. Ten years later (1896–1900) the relationship was 13 million to 106 million. All export data are from *Resúmen de la hacienda pública de Chile desde 1833 hasta 1914* (London, 1914).

22 Sepúlveda, *Trigo chileno*, p. 128. Barley exports fluctuated at about 400 000 qqm. Data include grain converted into flour.

23 *BSNA*, vol. xxi (1890), p. 882; vol. xxxiii (1902), pp. 604–5.

24 To arrive at a figure for wheat exported from the *central* zone, I have made the following calculations. Column i is from Sepúlveda, *Trigo chileno*, pp. 127–8, column ii is estimated from Talcahuano port records as shown by Sepúlveda, p. 100 and the data in *Estadística comercial* for the appropriate years (in 'ooo of metric quintals).

Years	National exports	From frontier	From central Chile
1871–5	1131		1131
1876–80	946		946
1881–5	1082	700	382
1886–90	836	750	86
1891–5	1409	1200	209
1896–1900	684	600	84

25 *BSNA*, vol. iv (1872), p. 467.

26 The diet of rural people is revealed in the contracts to supply food to construction workers (the contract specifies what they *should* receive), accounts of rural life, instructions to hacienda administrators and corroboration by travelers. Workers on the Cachapoal bridge in 1850, for example, were supposedly guaranteed the following rations: 'Almuerzo, dos panes de diez onzas cada uno o harina sernida con grasa . . . comida [would be] de frijoles con grasa, sal y hají . . .' *AMI*, vol. 236 (1850), no p. no. A similar ration was given to rural workers throughout the nineteenth century. See *BSNA*, vol. i (1870), p. 382. The *Boletín* has several references to diet, on how to improve nutritional value, and the importance of decent food in attracting seasonal workers. Quantities are varied but the basic ingredients remained the same. See also Claudio Gay, *Agricultura*, i, p. 374. There is an attempt to deal with diet statistically in F. Urízar Garfias, *Estadística de la república de Chile: provincia de Maule* (Santiago, 1845), pp. 77–8, and excellent description in J.M. Gilliss, *Naval expedition*, pp. 366–7.

27 Manuel José Balmaceda, *Manual del hacendado chileno* (Santiago, 1875), p. 119; George McBride, *Chile: Land and Society* (Baltimore, 1936), p. 154. Thomas C. Wright, 'Origins of the politics of inflation in Chile, 1888–1918,' *HAHR*, vol. 53, no. 2 (May 1973), p. 246.

28 Carlos Hurtado Ruiz-Tagle, *Concentración de población y desarrollo económico: el caso chileno* (Santiago, 1966), pp. 144, 173, 195.

29 Richard Morse (ed.), *The Urban Development of Latin America 1750–1920* (Stanford, 1971), pp. 1–21, 54.

30 The prefaces to several of the *Anuarios estadísticos* in the 1860s and 1870s contain apologies for the lack or unreliability of agricultural data. Often the ability of the men charged with gathering information is criticised by the director of statistics. The 1874 *Estadística comercial* shows that $15 859 000

pesos' worth of agricultural produce was exported during that year. The *Impuesto agrícola: Rol de contribuyentes* (Santiago, 1874) shows that total agricultural income amounted to $11 588 000. This inconsistency is pointed out in M. Drouilly and Pedro Lucío Cuadra, 'Ensayo sobre el estado económico de la agricultura en Chile,' *BSNA*, vol. x (1878). For discussion of livestock population see Luis Correa Vergara, *Agricultura chilena*, II, pp. 146–65; Teodoro Schneider, *La agricultura en Chile durante los últimos cincuenta años* (Santiago, 1904), pp. 63–8; *BSNA*, vol. III (1891), p. 68; and vol. II (1871), pp. 211–12, 301. The National Society of Agriculture thought that *aftosa* appeared in Chile for the first time in the 1870s. Anthrax (called *picada* in Chile) existed since the colonial years. For the 1906 data, see Correa Vergara, *Agricultura chilena*, II, p. 164; and *Censo ganadero de la república de Chile levantado en el año 1906* (Santiago, 1907).

31 Sergio Aranda and Alberto Martínez, 'Estructura económica: algunas características fundamentales,' *Chile hoy* (Santiago, 1970), p. 127; see Appendix I and Latorre Subercaseaux, 'Relación,' for prices.

32 Carlos Keller, *Una revolución en la agricultura* (Santiago, 1956), pp. 128, 230; Hurtado Ruiz-Tagle, *Concentración de población*, p. 162; Victor León, *Uvas y vinos de Chile* (Santiago, 1947), pp. 266–8.

33 Wright, 'Politics of inflation' pp. 252–3, deals with the 1905 'Red Week' riot; *BSNA*, vol. III (1872), p. 230 discusses changes in livestock production; on meat consumption, see Francisco A. Alcaíno, 'Estudio de las carnes contagiosas del matadero de Santiago,' *Anales*, LXXV (1889), p. 457; and Platt, *Latin America*, p. 260. The data arouse my skepticism.

34 Since the unit of measure in these prices is the single animal (a *vaca gorda*) a statistical problem is immediately introduced: how much did a 'fat cow' weigh and how much did its average weight change over the century? Undoubtedly there was a trend toward heavier animals but the magnitude of change is difficult to establish.

35 Sexual imbalance can be seen in the censuses, especially the 1930 census. See Arnold J. Bauer and Ann Hagerman Johnson, 'Land and labor in rural Chile,' *Patterns of Agrarian Capitalism* (Cambridge, 197?).

36 Bauer and Johnson, 'Land and labor.'

37 The 1854 and 1874 data are arranged on Lorenz curves in our 'Land and labor,' cited above. Rapid growth of *minifundia* further skews distribution.

38 Hurtado Ruiz-Tagle, *Concentración de población*, pp. 168–9; and the interesting discussion in Morse, *Urban Development*, pp. 4–19, on the lack of linkages in agricultural systems.

39 Arcadius Kahan, 'Notes on Serfdom in Western and Eastern Europe,' *Journal of Economic History*, vol. XXXIII, no. 1 (March 1973), pp. 86–99; and my 'Service tenancy in Spanish America' (Unpublished manuscript of paper delivered at the American Historical Association Convention, December 1973, San Francisco).

40 The quotation is from G. Feliú Silva, 'Medio siglo de la industria chilena,' *Anales*, no. 120 (September–December 1960), p. 113; for importation of livestock, see Correa Vergara, *Agricultura chilena* II, pp. 157–8; Wright, 'Politics of inflation,' pp. 239–59.

Capital, credit and technology in the rural economy

The expansion of the Atlantic economy created a growing demand for raw materials and a surplus of capital for export. These developments in Great Britain and Western Europe were accompanied in Chile by the rise of a group of merchant bankers and the evolution of a formal banking and credit system. Rows of figures in handsome ledgers and the imposing bank buildings are tangible proof of this aspect of economic growth, but credit itself flowed beneath the surface of rural society: at times in such proper forms as mortgage loans but also in common handwritten obligations or even as rude leather tokens redeemable at hacienda stores and its impact in these cases must be assessed from the evidence left in notarial records and hacienda account books. Credit is a barely visible and virtually unexamined element in the gathering forces that shaped Chilean rural society. To understand the later impact of credit and capital it is useful to begin with the informal, pre-banking decades prior to 1860.

After Spanish restrictions were abolished with Independence, Chilean trade turned naturally to the more powerful nations of the North Atlantic, and into the breach vacated by imperial merchants came the emissaries of Great Britain, Germany, France, and the United States, speaking both figuratively and literally the language of a more aggressive commercial age. By 1850, two-thirds (674 out of 909) of the tax-paying businesses and seventy per cent of the most important merchant houses in the port of Valparaíso were foreign-owned.[1] Some of these men who came out after the Napoleonic wars were simply employees of distant firms such as the Alsop house of New York or the Anthony Gibbs Company of London; but many foreign merchants married Chileans and settled in the country. The fortunes of the Edwards, Lyon and Délano families, for example, all grew out of the Valparaíso trade.

Before the development of a formal money market the Valparaíso and Santiago merchants were among the main sources of credit for Chilean agriculture. The merchants rarely advanced cash to *hacendados* but rather guaranteed an amount against which the landowners could pay for imports or cancel other accounts managed for them by the merchants. Since farm produce exported or shipped in the coastal trade was often handled by the same commercial houses, the credit operation merely consisted of the merchants honoring claims against the following year's harvest or round-up. Such a case may be found in the records of the large estate of Cunaco in San Fernando. Nicolás Albano, a Valparaíso merchant, sold Cunaco's produce in the 1840s. In 1846, Albano shipped about $13 000 pesos' worth of produce for the estate, and against this amount canceled debts in Santiago, issued drafts for imports, and remitted funds to relatives of the landowner on tour in Europe.[2]

The landowner's word or his signature in the company's books was usually the only guarantee required – or rather it was, however inadequate, the best security a lender could get. For this reason the volume of credit was low and the interest rates generally high. Since agriculture rarely yielded over five per cent on investment it could not afford to pay twelve to fifteen per cent on a very large loan.[3] There are some cases of 'general' mortgages inscribed in the public registries to guarantee loans, but mortgage legislation before 1850 was so vague and ill-defined that merchants considered it 'adventurous' to lend on that basis.[4] A credit system based on a verbal pledge depended upon public reputation and mutual faith: the more of both, the better were the chances of obtaining credit in adequate amounts at manageable rates. There is no way to determine the total amount of credit extended during these years as most of it was not recorded in the public records, but it is clear that compared to the post-1850 period the total was much less.

Before 1855, the Valparaíso merchants were Chile's *de facto* bankers. They stood behind an extensive system of bills, money orders, and credit. After the 1850s, the merchants joined and some became the dominant elements in a banking system they had originally opposed; and after the 1860s, commercial and mortgage banks tended to replace ordinary merchants as direct suppliers of credit to milling and agriculture. The merchants, however, retained their link with regional wholesale and retail outlets. Besides the more lucrative mining and import trade, merchants also – particularly before 1850 – provided capital for the commercialisation of animal products and grain and served as general agents for *hacendados*.[5]

Another source of credit in the nineteenth century was savings from individuals, miners, bureaucrats, relatives of landowners, wealthy widows interested in secure if rather low-yielding investments. Because of the imprecise legislation that in case of default made collection difficult, most of this money also circulated within a rather small group of well-known and responsible people. An example of early lending may be seen in the case of J. F. Larraín y Rojas, owner of the hacienda of Aculeo. For 1847, the hacienda's books reveal $72 000 in receivables. Most of this amount had been lent to other large landowners, often relatives of Larraín. Income from interest on these loans constituted about twenty per cent of the estate's earnings in 1847.[6] The total of credit advanced by private lenders was undoubtedly greater than the amounts shown in the mortgage registries, especially in the years before 1856. Money changed hands among friends and families or was lent on the basis of personal word or signature. For this we have no overall record, but the few private account books examined make clear that a certain but indeterminate amount was lent in this manner. A third of the $72 000 lent by the owner of Aculeo, for example, was not inscribed in the notary records. It is reasonable to assume that large loans not secured by mortgages went only to the most solvent and respectable landowners. As the economic pace quickened in the 1850s, almost all lenders, private or institutional, began to insist on formal guarantees, and the new mortgage laws spelled out in the 1856 Civil Code made rural property one of the best guarantees for loans in the country. Individuals continued, of course, to lend money to each other and in fact private lenders were the single most important source of credit for landowners in at least two Departments until the 1880s. After that, lending channeled through the formal institutions – mortgage and commercial banks – became far more important.

During the colonial period and early years of the Republic, inadequate guarantees for loans were an obstacle to credit expansion. Legislation at first was based on colonial precedent: the *Pragmática* of 1768 and a *Real Cédula* in 1783. These established 'oficios de hipotecas en las cabezas de partido en todo el reino,' and as a result, by 1783 in Santiago and Concepción mortgages were recorded by the Notaries of those cities. Later legislation built on these colonial laws. The 1845 *Prelación de créditos* and a *Reglamento de Censos e Hipotecas* three years later added other mortgage registries in the provinces and attempted to redefine 'general' and 'special' mortgages. Potential lenders still complained, however, that 'the law offered [the borrowers] infinite means of eluding or retarding their obligations.' By mid-century, as the need and request for credit became more frequent, laws in keeping with the times were promulgated. The vague 'general mortgage' – source of endless litigation in earlier years – was abolished by the 1856 Civil Code. A new instrument, the 'special' mortgage, more clearly defined the rights of the lender and established order of preference in case of default. Property registries were set up throughout the Republic which made information on mortgages, sales, and *censos* readily available to the public.[7]

The same year that new legislation on mortgages was published, the first source of long-term credit came into existence. The Law of 29 August 1855 established the Caja de Crédito Hipotecario, the first and most important of Chilean mortgage banks. Born in the trough of Chile's first modern depression, the Caja had a halting beginning but soon grew into the most powerful lending institution of its kind in South America.[8] To qualify for a loan from the Caja, the property to be mortgaged had to be worth at least $2000. The value was taken either from the tax rolls or based on special appraisal. No loan could be made for less than $500, nor in any case exceed one-half the value of the property. If approved, a process that could be trying and lengthy, the Caja did not lend directly but rather issued *letras de crédito* to the borrower in return for a mortgage on the property. Those *letras* were in the amount of $1000, $500, $200, and $100, and bore fixed rates of interest. The borrower sold these *letras* on the open market and the receipts constituted his borrowing. The bank thus stood between the collective borrowers and lenders: it was the general debtor of those holding *letras* and the creditor of the persons who had pledged property in return for the *letras*.[9]

In this system, the market value of the *letras* determined the interest rate. The reputation enjoyed by the Caja can be seen by the quotations of the *letras*. They fluctuated very little from their par value. Because of their stable value the Caja *letras* were the standard low yield/low risk security. All banks, insurance companies, and many other corporations included the *letras* in their portfolios. After 1884, the savings of smaller investors were channeled to the landowners through the Caja de Ahorros, a savings bank that was required to purchase Caja *letras*.[10]

After 1900 the Caja began, as a National Society of Agriculture President put it, 'a dizzy race to greatness.' The volume of loans which had tripled during the previous decade increased sixteen-fold to 1·5 billion pesos. Chileans as well as foreigners purchased Caja *letras*. As early as 1878 reliable writers estimated that foreign investment accounted for forty to fifty per cent of the total. In 1911–12 and in the 1920s several millions worth were bought in Paris and Berlin.[11] Table 15 shows the mounting volume of loans made by the Caja de Crédito Hipotecario.[12]

We will examine the importance of credit in more detail below but the importance of the mortgage banks can already be imagined. Perhaps some eighty per cent of the total amount was secured by mortgages on rural property; this enormous volume gave landowners the opportunity to obtain, fairly easily, long-term loans. A landowner who received

Table 15   Operations of the Caja de Crédito Hipotecario: 1860–1930 (in current pesos)

Year	Total value of outstanding loans $
1860	5 002 600
1870	4 514 600
1880	18 757 900
1890	32 153 400
1900	94 500 000
1910	205 426 000
1920	467 212 591
1930	1 471 669 975

Source: Adapted from: G. Subercaseaux, *El sistema monetario*, pp. 354–6; and Correa Vergara, *Agricultura Chilena*, vol. I, p. 374.

eight per cent *letras* in the 1870s, for example, was required to pay back over a period of twenty-one years the eight per cent interest, two per cent amortisation, and one-half per cent reserve fund.[13]

Not only were Caja loans limited to the owners of large estates but moreover to those who owned land in the Departments nearest to Santiago.[14] The value of land of course helps explain the concentration of Caja loans in the provinces of Santiago, Colchagua, Valparaíso and Aconcagua. But in addition to land value, there was the certain but imponderable advantage of influence and social connections. Indeed, a list of Caja loan recipients in 1880 would be barely indistinguishable from a list of members of the Club de la Unión, the Club Hípico, or Congress. From its foundation in 1856 down to 1930 at least, the Caja was a highly useful institution: 'dócil instrumento en manos de los terratenientes.'[15]

The last major credit source for landowners were the commercial banks, the first of which was founded in the mid-1850s. As a rule this type of bank evolved from the earlier *casas habilitadoras* that supplied the northern mines. The first important institution was the Banco de Valparaíso de Depósitos i Descuentos. It was organised by a group of the wealthiest Valparaíso merchants (the most outstanding was Augustín Edwards) in 1854 and incorporated in 1856. Other commercial banks – the Banco de Chile and the Banco Agrícola, for example – were founded in the 1860s and '70s. By 1890, fourteen were in operation throughout the Republic and their increasing volume of lending added to the already abundant stream of credit available to Chilean landowners.[16]

We have so far seen only the sources of credit that were *available* to agriculture. Let us now turn to a closer examination of the working of the credit system in the central Departments of Talca and Caupolicán. The first of these, before the boundaries were changed in the late nineteenth century, ran in a wide swathe from the cordillera to the sea, embracing a variety of soil types and farming systems. Caupolicán was a smaller Department and in many ways typified the central valley: close enough to be within the market district and social influence of Santiago but far enough away to avoid the distortions of too intense urban contact. Flourishing already in the eighteenth century it became the heartland of traditional rural Chile and the location of several fine estates. The following section is based on data for the years 1845–90 taken from the notarial archives of these two Departments.[17] By restricting the geographical area this statistical sounding enables us to examine more closely the actual working of the credit system from the time it came into existence to its maturity in 1890. Let us look first at Table 16 which gives the five-year totals of all loans secured by inscribed mortgages.

Table 16   Five-year totals of mortgage loans in Talca and Caupolicán: 1845–90 (in current pesos)

Years	Talca	Caupolicán
1845–50	198 000	44 000
1851–5	522 000	197 000
1856–60	1 764 000	1 343 000
1861–5	1 276 000	2 086 000
1866–70	1 927 000	1 275 000
1871–5	2 122 000	1 761 000
1876–80	3 391 000	2 958 000
1881–5	3 359 000	2 500 000
1886–90	4 107 000	4 930 000

Source: Table 16 was made from data found in *CN* (Talca) (1838–90), vols. 40A, 80A, 102, 111, 113, 115, 117, 119, 122, 123, 124, 125, 126, and *CN* (Rengo) (1848–81), vols. 37, 49, 51, 54, 57, 59, 62, 65, 67, 70, 76, 80, 84, 90, 94, 97, 102, and 106, and *AMR* (1882–90), vols. *Registros de Hipotecas* for those years. Before 1838 in Talca, and 1848 in Rengo (the department was later known as 'Caupolicán'), mortgages are scattered throughout the volumes of the notarial archive. Beginning with these dates, they are recorded separately in volumes entitled *Registros de Hipotecas y Propiedades*. In the larger cities, these records are kept by the *Conservador de Bienes Raíces*. Besides permitting the quantification of mortgage loans, these volumes are good sources for other aspects of agrarian history. The boundaries, evaluation, quality of land, and the produce and rental is often given of properties. For each loan, the lender, borrower, co-signer, amount, terms, and location of property pledged are given. Marginal notations often give date of redemption, extensions, bankruptcies, etc. After 1858, the profession of lender and borrower is occasionally shown but the use of the funds is seldom specified. In compiling these tables, I have recorded all loans awarded to property holders, whether rural or urban. The percentage secured by urban property grows, of course, with the size of cities. In Talca, with a large provincial capital city, the percentage based on urban property was about seventeen per cent in 1890, and less before. In Caupolicán, the urban portion is negligible. As both departments were predominately rural in the nineteenth century, and since even a larger city like Talca existed primarily in connection with agriculture, it is difficult and of little profit to separate urban from rural loans. The unpaid balances on land purchases that were guaranteed by mortgages have also been recorded. Thus, if a *fundo* were sold for $50 000 of which $10 000 was paid in cash and the $40 000 carried at interest for five years guaranteed by a mortgage on a departmental *fundo*, the latter sum was included in the tables. Mortgages to guarantee rentals, on the other hand, have not been included since these do not effectively involve receipt of credit. For the same reason, neither are the small amounts pledged in annual payments as '*Censos*' and '*Capellanías*' listed. These forms, which *did* constitute indebtedness, did not involve receipts of credit by the property holder.

Apart from showing the sharp increase in the 1850s, the totals alone are not especially useful. In the 1870s the total lending each year works out to about $2.5 pesos per hectare and $6.00 per inhabitant; according to the tax records, landowners would have received about the same amount in loans each year as they did in income.[18] But the aggregates are less interesting than the distribution of loans. It turns out that in Talca over seventy-five per cent of all lending was made in lots of $5000 or more. In Caupolicán, where the large estate was more dominant, that figure increases to eighty-four per cent while only four per cent was lent in loans of $999 or less. Over the entire period, the various shares of mortgage credit may be seen in Table 17. Since rural

Table 17 Mortgage loans by size of loan: total amounts during the period 1846–90

Loan size	Talca $	%	Caupolicán $	%
$5000 and up:	14 345 000	75	14 450 000	84
1000–4999:	3 431 000	20	1 970 000	12
0–999:	890 000	5	674 000	4

Source: Appendices 2 and 3.

property could not usually be mortgaged for more than one half its value an estate had to be worth at least $10 000 to qualify for a $5000 loan. Therefore a good-sized property – much larger than a single family farm – was required to obtain any loan over $1000. In effect, the increase in credit in this period of agricultural expansion went almost entirely to the large property owners.

As we saw above, landowners could obtain credit from a number of places. As these sources evolved in the last half of the nineteenth century, they constituted what may be called the organised or primary money market. From 1845 to 1890, these lenders – individuals and institutions – lent a total of $33 749 000 to property owners in Talca and Caupolicán that was secured by mortgages. This primary money market is represented diagramatically in Figure 2.[19]

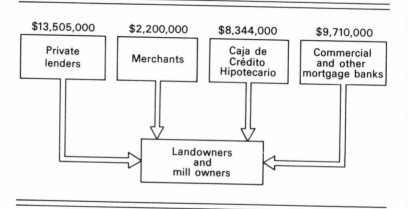

Fig. 2   The 'primary money market' in Talca and Caupolicán (totals lent during the period 1846–90 in current pesos)

Source: Appendix 2 and 3.

Often related by blood or social ties, the miners, bankers, landowners, and merchants forged an increasingly homogeneous group as the century progressed. Their access to economic information through the newspapers and telegraph and the common knowledge of local conditions made this a competitive money market as can be seen by the consistent and relatively low interest rates charged for the use of money: the rate varied only slightly from an average of around nine per cent throughout the period. This 'primary' money market functioned before the 1850s largely on the basis of private lending (in the 1840s for example, ninety-eight per cent came from this source) but as the century wore on, the new institutions became increasingly important. The impact of the most important of these, the Caja de Crédito Hipotecario, was felt immediately upon its foundation in 1856 and by the 1880s it was lending around a quarter million pesos each year in Talca and Caupolicán. The distribution of Caja loans is not unexpected. During the first years of operation the total $138 000 was lent to five important local land-lords and this pattern continued throughout the century. The Caja issued a small number of large loans to the most solvent and influential landowners. In 1880, an early peak year of Caja lending in Talca, the $534 000 was secured by only twelve mortgages on rural property. Two of these loans were for $140 000 and $150 000 – both at seven per cent for twenty-four years. The concentration of Caja loans to a few borrowers also held true for Caupolicán. In 1880, $715 000 was lent to fifteen large landowners – an average of $50 000 each.[20]

Commercial banks also extended credit to landowners but whereas mortgage loans were repayable over several years, commercial banks lent on the short term, three to six months, and the loan could be secured by a mortgage on land or animals. The interest rate on such loans was nine to ten per cent throughout the period 1865–90 and like the other credit operations we have seen, the large commercial banks lent only large sums to a few borrowers.[21] Table 18 indicates the

Table 18   Number of loans and total amounts lent by commercial banks: department of Talca, selected years (in current pesos)

Years	Number of loans	Amount $	Average size $
1869	15	275 000	18 000
1880	15	127 500	8500
1890	43	370 000	8500

Source: Appendix 2.

I have included loans guaranteed by urban property as well as rural. In Talca, a department with a large provincial city, the urban share was small (not over seventeen per cent in 1890). In Caupolicán, urban mortgages are insignificant. It is difficult, and I believe fruitless, to separate urban from rural in the nineteenth-century provinces.

distribution of commercial bank loans in Talca. In Caupolicán, the commercial banks were less important. Nearly all institutional credit came from the Caja de Crédito Hipotecario and the other mortgage banks. In 1863, for example, commercial banks made only two loans in the Department: $20 000 from McClure and Co. to Rafael Larraín Moxó; and $13 360 from Ossa and Co., to Ramón Valdivieso. In 1880, commercial banks made only three loans totalling $70 000.[22] Even in the later 1880s after three small local banks had been established, commercial bank lending remained small. These local banks (Banco de

Caupolicán, Banco de San Fernando, Banco de Colchagua) were small operations. They lent small sums at high interest rates to people who apparently could not qualify elsewhere.

For the larger landowners in Talca and Caupolicán the new institutions intensified and enlarged the pattern of the pre-banking, pre-1850 credit operation. The primary suppliers of credit – the merchants and other wealthy individuals – retained their importance in the later nineteenth century; their funds were now, however, often channeled through the new banks and corporations. On the receiving end, only the large landowners had been eligible for credit on a personal basis and they remained the only ones with adequate guarantees to obtain the later bank and mortgage loans.

Below the level of the main landowners in Talca and Caupolicán, credit was distributed differently and had different effects. Until well into the nineteenth century, hacienda workers were close to constituting a natural economy. Little money changed hands. The service tenants exchanged their labor for rights to subsistence plots and daily rations. The peon received a money wage in theory but his salary was more often – almost always before 1850 – simply held on account and goods drawn from the *pulpería* were charged against it. The larger haciendas often issued their own money in the form of pieces of lead, leather or other *señas* that bore the hacienda seal.[23] The hacienda, then, besides being the main productive unit in the country, was a distributional center for goods, and the commercial focus of rural society. Through this institution the merchandise obtained from Valparaíso, tobacco from the government monopoly, and local goods were exchanged for labor and produce. The *pulpería*, like the Mexican *tienda de raya* has been the subject of discussion. But whether the hacienda store was a convenience or burden it was certainly a necessity in a country of few towns or local markets and poor transportation. Most larger estates in the central valley maintained a store that offered a fairly wide variety of goods. The inventory of the hacienda of Cunaco in San Fernando reveals one such store. There was a selection of dry goods: coarse cloth of local manufacture, imported 'fine stockings,' white thread, indigo for blue dye from Central America, sugar from Lima and Pernambuco, Paraguayan tea, and tacks and ribbon. The *pulpería* was the rural social center as well. On Sundays and during the innumerable feast days of nineteenth-century Chile, the resident laborers, peons and nearby small proprietors gathered to gossip, trade farm information, and quarrel.[24] This last activity was lubricated by abundant quantities of *chicha* and *aguardiente* produced on the estate and dispensed by the store. Like vodka sold to Polish peasants, estate-produced alcohol in Chile made important contributions to rural drunkeness and hacienda profits.[25]

Through credit advanced by the hacienda store as well as through direct lending by landowners to *campesinos*, the large estate constituted the main source of credit for the lower classes of Chile's rural society. There is no way to determine exactly the total amount of credit extended to the thousands of small proprietors and workers. Some was advanced on the basis of a personal pledge or against a simple entry in the books of the hacienda store. Nor is it always possible to determine from the documents who the people were who received small loans. The notarial records occasionally state occupations (*agricultor, mediero, pequeño propietario*) and at other times the borrower's name can be found by cross-checking the lists of small-holders in the tax rolls. In other cases the nature of the security – animals, crops, or the size of the mortgaged plot – identifies the borrower. From the examples that can be identified in the notarial records, it appears that most of the loans were made to small holders and *inquilinos*. Table 19 shows the volume of the small loans during 1846–90.

Table 19 Five-year totals of small loans [0–99 pesos] in Talca and Caupolicán, 1846–90 (in current pesos)

Years	Talca $	Caupolicán $
1846–50	44 000	6000
1851–5	54 000	16 000
1856–60	82 000	23 000
1861–5	69 000	66 000
1866–70	102 000	55 000
1871–5	109 000	105 000
1876–80	182 000	153 000
1881–5	119 000	106 000
1886–90	136 000	114 000

Source: Appendices 2 and 3.

It will be noticed that just as the absolute amount of credit fell off after the early 1880s, so also did the share small borrowers got of the total. In the 1870s, small loans accounted for about five to six per cent but by the 1880s this fell to four and by 1890 to two per cent. Just why this decline occurred is not entirely clear. The 1870s was a decade of high cereal output in this zone and the relatively large amounts may reflect the advances made to smallholders and coastal sharecroppers against future harvests. We know that while the large estates prospered, the smallholdings underwent rapid fragmentation during the 1880s and so the decline may be an indication of their relatively worsening position during the last quarter century. These also were years when massive exports of grain from the newly opened lands of the United States and Australia caused prices to fall, a conjuncture that hit these cereal-growing regions of Chile particularly hard. This is speculation, but insofar as the inability to obtain credit is a measure of hardship, there is the suggestion here that the welfare of sharecroppers and small-holders was slipping.

The conditions under which the small borrowers received credit is revealing. Whereas large estate owners had access to twenty-four-year loans at eight and even six per cent, the interest rates increased for the more modest farmers and rose to quite unmanageable levels for the really marginal borrowers. Table 20 shows that most middling bor-rowers got loans below twelve per cent although a third had to pay that much or more. But the more humble tenants and smallholders were each year pushed to the wall by an interest rate that was almost always around fifteen and often twenty-four per cent. These rates – and the deteriorating conditions as one moves into the 1880s – can all be seen in Table 21. Moreover, one should recall that for these loans the

Table 20   Interest rates and average loan size among medium-sized borrowers: Caupolicán, selected years (in current pesos)

Year	No. of loans	Interest rate (%)			Average size loan $
		8–11	12–17	18–24	
1862	35	17	10	8	2935
1871	19	13	5	1	2510
1881	31	22	8	1	2150

Source: Appendix 3.

borrower was able to offer a mortgage inscribed in the public registry. Even with this demonstration of solvency half of the borrowers in 1862, for example, paid between eighteen and twenty-four per cent. People who had no mortgageable security – who were greater risks – received credit on less favorable terms.

Another group that paid the price of marginal existence were the sharecroppers, found mainly in the dry farming regions of the coast range. Here the spread of cereal cultivation after 1850 increased the economic interdependence between the estates and the lower rural society and put their relations more and more on a cash basis. Part of these estates' land was often let to sharecroppers, who, as the Spanish term for them (*mediero*) implies, usually shared the produce equally

Table 21 Interest rates and average loan size among small borrowers: Caupolicán, selected years (in current pesos)

| Year | No. of loans | Interest rates (%) | | | Average size loan $ |
		8–11	12–17	18–24	
1862	33	4	12	17	386
1871	60	12	39	9	302
1881	54	3	28	13	570

Source: Appendix 3.

with the estate. There were local variations of sharecropping. Sometimes the estate advanced or supplied the oxen; other times it paid half the cost of threshing or the salaries of seasonal peons. Besides this, the estate often advanced money on the future crop. This practice – then and now – is called *venta en yerba or venta en verde*, i.e., the sale by the grower of the green or standing grain.[26]

The agricultural year frequently progressed through the following cycle: The sharecropper or smallholder planted wheat in the fall, usually in May. By September, his savings from the last harvest began to run out, and the new season's fruit and *chacra* were not yet available. Unable to withstand this lean time, the marginal growers chose to sell their crop in advance. Because of the risk involved to the estate in buying standing grain, the seller was offered a price well below the going market price. In addition, the estate possessed certain advantages in dealing with its sharecroppers. As a rule and except for the occasional traveling wheat buyer, only the estate had money or goods to advance. Moreover, and perhaps more importantly, only the large estate had enough land to support sufficient numbers of oxen or mules to transport produce to markets. Even after the railroad reached the central valley, the estates kept a virtual monopoly on transport. Much local produce was marketed through the haciendas. Table 22 shows the difference between the price received by sharecroppers and the going market price.

These prices received by small producers were taken from the notarial records where the mortgages that guaranteed future delivery of the crop were recorded. Again we do not know the number nor the price of transactions which were not recorded in the public registry; most likely the majority of smaller transactions were simple verbal arrangements,

Table 22   Wheat prices in Talca: *Venta en yerba* and going market price, selected years between 1849–72

Year	*Venta en yerba* (a) $	Market price (b) $
1849	0.94	1.50
1852	1.12	1.88
1853	1.25	2.75
1858	1.50	2.75
1861	1.50	1.75
1862	1.37	2.25
1867	1.50	3.00
1868	1.87	3.50
1872	1.50	2.45

Source: (a) *CN* (Talca) 1842–72. (b) 'Precios corrientes de la plaza' from Talca newspapers and Intendents' reports.

a practice that can be seen, for example, in the case of a certain Manual Vargas. In the 1860s Vargas owned a *fundo* in the province as well as a house in the city of Talca. The inventory of his estate shows that during 1861–2 he made eighty-one loans totaling $6663 on future wheat harvests. Only four of these loans appeared in the notarial records.[27] At that rate, for each purchase of 'green' wheat recorded in the public registry, twenty actually occurred. Vargas' case may not be typical but it most certainly was not unique. The futures market was widespread and it is rare to find an inventory of a large estate in the grain growing region that does not list a number of transactions of cash advances against the coming harvest.[28]

The lower rural society, then, was only indirectly affected by the new banks and mortgage houses. Nearly all formal credit went to the few property owners who had assets and connections to acquire loans. Given the nature of Chile's agrarian structure this is not unexpected; yet it is instructive to contrast differences in other rural societies. Elsewhere credit occasionally provided an instrument to alter the agrarian system. In new lands like Australia or the U.S. West, local banks provided some assistance to new settlers; in other cases, cooperative credit societies (such as the German Raiffeisen–Haas group as early as the 1860s), helped finance small farmers.[29] But in rural Chile, credit more often provided a mechanism that enabled landowners to continue to control local production and appropriate a share of the income of small proprietors and sharecroppers. The clear advantage in access to credit that the large landowners enjoyed reinforced their original paternalistic domination over service tenants and surrounding smallholders. In those areas where sharecropping became important, credit permitted the landowner a larger share of produce. In all of these ways, far from creating tensions or new opportunities the expansion of credit tended to reinforce the existing agrarian system.

From first-hand accounts and the documents themselves, one gets a strong impression of low capital investment in Chilean agriculture. This can best be seen in the inventories of the larger estates. A *fundo* in Linares, for example, appraised at $94 962, had less than $200 in equipment (not counting animals). The great hacienda of Aculeo invested only occasional sums of 10 pesos and again 30 pesos for such things as nails, raw iron, etc., with no mention of new equipment. In the cereal-producing zone of Rancagua in 1866, a valley *fundo* valued at $149 396 had but $446 in farm implements.[30] These examples and others drawn from the Santiago Judicial for later years may be repeated many times over. Even the SNA acknowledged in 1887 that there was a 'reduced proportion of machinery of all kinds and above all, of agricultural machinery' in Chile. In more recent times, McBride in the 1930s was struck by the sharp contrast between the efficient mining enterprise, or the modern cities, and the primitive conditions on the land where agricultural methods on the great estates 'remind one of ancient Egypt, Greece or Palestine.'[31] The illuminated manuscripts of a fourteenth-century Psalter picture a plow and draft animals superior to those commonly found in modern Chile.

Technological backwardness, of course, is a relative matter and it is useful to examine the Chilean case in a wider context. The introduction of mechanical reapers and threshers provides an illustrative example. Horse-drawn machinery for harvesting small grains was introduced in the United States in 1834. By 1858 over 73 000 mechanical reapers were in operation west of the Alleghenies alone. Mechanisation of agriculture took place in other countries that experienced a similar market impulse. Threshing machines were first used in Great Britain in the late eighteenth century and soon afterwards in the United States. By 1850, 'machine threshing had practically superseded the older methods in the leading wheat-growing regions of the East and Ohio.' A few years later men and machines moved into the prairie districts and by 1860 very little grain was still threshed by hand. In California machines were introduced from the first years of United States' annexation and by 1869 the combined reaper/harvester was in use.[32] In Australia machinery was also necessarily employed in the first years of the colony: 'We have seen that the want of manual labor has had the effect of turning the attention of some of the most ingenious among the settlers to the means of devising mechanical contrivances which might supply the place of human labor,' the governor wrote in 1844. In 1860, two-thirds of the wheat was cut by machines and threshers were used widely.[33] In neighboring Argentina – the only other Latin–American country to export grain, high wages – perhaps eight to ten times the going rate in Chile – encouraged the use of machines on the Pampa. By 1894, 9000 reapers and 1500 threshers were imported annually.[34]

Machinery was not introduced in Chile until many years after it was common elsewhere. Then for a series of reasons its use was resisted. Even during the years of large-scale cereal cultivation, reapers and threshers were not widely used. The technological lag can be seen best in the resistance to threshers. The first mechanical thresher was tested in Chile in 1842 under the auspices of the National Society of Agriculture. The machine cost $500 pesos in London and had been brought to Santiago for $300 pesos freight charges. It required the work of fifteen horses a day. A report from a three-man commission especially chosen to 'examine with care and close attention this new apparatus' was favorable and newspapers carried enthusiastic advertisements; there is no record, however, that anyone bought a machine. Ten years later (1852), don José Gandarillas explained to a group at the University of Chile that attempts had been made to introduce machines but that no illusions should be harbored as to their value since 'few foreign methods or instruments can be used in Chilean agriculture.' Furthermore, 'the threshing of cereals will always be done by animals in Chile, the most suitable method given the [large] scale of operations.'[35] Four years later (1856) Horace Pitts, son of the well-known Buffalo manufacturer, arrived in person in Santiago with ten machines from a Paris exposition. The growth of cereal cultivation (exports were being sent to Australia at the time) awakened more interest than before, but Chilean *hacendados* were still not impressed with the machines. Even with a full-time mechanic from the United States to keep his machine in working order and eight specially trained mules for motive power, *Cunaco*'s 'progressive' owner saw no advantage in the Pitts thresher over the old system of treading out grain. He had already tried 'an infinity of new devices, some worse than others, that now lie unused in the sheds of the hacienda.' What was true of threshers can be said about other equipment. With rare exceptions grain was cut with sickle and scythe and only the most primitive plow used.[36]

For this reluctance to modernise there are some obvious explanations. Because of freight costs, prices of machinery in Chile were high. Repair of equipment in a non-industrial country posed other problems. Even with these rudimentary machines certain parts (castings, etc.) had to be procured abroad. The lack of mechanics, the frustrating unreliability of the equipment, and the constant breakage tried the owner's patience. Most haciendas had no competent local mechanic. In the case of *Cunaco* a North American technician was brought in especially for the threshers. In short, to operate farm machines thirty miles by a good road south of Chicago is a quite different matter from harvesting ten leagues below Rancagua.[37] By 1870, when California and the Midwest began to produce grain on an unheard-of scale, Chilean producers became aware of the vulnerability of their position. Falling grain prices and shrinking profits made investment in agriculture less attractive than other enterprises. *Hacendados* continued to mortgage their estates to obtain long-term credit but few were willing to invest their loans or earnings in modernising an agriculture so obviously unable to compete in the world market. The declining value of the peso from 1875 on would also have increased the cost of machinery relative to labor. Most machinery was imported and had to be paid for in foreign exchange equivalents; the price of labor lagged and was remunerated with increasingly worthless pesos.

Moreover, the full capital costs of mechanisation were much greater than the simple purchase price of machines. Machinery could not simply be introduced into the existing agricultural system of nineteenth-century Chile; it had to be accompanied by several significant reforms. In the usual method of planting, seed was simply broadcast on the uneven slopes or among rocks and tree stumps. A wheeled reaper required properly prepared seed beds and minimum grades. On the valley floor, the haphazard irrigation ditches (fields were never properly leveled) were another obstacle. A most important retarding factor and one that serves as an illuminating example was the lack of suitable draught animals. Machines require heavy-duty horses or at least mules bred for the task. 'Los bueyes,' an *hacendado* noticed in 1865, 'no sufren el trabajo de un dia de la maquina.' Horses or good mules were necessary for the sweeps or 'horse powers' used to operate most threshing machines, and the ox's pace was too slow to drive properly the sickle in the mechanical reaper. The work animal of Chile, however, was the ox: '[The ox] has been since the Conquest practically a dogma,' the

Agricultor remarked in 1841, and that remained true throughout the nineteenth century.[38]

In other Western cultures the change from oxen to draught horses or mules came about as population increase required greater food output. Fernand Braudel has followed this process in the countries bordering the Mediterranean. In other parts of Europe, 'the shift from oxen to horses, or in the south [of Europe] to mules, can be a result of increasing agricultural prosperity as it probably was in England in Queen Elizabeth's reign.' In any case, the change from one traction system to another is no simple matter. Horses require better feed and care. A widespread shift to draught horses in Chile would have required change in farming practices involving different crops and rotations. In Europe the substitution of horses was preceded by more intensive cultivation. Slicher Van Bath cites the 'late but exceptionally clear example of Poitou in 1790 where the change from two- to three-course rotation coincided with the change from oxen to horses. . . . This produced a greater oat harvest . . . [and] the way was open for horse-haulage.'[39]

Chileans were not unaware of the advantages that horses would bring to agriculture. A Chilean diplomat stationed in Paris and surprised at the difference ('There is not in these countries the profusion of ox teams [as in Chile]') urged the introduction of Percheron or Suffolk types of draught animals. The National Society of Agriculture discussed this need in 1886, 1890 and 1901, but it appears that except for carriages and wagons few draught horses were brought in. Indeed, the ox was not replaced until the 1930s and then by tractors, not horses.[40]

The larger grain market of the 1870s, and the migration of rural workers to Peru brought a certain urgency to the question of mechanisation. Exhibitions were assiduously held by the SNA to promote the use of farm equipment, tests were held, and comparisons made with traditional methods. Some machinery was introduced during these years, but threshers and even simple reapers still seemed more of a curiosity than a common means of production. We do not know how much machinery was actually used in central Chile. The official data in the statistical yearbook are either incomplete or missing altogether. Port records give ambiguous and inconsistent figures for machinery imported. The records of the large importing companies, such as the Rose Innes Company, for example, would be useful, but there is of course an important difference between machinery imported and machinery in use. The reports of the SNA and the impressions of contemporary writers are contradictory. In 1878 the *Boletín* of the SNA claimed that 'threshing machines were in use throughout the Republic.' Statements like this were supported by descriptions of haciendas. One near Santiago used three Pitts and one Ransome thresher and five mechanical reapers. Several other accounts deal with the 'spreading mechanisation,' insist that the *trilla a yegua* is a thing of the past, and so on. Apparently, these descriptions referred to a few estates near the capital that were in effect a kind of experimental station or model farm. We can see now, a century later, that they were not representative of central Chilean haciendas.[41]

Yet, one should resist too facile a judgement in the question of capital in agriculture. In recent times the advantages of investment in agriculture are obvious. There are the numerous tractors and a great variety of specialised farm implements such as grain drills, special plows, or combined harvesters, to say nothing of equipment for dairies and processing fodder and grain. But to the Chilean landowner in the latter nineteenth century and even down to 1930, the need for investment was less apparent and whatever technological change did occur was more subtle than today. Although labor-scarce countries like Australia or Argentina or the U.S. West did mechanise cereal production early on, older countries with large and stable rural labor systems were no more mechanised than Chile. In 1882, about seven per cent of the cereal acreage in France and only 3.6 of Germany's was cut by machine.[42] (Mechanisation defined as one reaper per 25 hectares.) Using the same gross criteria, Chile would have cut about five per cent by machine four years earlier. There is more involved than a simple surplus of potential labor in landowners' reluctance to modernise as we shall see below; but the fact remains that there were few places where capital could be usefully invested. We can see now that improved breeds of livestock for both dairy and meat might have been introduced on a wider scale; but to the *hacendado* who saw that the Chilean market did not demand high quality meat, the angular and hardy *criollo* steer was admirably suited to the sparse pastures, and the introduction of delicate breeds was often an unjustified risk. Some landowners did, of course, make such improvements but these *'agricultores progresistas'* that occupy so much space in the SNA *Boletín* and Correa Vergara's two-volume study were unusual.

Before 1930 there was one important exception to the pattern of low capital investment and significantly this was in irrigation – an investment that required few new techniques and was in keeping with the general Chilean response of more land and labor. Yet the impressive amount of land brought under irrigation between 1875 and 1930 was one place where credit could be usefully employed and undoubtedly increased per capita production. The area of irrigated land increased from 440 000 hectares in 1875 to nearly double that by 1900 and to over 1 100 000 by 1930. There were a few truly heroic engineering efforts such as the Mallarauco canal which involved pneumatic drills and a great deal of money and persistence; and ingenious devices were used such as the huge waterwheels that still lift water from one level to the next near San Vicente de Tagua-Tagua. Many of the most notable projects were carried through by men who had made their fortunes in mining – Subercaseaux, Bruno González – or in business, such as Domingo Matte, the Edwards, and Waddington. Into the 1930s irrigation was mainly the work of individuals or associations of landowners; only about ten per cent of all canals involved state assistance.[43]

If there was little inclination to invest in agricultural improvement, the rise of a formal credit system opened new opportunities for the important landowners in non-agricultural sectors. Mortgage banks, in effect, permitted landowners to give loans to themselves, repayable over a long period of time, and as it turned out, with greatly devalued currency. Contemporary observers and recent writers have often noticed the coincidence between easy credit and the increasingly comfortable life-style of the absentee landlord. New and often gaudy houses, the carriages, and jewels have all been presented as evidence of the misbehavior of a '*clase derrochadora*' that allegedly squandered its patrimony in pleasant living.[44]

Certainly the opportunities increased through the years of the Parliamentary Republic (1891–1920) – whose summers of opulence are well described in Orrego Luco's *Casa Grande* – and continued down to the eve of the 1930 Depression. By that year the Caja de Crédito Hipotecario alone – with all its importance, it still represented only a fraction of total credit – had nearly 1.5 billion pesos in outstanding loans at a time when the total value of Chile's rural property was assessed at 6.7 billion. Just how landowners could incur such indebtedness may seem extraordinary when agriculture rarely yielded profits of over five per cent.[45] Or put another way, if greater earnings could be obtained elsewhere why invest in land? The answer is that not everyone did. Many landowners driven to the wall through bad management or simply through the vagaries of farming, sold out to men who invested their mining or business fortunes in irrigation canals or improved stock to make the land more profitable. But quite apart from such non-economic rewards as prestige, status, or the rural values, a hacienda was a secure and ever-appreciating investment. As prices rose, land prices rose faster. And of course, since price inflation has been a Chilean fact of life since the 1870s, landowners were able to pay off their long-term loans with devalued currency, at times approaching a zero or even negative interest rate.

The difficulty of meeting mortgage obligations out of agricultural earnings was not lost on contemporaries. Pedro Lucío Cuadra, an influential cabinet member and landowner, pointed out in 1892 that interest could not be paid with the 'natural yield' of the mortgaged estates and that 'difficult moments would arrive if the peso recovered its legitimate value.' For this reason, he claimed, landowners had a 'deep interest' (*interés vivísimo*) not only in maintaining the current rate of inflation but in its acceleration.[46] The leap from motive to guilt has been facilely made by social critics seeking a link between landlord interest and inflationary policy. Frank W. Fetter's classic, *Monetary Inflation in Chile*, made the debt-ridden 'landed gentry' the principal culprits of Chilean inflation and the charge has been enthusiastically repeated by intellectuals and politicians eager to assail their cherished *bête noire*. Yet the relationship is not so simple. More than once the oligarchs of the Parliamentary era (including many landowners) apparently rose above self-interest in attempts to slow the inflationary pace; and once – in 1895, at the very apex of landowner influence of politics – managed to get the country back on a metallic standard that raised the value of the peso by some twenty-five per cent. After that disastrous effort – inconvertibility of paper money for gold was again declared in 1898 – the peso's value in terms of pounds sterling slipped and inflation increased at the rate of seven per cent throughout the period 1900–20. If this does not seem an exceptionally high rate to us today, it was much more alarming to people accustomed to financial stability; and if landlords cannot, as Hirschman argues, be singled out for blame as far as policy goes, there is no denying that they stood to benefit most from a generous long-term credit system and devaluation that lightened their burdens.[47]

But there was another way in which the interests of the wealthy classes were distinctly not served by the falling value of the peso. If devaluation aided exports and internal inflation made mortgage debts easier to pay, it also raised the cost of imported goods. And, of course, the people most often accused of wallowing in imported luxury are the landowners. We must recall that by the turn of the century, only a small share of agricultural income was obtained through sales abroad: Chilean landowners sold their produce for pesos and with these bought the 'ponchos of English cloth, the saddles made by the best leatherworkers in London, the real Champagne, Florentine lamps, Irish linen, silk shirts and jewels,' that devaluation made more expensive each year.[48] So we have a series of allegations: a landowning elite, given to wasteful spending, runs the government, and is responsible for monetary policies which make a continuation of its life-style increasingly difficult. There are still too many contradictions in the thesis of landowner culpability in Chilean inflation. Part of the problem lies in the difficulty of identifying the 'landowners' or their interests within a national elite that becomes more and more diversified and intertwined as we move into the twentieth century. When the matter is finally sorted out, the villains no doubt will shrink to human dimensions.

The wills and inventories of landowners' property among the papers of the cluttered Santiago judicial archive permit us to glimpse the social effect of credit. Let us look at three out of hundreds. First, a José Santos Lira Calvo: born in 1808 into a landholding family, he came into possession of the 2000 hectare estate of San José de Toro in Colchagua, assessed in 1885 at $176 000. In addition he owned a proper town house and a few minor rental properties. Lira's solidly *haute bourgeoise* life-style was apparently maintained by a loan of $100 000 from the Caja de Crédito Hipotecario: the small income from urban rentals and the $4000 annual rent for San José de Toro would hardly have been adequate.[49] In the case of the patrician José Ignacio Larraín Landa, large loans did nothing to improve slovenly agricultural practices but they did help maintain a large and demanding family in the accustomed style. In 1877, the family hacienda, Pudaguel (now the site of Santiago's international airport) and two smaller farms (*chacras*) produced around $28 000 annual gross income. But as one of the twelve surviving heirs lamented, 'as everyone knows, my father's income barely covered his expenses and in some cases even this was not achieved . . . [which] explains the necessity of almost all the loans . . .' The Bank of Valparaíso came to the rescue with $5000 and the Caja de Crédito Hipotecario with $110 000 in 1872, but if this postponed disaster it could not save a family whose agricultural base produced no more profit than 'one might expect from a *fundo* cultivated without investment or capitals.'[50]

Not all landowners inherited such heavy debts as Larraín, and others were better managers; but one has the unmistakable impression from the Santiago judicial records that huge loans from the burgeoning credit system were rarely enough applied to agriculture. A final example drawn from the same archive reveals the middling sort of estate owner, less noticeable than the magnate but more agriculturally important than is commonly supposed. Adolfo Formas inherited from his land-rich father a *fundo* – San Antonio del Cerro Negro – of some 300 excellent hectares together with a large house in Calle Huérfanos in Santiago. At the time of don Adolfo's death in 1897, rent from the *fundo* produced $6000 a year and enabled Formas to practise in Santiago the 'arts of engineering, astronomy and the novel.' At the same time, this absentee owner was able to obtain a $45 000 mortgage loan from the Caja de Crédito Hipotecario while the rental contract explicitly absolved the owner from any requirement for maintenance or improvement.[51] Since mortgage banks did not require that loans be put to a specific use, one finds several cases similar to that of Formas: the farm is rented and then heavily mortgaged. Since the rental contracts were rarely over nine years and often less, neither the renter nor the owner were encouraged to make salutary investment in the land.

Perhaps loans to landowners were useful in buying votes or influence for election to Congress. Another interesting connection might be found between loans secured by rural property and growth in the non-agricultural sectors of the economy. It is possible that a good share of the money received by landowners through the sale of mortgage bank *letras* were invested in the stock of banks, mining companies, commerce or urban property. Qualified through the ownership of land to receive long-term and relatively cheap credit, it is reasonable to assume that many landowners, resident in Santiago, living in the same streets and playing in the same clubs with wealthy bankers and miners, were often tempted to invest their loans in the higher risk/higher yield stocks of the burgeoning corporations founded in the early twentieth century.[52] If this were confirmed by research it would help explain the rural–urban flow of capital, the growth of Santiago and the continued undercapitalisation of agriculture despite a credit system ostensibly designed to improve the countryside. There are additional implications: since the savings of public employees and clerks were deposited in the Caja de Ahorros and since this organisation bought mortgage bank *letras*, we may have a case of urban wage earners investing in corporations through the medium of speculating landowners. Such a process could be diagramed as shown in Figure 3. The small investors of the savings bank were interested in a secured investment and a guaranteed – if low – yield; the mortgage bank *letras* met this need. Landowners with a better knowledge of the capital market, more resources, and inclined to speculate, could well have acted as the diagram suggests. In an inflationary economy they stood to gain as the interest rates on their mortgage loans were not readjusted. The yield paid to investors in mortgage book *letras*, however, in real terms declined. Undoubtedly, to some extent, the flow suggested here did occur; at this point, however, the magnitude or importance have not been determined.

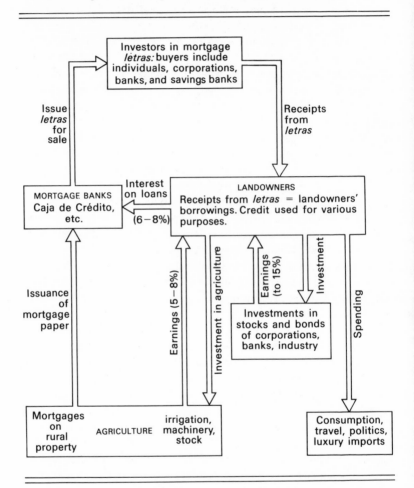

Fig. 3   Flow of mortgage credit, savings and investment

Although Chilean agriculture may be described as backward before 1930, it was not because agricultural earnings were low or capital unavailable. The years between 1860 and 1930 provided fine opportunities for agriculture and landowners prospered as never before or since. If the *rate* of return was low, the large scale of operations assured hundreds of *fundo*-owners of comfortable and sometimes – in the opinion of contemporary critics – quite indecent earnings. Moreover, beginning with the great silver strike of Caracoles in 1870 and continuing with the nitrate and copper activity, a great deal of wealth was generated in the export sector. Public revenue was drawn from these more easily tapped – and more politically vulnerable – sources freeing the landowners from taxation and sectoral conflict over rural produce. All this along with political stability and effective public administration gave landowners a long period of social tranquility in the countryside and a sophisticated and abundant credit system to serve their needs.

The explanation for low capital investment – or reinvestment – in agriculture must be sought in the nature of society itself and we will be concerned with this in subsequent chapters. For the moment it is sufficient to point out that an underemployed rural population reduced the need for labor-saving devices; neither the humble rural workers nor the sons of landowners – frequently bent on professional careers in the city – provided an intermediate enterpreneurial class that might have used credit to build a better agriculture. The landowners were the dominant political force in the country: they formed policy for the most important credit institutions and made themselves the principal beneficiaries of loans from the Caja de Crédito Hipotecario and the new banks. Some of this credit was used to clear land, construct irrigation works and buy equipment; but a great deal was undoubtedly used to preserve a traditional agrarian system and to provide the Santiago-centered landed elite with the ready cash it needed to reinforce its social and political control of the Republic.

CHAPTER 4

[1] Chilean trading patterns moved gradually, informally, and illegally away from the Spanish system during the eighteenth century; Independence marked a definitive step in this process. See Sergio Villalobos, *Comercio y contrabando en el Rio de la Plata y Chile* (Buenos Aires, 1965); and *El comercio y la crisis colonial* (Santiago, 1968). *AMH*, vol. 412 (1860), no p. no., gives complete list of all business houses that paid licence tax (*patente*). See also *Repertorio chileno* for years 1849 and 1859. There is no study available of Valparaíso, the merchants or commerce of the last century.

[2] For the eighteenth century, see María Eugenia Hórvitz, 'Ensayo sobre el crédito en Chile colonial,' (Unpub. *Memoria* in the Faculty of Philosophy and Letters, University of Chile, 1966), ch. III, pp. 161–5; *Cunaco*, pp. 43–5.

[3] For discussion of credit and banking before 1850, see Pedro Félix Vicuña, *Cartas sobre bancos* (Valparaíso, 1845), p. 37 and *passim*. This book is a compilation of letters that Vicuña wrote to the *Mercurio* of Valparaíso during 1844–5.

4 See the pamphlet signed by most of the important Valparaíso and Santiago merchants, 'Representación al Supremo Gobierno sobre la reforma de la lejislación' (Valparaíso, 1851), pp. 1–17.

5 See: 'Opinion del comercio de Valparaíso sobre bancos de emisión' (Valparaíso, 1855), pp. 5–15. For stockholders of Bank of Valparaíso, see 'Memoria . . . del banco de Valparaíso (Valparaíso, 1858), 1–10. The largest local merchant house in Talca was that of Donoso y Lois, founded in 1857 with a capital of $142 000. CN (Talca), vol. 76, p. 27. The operation and lending activities of local merchants and their connections with Valparaíso houses is seen in the notarial records. Provincial newspapers also contain information. See: El Alfa (Talca), 1849; El Eco (Talca), 1854–60; La Opinión (Talca) 1872–9; and La Libertad (Talca) 1880–1923. The records of Cunaco, for example, show a loan of $20 000 from Alsop and Co. at ten per cent interest.

6 Aculeo, pp. 115–30. Out of a total gross income of $39 427 on this estate in 1847, $7337 came from interest on loans.

7 For discussion of mortgage legislation, see Alejo Palma, Historia de la hipoteca especial en Chile (Santiago, 1866), pp. 1–16; and Enrique Tocornal, Análisis comparado de nuestra legislación hipotecaria (Santiago, 1859), pp. 26–32. The Civil Code, promulgated in December 1855, was the major nineteenth-century legislation on mortgages. It abolished the 'general mortgage' and established orders of preference in settlements. See Código Civil de la República de Chile, Ed. rev. and cor. (Valparaíso, 1865), p. iv.

8 For studies of nineteenth-century banking, see Guillermo Subercaseaux, El sistema monetario i la organización bancaria en Chile (Santiago, 1921); Ramón Santelices, Los bancos Chilenos (Santiago, 1893); Apuntes para una memoria sobre los bancos Chilenos (Santiago, 1889); Los bancos de emisión (Santiago, 1900); Agustín Ross, Chile, 1851–1910. Sesenta años de cuestiones monetarias y financieras (Santiago, 1911); Edward N. Hurley, Banking and Credit in Argentina, Brazil, Chile, and Peru (Washington, 1914); Frank W. Fetter, Monetary Inflation in Chile (Princeton, 1931); and the recent work by Marcello Carmagnani, 'Banques étrangeres et banques nationales au Chili (1900–1920),' Caravelle, no. 20 (1973), pp. 31–52; and Sviluppo industriale e sottosviluppo económico: il caso cileno (1860–1920) (Turin, 1971).

9 For discussion of a later but similar operation in Argentina, see H. S. Ferns, Britain and Argentina in the Nineteenth Century (Oxford, 1960), pp. 370–1.

10 Guillermo Subercaseaux, El sistema monetario, pp. 367–8. The Memorias Ministeriales give random data on quotations before 1872. For 1857–8, see vol. 14 (1858), in section 'Hacienda,' no p. no.; Frank W. Fetter, Monetary Inflation, p. 44; Subercaseaux, El sistema, pp. 374–5. See also: Ramón Santelices, Apuntes, pp. 106–7.

11 Santelices, Apuntes, p. 96, See also: Martin Drouilly y Pedro Lucío Cuadra, 'Ensayo,' p. 319. The quotation is from Correa Vergara, Agricultura Chilena, I, pp. 380–1.

12 Subercaseaux, El sistema, p. 364. The amounts issued by mortgage banks may be found in the various Memoria de Hacienda, 'Sección: Casa de Moneda.' Besides the Caja, several other mortgage banks and mortgage sections of already established banks came into existence in the later nineteenth century. They worked like the Caja, emitting mortgage bonds for sale by the borrower in return for mortgages on real property. Up to the early 1900s they had altogether issued half as much as the Caja itself; after that the Caja became relatively more important.

13 Santelices, Apuntes, pp. 94–5; Drouilly and Cuadra, 'Ensayo,' give the estimate of eighty per cent. Eight per cent letras were the most common in the beginning; but later, issues of seven, six, and five per cent were made and repayment time was lengthened to twenty-four years.

14 There were a number of explanations for this. First of all, in the nineteenth century before the railroad tended to equalise property values, land value decreased as one moved out from the Capital. In 1875, for example, land in Talca had about one-half the value of land in Rancagua. The lower the value of land the smaller the amount of the mortgage loan it could qualify for. Thus in the two sample Departments, Caupolicán, a much smaller department than Talca in terms of population and acreage, received $1 500 000 more in new loans than Talca in the period 1856–90. Drouilly y Cuadra, 'Ensayo,' p. 292, gives following land prices which provide at least some idea of comparative value, in 1875, in cuadras. (1 cuadra=1.57 hectares)

Province	Irrigated land	Non-irrigated land
Atacama	700	—
Coquimbo	450	—
Aconcagua	300	30
Valparaíso	300	30
Santiago	300	50
Colchagua	225	35
Curicó	175	25
Talca	160	20
Linares	150	20
Maule	150	20
Nuble	135	25
Concepción	135	20
Bío-Bío	115	25
Arauco and Angol	100	15

15 Borde and Góngora, *Puangue*, I, p. 126.

16 Hernán Ramírez Necochea, *Historia del movimiento obrero* (Santiago, 1957), p. 39. See also Subercaseaux, *El sistema*; 'Estatutos del banco de Valparaíso,' (Valparaíso, 1854). The law permitting and regulating *Sociedades anónimas* was promulgated in November 1854. The name of this bank was finally settled as Banco de Valparaíso in 1860.

17 The choice of Talca and Caupolicán was partly dictated by the sources. Few of the provincial archival collections for the years past 1870 are in the National Archive in Santiago. The notarial collection for Talca up to 1890, however, is in Santiago; and the collection for Caupolicán up to 1880. I consulted the Caupolicán collection for the years 1881–90 in Rengo, the capital of the old Department of Caupolicán.

18 The tax records undoubtedly underestimate income. Notice also that the data in Table 16 represent new loans; therefore, the amount of outstanding loans, being cumulative, would be greater.

19 The 'primary money market' has been drawn up to include all loans made on the basis of mortgages of over $1000 in each.

20 *CN* (Talca), vol. 40A (1856), fs. 138, 150, 151, 157, 158; *CN* (Talca), vol. 115 (1880); *CN* (Rengo), vol. 122 (1880). The other mortgage banks supplemented the Caja de Crédito Hipotecario. Second in importance was the Banco Garantizador de Valores and the mortgage section of the Bank of Valparaíso. They followed the pattern of the Caja by lending large amounts to a very few borrowers. In 1870, in Talca, the Banco Garantizador made four loans of $23 000; $40 000; $15 000 and $24 000 each. In Caupolicán, loans averaged around $22 000.

21 Subercaseaux, *El sistema*, pp. 335–8. The interest rates are also given in the *registros de hipotecas* in the notarial collection.

22 CN (Rengo), vol. 59 (1863), fs. 12, 37; CN (Rengo), vol. 122 (1880), fs. 23, 35, 64.

23 Guillermo Subercaseaux, *El sistema monetario*, pp. 92–3 has discussion of this problem. The complaints of the Intendents to the Minister of Hacienda also show the scarcity of coin. See *AMH*, vol. 318 (1855), no p. no. Some of the legislation made to deal with the problem is in: *BLEY*, Libro VIII, no. 5, p. 30 (14 May 1838), and Libro XX, no. 10 (26 October 1852). For late eighteenth century see Romano, *Una economía colonial*, pp. 35–6 for use of *macuquino*. José Toribio Medina, *Las monedas chilenas* (Santiago, 1902), has the amounts and types of coins minted in the nineteenth century. Travelers noticed the nearly total lack of small coins: e.g., Graham, *Journal*, p. 220.

24 Appendix 5 gives a fair sample of the inventory of a large hacienda's store. See also *CJ* (San Fernando), Leg. 141, p. 1, for the store of the hacienda of Chimbarongo. For description and criticisms of the institution, see Ramón Domínguez, *Nuestro sistema de inquilinaje*, pp. 43–4; Atropos, 'El inquilino en Chile,' pp. 205–6; Claudio Gay, *Agricultura* (Paris, 1862), I, p. 187. There were some ninety-five feast days per year celebrated in rural Chile in the nineteenth century: *BSNA*, vol. XXI (1890), p. 391.

25 Stefan Kieniewicz, *The emancipation of the Polish peasantry* (Chicago, 1969), pp. 90–1, 116.

26 Different sharecropping arrangements may be seen in Pichidegua; *CJ* (Talca), Leg. 359, p. 2; and *CJ* (Linares), Leg. 88, p. 13. There were early attempts to legislate against the practice of advancing money for future crops, e.g., *BLEY*, Tomo I, Libro I, no. 230 (10 February 1824), but many testify to its continued widespread practice. Fernando Urízar Garfias, *Estadística*, p. 77, mentions the 'common necessity of the poorer workers to sell their produce in advance for which they only received half of their true value . . .' Charles Darwin, *Voyage of the Beagle*, noticed the practice in Copiapó. Reports by the Intendent on this subject were common during the nineteenth century. J. M. Bascuñan (Talca) in 1846 talks of 'the state of frustration and misery that the workers and smallholders are being progressively reduced to . . .;' and says that among the causes the most important was 'the sale of produce in advance of its harvest, which is called "venta en yerba." This way, only half the price is received which is the same as paying 100% interest . . . if a good crop follows, the small man can break even, if not he begins by selling his cattle, then land, and he ends ruined. There are a greater number loaded with debt.' *AMH*, vol. 152, p. 117 (1846). In Colchagua, there was a similar lament: '. . . already in May the produce has been sold "en yerba" and since the proceeds are so small received in this manner, by November they have completely disappeared and there is not enough left to satisfy the necessities of life.' *AMH*, vol. 403, p. 110 (1860). Daniel Barros Grez, *Proyecto de división de la Provincia de Colchagua* (Santiago, 1858), p. 5, says that the people of the coast range 'move between misery and monopoly.' Because the 'ricos compran a los pobres sus trigos "en verde" [and sell them two months later at double the price].' Cattle were purchased the same way. Ramón Domínguez, *Nuestro sistema de inquilinaje* pp. 44–5, writes of a, 'contrato mui común en nuestros campos' [venta en yerba] in which the 'hacendados buy at half the price.' Finally, Claudio Gay, *Agricultura*, I, p. 111, mentions, 'private contracts' to purchase future crops as being widespread among smallholders.

27 *CJ* (Talca), Leg. 802, p. 13. Vargas had also lent $9871 in small cash loans.

28 Examples of such estate inventories are in *CJ* (Talca), Leg. 802, p. 13; *CJ* (Linares), Leg. 81, p. 18; and Leg. 98, p. 1; *CJ* (Rancagua), Leg. 135, p. 10.

29 Dunsdorfs, *Australian wheat-growing economy*, p. 125, tells of credit (and

credit difficulty) among small growers; for the U.S. see two recent articles: Robert F. Severson *et al.*, 'Mortgage borrowing as a frontier developed: a study of mortgages in Champaign County, Illinois, 1836–1895,' *Journal of Economic History*, vol. XXVI, no. 2 (June 1966) pp. 147–68; and Jay Ladin, 'Mortgage credit in Tippecanoe County, Indiana, 1865–1880,' *Agricultural History*, vol. XLI, no. 1 (January 1967), pp. 37–44.

30 *CJ* (Linares), Leg. 97, p. 7; Aculeo, pp. 15–74; *CJ* (Rancagua), Leg. 125, p. 10.

31 *BSNA*, vol. XIX (1887), p. 630; George McBride, *Land and society*, p. 177.

32 Leo Rogin, *The introduction of farm machinery . . . during the nineteenth century* (Berkeley, 1931), pp. 72–8, 165, 170–1; Wayne D. Rasmussen, 'The impact of technological change on American agriculture,' *Journal of Economic History*, vol. XXII (1962), pp. 578–91; Paul David, 'The mechanization of reaping in the ante-bellum Midwest,' *Industrialization in two systems*, Henry Rosovsky (ed.), (New York, 1966), pp. 3–39.

33 Quoted in Dunsdorfs, *Australian wheat-growing economy*, pp. 102, 75–6. The entire white population of Australia in 1830 was only 70 000.

34 James R. Scobie, *Revolution on the Pampas: A social history of Argentine wheat, 1860–1910* (Austin, 1964), pp. 60–1, 80–4, gives an average monthly wage of around £10 or roughly 60–70 Chilean pesos.

35 The earlier article is reprinted in *BSNA*, vol. X (1878), see especially pp. 239–40.

36 *El Mensajero*, vol. II (1856), p. 346. The Pitts machine cost $1000 pesos roughly then the same value as 1000 dollars—delivered in Chile. There is a review of rural technology in Silvia Hernández V., 'Transformaciones tecnológicas en la agricultura de Chile central. Siglo XIX,' *Cuadernos del centro de estudios socioeconómicos* (Santiago, 1966), no. 3. pp. 1–31.

37 *El Mensajero*, vol. II (1856), p. 348. The owner of the large hacienda of Cunaco, Ignacio Valdés Larrea, complained that the North American's 'profound desire to make a fortune' caused him to overcharge for services. The records of Vichiculén demonstrate the difficulty of maintenance and repair. A new belt for a thresher cost more in the 1870s than the wages for several hundred man-days of peon labor. See Vichiculén account book, no page no.; kindly lent by the González Echenique family, Santiago.

38 Quoted in, *BSNA*, vol. X (1878), p. 241. See Rogin, *Introduction of farm machinery*, pp. 173–4. A mechanical reaper requires a certain minimum forward speed. If the machine moves too slowly, the sickle will not move rapidly enough; if the gear ratios are changed to compensate for the ox's slower pace, the drive wheels of the machine will slip. Insufficient forward speed will also cause the grain to fall forward when cut instead of backward over the sickle. Some oxen may have been used to pull reapers but they would have been fairly ineffective. *El agricultor*, vol. II, no. 19 (1841) pp. 117–19.

39 Braudel, *El Mediterráneo*, I, pp. 319–20; G. H. Slicher Van Bath, *The agrarian history of Western Europe*, pp. 289, 60–4.

40 Francisco Javier Rosales, *Progresos de la agricultura Europea y mejoras practicables en la de Chile* (Paris, 1855), p. 14; *BSNA*, vol. XXXII (1901), pp. 775–9. There were other reasons why rural Chileans were reluctant to give up oxen for example, they could always be converted into meat or hides when too old to provide traction.

41 Drouilly and Cuadra, 'Ensayo,' p. 297. Basing their estimates in the customs data the authors believe that 973 threshers at an average cost of $625 pesos each and 1076 reapers at $220 each had been brought into Chile by 1878. See also *BSNA*, vol. III (1872), p. 242; Julio Menandier, 'La hacienda de Viluco,' *BSNA*, vol. III (1872), p. 209; and *BSNA*, vol. XI (1880),

p. 393 has a description of La Compañía, an often-cited example of a model hacienda.

[42] E. J. T. Collins, 'Labour supply and demand in European agriculture, 1800–1880,' *Agrarian change and economic development* (London, 1969), p. 75. My estimate is based on data in Drouilly and Cuadra, 'Ensayo,' which gives 1076 reapers and Roberto Opazo, *Ha disminuído la fertilidad de los suelos en nuestro pais?* (Santiago, 1934), p. 15, which estimates wheat acreage for the same years at 400 000 hectares. I have added 100 000 for barley.

[43] Correa Vergara, *Agricultura Chilena*, I, p. 130; and II, ch. XII.

[44] Out of a large literature critical of the spending habits of the upper class, see Marcial González, 'Nuestro enemigo el lujo,' *Estudios económicos* (Santiago, 1889), pp. 429–62; *derrochadora* translates as 'squandering.'

[45] For discussion of agricultural yield and indebtedness, see *BSNA*, vol. XXXIII, nos. 21 and 22 (1902), pp. 538–41, 563–6. For volume of Caja de Crédito Hipotecario, see Correa Vergara, *Agricultura Chilean*, I, p. 374. Not all mortgage credit was based on rural property and in the twentieth century the urban share steadily increased.

[46] Pedro Lucío Cuadra, 'La moneda i los cambios,' *Anales*, vol. 81 (1892), pp. 125–6.

[47] Albert O. Hirschman, *Journeys toward progress* (New York, 1963), pp. 169–71.

[48] The list of imports is paraphrased from Claudio Véliz, 'La mesa de tres patas,' *Desarrollo económico*, vol. 3, nos. 1–2 (April-September 1963), pp. 231–47.

[49] *CJ* (Santiago), Leg. 107, no. 2. (The *fundo* was rented to a son.)

[50] *CJ* (Santiago), Leg. 59, no. 1.

[51] *CJ* (Santiago), Leg 134, no. 35. See also Figueroa, *Diccionario histórico*, III, pp. 208–10.

[52] Kirsch 'Industrialisation of Chile,' pp. 112–30. During the years 1915–30, the rates of return on investment in industry averaged around sixteen per cent, much higher than the rate normally earned in agriculture.

CHAPTER 5

Agriculture, tenure patterns and agrarian structure

> Children may live for years within
> sight of the eternal snow fields of the
> mountains, yet never know the sight
> or feel of snowflakes.
>
> *George McBride, 1936*

The dozens of foreign travelers who passed through Chile in the 1820s and '30s were presented with ample opportunity to indulge their pens in rapturous descriptions of the natural glories of the countryside as well as scorn for the way it was settled and farmed. The imposing mass of the cordillera, sparkling streams, the pastel hues of luxuriant vegetation, were always contrasted with the slovenly agriculture practised on the vast, neglected haciendas. The North American visitors might be excused for their provincial surprise at the absence of the 'family farm,' but even the British and French, no strangers to estate agriculture, were astonished at the size of the great haciendas in such a small country. Maria Graham wrote that 'only three superior lords' possessed the entire region between Santiago and Valparaíso. Most of these properties – and especially as one moved out from the capital – lay in isolated neglect, unfenced, largely untilled, populated by droves of cattle and too many peons. There was a distinctly overgrown quality about these large estates and often it seems in the travelers' accounts that only the inevitable packs of barking dogs interrupt the silence of a langorous countryside. A century later the dogs were still there, and generally as well 'an abiding reverence for a simple mode of tillage' whose oxen and crude plows had reminded one observer of the technology of Cincinnatus.[1]

From the 1860s on, however, the rise of a wider market and with it the better roads, rail, steam, and telegraph that permitted produce from land deep in the country to reach the growing cities was a powerful stimulus to agriculture. Output was still laboriously wrung from the land but throughout Chile's agrarian system slow but inexorable change in land distribution and management occurred. The older haciendas gradually gave way to more manageable *fundos* and greater production yielded more income for a more numerous landowning class.

Our subject in this chapter is the change in tenure patterns and agrarian structure between 1850 and 1930; but we should first notice that change took place within a context of fortuitous circumstance and governmental benevolence.

The last legal impediments to a free land market were removed with the abolition of entails in the 1850s, and beyond this the government took positive steps to ease and regulate sales, rentals, and mortgage of property. Mortgage registers and notaries with special responsibility for title search and property transfers were established in the main provincial cities in the 1830s and '40s. A number of vexatious taxes held over from the colonial era, such as road and bridge tolls, were ended. More importantly, the ecclesiastical tithe that aimed to collect a tenth of the value of agricultural produce was abolished in 1854, and six years later the *catastro* or land tax was also done away with. The tithe and *catastro* were replaced by a single *contribución territorial* (later called *impuesto agrícola*) which was a tax not on property as such but rather on agricultural income (*renta agrícola*); thus, idle land was not penalised. Nor did the tax increase in proportion to increased production; rather the government aimed to raise a certain amount and taxed only up to that point. Throughout the years 1861 to 1874, for example, the amount collected annually was always about $650 000 pesos. From 1875 (after the 1874 reassessment) to 1890, the annual tax collected was constantly around $1 000 000. Since prices for agricultural produce rose steadily during the last third of the century and the volume increased as well, landowners enjoyed an ever-decreasing tax burden. If measured in £ sterling, for example, the yearly tax dropped from £191 000 to £116 000 between 1875 and 1892.[2] And finally, after the triumph of the 'Constitutionalist' forces over Balmaceda in the 1891 civil war, the land tax was sharply reduced and assessment and collection were turned over to the local municipality.

The circumstances that made it unnecessary for the government to rely on agriculture for public revenue will be examined later; but the absence of conflict between the government and the landowners over agrarian resources is worth noting here. Unlike more purely agrarian societies such as eighteenth-century Russia or Poland where state and gentry competed for peasant taxes and produce, in Chile the government was able and generally willing to pursue a hands-off policy toward the landowners. In those areas where the government did interfere in the countryside, the effect was to strengthen the position of the landowning class. At various times during the years we are concerned with, the government yielded to landowners' pleas for protection against imports of Argentine cattle, and assisted with subsidies on freight rates and fertilisers.[3]

One area in which governmental action proved most beneficial toward landowners involved the redemption of ecclesiastical debts. Although the Church was never as important as in Mexico or in the more densely populated Andean countries to the north, it was involved in various ways in the Chilean agrarian economy. First of all were charges for the multiple spiritual services the clergy provided, such as baptism, marriage, or extreme unction, which punctuated the lives of most believers. Besides this, most education, medical care, and programs of social welfare were in the hands of the Church. All of these things had to be paid for and the tithe, alms, and meager income from real estate was not adequate. For this reason the Church drew on the produce of the agricultural sector in another way and this was through the vast network of encumbrances and liens – called variously *capellanías*, *obras pías*, and *censos* – placed on property that guaranteed income for the Church. These were established by a landowner – not infrequently on his deathbed, urged on by a cleric – by placing a perpetual lien on his property. The capital value of the lien was calculated in monetary terms and the annuities paid the Church usually represented a five per cent yield on this amount. Thus a $3000 peso lien (the normal value of a single *capellanía*) would yield $150 pesos a year to the Church. Such encumbrances were widespread and over the years many estates came to be burdened for up to a third or even half of what they were worth. The foundations were cumulative and usually perpetual. They could be paid off but rarely were; and as property changed hands the obligations went with the land.[4] *Capellanías* and the other obligations were recorded in ecclesiastical records and often in the public notaries as well. All of the private estate records I have examined show a number of these obligations: Aculeo, for example, had such obligations to La Merced, the Agustinas and Capuchines; Vichiculén to hospitals in Santiago; El Huique made semi-annual payments to the Capuchines and others.[5] A prospective buyer of any of these estates took the amount of such obligations into account. For an estate appraised at $100 000 and burdened with $30 000 of clerical obligations, the buyer paid $70 000 and assumed payment of the obligations. Through a large number of such foundations, the Church skimmed off the top an important share of rural income.

The devices we have just mentioned were not limited to guaranteeing annuities to the Church; the *censo* could be used to guarantee a share of income to private individuals. If, in the settlement of an estate, one or two sons got the hacienda, other heirs could be compensated by 'imposing' a *censo* on the property. Another use of the *censo* and one that involved large sums of money occurred during the exvinculation of the *mayorazgos*. The law of 14 July 1852, spelled out the following procedure for disentailment. The property was first assessed and given a monetary value. The owner of the *mayorazgo* (the property) had then to 'impose a *censo*' at four per cent on this amount to guarantee an annual payment to the would-be heir (also called the *mayorazgo*). After this was done, the estate could then be alienated like any other property.[6]

Now obviously these *capellanías* and *censos* represented a drain on rural income and produced a tangle of legal confusion when property changed hands. Annuities had to be paid in both good and lean years and although the Church's recourse in case of default was cumbersome and slow it does seem that payments were regularly kept up. But in 1865 the first of a series of laws were passed that enabled landowners to free themselves from these income-sapping obligations. On 24 September of that year (the need for cash during the war with Spain was the immediate reason), legislation made it possible for landowners to redeem *censos* and *capellanías* by paying between forty and fifty per cent of their capital value to the national treasury. The state then assumed payment of the annuities. Thus, in our earlier example, the landowner with a $100 000 estate that had $30 000 in *censo* or *capellanías* (representing an annual obligation of from $1200 to $1500) could now remove the obligation and obtain immediate capital gain of $30 000 pesos, by paying from $12 000 to $15 000 to the National Treasury. By 1919, nearly $38 000 000 pesos had been paid into *arcas fiscales* representing the redemption of about twice that figure in clerical and private obligations. Thus the government acted as intermediary in a vast operation to relieve landowners of their debts. The impact of all this on the ability of the Church to continue in its traditional role has not been adequately studied but it is reasonable to suppose that the lowly and desperate poor found even less succor with the principal source of charity and social welfare sharply restricted.[7]

Within an increasingly helpful institutional setting the rise of a wider market began slowly to transform the countryside. It is necessary here to distinguish between two general types of farming within central Chile: the dividing line is formed by the irrigation canals that enclose the level valley floor and set off these verdant and often lush fields from the rolling land of the coastal range on one side and the foothills of the cordillera on the other. Rain generally falls only three or four months of the year above 37° or 38° latitude, and the amount is often insufficient for crops or pasture. Happily enough for those fortunate to have property in the valley, the great masses and elevation of the Andes – much of the range is above the eternal snow line – means that irrigation water is available through the hottest and dryest months of the year. It is most necessary to understand the important differences between dry and irrigated land in central Chile; one can say with little exaggeration that irrigation canals trace a cultural line through Chilean farming patterns.

Let us consider first the dry lands of the coast and cordillera ranges. In the colonial epoch and up to the mid-nineteenth century at least, this was open range, loosely defined, cattle country. Usually the large haciendas spread over large sections of hill and land and often contained a certain area of irrigated land as well. The great estate of La Compañía toward the cordillera from Rancagua, for example, had several thousand hectares of level land and *'inmensas serranías'*; Aculeo, just across the valley floor, contained in 1888 six classes of land ranging from some 700 hectares of excellent irrigated land, to thousands of 'gentle slopes', and finally over 10 000 hectares of the *'serranía'* of the Coast Range.[8] In such an estate, the various sections were used in combination. Cattle wintered in the protected canyons and were brought down to the annual rodeo in the springtime. The larger animals were cut out of the herd, put to pasture on the irrigated alfalfa on the valley floor and slaughtered. The rest of the herd was driven on to the still green slopes until the rainless summer forced the animals to higher and wetter altitudes for pasture.[9]

Sparse forage or unsystematic techniques of animal nutrition meant that livestock were kept from six or seven years before slaughter, an understandable practice with the rugged *criollo* when the aim was tallow and hides, but one that made steaks tough and yields low for modern tastes. Reliance on scrubby hill pasture made it difficult to change over to the finer Shorthorn or Hereford breeds, designed for Europe or North America and Argentina where a large domestic market and the development of *frigoríficos* made a meat-yelding animal desirable. In nineteenth-century Chile, the feeble internal demand provided little incentive to change the system of extensive pasturage. It was upon this kind of livestock industry that a rapidly growing demand fell in the twentieth century. The result was explosive riots by the urban mass over high meat prices, imports to relieve the pressure, a number of first-rate cattle-raising enterprises, but on the whole, an industry that has not been able to satisfy even internal demand. The number of bovine stock in the entire country actually dropped between 1907 and 1930 (from 2 675 000 to 2 388 000) and had barely recovered the earlier level in 1965 when the agricultural census counted only 2 870 000 head.[10]

The favorable conjuncture in the 1860s and '70s that permitted Chilean grain to compete on the world market had a strong impact on the dry lands used for grazing. In the course of the nineteenth century thousands of hectares in the coastal range were broken up which diminished the area of natural pasture. Much of the grain subsequently produced in this region from the Itata through Curepto to the north was and still is grown by stoutly independent sharecroppers.[11] If the sharecropping did provide some incentive and a measure of independence from the estate system, it led to disastrous agricultural practices. The technique of 'dry farming' was virtually unknown, hills were plowed vertically, little care taken in preparation of seed beds. The eroded red soil of the coastal range from the Rapel to Concepción, and the silt-clogged rivers such as the Itata, provide evidence today of that careless and exploitive cultivation. The rusted iron wharf in the abandoned port of Llico is a pathetic monument to the lost prosperity of this now desolate coast.

Beginning in the 1850s as demand from California and Australia began to stir Chilean agriculture, Vicuña Mackenna noticed that changes were occurring, 'if not in the methods of cultivation' at least in the amount of output.[12] To employ additional units of land and labor was a natural reaction in a country where both were abundant. As the railroads pushed south from Santiago, level land that had been idle or used for pasture was irrigated and converted into grain fields. This sort of transition may be seen on the estate of Viluco just south of the Maipo River. In 1861, livestock was the primary source of income. Only 700 hectares out of 4700 arable were cultivated. A decade later wheat was planted in 1500 hectares and the number of animals was reduced. Similar changes occurred on the estates of Cunaco and Pichidegua. In central Chile as a whole the same process was at work. Between 1850 and 1875, cereal cultivation increased about four times – from perhaps 120 000 to 450 000 hectares – to meet foreign demand.[13] No one can decide on the total amount of new land brought into production between the 1860s and 1930, but everyone agrees that a great deal was.[14] The data on exports, which are easier to gather and fairly reliable, provide one indication of growth; and it is clear that the national market became increasingly important and more than made up for the decline in the foreign market after 1890. It would be an easy matter to present the increased volume of agricultural output in neat tables; but this is largely a futile exercise since these data are notoriously inadequate and permit only rough approximations. In the central nucleus, the acreage planted to grain probably did somewhat decline after 1890, but then prices steadily rose and the decrease in volume was more than made up by increased total revenue. Much more important was an ever more diversified output. Dairies and grain for fattening livestock, a great expansion in vineyards, tobacco (after the state monopoly was abolished in 1882), horticulture, sugar beets, alfalfa, and better beef cattle, and a host of lesser items, were all developed in response to a stronger national market as we move into the twentieth century.

Given the nature of agricultural statistics and difficulty in calculating total revenue, the prosperity of agriculture can be conveyed as well by prose as by numbers. The large number of glossy accounts by foreigners in the first years of the century all point to the thriving state of agriculture and of the country as a whole. Chileans themselves certainly thought that agriculture was booming: 'If we look back over our history,' wrote Correa Vergara in the bleak days of the 1930s, 'we are obliged to confess that the most interesting, the most satisfactory period, for our national pride is the second half of the nineteenth century.' Augustín Ross estimated that the value of agricultural production increased from $33 000 000 (undoubtedly too high) in 1871 to $142 000 000 in 1908. Certainly there was a general appearance of well being in the agriculture sector at the turn of the century and the upward trend continued down to 1930. The Ballesteros–Davis data, although unreliable for per capita output calculations, indicate continued growth after 1908 while the volume of land used for agriculture and stock raising obviously increased, in the official statistics, from 6.2 to 8.1 million hectares in the central nucleus we are discussing.[15]

Our main interest here is not a futile quest for numerical accuracy but rather the effect that an undoubted expansion had on agrarian structure and rural society. The outline of the changes in land distribution can be seen in the tax records; and I have tried to piece together enough information from other sources to show how the land was exploited and the changing pattern of estate organisation and administration. We have seen earlier – in Chapter 2 – a description of rural Chile in the 1850s; let us now examine the impact of the post-1850 expansion.

In order to understand the complexity of tenure changes it is useful to examine a number of different regions within central Chile. One place for which good records survive is the department of La Ligua, a niche off the main central valley, some 150 kilometres north of Santiago and just below the arid *norte chico*.[16] Here in 1854 eight sprawling livestock haciendas – five of which were still in a single colonial *mayorazgo* – held 143 000 of the department's 149 000 hectares of 'agricultural land.' The expanding market encouraged the owners of these huge estates to increase their herds of livestock. This internal expansion gives the impression of increasing hacienda size when in fact the haciendas were merely filling out the boundaries to which they had a prior claim. By 1926, the eight mid-century haciendas had become twelve; but because the statistical service now designated 226 000 of the estates' land as 'agricultural' their average size increased from 18 000 hectares to around 19 000. The constancy of tenure patterns in La Ligua as shown in Table 23 was unusual but not unique. Rafael Baraona's detailed study of the neighboring valley of Putaendo demonstrates a similar stability.

The department of San Felipe, only a few kilometres to the south of Putaendo, was an entirely different sort of place. Landowners in this small but well-watered and fertile valley tended the vine, planted fruit trees and from the late eighteenth century enjoyed a lively commerce with Santiago and Valparaíso. The largest estate in 1854 (J. M. Hurtado's San Regis) was one-sixth the size of the largest in La Ligua but produced much more. As agriculture flourished there was a tendency toward greater inequality. Although there were no really large haciendas here – none over 5001 hectares – the *fundos* in the 1001–5000 category doubled their share of the land by 1965. Apparently most of the land brought under cultivation through irrigation or clearing was within the original boundaries of these farms. The medium and smaller properties (5 to 200) increased in number but kept the same average size and roughly the same share of total land. At the very bottom of the scale the smallholder plots fragmented: their number increased from 353 to 978 in 1917, and to 1706 by 1965. Table 24 gives land distribution in San Felipe. By 1965, the prosperous 'yeoman farmers' for which this department is noted were still there but they were being eclipsed by the larger estates.

Modern studies of two other special regions further demonstrate the diversity of tenure patterns. The Borde and Góngora work on the valley of Puangue, just west of Santiago, shows the development of large estates through the colonial years, their persistence down to around 1880, and rapid fragmentation down to the 1950s. Puangue, like

Table 23 Land distribution in La Ligua: 1854, 1916, 1926

Category in hectares	0–5	5–20	21–50	51–200	200–1000	1001–5000	5000 up	Totals
1854								
No. of owners	95	40	9	4	5	1	8	162
Percentage	58.6%	24.6%	5.6%	2.6%	3.1%	0.6%	4.9%	100%
Total ha	243	394	252	385	3006	1570	142 850	148 700
Percentage	0.2%	0.3%	0.2%	0.3%	2.0%	1.0%	96.0%	100%
1917								
No. of owners	22	19	5	2	10	1	10	69
Percentage	32.0%	28.0%	7.0%	3.0%	14.3%	1.4%	14.3%	100%
Total ha	65	151	153	193	4185	2272	194 998	202 017
Percentage	0.03%	0.09%	0.08%	0.09%	2.1%	1.1%	96.5%	100%
1926								
No. of owners	190	57	12	4	7	5	12	287
Percentage	66.2%	19.9%	4.2%	1.4%	2.4%	1.7%	4.2%	100%
Total ha	325	507	391	528	3443	13 483	226 523	245 200
Percentage	0.1%	0.2%	0.1%	0.2%	1.4%	5.5%	92.5%	100%

Source: *AMH*, Vol. 306 (1854), *AE*, vol. VII (1917), pp. 5–15; and *AE*, vol. VII (1926–7), p. 5.

Table 24 Land distribution in San Felipe: 1854, 1916, 1965

Category in hectares	0–5	5–20	21–50	51–200	200–1000	1001–5000	5000 up	Totals
1854								
No. of owners	353	134	40	22	5	2	—	556
Percentage	63.4%	24.2%	7.1%	4.0%	0.9%	0.4%	—	100%
Total ha	739	1421	1423	1839	1605	3225	—	10 260
Percentage	7.0%	14.0%	14.0%	19.0%	15.0%	31.0%	—	100%
1917								
No. of owners	978	134	35	28	8	6	—	1189
Percentage	82.2%	11.3%	2.9%	2.4%	0.7%	0.5%	—	100%
Total ha	1023	1283	1027	2906	4009	11 038	—	21 286
Percentage	4.8%	6.0%	4.8%	13.7%	18.8%	51.9%	—	100%
1965								
No. of owners	1760	272	61	49	6	9	—	2157
Percentage	81.2%	12.9%	2.9%	2.3%	0.3%	0.4%	—	100%
Total ha	2352	2812	2135	5325	2500	19 500	—	34 624
Percentage	6.8%	8.1%	6.2%	15.4%	7.2%	56.3%	—	100%

Source: *AMH*, vol. 304 (1854–6); *AE*, vol. VII (1917), pp. 5–15; and *AE*, vol. VII (1926–7), p. 5.

San Felipe, is a well watered, mixed farming area within the market area of Santiago. Both areas had the resources and were close enough to Santiago to be able to supply the city with specialty items such as dairy products, fruit, and vegetables. These possibilities made smaller units feasible and contributed to a more equitable distribution of land. Putaendo on the other hand is geographically similar to La Ligua and followed a similar pattern of development. While these examples demonstrate the variety of tenure patterns within central Chile as well as the risk of loose generalisations, all four lie off in nooks and crannies peripheral to the main central valley.

A more typical region is represented by the department of Caupolicán which lies just below the Cachapoal River in the heartland of the traditional large hacienda country, and represents perhaps better than any other single department the classic *criollo* rural society.[17] Most of its territory was staked out by the seventeenth century and in 1854 the department had twenty-six estates that averaged about 5600 hectares each. As Table 25 shows, they accounted for about eighty per cent of the land then considered to be 'agricultural.' As the market grew after 1850 and more land was brought under cultivation, more farms appeared through division of the larger units. By 1917, there were important increases in the number of all sizes of farms, and the statistical service now found 60 000 additional hectares of agricultural land. Much of this was undoubtedly developed within the estates; there were now thirty-nine in the largest categories.

The 1854 manuscript sources that I have used for La Ligua, San Felipe, and Caupolicán are not available for the entire central nucleus, and for this overall view we must skip to the first published acreage data, those for 1917 and 1935. Between those dates the amount of agricultural land continued to increase (from some six million hectares to a little over eight million in 1935); the large estates persisted (in 1935 they still contained sixty-seven per cent of all land); there was an increasing number of small- and medium-sized farms (there were over fifteen thousand more in 1935 than in 1917); and a very rapid increase in dwarf holdings (or *minifundia*). Table 26 permits an overall picture of tenure pattern by 1935.

We must be careful not to overstate the persistence of the 'latifundia.' In a few cases, the great sprawling haciendas of colonial origin and style did remain intact down to recent times. Such a place as Rio Colorado, a vast livestock hacienda in the cordillera of some 160 000 hectares, or Las Condes behind Santiago, or the hill country spreads we have seen in La Ligua or in Putaendo, are examples. But the presence of

Table 25 Land distribution in Caupolicán: 1854, 1916

Category in hectares	0–5	5–20	21–50	51–200	200–1000	1001–5000	5000 up	Totals
1854								
No. of owners	358	440	164	90	36	21	5	1114
Percentage	32.1%	39.5%	14.7%	8.1%	3.2%	1.9%	0.5%	100%
Total ha	1067	4783	5263	8945	17 268	43 448	103 608	184 382
Percentage	0.5%	2.6%	2.9%	4.9%	9.4%	23.7%	56.0%	100%
1917								
No. of owners	3041	555	162	163	78	31	8	4038
Percentages	75.3%	13.3%	4.0%	4.0%	1.8%	0.7%	0.2%	100%
Total ha	4212	5353	4780	17 483	43 214	59 565	108 535	243 142
Percentage	1.7%	2.2%	2.0%	7.2%	17.8%	24.5%	44.6%	100%

Source: *AMH*, vol. 306 (1854–6); *AE* (1917), vol. VII, pp. 10–11. It is impossible to isolate the Caupolicán data in 1926–7 *AE*, or in the 1935–6 agricultural census.

Table 26 Land distribution in central Chile: 1916, 1935

Category in hectares	0–5	5–20	21–50	51–200	200–1000	1001–5000	5000 up	Totals
1917								
No. of owners	26 033	13 627	6268	4867	2131	731	216	53 873
Percentage	48.2%	25.4%	11.6%	9.0%	4.0%	1.4%	0.4%	100%
Total ha	41 987	127 851	196 878	469 843	943 913	1 539 538	2 898 212	6 218 222
Percentage	0.7%	2.1%	3.2%	7.6%	15.2%	24.6%	46.6%	100%
1935								
No. of owners	59 922	22 482	9799	6995	3143	939	246	103 526
Percentage	57.8%	21.8%	9.5%	6.8%	3.0%	0.9%	0.2%	100%
Total ha	95 385	239 602	315 732	690 452	1 360 718	1 909 702	3 504 698	8 116 289
Percentage	1.2%	2.9%	3.9%	8.5%	16.8%	23.5%	43.2%	100%

Source: *AE* (1917), vol. VII, pp. 4–14; Dirección general de estadística, *Agricultura 1935/6 censo* (Santiago, 1938), pp. 125, 248, 268.

such large units unduly inflates the land distribution statistics where the exaggerated number of hectares in the category of 5001 and over often are used to give the impression of huge 'feudal' estates. But much of the land in such haciendas is practically worthless. Only 250 of Rio Colorado's 160 000 hectares, for example, were arable and one could point to many similar cases.[18]

Also, owing to the fact that more acres were being used – or at least the statistics gatherers were more inclined to designate land as 'agricultural' land, there is the impression – as we move into the twentieth century – that larger units are being put together. The official data show, for example, that there were thirty more haciendas of 5000 hectares or over in 1935 than in 1917. But this is surely mis-leading; in fact, the increased number of very large haciendas reflects an increased use of land and changing definitions. Thus, for example, a hacienda might in 1912 have had 15 000 total hectares of level, hilly and wooded land within its legal boundaries, but may have actually used only 3000. In many cases, the owner of such an estate increased output by clearing land or by simply increasing his herds and conse-quently the area on which they pastured. By 1935, such land might now be called 'agricultural' and in that case the estate would pass into the '5000 and over' category. Such statistical mirages do not describe an extension of 'latifundism' nor an increase in the number of large estates, but rather, the increased use of resources.

The much more common practice was subdivision of all sizes of properties. There are a number of straightforward explanations for this. As the market for diversified output increased, more land was cultivated or planted to vines, and dairies or creameries were installed. This usually took the form of internal expansion: land within the boundaries of the estate that was previously unused was now cleared, plowed and irrigated. Increased activity brought problems of management and the huge colonial spreads were too unwieldy. At the same time, increased estate income meant that more than one family could be supported in a comfortable fashion. Where in the 1840s the owner of such an estate as El Huique opposed subdivision on grounds that less than 3800 hectares (of excellent land) would reduce an heir to 'scant fortune'; by 1920 that amount of land could easily maintain a family in upper-class style.[19] Before, one or perhaps two children would inherit the hacienda and the others might practise law, go into business or politics.

Increases in agricultural income – and better transport that made estates more agreeably accessible from Santiago – meant that the land could support more people; and consequently the number of wealthy landowners increased. La Compañía, for example, provided its sole owner, don Juan de Dios Correa de Saa, with an excellent income in the 1850s; and when he died, eleven still large *hijuelas* (or 'little daughters' of the parent estate) were carved out of the original hacienda and each of these in the later nineteenth century supported a son or daughter in the appropriate style.[20] La Compañía was exceptional for its size and the number of large *fundos* that derived from it, but the pattern was common. Most of the great haciendas – especially the valley estates – of 1850 were divided by 1920 or 1930 into two or three still large *fundos*. If we consider only the period between 1917 and 1935 the number of properties between 201 and 5000 hectares in central Chile increased from about 2800 to nearly 4100.

There are no published statistics before 1917 for the entire central nucleus but the single department of Caupolicán may be taken to indicate the general trend. From 1854 to 1917 in Caupolicán the number of medium–large estates increased from 57 to 109. The same process of subdivision was at work among the smaller properties: the number in the category of 21–50 hectares increased from 6300 to 9800 between 1917 and 1935 and, as we shall see, subdivision among the smallholders occurred at a much faster rate here and throughout central Chile.

While the tenure pattern of larger estates only gradually changed, the really small plots were rapidly fragmented. Actually this began much earlier than is commonly supposed but the increase in minifundia is somewhat clouded by statistical difficulty. Let us begin with the nineteenth-century sources. The 1854 tax roll attempted to list all properties above $25 or more of annual income but unfortunately there is no way of knowing how many properties existed below this minimum figure.[21]

If we do not know the number under $25 in 1854, the problem is more perplexing for 1874, for then the minimum was raised to $100. It was obvious that such a policy left out many farms and the National Society of Agriculture managed to persuade the government to carry out a special survey in 1881 to count the smallholders ignored by the previous tax rolls. Here a definitional problem entered as well: were the smallholders rural or urban? Ambiguity on this point continues down to the present as we shall see, but let us first attempt to make sense out of the data at hand.

The 1881 survey is a good place to begin our examination of the smallholder problem. This survey found 57 578 rural properties (*fundos rústicos*) that had been left off the 1874 roll. A handful of these were

large properties inadvertently overlooked in 1874, but the rest were
in the less than $100 category.[22] This astonishing growth of tiny plots
reflects the changing settlement pattern of central Chile and the impact
of agricultural expansion. Although some of the new minifundists
were undoubtedly ex-*inquilinos* or relatives, a great many were floating,
seasonal workers and squatters who came to settle in quasi-urban
clusters and hamlets – the *caseríos*, *aldeas*, and *villorios* – that sprang
up everywhere during these years. The new settlers grew a few
vegetables, kept a pig or chickens, and supplemented this meagre income
with wages earned on the large estates. It was never entirely clear to
census takers whether these properties should be called urban or rural,
and of course both the reality and definition were constantly changing.[23]

In 1935–6, the statistical service tried to resolve the definitional
problem by categorising proprietors by the produce: the 'principal'
ones produced livestock, cereals, and garden crops; the 'secondary'
ones anything but those items. It is undoubtedly these 'secondary'
producers that best correspond to the type of minifundists that emerged
in the 1860s and '70s and that constituted the majority of dwarf holdings in 1935.[24] By this time, however, many of the minifundists had
been absorbed into the smaller rural hamlets. I hope this extended
statistical exegesis makes clear that although the minifundists are not
always visible in the censuses, they came into existence fairly early to
satisfy the need for a more stable hacienda work force and have lingered
on as a marginal class, by and large ignored by landlord and reforming
governments alike.

By 1935 much of the floating mass of men who had provoked so much
comment in the mid-nineteenth century had disappeared. Most of these
people were absorbed by the transformed hacienda system which required higher labor quotas. The estates could absorb some of the
population increase that because of fragmentation could not remain on
the minifundia. But rural population grew faster than labor requirements and, beyond a point, fragmentation was devastating. The resulting population pressure was at first somewhat relieved through migration to the northern mines and newly-opened Araucanía in the south.
There was also some minimal emigration to Peru and Argentina. Within
central Chile itself, the population was likewise on the move. Men went
to Valparaíso to work on the dock and railway projects and both men
and women, but especially women, moved to the cities, attracted by
the prospects of domestic labor for the flourishing upper class.

To say that most great colonial haciendas were divided into smaller but still large *fundos,* or to acknowledge that total agricultural output increased a great deal in the process, does not necessarily imply that the new individual units were operated more efficiently than before. It is difficult to calculate production costs because labor input for each crop or operation, the cost of overhead, or even a reliable cost of living index to establish real levels of income, are not available. Our best indications are still the estimates made by contemporaries and Table 27 presents two such schedules, one for the beginning of our period and

Table 27   Comparative cost of wheat production in central Chile: 1856 and 1929

	B. J. de Toro's data (1856)		*Estudio* data (1929)	
	Cost	% of total cost	Cost	% of total cost
	$		$	
OPERATION				
Rent of 1 cuadra	15.00	27%	200.00	28%
Plow, harrow, and plant	6.75	12%	144.50	20%
	[18 man days]		[19 man days]	
Seed	6.00	11%	150.00	21%
Irrigation	2.00	3%	42.50	6%
Reaping	4.10	7%	80.00	12%
Threshing, sacking and storage	11.20	20%	75.00	11%
Carriage and freight costs	11.00	20%	13.00	2%
Totals	56.00	100%	705.00	100%
PRODUCE (in *fanegas*)				
(72 kg each)	30.00		38.00	
Price (each)	3.00		24.00	
Total revenue	90.00		912.00	
Less costs	−56.00		−705.00	
Gross profit	34.00		207.00	

Source: B. J. de Toro's data from Gay, *Agricultura,* II, p. 44; *Estudio sobre el estado de la agricultura,* p. 15.
Note: 1 cuadra equals 1.57 hectare; 1 fanega equals 72 kilograms.

the other at the end. Both estimates are for the cost of producing on 1 cuadra (1.57 hectare) of irrigated land in the central valley.

From these estimates it appears that the number of man-days for field work very slightly decreased. Taking just operations of plowing, harrowing, and planting – the only ones for which labor inputs are given – 0.6 man-days per fanega of output were required in 1856 and 0.5 man-days three-quarters of a century later. Neither these nor the other labor costs, with the exception of threshing where by 1929 machines were used, suggest much improvement in technique or capital investment. Table 27 also points to shrinking average revenue despite an increase in yield (from 30 to 38 fanegas): total costs increased over twelve times between 1856 and 1929; wheat prices eight times; total revenue ten times and total profits only six times. (I have presented the data in this way in the absence of a suitable index to establish real income.) It would be somewhat adventurous to extend these estimates to central Chile as a whole; yet these figures are in agreement with the general picture of agricultural development that we are examining. More land was cultivated, estates broken into somewhat smaller units, a small amount of capital investment and a bit better supervision slightly increased labor productivity. But costs remained high. Landowners were making more money – for many, in fact, the 1920s were golden years – but it was because the scale of operation – more land under cultivation; more man-days applied to it – was larger than before.

For a picture of the characteristic rural system that emerged in central Chile after a century of growing markets, easy credit, social tranquility and the full blessings of government, we may look beyond the statistics to a description by a distinguished social geographer. When George McBride traveled through the country in the early part of his century he was impressed with the large scale of agricultural industry. There were 'league-long rows of eucalyptus and Lombardy poplar trees stretching across the landscape; high, well built mud walls lining the road for miles without a break; irrigation canals following these in a single extensive system; dozens of connected fields, not large in themselves but joined by gates showing that they are all sections of the same property.' The increase in the number of resident workers and a more stable settlement pattern that made the estate the center of rural society and reinforced the sense of hacienda community was also apparent; '[there was] an absence of houses in most of the fields; private roads uniting the fields with an extensive central settlement perhaps several miles away; a great rambling hacienda house set in an attractive grove of giant eucalyptus trees, surrounded by beautiful Mediterranean gardens, and separated from the other houses of its type by leagues of agricultural land; and in back of the house, covering a distance of several city blocks, granaries, storerooms, wine *bodegas* . . . and not far away numerous small dwellings of laborers, strung out along both sides of the main hacienda road like a village with a single street – a town of workers and their families all connected with the farm.'[25]

In the 1920s there were at least a thousand estates of over 1000 hectares that fit McBride's description, and if we included *fundos* down to 200 hectares – which, of course, are multi-family operations – another two thousand could be added. A study that purported to list all of the 'most important *fundos* and haciendas' of central Chile contains about 1800 properties.[26] These held around eighty-five per cent of all 'agricultural land' and probably produced at least that percentage of all commercial agricultural output, and gave subsistence as well to a majority of the rural inhabitants. By far the greatest part of the estate production came from the 'demesne' in medieval usage or the 'land-lord's enterprise' in modern parlance. That is to say that Chilean agriculture did not develop the tripartite system of landlord, capitalist tenant farmer, and hired laborer, that was common, for example, in England; nor a system of peasant rentals or sharecropping found in other traditional agrarian societies. Rather, most output was produced on estate land, with direct estate administration of capital and labor. A sense of the organisation of these larger estates and the flow of services can be obtained from Figure 4.

By 1935, when the statistical service first gathered this kind of information, some seventy-five per cent of the estate work force was made up of service tenants (*inquilinos*) and the extra hands they supplied from their households, together with the clerks, specialists and middle-range administrators or 'employees' (*empleados*). A large group of simple day laborers called 'peons' (or more recently, *afuerinos*) were employed on a seasonal basis. The system of rural labor is discussed in Chapter 6; the only point to be made here is its relationship to estate production. Service tenants and peons exchanged their labor for payment in the form of subsistence plots, lodging, rations, and only to a small degree, in money. They were landless and rarely able to sell the things they helped produce. It is not possible to determine for these years how much estate land was worked by sharecroppers. Some estates made arrangements with charcoal makers (*carboneros*), exchanging scrub trees and bushes for a third of the product. Occasionally the more trusted or able *inquilinos* were allowed to work sections of land in '*media*', but the amount was probably insignificant. In 1955, when the first data that I am aware of appeared, the subtenancies under the control of *inquilinos*, hacienda employees and sharecroppers together, exploited only 2.4 per cent of the total arable land in the country.[27] It may be, as some have argued, that sharecropping or production by the 'peasant enterprise' was more important in the eighteenth or even in the later nineteenth century; but it appears that such arrangements were mostly limited to the marginal lands of the coastal range.[28]

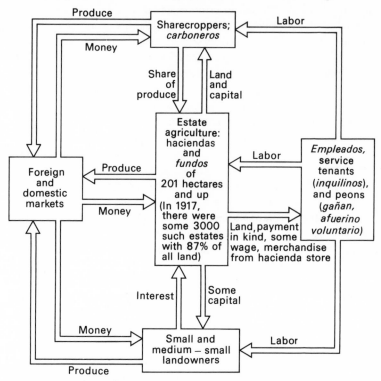

Fig. 4   Market relations and flow of produce and services in the rural economy

A greater and more diversified agricultural output created the need for an ever-increasing staff to assist in estate management. Spreading outward below the owner or his delegate was a complex hierarchy of *mayordomos*, and *capataces* (foremen): *potrerizos* (field bosses), *llaveros* (warehousemen), and clerks, needed to supervise the large number of direct laborers. Figure 5 shows the hierarchy of estate workers arranged along lines of authority and also in layers according to their form of payment. This is a simplified and idealised sketch: estate organisation

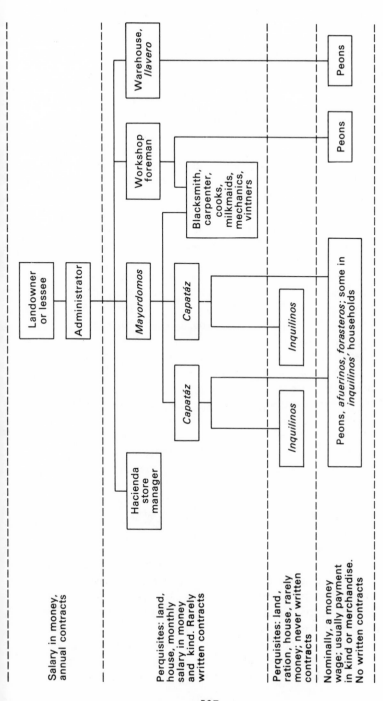

Fig. 5 Hierarchy of estate work force and modes of payment

would vary with location, size and the type of activity. And as we move into recent years, more specialised employees – mechanics, tractor operators, accountants – would appear.

The wives and daughters of these *empleados* or '*sirvientes del campo*' found work on the estates as maids, cooks, and washerwomen. On a level just below the *mayordomos* and foremen was a growing group of specialists such as carpenters, blacksmiths, and by the 1930s, the occasional mechanic or machinery operator. Some of the *empleados* were craftsmen brought from the city, but most were recruited from among the most reliable of the service tenantry, and this provided one of the few opportunities for improvement in rural society. In the main dining room of the hacienda El Huique is a large oil portrait of a worker so favored: the *inquilino* who became the trusted *peón de confianza* of the *hacendado* (and President of Chile), Federico Errázuriz Echaurren.[29]

The censuses show 50 000 more *empleados* in 1907 than in 1875 and although not all of these were rural, there is no doubt that they constituted a growing class in the countryside. Like the lengthening rows of *inquilinos*, the *empleados* were brought into the hacienda community. Instead of giving rise to a rural proletariat external to and possibly in opposition to the hacienda, agricultural development brought more workers and administrators onto the estate and strengthened the bonds of dependence and affection between patron and employee. Instead of alienating workers through a modern, impersonal, and perhaps more efficient system of rural economy, many more men were brought within the shadow of the hacienda house and within the paternalistic orbit of the owner. Labor service was exchanged for shelter, a daily ration, often the benevolent interest of the owner, a monthly salary, and most importantly, a sense of participation. The estate *empleados* came in time to occupy a middle layer in rural structure and in recent years have been among the most conservative of rural inhabitants.

Above the increasingly complex hacienda hierarchy – and often physically removed from the estate as well – were the landowners. As Santiago became more and more the center of political, social, and economic life, landowners were more likely to be absentee owners. Absentee owners are not necessarily careless ones but the Chilean custom does seem to have worked against the practice of effective agriculture or a proper conservation of resources. As the capital grew in population and prestige and as better roads and especially the railroad improved mobility, more landowners from the provinces built houses in

Santiago. For a person interested in education for his children or an urban culture there was little choice outside the capital. Only Talca in the entire region between Concepción and La Serena provided a measure of the amenities that the wealthy came to expect as the nineteenth century wore on.

There were two principal ways that a landlord could enjoy the income of his rural property without excessive exposure to the rustic life. The first was through rental or long-term leases. The notarial and judicial archives are full of such contracts and they tell a common tale. In 1881, for example, don Lucio Formas leased his 320 hectare *fundo* (Cerro Negro) for a six-year term for $4800 annually. The contract specifies that the owner will pay $100 a year for repairs of buildings and fences but other expenses or improvements will not be compensated.[30] Another illustrative case is that of señor José Luis Larraín, a businessman in the farm produce firm of Tattersal in Santiago, and son-in-law of former President Manuel Bulnes. Apart from the usual house in Santiago, Larraín owned a *conventillo* (or tenement) in the city and a *fundo* in San Fernando of some 1500 hectares (190 irrigated) appraised at $102 000 in 1898. This he rented for $3000 a year and then obtained a Caja de Crédito Hipotecario loan for 60 000 at six per cent which he invested in higher-yield stocks and in the business.[31] Often widows rented their property. Trinidad Larraín, daughter of the Marqués de Larraín received $10 000 a year from San Javier just south of Santiago and she too mortgaged the place to the Caja de Crédito Hipotecario ($30 000 at six per cent). Doña Trinidad held stock in two banks and the Gas Company.[32]

It takes little imagination to see the relationship between such owners and their land. They lived most of the year in Santiago, rarely saw the hacienda whose rent paid the bills. At times the contract reserved part of the hacienda house 'to inhabit when suitable' or asked the renter to keep houses for the owners' periodic use.[33] Landowners were not required to reinvest borrowings in the land or even mention the purpose of the loan. The owners were under little obligation to maintain let alone improve the estate and all too often the renter was motivated only to obtain as much profit as possible from the estate during his brief tenure. Nine years or less was the usual length of the lease.[34] It would be misleading, however, to leave the impression that all or even the majority of estates were operated in this way. Whenever possible *fundos* were rented to close relatives. The señora Tagle de Echenique acknowledged what most knew when she rented Huique to two sons: 'strangers [non-family members] always exploit to the maximum diminishing the value of land and buildings.'[35] And it is not possible at this point to determine how many or what percentage of all estates were rented. The Valenzuela O. *Album* occasionally mentions rentals and in nearly all of these cases, the renter was either the owner of a neighboring estate or a relative of the landowner. But whether the landowner rented his rural property or not, he still generally directed the operation from a distance through an administrator; and this feature, too, seemed to work against more effective exploitation of the land.

An important number of landowners were only secondarily farmers; people such as widows or spinsters did not ordinarily directly manage land but neither did many businessmen, professionals, politicians, and bureaucrats who although by all means were interested in income, saw the rural estate, 'as first of all a place to enjoy life.' The growth of Santiago enhanced the value of land in this way; for while a farm to a farmer is not especially glamorous, to the city dweller it becomes a retreat, a delightful place for summer vacations, a place for a honeymoon, a showplace for visitors, a place where business and political companions can be entertained and impressed.[36] All this, of course, may serve an economic purpose just as does the modern executive's paneled penthouse office, but not usually an agricultural purpose. Such owners often hired an administrator who might be the proprietor of a neighboring farm, a trusted friend or relative, and occasionally a trained agronomist. Like the renter, administrators generally came from the same social class as the landowners themselves. In these arrangements where the landowner had little time or inclination and the administrator scant incentive, there was not much effective leadership toward better agricultural practice. The estate was valued as a social base that helped keep the family together and where during summer sojourns, kinship ties could be renewed and strengthened, where one had the gratification of commanding and being obeyed, and the solicitous care of dozens of domestic servants softly padding through the cool and quiet corridors of the hacienda house. We have an impression of this life through the eyes of visitors and such diplomats as Henry Lane Wilson who visited Francisco Undurraga's hacienda once toward the turn of the century and was 'met by a procession of probably a thousand of the tenantry and escorted to the family mansion for luncheon.'[37]

The very social development of Chile, and the growth of the urban values of its elite, were thus important influences in agriculture. This, of course, is another way of saying that rural society cannot be understood in isolation from the rest of the country. Moreover, it would be misleading to leave the impression that all estates were neglected or cherished completely for recreation. We will be able to elaborate this theme in a later chapter; what is important here is that the system and values that I have briefly mentioned helped preserve a traditional agriculture. In regard to estate organisation this implied a hacienda community valued nearly as much for loyalty and obedience as for productivity. The disproportionate growth of Santiago for reasons unrelated to agriculture – above all, because of a thriving export sector – nevertheless drew landowners into the city who exercised their influence in society and politics, and were content to leave the rustic business of estate management to others. The renters, administrators, and *mayordomos* to whom this task fell had little inclination to prepare for the long run or plant trees for grandchildren. Under the circumstances, capital investment was low, technology backward and the turnover of land frequent. The landless resident workers formed a closer attachment to the soil than did the distant *hacendado*.

Perhaps we can better understand rural Chile if we keep in mind the repercussions in other parts of the world of similar pressures. In the new lands of the trans-Mississippi West, the Canadian plains, Australia or New Zealand, European emigrants led on by the prospects of the rising market, created wholly new rural societies, often based on communities of family farmers. Not finding native people whom they could induce to work, they were quick to take up the new implements of modern agriculture. In older agrarian societies the competition and heightened demand of the latter ninteenth century made a series of adjustments necessary. In England and such parts of the Continent as Denmark and Holland, agriculture was mechanised and diversified and a reduced rural population was more intensively employed. Elsewhere in Western Europe responses varied but everywhere a more efficient agriculture base was created and as surplus population and produce flowed toward the cities so also did political power. But out on the periphery of the burgeoning capitalist world, economic expansion had different social effects. The Chilean countryside was changed but in such a way that the older agrarian system was preserved and even strengthened.

CHAPTER 5

1 Graham, *Journal*, p. 230; Henry Willis Baxley, *What I saw on the West Coast of South and North America* (New York, 1865), p. 225.
2 *Resúmen de la hacienda pública de Chile desde 1833 hasta 1914* (London, 1914), pp. 26–8. The tax amounted to about nine per cent of income.
3 The role of the landowners in politics has been studied by Thomas C. Wright,

'The Sociedad Nacional de Agricultura in Chilean politics, 1869–1938' (Unpublished doctoral dissertation, University of California, Berkeley, 1971); and in Wright, 'Politics of inflation,' pp. 239–59.

4 *Censo* was a generic term used to denote several different kinds of obligations or contracts in nineteenth-century Chile. It also was used interchangeably with *capellanía*, although the latter was generally used in the strict sense of supporting a *capellán* or to guarantee those funds destined to pious works. A *censo* was different from a mortgage in that a property owner did not receive capital, but rather, he 'imposed a *censo*' or pledged a certain area of land (expressed in money value) to guarantee annuities. The payments could be used to support a priest, build a chapel, pay for masses for deceased relatives, pay tutors, and so on. *Censos* were recorded in notarial records. They could be for a limited time or in perpetuity, and were transferred with the property; thus, although a *censo* did not mean capital received it did mean a burden on the land. For discussion of *censos* and *capellanías* see J. M. Ots Capdequí, *El estado español en las Indias* (México, 1957), pp. 33–40; and *Manual de historia*, vol. II, pp. 161–85; and Arnold J. Bauer, 'Church and Agrarian Structure,' pp. 86–91.

5 *Capellanías* are recorded in 'Indice de poseedores y fundadores de las capellanías eclesiásticas o colativas que se proveen de esta curia . . .' (Archive of the Archbishopric of Santiago, 1895), no vol. no., pp. 784. *Censos* are listed in *Dirección general de impuestos internos*, 'Rol de valores mobiliarios de la república' (Santiago, 1919), pp. 97–125.

6 The details of the law are spelled out in *BLEY*, VII, Libro XX, pp. 73–4.

7 The legislation of 24 September and 23 October 1865, providing that 'censos, *capellanías i cualquiera clase de capitales vinculadas*' could be redeemed by paying one half (and at times forty per cent) of the capital value of the *censo* to the Ministry of Hacienda. An example of the way this worked in practice may be seen in the case of Irene Cuevas de Ortúzar. In 1881 she transferred a *censo* amounting to $9270 by paying $4635 to the Ministry of Hacienda which then paid the *censualista* (a priest in this case) an annuity of $370 ($9270 × four per cent). *CN* (Rengo), vol. 125 (1881), p. 1. Inflation, of course, simply made such fixed payments worthless. In 1970, for example, the $370 pesos paid to the priest in 1881, would have amounted to about one tenth of one U.S. cent. For laws permitting transfer of *censos*, see *BLEY*, vol. XXXIII, no. 9, pp. 518–19. For amounts redeemed see *Resúmen de la hacienda pública*, pp. 23–6; and 'Rol de valores,' p. 96. Obviously some landowners defaulted on payment of *réditos* to the Church or individuals, but the private records I consulted all show regular payment. Notice too, that not all of the $38 000 000 redeemed had been imposed on rural property, but most was.

8 *CJ* (Santiago), Leg. 107, no. 4.

9 The angular *criollo* breed survived on this pasture and by eating the leaves off the lower tree branches (the Spanish verb *ramonear* describes this unnourishing practice), but inadequate forage for livestock remained a problem even after the wider planting of alfalfa and clover. There is no better indication of the poverty of Chilean pastures than the widespread use of wheat straw for forage. In most countries since straw has so little nutritional value it is used only for bedding; in Chile it was commonly fed to animals and, in fact, one of the major objections to mechanical threshing (compared with *trilla a yegua*) was that it made the straw unfit for forage. See *BSNA*, vol. IV (1873), pp. 278–9, and Baraona *et al.*, *Valle de Putaendo*, p. 25, for the same complaint.

10 Correa Vergara, *Agricultura chilena*, II, 175; *Chile hoy*, p. 127.

11 In the early nineteenth century Claudio Gay thought the extension of share

cropping would be a marvelous way of uplifting the rural lower classes by giving them incentive, dignity, and interest in the land, and some of the more scolding passages of his classic work are devoted to this theme. And he believed that in the long run sharecropping would 'become more common thanks to the philanthropic spirit of the landowners.' But from the 1830s when Gay noticed that sharecropping was rarely practised except for 'the cultivation of cereals in dry lands,' down to recent times, this form of exploitation seems to have followed geographical lines. Claudio Gay, *Agricultura*, I, p. 120; cf. Cristóbal Kay, 'The development of the Chilean hacienda system, 1850–1972,' to appear in *Patterns of Agrarian Capitalism* (Cambridge, 1975).

12 *El Mensajero*, I (1856), p. 346.

13 *BSNA*, vol. III (1872), p. 227, account books of Cunaco and Pichidegua; *BSNA*, vols. XXI (1890), p. 89, and VI (1875), pp. 527–31, discuss barley trade and beer making. In 1874–5, sixty per cent of the harvest went to the export trade. In addition to wheat, barley became important for foreign and local brewers, and after 1870 the value of barley exports was about one-third that of wheat.

14 Departamento de Agricultura, *Estudio sobre el estado de la agricultura chilena* (Santiago, 1929), pp. 5–7, points out the 'diverse opinion' on what can be considered 'agricultural land.' Encina estimated a total of 193 000 square kilometers in the entire country while Luis Risopatrón gave 320 000 square kilometers.

15 Correa Vergara, *Agricultura chilena*, I, p. 121; Guillermo Feliú Cruz, *Chile visto a través de Agustín Ross* (Santiago, 1950), p. 89; Marto Ballesteros and Tom E. Davis, 'The growth of output and employment in basic sectors of the Chilean economy, 1908–1957,' *Economic development and social change*, vol. XI, no. 2 (January 1963), pp. 152–76; *Chile hoy*, pp. 126–9.

16 The manuscript worksheets for the 1854 tax roll are contained in *AMH*, vols. 304–6 (1854–6). They are incomplete: records for only seven Departments exist. The worksheets include information on irrigated, *de rulo*, and *serranía* acreage, the number of livestock and vines. I am grateful to Mr Robert McCaa for the reference. Because of frequent boundary changes it is difficult to find Departments whose limits remained unchanged over the long period of time we are dealing with. And because of the pecularities of reporting, it is not always possible to isolate data for certain Departments in the same years. Thus, we have La Ligua for 1854, 1917, 1926; San Felipe and Caupolicán for 1854 and 1917; and for San Felipe, I have included the most recent (1964–5) data as well.

17 *AMH*, vol. 304. Part of the Department of Caupolicán—the *comuna* of San Vincente de Tagua-Tagua—was selected as a test area in 1955 because it was considered as most representative of central Chile. See República de Chile, Dirección de estadístico y censos, III *Censo nacional agrícola-ganadero* (6 vols., Santiago, 1955?), vol. 6, p. xv.

18 McBride, *Land and Society*, pp. 126–7.

19 *CN* (Santiago), vol. 342.

20 *Rol de contribuyentes* (1874).

21 In the manuscript worksheets of this tax roll we found that several of the *funditos* evaluated at $25 had no more than half a hectare. It would seem, therefore, that only the tiniest of plots – the sort found in back of rude huts or the pigsty/chicken coop/garden patch syndrome – still found in rural hamlets were the only properties left out.

22 The 10 000 worksheet pages of this remarkably detailed survey on acreage, quality of land, animals and production have not been uncovered but the SNA published a 'pre-report' in the 1881 Treasury Yearbook that gives the

total number of properties by Subdelegación (the political division within a Department). Moreover, local newspapers published complete lists of proprietors, giving their annual income, which was often only 4 or 5 pesos. The 'pre-report' is in *Memoria de Hacienda* (1881), 'Anexo Sociedad Nacional de Agricultura,' pp. 28–41. Most of the local newspapers that published lists of these newly-found smallholders have apparently been lost. *La Libertad* (Talca) devotes several issues to the lists.

23 The 1881 survey considered 'rural' all householders who did not pay the night watchman or lighting tax ('derecho de sereno y alumbramiento') and thus must have included almost everyone outside the large provincial towns. This, too, must have reflected reality since at this time few proper towns existed; the bulk of provincial villages were functionally rural. See Anguita and Quesney, *Leyes promulgadas*, II, p. 212; *BLEY*, Libro XLII, vol. I, pp. 431–4.

24 *Agricultura, censo* (1935–6), p. 3.

25 McBride, *Land and Society*, pp. 122–3.

26 Juvenal Valenzuela O., *Album de informaciones agrícolas; zona central de Chile* (Santiago, 1923).

27 *CIDA*, p. 161; III *Censo nacional agrícola-ganadero*, (1955) vol. VI, p. 14, has a lower figure, only 1.9 per cent of all arable land.

28 It is not entirely clear where this class of petty entrepreneurs came from or why such arrangements were not used more widely on the irrigated *fundos* of the central valley. Nineteenth-century observers thought that sharecroppers were drawn from among the 'more elevated class' of the rural population: the *inquilinos*, *mayordomos*, and small or medium holders. See *El Mensajero* (1857), pp. 204–6; *BSNA*, vol. II (1871), p. 384. Cristóbal Kay, 'Comparative development of the European manorial system and the Latin American hacienda system: an approach to a theory of agrarian change for Chile' (Unpublished doctoral dissertation, University of Sussex, England, 1971), pp. 82–121, suggests the application of the ideas of 'peasant' and 'landlord' enterprise to Chile.

29 Bauer, 'El Huique,' p. 461.

30 *CJ* (Santiago), Leg. 148, no 15.

31 *CJ* (Santiago), Leg. 169, no 7.

32 *CJ* (Santiago), Leg. 107, no. 7.

33 *CJ* (Santiago), Leg. 23, no. 4. This is what the nitrate king, José Santos Ossa, requested.

34 For an instructive comparison between French and English rural leasing practice, see Robert Forster, 'Obstacles to Agricultural Growth in eighteenth-century France,' *American Historical Review*, vol. LXXV, no. 6 (October 1970), pp. 1600–15. Chile is similar to the French pattern.

35 *CN* (Santiago), vol. 342.

36 McBride, *Land and Society*, pp. 42, 60; Tornero, *Chile illustrado*, p. 451; Subercaseaux, *Memorias*, ch. V, pp. 218, 361.

37 Henry Lane Wilson, *Diplomatic Episodes in Mexico, Belgium and Chile* (New York, 1927), p. 52; see also McBride, *Land and Society*, p. 181; Marie Wright, *The Republic of Chile* (Philadelphia, 1904), pp. 231–42.

Lower rural society from 1850 to 1930

It is understandable that people writing on rural Chile in the 1930s believed that 'nothing had changed since colonial times.' The city has rarely been able to understand the mysteries of the farm and most of our information at this time comes from urban critics and artists too often inclined toward disdain or idyl. The picture of a backward, 'feudal' countryside also coincided with the emerging view of the land-owners as social troglodytes. But beyond that, the grinding poverty associated in the popular mind – especially in the Anglo–American mind – with Spanish rule, the oxen and wooden plows, peons with hat in hand, and also the horses and guitars, fresh water and cool tile, the unhurried pace, seemed to many a simple prolongation of the eighteenth century.[1] But, in fact, in the years after 1860, the impact of rail and steam and the greater market forces they unleashed had repercussions in the most remote corners of rural Chile. This was not change along the lines of mechanisation or proletarianisation familiar to students of North American or Western European social development; rather, in Chile, the already archaic system of rural labor was reinforced.

Although it is obvious that urban life and the visible layers of society were rapidly transformed by economic growth while the country itself stretched out hundreds of miles both north and south, changes in the countryside are more dimly perceived. At the upper levels, some con-temporaries were aware of change and the National Society of Agriculture's *Boletín* records the landowners' optimism and doubt. Sadly, however, we have no such comparable source for the lower rural classes. More obscure by far than George Eliot's provincials who 'lived faithfully a hidden life and rest in unvisited tombs,' the thousands of Chilean peons and tenants have not even graves to visit, no monuments, no memoirs, no poet. One is forced to infer from the demands placed upon them and from the opinion of others something about their quality of life and the changes they underwent.[2]

Let us turn first to the lowest stratum of rural society, the large number of under-employed, rootless, often ambulatory masses. In the course of agricultural development many of these people found their way into the somewhat more stable rural hamlets – *villorios* and *caseríos* – that sprang up everywhere in the central valley; others were taken on by the estates to augment the service tenantry; the rest sought their fortune in the northern mines, fought the war of the Pacific (1879–84), or drifted into the cities.

From around 1700 to the early nineteenth century population grew rapidly throughout most of Europe and America. Although Chile shared with more economically advanced countries much of the knowledge and improvement that made demographic growth possible, unlike other regions she lacked the means to employ the increased numbers.[3] Only a fraction of the population could be absorbed permanently on the estates as tenants. Some men sought work in the mines, a few signed up for construction work on the Copiapó rail line, and others helped build the new cart roads and bridges in the 1840s and 1850s. The great majority, however, formed a loose, unattached mass of people who squatted on marginal land along the coast or on the edge of cities, lived in rude huts on interstitial plots in the valley, or simply moved along the length of central Chile in search of sustenance. The benign climate and fertility of the land made it possible for them to exist; lack of economic activity gave them no alternative. Most of them could work but few would do so for the remuneration offered. Under the circumstances many preferred to live off the land and supplement their foraging with petty theft.

Occasional attempts were made to encourage the floating population to settle in hamlets, but there was too little incentive for the peon or too little control by the authorities to accomplish this. The peon undoubtedly understood that concentration would threaten his semi-legal means of support, and given the choice of organised or free poverty he chose the latter. In 1839 a Franciscan friar wrote that in the 'vast and wide fields [near Rosario on the coast] there are more than 10 000 souls who have no place to pitch their "*tristes ranchos*".' He proposed to settle them on Church lands and enlist the cooperation of local *hacendados*. The plan failed but the proposal suggests the magnitude of the problem.[4] Many documents of the 1840s and 1850s refer to the floating population. A proposal to develop the port of Llico, for example, suggests that work crews could be formed out of the vagrant population ('de los muchos vagos que hay en el puerto'). The intendency archive of Talca contains countless references to theft and vagrancy that resulted from 'the large number of evildoers' in the province. Moreover, the mobility of the peons is impressive. They moved from one work gang to another several miles away for an additional six centavos or an 'extra bean in the pot.'[5]

For the less arduous labor on the haciendas peons were attracted for little pay. For tasks such as harvest or roundup when outside labor was required, quantities of local wine (or *chicha*, a fermented grape drink) and food and the promise of frolic were sufficient inducements for the floating laborer. The name for this form of 'fiesta labor' is a word of Quéchua origin: the *mingaco*. It may be defined as a 'fiesta or reunion celebrated to do something in common, a work that requires the participation of many people . . . The characteristics of a *mingaco* are that nothing is paid except . . . a *comilona* [gluttonous meal] accompanied by drink, song, and dance.' In 1840 the Society of Agriculture circulated a questionnaire to several landowners asking, among other things, 'Which are more advantageous: the *mingacos* or the daily wage earner?' Unfortunately, few responses were recorded. One respondent from near Rancagua replied that his *inquilinos* were adequate for the task, but if they had not been he would be disinclined to use the *mingaco*, 'because with them it is necessary to tolerate drunkenness.' The tone of the article suggested that the *mingaco* was a common labor form. And Gay notes that 'the expense in money is almost nothing when the use of the *mingaco* is adopted . . . Workers are always ready to lend their services to this kind of fiesta.'[6]

That seasonal labor could be attracted through the *mingaco* reveals at once the low labor requirement, the casual nature of agriculture, and the precariousness of a large body of the rural population. If this was the peons' income at harvest time it is not difficult to imagine the extent of their resources in the off-season or to understand why the *inquilinos* must have considered themselves fortunate.

Most writers made a clear distinction between the *inquilino* and the peon. Gay, for example, after complementary remarks about *inquilinos*, condemned the peons: 'The major portion [of peons] lead an entirely nomadic life . . . have no notion of order . . . and are incapable of appreciating the value of time. The rural peon, generally called *forastero* [outsider] is more thieving than the city worker . . . [Rural peons] move from field to field looking for work and often they descend on the orchards like the plague stripping the trees to satisfy their craving for fruit.' In winter they were even less industrious, and few observers fail to comment on their 'sloth.' 'A pernicious and vituperable lassitude – which they themselves call apathy – dominates the inhabitants.'[7]

A peak in the quantity of the floating population was reached in the late 1850s. Writing of the fertile province of Colchagua in 1858, a prominent Chilean had this to say: 'Open your eyes and you see daily entire families abandoning their homes and setting out – to where? Even they do not know. Their only purpose is to leave a place that does not provide a living . . . many head toward Santiago. The refrain, "me voi pa'la ciudad" is very common among the poorer people. Travel our roads and you will see many families moving with their equipment on their backs toward the capital to augment the already present pauperism . . . even now the "vagos" cannot be controlled as they should be.'[8]

Central Chile, therefore, was an area with plentiful if idle hands. In one section alone nearly sixty per cent (59 000) of the 101 000 adult male population were considered by the census takers to be 'persons without a fixed destiny.' It was this group of men that landowners felt obliged to draw into agricultural production, during seasons of peak need, but they were up against an attitude very different from that held by the modern industrial worker and one that would have to be fundamentally changed before the peon could become a reasonably efficient cog in production. The problem – from the point of view of the landowners – rested in the fact that the peons were not overly interested in security and their basic drive seemed to be for subsistence or immediate gratification rather than gain. Julio Menandier, editor of the National Society of Agriculture's *Boletín* and a man who knew the Chilean countryside as well as anyone in the nineteenth century, was appalled: '[The peons] have no real needs. To them it is the same whether they have a roof over their heads or live in the open air, whether they have good and abundant food or bad and scarce [meals]. The majority of them do not work unless driven by hunger; the income from a whole week's arduous labor is lost with indifference in a single night of gambling and disorder.'[9]

Now, a group of men that will not work 'unless driven by hunger,' who will not respond to the allurement of wages, is a distinct obstacle to the formation of a labor market. Yet experience in the 1870s, a transitional decade for the Chilean peon, seemed to confirm Menandier's observation. In one example 'out of a thousand' the daily wage of seasonal workers on the hacienda El Pirque was raised in the middle of the wheat harvest from 40 to 50 centavos; but instead of working more, the peons took off Monday and Tuesday: 'the wage increase had no other effect than to convert steady workers into drunken slackards.' All through these years we find a similar lament. In 1882 a landowner wrote, 'studying with an attentive eye the lower orders [*capas inferiores*] of our *campesinos*, what stands out is their indolence or lack of ambition in improving their habitual laziness.' A wage increase would only 'foment their habitual sloth.'[10]

The solution urged in the face of the workers' apparently negative reaction was not much different from that in other regions where an expanding market came in contact with archaic behaviour. The more visionary thought that education and moral examples pointed by 'philanthropic' landowners were the long-run solution, but practical men saw that a fuller incorporation in the national economy was necessary. Beginning in 1881, the landowners' association carried out a thorough survey to determine the number of smallholders (by this time a source of estate labor) who under the provisions of the 1874 law were exempt from the land tax, and then pressured the government to end the exception. 'Nothing,' decided the SNA Directory, 'would contribute more effectively to the increase of production than the peons' need to cover urgent obligations.'[11] Others thought that the problem could be overcome by extending the system of *inquilinaje*, bringing more people onto the estates, and tying them down by withholding their salary or through the mechanism of the hacienda store. But such an extension could only be carried so far. More people were settled but it was not advantageous to the owner to clutter his estate with workers who might be employed only a few months or even weeks of the year. Another powerful influence was the reduction of alternatives. As owners put more land under cultivation, broke large areas of the coastal range, and fenced and extended grazing areas, the nomadic peons, accustomed to pitching their shacks on vacant land, were evicted or their possibilities for foraging or petty theft made more difficult.

But none of these methods was really effective. The government did institute the new tax – some 60 000 miniscule holdings were liable – but the problems of collection were so costly that it was soon abandoned. Outright coercion or social control was exceedingly difficult given the lack of effective local or national police. The expanding market itself had some effect as peons began to perceive their needs differently. As we move into the twentieth century the difference between rural and urban dress diminishes, an indication that peons were spending more pesos on ready-made clothing. As they settled into the straggling hamlets or rude huts in the interstices of the central valley the odd pot or stick of furniture became necessary.[12]

In the 1870s the problem of sufficient hands became especially acute. The sluggish response of potential workers was first noticeable during the wheat harvest. Low freight rates and insufficiently prepared competitors enabled Chilean *hacendados* to sell grain at a profit in England for a few decades of the nineteenth century and although some machinery was employed in reaping and threshing, increased output depended on a massive use of labor.

The need for seasonal labor may be best seen in reaping. Between

Chilean Rural Society

1850 and 1875 Chilean grain cultivation increased from about 120 000 to 450 000 hectares. In the common measurements of the time this meant an increase of about 173 000 cuadras or 1 730 000 tareas. The maximum output per worker was 1 tarea a day. In any one Department there was a period of two to three weeks during which grain must be cut. If harvested too green, the kernel shriveled; if too ripe the grain shattered and was lost. But over the entire length of central Chile – because of different growing seasons – this period was extended to about forty-five days. Reaping began in Aconcagua in early December and continued until late January south of the Maule. Given this fact and the knowledge that some workers followed the harvest from north to south, one may assume that each worker could have cut 30–50 tareas a season. At this rate all of central Chile would have required between 35 000 and 50 000 additional workers for the wheat harvest alone. It is against the background of rapidly increasing need for field hands, combined with the reluctance of the floating mass of men to give up their accustomed leisure for a tiny wage, that the constant complaints about the scarcity of labor must be read. Compared with other regions just then also responding to the European demand for grain, Chile had an abundance of potential workers. Table 28 gives an indication of population density in three regions primarily dedicated to grain in the 1870s and helps explain why in Australia and the new lands of the American West farmers were quick to use the new machines.

Table 28   Ratios of population to land area: selected areas, 1875–82

Area and population density	Central Chile[a]	Victoria (Australia)[b]	San Joaquin valley (California)[c]
Total area (km²)	33 500	34 000	50 500
Wheat area (km²)	1500	3656	3628
Population	450 000	117 000	80 000
Pop. per km²-area	14	3.4	1.6
Pop. per km²-wheat	300	32	23

Sources:

a Data are for the present-day provinces of O'Higgins, Colchagua, Curicó, and Talca—the area between the Maipo and Maule Rivers. Population data are from *Censo* (1875); wheat harvest and acreage data are from *AE* (1874).

b Data on area under wheat from twenty wheat-growing shires in Victoria are for years 1881–2. See Dunsdorfs, *The Australian Wheat-Growing Economy*, pp. 489, 532–4. Population data are from the same source.

c California data for area under wheat represents the counties of Calaveras, Fresno, Mariposa, Merced, San Joaquin, Stanislaus, Tulare, and Tuolomne. See E. E. Martin, 'The Development of Wheat Culture in the San Joaquin Valley 1846–1900' (Master's thesis, University of California, Berkeley, 1924), p. xi.

In neighboring Argentina – the only other Latin-American country to export grain – landowners began to fill this same need by attracting thousands of seasonal workers from Italy and Spain. But these immigrants commanded fairly high wages – perhaps eight to ten times the going rate in Chile – and machines increasingly came into use on the Pampa.[13] Chile, in contrast to all of these countries, had the possibility of a great many inexpensive laborers. Yet, there is hardly a volume of the SNA's *Boletín* that does not lament the 'shortage of hands' ('escaséz de brazos'). More than anything else, these complaints reflect the stress of a more demanding system of production. Up to then this 'masa flotante' was unaccustomed to the discipline or sustained output found in countries where the triumph of liberal capitalism had wrenched men out of traditional environments and more fully integrated them into the market. At the same time, landowners whose prospects for gain were now so promising, insisted on a rapid turnabout in the attitudes of the peons and were appalled but quite powerless to do much about it when they did not respond.[14]

There is no doubt that the peons were slow to respond in part because what was now called 'sloth' and 'apathy' were built into the society. Nearly a hundred feast days and holidays were celebrated a year, alcoholism was always a problem, and although the peon was capable of backbreaking work for a few days, he could leave as quickly as he came. There was the 'inveterate custom' of not working Mondays and often Tuesdays, and in any event, the organisation of agriculture in the nineteenth century meant that most tasks were seasonal, and workers were unaccustomed to sustained effort. During the critical period of the grain harvest landowners often paid for piecework, or in the case of reaping, by the tarea. Yet it appears that the daily cutting rate of Chilean workers – perhaps because they held to the sickle in place of the scythe – was much lower than elsewhere.[15] Another indication of the massive use of labor in Chilean agriculture is seen in Table 29. The data show the number of man-days used to produce 30 metric quintals (about 110 bushels) on one cuadra of land. Chilean labor use was at least three times as high as in the United States for a given output. The explanation for the difference is that capital investment was greater, technology (even for hand tools) better, and despite lower yields in the United States, North American labor was more efficient.

Accustomed to attracting easily a large number of unskilled men with little cash outlay, the *hacendado* looked upon any temporary bottleneck that restricted his supply of labor and forced him to pay a slightly higher money wage as 'escaséz de brazos'. But in fact there was a surplus of men. From 1850 on, large numbers of people migrated from the agricultural zone. From 1865 to 1895, the population of rural central Chile stayed almost constant at 960 000 to 990 000. But in the urban departments of Valparaíso and Santiago and the northern mining districts the increase was from 469 000 to 828 000, an annual rate of 1.9 per cent. The first large-scale attraction for peon labor was the Valparaíso to Santiago railroad.

Table 29   Labor use in wheat production: United States and Chile, 1829–95

Year	Method	United States	Chile
1829–30[a]	All hand labor	32 man-days	—
1856[b]	All hand labor	—	92 man-days
1873[c]	Machine threshing	—	53
1880[d]	All machine	15	—
1894[e]	Machine (Kansas)	11	—
1895[f]	Machine (California)	1.3	—

Sources:

[a] Leo Rogin, *The Introduction of Farm Machinery*, pp. 72–8.

[b] Claudio Gay, *Agricultura*, vol. II, p. 44. I have added 8 man-days for threshing and adjusted for different yields.

[c] *BSNA*, vol. V (1873), p. 9.

[d] *The Statistical History of the United States from Colonial Times to the Present* (Stanford, 1965), p. 281.

[e] Rogin, 218 (unit D).

[f] Rogin, 217 (unit 26). For corroboration of Rogin's data, see W. P. Rutter, *Wheat Growing in Canada, The United States, and the Argentine* (London, 1911), p. 110.

Begun in 1852 and completed in 1863, construction through the rugged coast range required a work force of about 10 000 men a year. In 1868 Henry Meiggs, the famous 'Yankee Pizarro,' turned his talents to railroad construction in Peru and for the next four years migration from central Chile occurred on an unprecedented scale. Upward of 25 000 peons went to Peru between 1868 and 1872. This movement of people, most of them peons from central Chile, provoked long speeches in Congress and several introspective articles by members of the SNA. Threatened by the prospect of higher wages if workers could not be retained in the agricultural zone, the landowners enlisted the help of the clergy. Directives were sent by the bishop to each parish priest that instructed them to inveigh against the destruction of family life that emigration would cause.[16]

A proposed law to limit the exodus was ignored, however, and the

SNA shrank with horror from the suggestion that 'coolies' might be brought in to work the fields. There is no evidence that agricultural wages were driven up because of the emigration to Peru. Nor did agriculture suffer; on the contrary, the years bewteen 1868 and 1872 were ones of peak cereal output. Amid the pages of discussion on the 'escaséz de brazos' in the SNA *Boletín*, the always perspicacious Menandier noted that 'the peon emigrates for lack of work.' Indeed others thought that without the safety valve of emigration the rural population would sooner or later 'conspire against the established order.' Emigration from the agricultural zone continued – as may be seen in the nearly constant population of rural Chile – while the cities and mining districts grew at a rapid rate. Some Chileans crossed the Andes to acquire small holdings in Mendoza and others worked on the early attempts to dig a Panama canal.[17]

The records of the hacienda of Vichiculén, some 80 kilometers north of Santiago in Aconcagua, provide a rare glimpse of rural labor from the point of view of the estate's accountant. Anywhere from sixty to eighty peons worked on Vichiculén throughout the year at an average wage of 19–20 centavos a day. In January 1872, precisely the time when landowners' complaints about 'escaséz de brazos' are most noticed, Vichiculén paid 20 centavos a day for over a hundred peons [2214 man-days]. Table 30 shows the number of man-days and the average daily wage paid at Vichiculén during 1872–3.

Table 30   Number of man-days and average daily wage paid at the hacienda of Vichiculén, 1872–3 (in centavos of current pesos)

Month (1872)	Man-days	Average wage	Month (1873)	Man-days	Average wage
January	2214	0.20 cent.	January	—	—
February	1269	0.21	February	1109	0.21 cent.
March	924	0.23	March	1084	0.20
April	1656	0.22	April	1084	0.20
May	1659	0.19	May	1351	0.21
June	915	0.19	June	—	—
July	778	0.19	July	661	0.23
August	—	—	August	363	0.23
September	—	—	September	661	0.29
October	784	0.20	October	596	0.28
November	1206	0.24	November	757	0.29
December	—	—	December	861	0.23

Source: Account book of the hacienda of Vichiculén (Aconcagua province).

Here we see a remarkably constant wage of around 21 centavos a day during 1872 regardless of the season. The records of Vichiculén do not reveal all the activities on the hacienda. There were some 260 hectares of wheat and barley, about 2400 head of cattle and 460 horses, and unspecified acreage in *chacra* or horticulture. Within the hacienda there were also a number of small copper mines whose records were kept separately, but it is interesting to notice that miners' wages were generally about 40 centavos or twice that of agricultural workers. Since there is so much we don't know, it is difficult to explain why the numbers of peons employed fluctuate as they do. Certainly it seems unusual that 28–9 cents were needed to employ the small numbers of off-season workers in September and October of 1873 or that as the wage fell to 23 centavos in December, the number of peons willing to offer their services should increase. There may be local explanation for this but the hacienda records alone are inadequate. We do have a picture, however, of the massive labor inputs in this estate and an indication of an elastic supply curve for labor, a picture that conflicts with the land-owners' complaints of labor shortage.[18]

The uncertainty about wages that is apparent in the Vichiculén records is compounded as one tries to construct a picture of peon wages for central Chile over a long period of time. First of all, any kind of wage data are scarce. The best source are hacienda account books but few of these exist either from private or ecclesiastical estates. Scientific farming and the best rural accountants were both done away when the meticulously managed Jesuit estates were sold in the late eighteenth century. A few *libros de cuenta* can still occasionally be found in private libraries or abandoned trunks, and others are filed in the Judicial Archival collections that pertain to lawsuits where owners or administrators were forced to 'render accounts.' Even when private accounting records can be found the problem is not solved. In the Vichiculén records, the wage is expressed in total man-days paid, and in the case of the voluminous records of El Melón, only the total peon wage bill for each month is given. Beyond this, there are the normal complications. Peons were remunerated with money, payment in kind, perquisites, tokens for exchange in the hacienda store, and combinations of all these. They were paid by the day, week, and month, and they were paid differently in different regions. The testimony of Luis Galdames, a scholar and reliable witness, is worth quoting at length: 'It is surprising to notice the extreme inequality of salaries in the country-side . . . From one *fundo* to another, separated by no more than a range of hills, or a stream, the daily rate varies from $.40 to $1.60. This is not due as one might think to the abundance or shortage of hands in a given moment (which does influence the rate but is far from being the most important factor), but rather to the various systems of remuneration and the diverse kinds of workers that are used in agriculture.'[19]

I have taken some pains to indicate the difficulty of putting together a proper index of peon wages because when I began my work I thought it would be possible. However, without long runs of data, the sort that might be found in well-kept hacienda account books, we can only admire the diligence and good fortune of Jan Bazant in Mexico and fall back on scattered data and published accounts. Few observers failed to comment on peon wages. Many of these informants were casual travelers but a few – Gay, Gilliss and Rumbold among them – were knowledgeable and critical. There are also a number of painstaking statistical surveys of various years. Urízar Garfias' *Estadística de Maule,* for example, the 1874 and 1923 *Anuario estadístico,* and after 1906, the *Oficina del Trabajo,* although primarily concerned with industrial labor, occasionally reported on rural conditions. Finally, the SNA *Boletín* especially in the 1870s when *hacendados* and politicians were agitated by problems of rural labor, provides several unsentimental and perceptive reports. With these I have combined the data from a number of private hacienda records to make Table 31.

During this same period the cost of living for rural peons increased as well but it is exceedingly difficult to determine how much. Even if we had the prices for clothing and shelter the task would be arduous; as it is, I have assembled the prices for three main items in the peons' diet to serve as a rough indication of well-being. The prices are the average wholesale quotations in Santiago. The weighting of the index is based on various descriptions of peons' diet, assuming that it did not appreciably change over this period. When the two series are put together the general indication of the real wage trend can be seen in Figure 6.

From the 1860s on, peon wages steadily fell behind the more rapidly rising cost of food. We must be clear what this means. It does not mean that laborers were necessarily worse off by 1925, because by then they most likely worked more days of the year. The pay lists of haciendas and the impressions of a great many observers in mid-nineteenth century give the unmistakable impression that peons worked only a few weeks of the year and often only a few days of the week. A better market from the late nineteenth century on led to a more diversified agriculture. This required more year-round hands, and a reduction in the number of holidays permitted fewer excuses and less dissipation. Despite a con-

Table 31   Estimates and indexes of peon wages in agriculture and index of basic food prices: central Chile, 1850–1925 (in centavos and pesos)

Years	Peon wages			Food price index
	Range	Average	Index	
1846–50	20–5 cents	22.5	90	57
1851–5	20–5	22.5	90	86
1856–60	20–5	22.5	90	111
1861–5	20–30	25	100	85
1866–70	20–30	25	100	100
1871–5	25–30	27.5	110	123
1876–80	25–30	27.5	110	134
1881–5	25–35	30	120	157
1886–90	25–35	30	120	184
1891–5	30–40	35	140	204
1896–1900	40–5	42.5	170	255
1901–5	60–100	80	320	355
1906–10	1.00–1.40 pesos	1.20	480	656
1911–15	1.20–1.60	1.40	560	874
1916–20	1.50–2.20	1.85	740	1161
1921–5	2.00–3.00	2.50	1000	1495

Sources: Food price index from Appendix 1; peon wages from the notarial collections of Santiago, Rancagua, Rengo, and Talca; *AE* (1874) and 1923, vol. VII, p. 123; innumerable travelers' accounts and other books; and the account books of the haciendas of Cunaco, El Huique, Vichiculén, La Quinta (Colchagua), and Ñuble.

Our data are too uncertain to indicate anything beyond a general trend. There are important difficulties in using food prices as an indicator. First, the prices are Santiago prices whereas the wage data are drawn from throughout central Chile: secondly, there may be some qualitative changes in the items; for example, the unit prices for a cow may be misleading because the average weight of the animal probably increased. Peon diets may have slightly changed in proportion but the three items we have listed were basic throughout the period. The use of food prices at all may be questioned since some peons received a ration or were able to produce some of their own subsistence on tiny plots; thus, to the extent they were remunerated in food—and this is more the case with *inquilinos*—their well-being was less prejudiced by rising food prices. Yet, with all this it remains true that rural laborers had to obtain food for themselves when not working and help to support relatives so it is obvious that prices did affect them. Moreover, food prices are the only indicator we have; and although one may quibble with details, the tendency seems clear.

stant or slightly falling real wage it appears that labor productivity increased; in part because of some investment in clearing, irrigation, fertilisers and slightly improved equipment, but also because of longer days and closer supervision. More clerks, *mayordomos*, and section bosses were employed for this purpose, leading to an important increase in estate *empleados* after the 1860s.

None of these changes – a more stable work force, more output per man – makes sense unless we understand the changes in settlement pattern that shifted the supply of labor in central Chile. Once again we are confronted with the problem of faulty data and changing definitions. The nineteenth century defined a *gañán* as a person, 'without

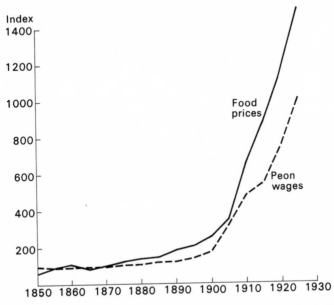

Fig. 6   Indexes of daily peon wages in agriculture and basic food prices,
1850–1925

residence or fixed destiny who prefers manual labor in rural or urban tasks,' and the census of 1865 put about 120 000 in this category. Obviously some of these people worked in the ports, others helped build roads or worked on urban construction projects. Many found part-time employment in agriculture, helping with the harvest or roundups, often for only a few weeks of the year and for little pay other than the abundant drink and food handed out on such occasions.

As time went on, some of these people left for the mines or cities and others settled into the dusty hill towns of the coastal range or gathered in the clusters of shacks that were knocked together all through the central valley in the later nineteenth century. Closer to the haciendas and *fundos* that could more regularly use their labor, these future minifundists could often supplement their daily wage with the produce – a few hens, a pig, a few rows of vegetables – from the back yard. The population in these settlements increased through internal growth as larger plots were fragmented for heirs, or through *de facto* occupation by squatters, an action generally overlooked by landowners since the land occupied was usually marginal strips lining roads or streams and the families settled in this way formed a convenient source of casual labor. The 1930 census likened these 'groups of small agricultural plots . . . to what in Spain is called *huerta*.'[20] Still, although many new groups of squatters formed in the valley, many remained in the small string villages in the dry land of the coastal range and came down for the wheat and *vendimia*. This pattern, in fact, has persisted to the present; the *costinos* are considered indispensable for harvests.

These loose settlements in the coastal range or valley hardly provided a basis for community life; a family's livelihood depended on employment on the estates and many days were spent on the move, seeking work. One must be certain not to see in these straggling settlements anything resembling an established traditional peasant community. Contemporaries saw the accelerating change in occupational patterns; already in the 1870s a landowner and Senator noted with satisfaction that, 'one no longer sees as many of those ambulatory peons [*peons ambulantes*] as before.'[21] But it was not just that existence was precarious in the extreme but the resources in even these marginal resting places were sharply limited. Some plots could absorb or be subdivided to accommodate larger families or heirs but an irreducible minimum was soon reached and then sons or daughters had to find a place on the estates or leave. It is from this element of rural society that most rural-urban migrants undoubtedly came. By 1935–6, the agricultural census shows that 60 000 smallholders (0–5 hectares) but a great many more families (twenty, thirty thousand?) were inhabitants of the straggling *caseríos* and while not counted as smallholders or minifundists, they actually filled that role.

The data in Table 32 are offered to provide only the most general notion of population and occupational change. It is clear that rural population, and by inference the number of people engaged in agriculture, grew very little between 1865 and 1930: the censuses show an increase of 952 000 to 1 047 000. Obviously many migrated. We have as yet no close study of internal migrations for this period but Carlos Hurtado estimates that 481 000 left the rural areas of central Chile between 1865 and 1907 alone.[22] Service tenants and *empleados* also increased: the 1930 population census and the 1935 agricultural census agree on nearly 60 000 *inquilino* and 18 000 *empleado* families. As near as I am able to calculate, the comparable figures for 1865 were approximately 30 000 and 5000 respectively. The figures for day laborers and marginal, underemployed, are meaningless without our previous discussion of labor quality. There may have been about the same number of men around in 1865 as in 1930, but it is clear that by the later date they were putting in more and longer days. A clearer

Table 32 Estimates of population and agricultural occupations in central Chile, 1865 and 1930

Population categories	1865	1930
Total population	1 252 000	2 375 000
Total rural population	952 000	1 047 000
Service tenant (*inquilinos*) and	[30 000]	59 000
Empleado households	[5000]	18 000
Day laborers	125 000	133 000
Marginal, underemployed	[35 000]	[8 000]

Source: *Censos* of 1865 and 1930. Figures in brackets are rough estimates.

picture of changing settlement patterns and occupations can be obtained from Figure 7 where approximate proportional changes are presented. Movement of people was in several directions and the arrows only indicate principal flows. Some of the marginal, 'floating mass' became more stable by settling in valley hamlets but people from both groups account for the growing urban migration; a few service tenants fulfilled a persistent goal of getting enough money together to buy a small *fundito* or *parcela* in the neighborhood; but up to 1930 at least, the net flow of those who stayed in the country was toward the large estates whose increased area and diversified output required more dependable labor. It is to this process that we now turn and we shall see that during the years following 1860, the institution of *inquilinaje* was extended and by 1930 had hardened into a conservative symbiosis with the hacienda system that was not shaken until recent years.

Under the impact of a growing market, the system of *inquilinaje,* or service tenantry, was modified in a number of ways. First those tenants who from earlier times had been allotted relatively generous perquisites were required to supply the estate with additional workers. Whereas one *peón obligado* was the maximum service required of an *inquilino* before 1850, now he was asked to provide two and even three full-time workers. Already in 1862, for example, as the hacienda of Pichidegua turned to wheat cultivation, the number of *peones obligados* required of each *inquilino* was stepped up. Of the twenty-one *inquilino* households, twelve had to supply two peons each. By 1870 this process had become commonplace. Menandier noted that 'the work load imposed on the *inquilino* has increased many times over.' In Caupolicán the 'better class' of *inquilino* (or the *inquilino de a caballo*) supplied two year-

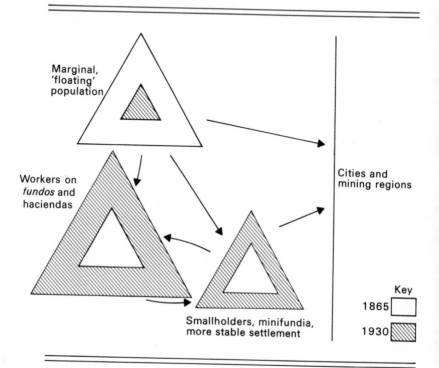

Fig. 7   Changing settlement patterns in central Chile, *ca* 1865 and 1930

round laborers each. Even the *inquilino de a pie*, who enjoyed fewer perquisites, was expected to work himself and furnish as well any son old enough to 'swing a hoe.' Adults living in his household (*allegados*) were also required to work.One can see in the upland hacienda of El Peumo a clear picture of the relationship between perquisites and service requirements as well as the complex and varied arrangements that had evolved. The 'first-class' *inquilino* furnished two peons for the entire year. The *inquilino* was responsible for remunerating the peons; the hacienda only provided the daily food ration. It was calculated that each worker cost the *inquilino* 50–60 pesos a year (about 20 centavos a day). Since the peon was often a member of the *inquilino*'s household, the 'wage' was probably most often paid in kind. Even if the *inquilino* had to go outside his own kin for the peon, he must rarely have paid in cash. The *inquilino* was expected to remunerate his workers from his own earnings on the hacienda.[23]

At the same time that the labor requirements of the original *inquilinos* were stepped up, new tenants settled and received reduced land allotments. This extension of *inquilinaje* in a modified form was particularly noticeable in the 1870s and 1880s. A well-known manual of operating instructions for rural estates speaks of the *inquilino–peón* who was allotted a dwelling and a small piece of land 'not exceeding forty varas [about 35 metres] to a side in order to raise hens and vegetables when there is water.'[24]

These new tenants were selected from among the families of the *inquilinos* or from the *peón–gañan* class. Many peons preferred to deal directly with the estate rather than work through the *inquilinos*. The tenant-peons then received a smaller *cerco* than had *inquilinos* before 1850, and if necessary this was supplemented by a small salary. This process was at work in 1871 on the hacienda of Viluco just south of Santiago where more than 200 *peones sedentarios* each received a house surrounded by a $\frac{1}{2}$-cuadra ($\frac{3}{4}$-hectare) garden plot. Menandier repeatedly urged the extension of *inquilinaje* and thought that the sole defects of the new dwellings on Viluco were their unnecessary comfort and high cost; it would have been better to build more and cheaper buildings to house all the hacienda peons. Furthermore, 'in order to procure a good number of able, moral, and constant workers' it was necessary to increase the number of dwellings of the sedentary peons.[25]

The 1870s was a time of economic leveling off of lower rural society. More prosperous tenants were required to contribute labor service commensurate with their perquisites, while the landless peon was raised to the only slightly higher level of tenant–peon in return for more reliable labor. This tendency was not lost on contemporary observers. An article in the *Boletín* noted that whereas in earlier times the *inquilino* as head of the household had also been the *patrón* of several cuadras of land, an increased cereal cultivation had effectively led to diminished perquisites. A comment on the 'growing poverty' of the *inquilinos* that is probably only slightly exaggerated will serve to sum up the process taking place in the 1870s: '[In earlier years] the horses, cows, and sheep that often were numerous formed for the *inquilinos* a relative fortune. Does any of this exist after sixty years of independence and free commerce? . . . Unfortunately everything has been changed . . . the proprietor is obliged to obtain all the possible advantage out of the worker who now lives on his land.'[26]

Up to now we have mainly been concerned with men, but as any farmer or observer of rural Chile knows, this is a serious omission. For each *empleado* there was at least one *empleada* who worked as a household servant, or milkmaid. But wives and daughters also worked in the fields tending the crops of the tiny *posesión*, or herding livestock and assisting in heavier tasks on the estates. 'It is not possible to excuse women from [field work] if labor shortage threatens to delay the hacienda's operation,' admonished Manuel José Balmaceda in his well-known *Manual*, but evidence from Claudio Gay to the present makes clear that women contributed a great deal to the estate labor force and not just in times of peak labor needs. Just how much is difficult to say but any attempt at a quantitative calculation of labor productivity that omits women is further removed from reality.[27]

It is difficult, however, to determine the value of women's contribution to agriculture (and in addition to field work, homespuns, handicrafts, and cottage industry would have to be considered). Even with better census data the same problem we saw with men is present here: did 1000 female workers put in as many days or hours in 1875 as in 1930? As the word spread of opportunities for maids and washer women in the cities and new roads and railroads made it easier for them to get there, women left the rural areas. This sexual imbalance can be clearly seen in the 1930 census where in such typical rural communities as Requínoa or Palmilla (province of Colchagua) the number of single men aged 20–9 was almost double the number of unmarried women while Santiago was fifty-four per cent female. But simply because they were fewer does not necessarily mean that women's contribution was less. It may well be that in a more stable and disciplined rural setting with demand for more diversified tasks, women contributed more; but I know of no statistical evidence or method that would support such a hypothesis.

The labor system described in its protean form by Gay in the early years of the Republic reached maturity in the later nineteenth century and Chilean landowners soon regarded *inquilinaje* as their peculiar institution. Where before few demands were put on *inquilinos* and they worked in isolation and lived virtually unnoticed lives, now as we move into the later nineteenth century, discussion on both the justification and the evil of the system multiplied. 'What would agriculture be without this element of vital importance?' a writer for the National Agricultural Society asked in 1887. Without *inquilinos*, he thought, 'modern agriculture' would be impossible. Service tenants provided security, stability and routine.[28]

These were ideas born of necessity and a growing conviction that the lower rural society was beyond redemption and much of it hopelessly if not dangerously inept. Shortly after Independence there was the occasional view that reform might rescue the lower rural classes. But this optimism faded as landowners' opportunities widened and life became more individualistic while the *bajo pueblo* showed little sign of losing its 'nomadic spirit,' sloth, or addiction to alcohol.[29] The common assumption of many landowners which permitted them to see poverty in the natural order of things was compounded by their racial views. It was otherwise, thought Horace Rumbold, 'not easy to account for the somewhat desponding views held here by many liberal-minded persons as to the possibility of imparting culture and habits of morality to the lower orders by means of education.' The 1919 Assembly of Landowners heard an explanation that many must have shared: 'The weakness of our agricultural production . . . is the consequence of mental retardation [*retroceso mental*] produced in Chile and in all Spanish America, by the crossing of the conquistador with the aboriginal race.'[30]

It would be a mistake, of course, to think that all landowners held these views and as we shall see below, much of the criticism that developed around the growing 'social question' at the turn of the century was directed at the system that made victims of the working class. Most landowners were probably uninterested in explanations or justifications but simply saw before them potential workers who had to be forced if possible, cajoled if necessary, but in any event formed into an obedient and stable work force. As it turned out both the stick and the carrot were employed in the formation and preservation of *inquilinaje*.

Before resident workers were in great demand, rural people lined up to obtain a *posesión* on the estate and this favorable land–labor ratio gave landowners a distinct advantage in dealing with *inquilinos*. Few observers fail to point out the extreme respect if not subservience with which *inquilinos* treated their master. In some cases they humbly removed hat and spurs before an audience with the *hacendado* and the form 'usía' was used in address to Su Merced, that is, to the master, the 'semi-Dios, owner of the hacienda and the wills of all his faithful vassals.'[31] Agreements between owner and worker were always verbal (few *inquilinos* could tell one letter from the next); disputes were summarily settled by the owner, tenants could be evicted in a moment's notice – in short their welfare depended in large measure on the whim of the landowner. Paradoxically the best evidence for the tenants' inferior position is the nearly complete lack of notice of them in local courts or in the records of private estates. *Inquilinos* are the most anonymous, least visible of rural inhabitants. They were rarely given a money wage and although there are occasional mention of fines in the 'credit' side of hacienda account books, usually the *inquilinos'* complaints or crimes were too insignificant to be recorded in the private records or in the provincial court.[32] The countless pages of litigation useful for information on the lower classes in the colonial epoch are here in the Republic, nearly non-existent.[33]

The relationship formed between owner and tenant was not much different from other areas of Spanish America where a similar agrarian system developed. In Mexico, 'The hacienda owner [assumed] the rôle of a stern and irascible father, prepared to guide the steps of his worker-children, ready to unleash his temper and anger upon them when provoked.' But the ties that bound worker and owner were not only those of fear and repression: 'The *inquilino* has those ties which unite him with the owner or land on which he has been born and passed his life working; ties, which although weak, establish nevertheless a certain community of interest and compassion.'[34] A principal duty of service tenants was to guard the estate against *forasteros* – the outsiders – and to ride in escort with the owner, or to carry messages. Most came to identify with the estate itself; the land was his land, the cattle better, the bulls braver than on other haciendas. This attachment between *inquilino* and hacienda went deeper than the owner himself. Landowners bought and traded property with surprising frequency and someone has correctly pointed out that Chilean landowners appear to love the land but not any particular piece of it. This was not so with the service tenantry who often in fact had a longer history of residence than the owner. This long-standing 'attachment to place' can be seen in the suspicion with which all *forasteros* were seen during the recent agrarian reform or how ready *inquilinos* were to organise 'their' *fundo* and quickly exclude other workers.[35]

The landowner's ability to dominate his estate like a 'veritable monarch' or a 'semi-Dios' was possible in the absence of competition for labor or the lack of any alternatives for workers, but this began to change in the later nineteenth century at the same time as the need for workers increased. '*Inquilinaje* is an institution *sui generis* and far from combating it, landowners and legislators should make an effort to develop it on a larger scale,' wrote Julio Menandier, the astute editor of the *Boletín*. Menandier and a great many thoughtful landowners were troubled by the difficulty of obtaining sufficient workers at the going wage, a situation that became acute for the first time in the 1870s as thousands of men and women from the rural districts followed the new rails and roads into the mining zones and the cities. The solution put forth by a number of *hacendados* and observers was not to compete on a wage basis because an increased salary often had adverse social effects: workers would squander the entire week's salary in a few hours of revelry or trivial knick-knacks. Rather – and here the ideas of both *progresista* and more traditional landowners coincided – the ill-fated assumptions of *laissez-faire* should be abandoned. If a wage must be paid let only a small part be in *moneda sonante*, i.e. jingling coin, and the rest in vouchers redeemable at the hacienda store. This would make it more difficult to buy foolish and needless items in the towns or from ambulatory merchants and also, hopefully, reduce the amount thrown away on drink and gambling. Beyond that, the psychological importance of payment in kind was well understood. The handout of rations was a daily reminder to workers that their well-being depended on the estate while the absence of spending money restricted to the hacienda store whatever acquisitive urges the *inquilino* had and dampened his interest in things the outside world offered.[36]

There were a number of ways workers could be brought into the system without payment of money. Where before a man and his family would simply be shown a small plot on the estate and be expected to put up their own flimsy shelter, in the 1870s and after landowners often offered a ready-made shack and used this device to *arraigar* (root) workers to the estate. The SNA pointed to the examples of Pomerania and East Prussia where landowners trying to increase the service tenant̃y obtained excellent results by building shelter for their workers. Other 'philanthropic' landowners made a practice of distributing watermelons among their workers or advancing on credit items from the hacienda *pulpería*.[37]

Although suggestions were made early on about the need and use of 'algunas distracciones,' such as horse races or festivals of folk dances, that would help gather the working classes around the estate and create a better sense of community, the suggestions were rarely followed up and rural people had little distraction save the Sunday or holiday gatherings around the *pulpería*, occasions that frequently ended in drunken brawls. Many *hacendados* in fact were assailed by the twin onslaughts of greed and doubt when it came to such gatherings. On the one hand the sale of drink – *aguardiente*, wine or *chicha* – was an excellent source of revenue but on the other, especially before the countryside had an effective police force, the dissipation and violence were excessive. In the 1920s, several estates marked off fields for football and although this may have contributed to hacienda solidarity as long as games were strictly local affairs, organised league play soon brought rural workers in contact with outside teams and, as trucks and buses began to appear, inevitably with men from other regions and cities. In recent times such organised sports have been an important agent in transmitting fashions and values.[38]

These rather rustic bread and circus devices were effective in molding around the estate the kind of labor force landowners wanted. The distribution of daily rations, gifts at weddings and births, handouts during times of food shortage, 'which are a work of charity and also advantageous to the [landowner's] interests,' and even a watermelon for 'the grateful workers' were reminders of the source from which blessings flowed. Even next to an obvious labor source – for example on the outskirts of Santiago – landowners set aside valuable plots of land on their estates and took on the task of administration in order to have at their beck and call the loyal servant, dependent on the well-being of the estate and the landowner's whim.[39]

It is commonly supposed that the landowner's ability to enforce his will on the service tenantry was greater than in fact it was. We should recall that although the larger cities had quite effective police forces the countryside until the late 1920s depended on a handful of ill-equipped constables, *ad hoc* vigilante units led by the *hacendados*, and the watchfulness of the tenantry. Thus for most of the period we are concerned with, bandits and the rare armed group of maurauders were an occasional menace and the means of enforcing civil law – of collecting small debts, for example, or bringing trespassers to justice – were informal. Here the Church was of some importance. Most haciendas had their own chapel where both the *hacendado*'s and workers' families heard Mass, there were joint celebrations of saints' days, and the resident priest who gamed and supped with the landowner could be counted on to inveigh against disloyalty and immorality from the pulpit. Occasionally religious brotherhoods such as the Corazón de Jesus, established by a Larraín on a *fundo* near Rancagua, were instrumental in converting the 'vice-ridden' into model workers, men who 'faithfully fulfilled all their obligations.' In other cases the *missión* – a series of processions and Masses that involved the entire hacienda population – helped bind the social unit together. 'My mother,' recalled Ramón Subercaseaux of one such occasion in Pirque, 'was always satisfied with the result [of the *misión*] because marriages were performed, a truce was imposed on drinking and theft and finally, stolen money, animals and other objects were returned to the surprised owners.' A principal aim of such ceremonies was to 'strengthen the attachment and affection of the workers towards their masters,' but here again the effectiveness of the Church was limited to the use of suggestion and admonition.[40]

Under the circumstances, landowners were required to exercise considerable discretion in their control in the countryside. This became more and more the case as better communications and the intrusion of the city permitted rural workers to glimpse an alternative way of life. The limits to a landowner's authority come through clearly in the rude language of one Rafael Herrera, the administrator of Las Condes, a livestock hacienda stretching for uncounted kilometres into the cordillera behind Santiago.[41] An administrator, Herrera tells us, must often be 'strong and just' (*recto i fuerte*) but the job requires much tact and one must 'loosen the reins to tranquilize the people and make them understand with good and prudent declarations the way things must be done.' With the *inquilinos* and other workers ('la jente sirbiente, ho inquilinos') there are many times when one must 'tolerate any number of demands because on this hacienda there are so many places where a worker can go to live . . . one fires an *inquilino* and he says "well I'm not going" and then when he sees there's no hope of staying what he does is move to another place or some settlement or along the road and there mocks the sentence. One complains again to the owner on whose land he lives and the man moves again and now besides mocking he declares himself an enemy and since it's never good to have enemies even though there is nothing to fear for one's self, the master's [*patrón*] interests are endangered . . . this is why one must put up with impertinences of the workers and before firing one, try to arrange things with prudence and patience.' It is not, as Lawrence Stone has pointed out, either willful romanticism or black reaction to recognise that important restraints were imposed on landowners by public opinion or that paternalist employers demonstrated a sense of obligation toward their workers that was often advantageous to both parties.[42]

As threats to the hacienda system began to appear, efforts were made to strengthen paternalistic ties. One of the arguments presented in a 1913 Catholic University seminar designed 'to orient and shape the consciousness of those who direct, the *patrones*,' succinctly expressed the prevailing ethic: 'Given the state of dependence in which the field worker of Chile normally lives and his rudimentary culture, one cannot expect the improvement of his material and moral condition through his own initiative. This is a Christian and humanitarian task of the highest degree, which it is incumbent upon the social class which utilises the efforts of the worker to carry out. The masters, then, are those called upon to take the initiative in this chore in Chile and they are the only ones whose intervention will always be effective, given the unrivalled influence they enjoy over their subordinates.'[43] The halting steps taken toward improving the lot of the service tenantry about this time (the 1920s) were in keeping with the view landholders held of 'their' *inquilinos*. The first of the houses that one commonly sees now in the countryside were built then. Instead of mud and straw, *sólidas casas* of adobe and tile were put up, and the occasional latrine dug. The best indication that these measures were woefully inadequate – although the fact was obvious to any casual observer – may be found not in the increasingly strident attacks of critics but in the words of the system's defenders. The SNA *Boletín* pointed out, 'even though our distinguished habitual readers may feel offended,' that *hacendados* had done little, very little, to improve the condition of their workers. *El Mercurio*, the principal daily paper, charged in 1911 that the condition of labor 'is simply monstrous, unworthy of a civilized country and an affront to Chilean landowners.'[44]

By 1935–6, the second Agricultural Census gives a fairly reliable statistical picture of the service tenantry.[45] Although *inquilinos* (here the term refers to heads of households) themselves made up about thirty per cent of the total rural labor force, they provided the estates with nearly 65 000 more workers out of their own households. These 'peons o gañanes, miembros de la familia de inquilinos i empleados' were just that: sons, daughters or more distant relatives who lived *allegado* in the *inquilinos*' houses. These were the *obligados* or extra hands required by the landlords of the *inquilinos* and their large number here reflects the mounting pressure applied to the service tenantry, the culmination of a process begun some seventy years earlier. (See Table 33.)

There has been some confusion over the composition of the labor force, partly because Correa Vergara's widely quoted *Agricultura Chilena*, although taking its data from the 1935 Agricultural Census, gives only the number of heads of *inquilino* households and their percentage of the total work force. Thus it has been assumed that the importance of service tenantry was shrinking and landowners turned to a wage-labor system. But as the figures in Table 33 show, down to 1935 at least, one does not discover in the Central Valley a 'proletarianisation' of the rural work force, but on the contrary, an intensification of an older paternalistic system.[46]

Table 33 Composition of the rural labor force in central Chile, 1935

Categories	Inquilinos (heads of households)	Peons or gañanes (workers who are members of inquilino or empleado households)	Afuerinos (workers who are not members of inquilino or empleado households)	empleados (black-smiths, car-penters, warehouse keepers, etc.)	Total workers
No. of workers	58 701	64 889	54 785	18 492	196 867
Percentage of total	29.8%	32.9%	27.8%	9.5%	100%

Source: Dirección general de estadística, *Censo de Agricultura*: 1935–6 (Santiago, 1938), pp. 34, 265, 284, 498.

There is a convenient symbol to illustrate the changes that made everything remain the same. At the beginning of our discussion the hacienda chapel and store, built on the estate by the owner, stood near the center of rural life. The first helped forge ties of dependence and loyalty between estate and worker; the second contributed to the hacienda's social and economic control of the local society. By 1930, two new buildings were commonly in sight: the rude schoolhouse and the office of the state police (*retén de Carabineros*). These were frequently not on the estate itself and often built without the landowner's permission. But the lesson of the school no less than the chapel was conservative and the Carabineros stood ready if needed to maintain firmly in control the traditional system of property and privilege.[47]

Actually not much restraint was needed. The service tenantry continued to supply landowners with the labor and votes that underlay their social and political position in the nation. The 'mutually advantageous' arrangements that developed over the previous half century as the rural labor system took on its modern shape hardened into a conservative symbiosis. In 1919–21 the intrusions of urban labor leaders provoked some disturbances; but once they retreated, the country remained essentially passive and quiescent until the heavy urban pressure of recent years.[48]

The absence of even the most feeble revolt by rural workers cannot be easily dismissed, especially when Chile – and much of Spanish America for that matter – is seen against a history of frequent peasant revolts in other parts of the world. Rural isolation and landlord autonomy permitted exploitation, but they also led to a remarkably stable relationship between owner and service tenant. Ties of dependence and obedience grew out of the sixteenth-century Conquest itself but were then reinforced as owner, administrators, *empleados*, and service tenants came to form a hacienda community isolated from city and village community alike. Some observers of the Spanish American hacienda have sought comparisons with large estates in Western and, more recently, with Eastern Europe. In the landlord's insistence on labor services instead of rent, in the expansion of the demesne, in the institution of *robot* labor, the estates east of the Elbe are similar. But the major difference in all the European examples is the presence of a traditional smallholder peasant village that produced a distinct peasant culture and a base for community action. The Chilean estate was itself the community with no elected leaders or public functions or responsibilities beyond the hacienda. Workers heard Mass at the estate chapel, celebrated the saint's day of the owner, rarely produced for an independent market, and accepted the landlord's guidance, discipline and paternalism, and if called upon, voted for him. Rather than the European manor, we may find a closer parallel in the textile factories of the early industrial revolution. Here too, the work force was sealed off from the larger society and made part of the factory 'family.' Workers were disciplined and fined by the owner who was given a free hand by the State, and besides, the threat of being cast out into the desperate sub-proletariat beyond the gates was a powerful stimulus to greater output.[49]

It is no accident that the main place in modern Spanish America where rural revolt did occur was a region of strong, independent villages where a proper peasant – Zapata – emerged as community leader. In Chile the hacienda system remained intact until the 1960s, when governments based primarily on the urban mass and under heavy pressure for lower food prices and political support encouraged rural workers to organise into unions and began to expropriate the haciendas. Even then, the service tenantry was as apt to revolt against modern wage payment and meddling outsiders as against the landowners.

CHAPTER 6

[1] McBride, *Land and Society*, p. 148; Carlos Suera Salvo, 'Tipos chilenos en la novela y en el cuento nacional.' *Anales*, pp. 5–85; Graciela Illanes Adaro, 'Sentimiento estético de la literatura chilena,' *Anales* (1939), pp. 201–41.
[2] For discussion of the reliability of census data and categories, see Appendix 6.

3 Carmagnani, 'Colonial Latin American demography,' pp. 179–91.
4 An example of these labor contracts is the one drawn up by William Wheelwright for 119 peons for six months at 3 reales a day plus rations. This was for the Copiapó railroad in 1850. *CN* (Valparaíso) vol. 86, fol. 355, vol. 88, fol. 94. See also *El Mercurio* (Valparaíso), no. 7606, 7 January 1853, for a note on 'gran caravana de hombres enganchados para las minas de Copiapó y el Huasco.' For a discussion on vagabondage and floating population for an earlier period, see Mario Góngora, 'Vagabundaje y sociedad fronteriza,' pp. 1–41. Gay, *Agricultura*, I, p. 155; *El Mensajero*, 2 (1856), pp. 270–6. The friar was Padre J. J. Guzmán, whose candid description of rural Chile, the *Mensajero* reminded its readers, 'was that of a worthy priest, not a "socialista o republicano rojo".'
5 For Llico, see *AMH*, vol 250 (1853), no fol.; *Archivo de la Intendencia de Talca*, vols. 12, 15, 18. This is the only *intendencia* archive of the central agricultural provinces that is even partially organised. In 1967–8 a group of students cataloged the *Archivo de la Intendencia de Concepción*. *AMI*, vol. 163 (1842), no fol.
6 Manuel Román, *Diccionario de Chilenismos* (Santiago, 1913), 3, pp. 508–9. For a discussion of the present-day practice of *mingaco* (in the Araucanía), see Charles Erasmus, 'Reciprocal Labor: A Study of Its Occurrence and Disappearance among Farming People in Latin America' (Ph.D. diss., University of California, Berkeley, 1955). *El Agricultor*, no. 10 (April 1840), pp. 1–16; Gay, II, p. 34.
7 Gay, *Agricultura*, I, pp. 198–203; F. Urízar Garfias, *Repertorio chileno* (Santiago, 1835), p. 7.
8 Daniel Barros Grez, *Proyecto de división*, p. 4. The data apply to the area between the Maipo and Maule in Map 1. See *censo* (1865). The definition is that used by the nineteenth-century census takers. See *Censo* (1885), I, pp. xiv–xv.
9 *BSNA*, vol. I (1869), p. 381.
10 *BSNA*, vol. III (1872), p. 185; and vol. XIV (1882), p. 80. This 'uncommon' preference for leisure over labor, described by economists through 'a backward bending supply curve for labor,' is interestingly discussed by Karl Polanyi, *The Great Transformation* (Boston, 1968), pp. 130–209.
11 *BSNA*, vol. XIV (1882), and see the discussion in Chapter 5 above; for discussion of other regions, see Jonathan Levin, *The Export Economies* (Cambridge, Mass., 1960), pp. 125–43.
12 The tax on smallholders was abolished in 1882; for changing dress, refer to the various illustrated studies: *Twentieth Century Impressions of Chile* (London, 1915), Adolfo Ortúzar, *Chile of Today* (New York, 1907); Eduardo Poirier, *Chile en 1910* (Santiago, 1910). Rural workers were exhibiting less 'indifference to consumption,' in the language of economics.
13 James R. Scobie, *Revolution on the Pampas*, pp. 60–1, 80–4, gives an average monthly wage of around £10 or roughly 60–70 Chilean pesos. The scale of agricultural output in the late nineteenth and early twentieth centuries in Argentina far surpassed that of Chile.
14 For a summary of the literature on labor shortage, see Gonzalo Izquierdo, *Un estudio de las ideologías chilenas: la sociedad de agricultura en el siglo XIX* (Santiago, 1968), pp. 133–58.
15 *BSNA*, vol. XII (1880), p. 391; and vol. XIX (1887), p. 632. Newspapers advertised for workers at as much as 1 peso per tarea in 1859. See *El Ferrocarril* (Santiago), 15 January 1859. The accounts of a *fundo* in Linares show a daily wage of 20 centavos while 80 were paid per tarea: *CJ* (Linares), Leg. 88, p. 13. See also, Gay, *Agricultura*, II, pp. 33–5. For the results in changing from sickle to scythe, see, E. J. T. Collins, 'Labour supply and demand.'

Chilean Rural Society

[16] Censuses of 1865 and 1895; Carlos Hurtado, *Concentración de la población*, pp. 166–72, 65, quoting Henry Meiggs, *Reseña histórica del ferrocarril entre Santiago y Valparaíso* (Santiago, 1863), p. 130. For a summary of the literature on emigration to Peru, see Watt Stewart, *El trabajador Chileno y los ferrocarriles del Perú* (Santiago, 1939), 5–48; *BSNA*, vol. II (1871), p. 286; *Sesiones de la cámara de senadores* (ordinarias), 31 July 1871, pp. 60–7. 'Circular a los párrocos,' *BSNA*, vol. II (1871), pp. 286–7.

[17] *BSNA*, vol. XIII (1882), pp. 164–7. Testimony from a former San Francisco consul was used to point out the 'unsuitability' of Asiatic labor. *BSNA*, vol. II (1871), p. 346. *Sesiones de la cámara de senadores* (ordinarias), 31 July 1871, p. 63. *Primer censo de la Republica Argentina verificado en los dias 15, 16, 17 setiembre, 1869* (Buenos Aires, 1872), pp. 338–50. *BSNA*, vol. II (1871), p. 387.

[18] On the question of labor scarcity or abundance, see Ernesto Laclau, 'Modos de producción, sistemas económicos y poblacíon excedente: aproximacíon histórica a los casos argentinos y chileno,' *Revista Latinoamericana de Sociología*, vol. V, no. 2 (July 1969), pp. 276–342.

[19] Luis Galdames, *Jeografía económica*, pp. 171–3.

[20] *Censo* (1930), p. 10.

[21] *Sesiones de la cámara de senadores* (ordinarias), 31 July 1871, p. 65.

[22] Hurtado Ruiz-Tagle, *Concentración de población*, p. 146.

[23] Pichidegua (1862–4); *BSNA*, vol. I (1869), p. 380; vol. II (1870), p. 387; C. G. U., 'Los inquilinos de "El Peumo," ' *BSNA*, vol. VI (1875), pp. 306–8; Balmaceda, *Manual*, pp. 127–8.

[24] Balmaceda, *Manual*, p. 128. M. J. Balmaceda, a Senator and a great land-owner in the latter nineteenth century, was the father of J. M. Balmaceda, President of Chile (1886–91).

[25] Félix Echeverría, 'Las máquinas y el trabajador agrícola,' *BSNA*, vol. II (1870), p. 376; and *BSNA*, vol. III (1871), pp. 183–4.

[26] *BSNA*, vol. II (1870), p. 376, speech by Senator Félix Vicuña, *Sesiones de la cámara de senadores* (ordinarias), 31 July 1871, p. 62.

[27] Balmaceda, *Manual*, pp. 128–9. Judging from the *ca* 1900 photographs in Victor E. León, *Uvas y vinos*, p. 56, there were many female grape pickers.

[28] *BSNA*, vol. XIX (1887), p. 593.

[29] *El Mensajero*, vol. I (1856), p. 346; Agusto Orrego Luco, 'La cuestión social en Chile,' *Anales* (January–June, 1961), p. 52.

[30] Rumbold, *Report*, p. 320; Francisco Encina, *et al.*, 'La subdivisión de la propiedad rural en Chile en 1919,' *Mapocho*, vol. 13, no. 1 (1966), p. 22.

[31] Ramón Domínguez, *Nuestro sistema de inquilinaje* (Santiago, 1867), p. 41; Tornero, *Chile ilustrado*, p. 470.

[32] *El Huique*; Paola Moltoni, 'Il passaggio dalla conduzione diretta all' affittanza capitalista nell 'economia agraria cilena: il caso dell' hacienda "El Melón" nel Cile centrale (1890–1898)' (Thesis in History, University of Turin, 1972), p. 26.

[33] For an idea of how provincial justice was supposed to have been dispensed, see *Manual o instrucción*. The system described was reorganised in the 1870s.

[34] Eric Wolf, *Sons of the Shaking Earth* (Chicago, 1959), p. 208; Orrego Luco, 'La cuestión social,' p. 50.

[35] Atropos, 'El Inquilino en Chile,' p. 200.

[36] This discussion is based on a series of articles by Menandier and prominent *hacendados* in the *BSNA* during the years 1870–5. See especially vols. I, II, and IV.

[37] *BSNA*, vol. II, p. 320; vol. III, p. 185; vol. IX, p. 90.

[38] Wright, 'Sociedad nacional de agricultura,' p. 272; McBride, *Land and Society*, pp. 168–9.

39 *BSNA*, vol. XIX, p. 635; there are numerous cases of *inquilinos* on the outskirts of Santiago: Valenzuela O., *Album*, pp. 52–63.

40 *BSNA*, vol. III, p. 187; Subercaseaux, *Memorias*, vol. I, p. 47.

41 Rafael Herrera, 'Memoria sobre la hacienda "Las Condes" en 1895,' Intro. by Gonzalo Izquierdo, *Boletín de la Academia Chilena de la Historia*, no. 79 (1968), pp. 121–205, esp. pp. 202–3.

42 Lawrence Stone, 'News from everywhere' (review of Barrington Moore, Jr, *Social Origins of Dictatorship and Democracy*), *New York Review of Books*, vol. 9, no. 31 (24 August 1967).

43 Wright, 'Sociedad nacional de agricultura,' p. 267, quoting Carlos Reyes P., 'La habitación del obrero agrícola,' *Primera Semana Social Agrícola* (Santiago, 1914).

44 Wright, 'Sociedad,' p. 266.

45 Carlos Keller has an informative critique of agricultural censuses in *Revolución en la agricultura*, pp. 11–19.

46 Correa Vergara, *Agricultura chilena*, I, pp. 162–3.

47 Borde and Góngora, *Puangue*, I, p. 159; Valenzuela O., *Album*, notices the recent appearance of rural schools. See also the interesting discussion in Tancredo Pinochet Le-Brun, 'Inquilinos en la hacienda de su Excelencia,' *Antología chilena de la tierra* (Santiago, 1970), pp. 104–5.

48 Wright, 'Sociedad nacional,' p. 268. Brian Loveman, 'Property, politics and rural labor: agrarian reform in Chile, 1919–1972' (Unpublished Ph.D. diss. in Political Science, University of Indiana, 1973), pp. 47–109.

49 I owe a great deal to my colleagues, T. W. Margadant and W. W. Hagen, for discussion and information on these points.

Landowners in Chilean society

In the decades after 1860, the stimulus to Chilean development continued to come from the outside: the British demand for grain was the first impulse in this period, but with full-scale exploitation of nitrate and then copper, the pace of economic activity rapidly increased. The creation of a modern and wealthy mining enclave had several repercussions on what had been up to then essentially a traditional agrarian society. Although the mines themselves were for the most part isolated in the northern desert, their effect was felt not only in the new towns or such nearby ports as Antofagasta or Iquique, but above all in Valparaíso and Santiago where bankers and bureaucrats and a multitude of services came into existence to support and also to tap the new industry. The mining economy created simultaneously a market for agriculture, a group of eager buyers for rural estates, and a modern proletariat, ideologically a century ahead of its rural counterparts, which in the end forced the destruction of the hacienda system that we are studying here.

It is important to understand the implications of Chile's uneven development for rural society. Although a few Chileans became wealthy directly through mining, most participated indirectly through government taxation or through such activities as banking, insurance, or through payment by the new companies for legal council. Since Chile's was a highly centralised government, most of the mining revenue was channeled to Santiago where modern sewage and transportation systems were installed and the houses of the wealthy began to line the new broad and well lighted avenues. There were no important regional mining centers such as Guanajuato or Sucre in Chile: the income from nitrate and copper went either to foreign corporations or the thriving capital city. As the contrast with provincial towns became more obvious every landowner able to bear the cost sought the amenities of urban life and built his house in Santiago. At the same time, the *nouveaux riches* created by the mining industry invested in rural estates; for if the motor of the Chilean economy was in the northern desert, the national government and social leadership were firmly in the hands of a traditional elite for whom landownership was one of the principal values.

Landowners in Chilean society

We have already seen in Chapter 5 the changes in land distribution and estate organisation; here we will be concerned less with land itself than with the people who owned it. But first two points need to be made about the number and location of the large estates. As we move through the last half of the nineteenth century and into the twentieth, many of the great haciendas of the late colonial period were split into three or four smaller *fundos*. As mixed and more specialised farming replaced livestock, subdivision permitted closer management; but besides that, increased agricultural output meant that each of the smaller *fundos* could now support a landowning family in an appropriate upper class style, where before a huge and largely unexploited hacienda provided for one owner. The trend toward somewhat smaller units was especially clear in the irrigated zones near Santiago, but as the railroad and better access roads enabled landowners deep in the provinces to send their produce to the new markets, estates everywhere increased in value and were often divided. Between 1854 and 1874 the tax records show an increase in total agricultural income from 5.8 to 9.7 million pesos. Most of this increase was produced on the larger estates: in 1854 there were 145 with an income of 1 545 000 pesos and twenty years later, 338 that produced 3 880 000 pesos.[1]

Despite better transportation, the most valuable estates were still centered around Santiago, a fact that can be seen clearly in the data for 1854 and 1908. As the railroad and local markets (Talca; Concepción) led to greater prosperity in the southern provinces, more highly appraised estates show up in the tax rolls. Below Curicó, there were only four in 1854 whose income exceeded 6000 pesos, while in 1908, sixty-nine were appraised at 200 000 or above. Still, value did not closely coincide with area as can be seen in the 1916 figures which are based on hectares. Santiago province had about the same number of haciendas of 5000 hectares or more as Aconcagua; but in terms of 1908 appraised value, Santiago had five times as many. Maule had twelve per cent of the larger area estates, but only five per cent of the most valuable. The discrepancy between size and value can be partly accounted for by the quality of land and proximity to a large urban market which presented opportunities for specialised agriculture such as dairy or garden crops. But beyond the commercial qualities, estates close by the capital were also cherished for their recreational value: the better houses and gardens were built on *fundos* within an easy journey of Santiago, and the competition for these delightful spots undoubtedly bid up the value of rural property.

What we have seen so far, then, is an increase in the ability of land to support more families at a high income. There were 193 more large estates (over 6000 pesos income) in 1874 than at mid-century; and – if our appraisal figures are comparable – another 166 by 1908. The increased value of land led to both subdivision and improvement (houses, fencing) and more units; it meant that more heirs could be given land

Table 34   Geographical distribution of large estates in central Chile based on income or evaluation in 1854 and 1908, and acreage in 1916

Province	1854 number	%	1908 number	%	1916 number	%
Aconcagua	18	12	51	10	50	23
Valparaíso	18	12	36	7	15	7
Santiago	78	54	247	49	58	27
Colchagua	22	15	75	15	23	12
Curicó	5	4	26	5	16	7
Talca	1	1	28	6	17	7
Maule	3	2	27	5	25	12
Ñuble	0	0	14	3	12	5
Totals	145	100%	504	100%	216	100%

Sources: *Renta agrícola* (1854); *Indices de propietarios rurales* (Santiago, 1908); *AE* (1916–17), vol. VII. After 1891, the basis for taxation was shifted from annual income (*renta anual*) to an appraised value of the estate (*avalúo*), and this presents a certain problem in establishing comparable values. I have converted appraised value to annual income by estimating a yield of six per cent and then roughly compensating for the deteriorated value of the peso by dividing the yield by a factor of two. Thus, an estate appraised at $200 000 in the 1908 tax roll would have a 6000 peso 'income'. 'Large estate' in this Table is defined as follows: in 1854: $6000 or more annual income; in 1908: $200 000 appraised value; in 1916: 5000 or more hectares.

and be maintained at an adequate level of income; and it meant that more proper rural estates were available for purchase by the wealthy miners, bankers, and bureaucrats. While the lot of rural workers and methods of farming were only slightly changed down to the 1920s, the estate system itself was strengthened by a wider market and the attraction of outside capital. It is worth examining now the effect that all this had on patterns of land ownership.

Some studies have stressed the rapid turnover of landownership while others notice the persistence of the 'Castilian–Basque landed aristocracy' from the eighteenth century until well into the twentieth.[2] In fact, these two phenomena are not incompatible. Rural estates did change hands regularly. An heir, for example, might sell his inheritance and enter a business or practice law; but having made money in such a profession, he or his descendants would then very likely invest their earnings in another estate. Part of the explanation for the high rate of estate turnover lay in the nature of Chilean society. Unlike northern Europeans, the Chilean landowners, true to their Mediterranean heritage, were city dwellers. The difference between the English and Chilean landowning class, for example, is the difference between the subjects of Jane Austen or George Eliot and those of Blest Gana. Unlike the provincial gentry in *Pride and Prejudice* or *Middlemarch*, the landowners of *Martín Rivas* rarely stayed for long in the countryside. In the city, estates were bought or traded and leases arranged. The predominantly urban interests of Chilean landowners compared with those of northern European can also be seen in the absence of the great manorial house. Except for a few ostentatious mansions easily accessible from Santiago, there were few impressive hacienda houses. In those few cases where rural mansions did exist – the complex of the Casas del Huique, or Alhué, for example – the land, or at least a section immediately surrounding the estate house, was retained in the same family for several generations. (Both Huique and Alhué, in fact, were retained by heirs of the colonial Echenique and Toro families until their recent expropriation by the Agrarian Reform in 1966–8.) The fact that a tradition of sentiment for an ancestral home was rarely associated with Chilean rural estates undoubtedly made it easier for owners to sell uninhibitedly or exchange haciendas and *fundos*.

But it is also true that regardless of much buying and selling a number of families have been traditionally associated with land ownership. It would be an excessively arduous if not impossible task to trace the owners of large estates through seventy-five years of tax records and Notary documents. The names of some estates change and others completely disappear through fragmentation, and while it may be possible to follow two or three notable families through the genealogical jungle, such a procedure is not feasible for most landowning families. As an alternative to this and in order to test the idea of the persistence of a few families, I compiled the 1874 tax records to determine the twelve largest landowners by surname; these were – in order of size – the Ossa, Larraín, Correa, Ovalle, Valdés, Balmaceda, Errázuriz, Vicuña, Echeverría, Subercaseaux, Ruiz-Tagle, and Garciá-Huidobro. In 1874 there were 105 large estates (of $6000 or more annual income) owned by people with these surnames and they produced, according to the tax records, 1 128 000 pesos. This was about thirty-three per cent of the income from all large estates and thirteen per cent of all taxable rural income in central Chile.[3]

A generation earlier, in 1854, there were forty-five estates under the same twelve surnames. Their taxable income was less in pesos but five per cent larger in terms of total large-estate income. (See Table 35.)

Table 35 Income from rural property in central Chile, 1854, 1874, 1908 (in current pesos)

Income groups	1854	1874	1908
Total number of taxed farms in central Chile	19 100	11 920	21 600
Total taxable income in central Chile	5 803 000	9 693 000	14 143 000
Number of largest estates ($6000 and up annual income)	145	338	504
Taxable income of these largest estates	1 545 000	3 880 000	5 402 000
Percentage of all central Chilean rural income obtained by larger estates	27%	40%	38%
Number of these larger estates held by twelve family surnames	42	105	88
Taxable income obtained by twelve family surnames from their larger estates	1 545 000	3 880 000	5 402 000
Percentage of all larger estates' income obtained by twelve family surnames	38%	33%	21%
Percentage of total taxable income in central Chile obtained by twelve family surnames	10%	13%	8%

Sources: *Renta agrícola* (1854); *Rol de contribuyentes* (1874); *Indice de propietarios rurales* (1908). Note: The minimum taxable income in the tax rolls is: $25.00 in 1854; $100.00 in 1874 (this accounts for the decreased number that year); and $2000 in evaluation in 1908. In all cases, the very smallest minifundia were excluded.

The definition of 'large estate' is: $6000 or more annual income in 1854 and 1874; $200 000 or more appraised value in 1908.

Since the 1854 and 1874 tax was based on annual income (*renta anual*) while the 1908 tax was based on the appraised value of the estate (*avalúo*), I have settled on the following formula: a six per cent yield on value, reduced by a factor of two to compensate for price inflation. Thus an estate with an appraised value of $200 000 would yield $12 000, which divided by two equals $6000. The factor of two is based on the index of basic foods (see Appendix): in the first years of the twentieth century, the index number is about double that of 1874. The 1908 tax is often based on earlier evaluations, so besides being convenient, 'two' is roughly accurate.

The 'twelve family surnames' are (in order of size): Ossa, Larraín, Correa, Ovalle, Valdés, Balmaceda, Errázuriz, Vicuña, Echeverría, Subercaseaux, Ruiz-Tagle, and Garcia-Huidobro.

After 1874, the property owned by our twelve surnames began to decline. In 1908, the Ossa, Larraín *et al.*, owned eighty-eight properties but their share of total large-estate income had dropped to twenty-one per cent; and to only eight per cent of all rural income. This trend continued into the twentieth century, and some of the most important names dropped entirely out of the rural scene. The Ossa, who by 1874 had invested millions of their mining wealth in fifteen large estates, owned only one *fundo* in 1923. The holdings of the Balmaceda – mainly they had belonged to the martyred President's father – shrunk from eight haciendas in 1874 to only one in 1923. Our information does not give a completely accurate picture, of course, since land was often passed to daughters and thus, in two generations, out of the family name; but there is no denying that the great landholding names of the eighteenth and nineteenth centuries were being replaced by a host of new buyers.

The new buyers came primarily from commercial and mining circles. Merchants such as Enrique Möller, Nicolás Albano, and José Ceveró of the Valparaíso trade, or Pablo H. Délano, 'one of the most competent businessmen in Chile,' Roberto Lyon, one of the founders of Balfour, Lyon and Co. merchants house, Nathan Miers Cox, Waddington, and other descendants of foreign merchants had by the last third of the century made money, bought rural estates, and often by this time married into the older elite Chilean families. The main banking families – the Ossa, Edwards, Cousiño, Arlegui, and Besa – all bought large rural properties, as did the wealthy miners whose investment in Chilean agriculture is a historical commonplace. Valentín Lambert, Severo Vega, Eduardo Charme all made fortunes in the north and sunk their millions in the land of rural Chile. A tin miner, Orlando Ghigliotto Salas, paid 1 800 000 for the hacienda Hauquén, in 1919.[4]

After the remarkably successful War of the Pacific (1879–84), nitrate became the main force in the Chilean economy. Although much of the actual mining and processing passed into foreign hands, a tax on exports tapped the flow of wealth and enriched a generation of bureaucrats and local professionals who grew up on the periphery of the export enclave. Customs inspectors, tax officials, accountants and lawyers were indirect beneficiaries of nitrate. There is a good example of such a person in the case of Luis Claro Solar, the head of an important law firm that was linked to the Compañía de Antofagasta. By the early twentieth century, don Luis had made millions and like a great many others, put much of his money into land. In 1908 he owned over 1 100 000 pesos worth of rural estates.[5]

The 1908 tax rolls reveal the changes then occurring in landownership. The familiar names of the 'Castilian–Basque aristocracy' are still there – as we have seen, our twelve surnames still owned nearly ninety large estates – but the names of Edwards (the largest landowner in Chile in 1908), Lyon, Rivas, Eastman, Cousiño, Soto, and Letelier, were now increasingly important. For most of these men, rural property undoubtedly helped legitimise a claim to social status that was commensurate with their wealth, and one has the clear impression of their success from the genealogical dictionaries. Although the first generation of local and immigrant merchants and miners generally married among themselves, money and land enabled them to enter the best social circles. This process can be seen early in the nineteenth century in the case of Ramón Subercaseaux, the son of a French immigrant. By 1835 he was rich from trade and the silver mines of Arqueros, the owner of opulent estates, and had married Magdalena Vicuña, daughter of a prestigious family. All of their children married 'encumbrados personajes de la sociedad santiaguina.' The same was true a century later of an obscure miner, Juan Francisco Rivas, who made his fortune in mining, married a local woman, and bought the huge hacienda of Virhüin y Zemita. His three daughters married an Errázuriz, Riesco, and Subercaseaux.[6]

The flow of capital was not just in one direction. Miners and merchants bought haciendas but landowners in turn invested in banks, insurance companies, commercial firms and the incipient industrial sector.[7] Neither the move from commerce to land nor the role of landed property in social mobility is, of course, peculiar to Chile. But the particular conjuncture in Chilean history when great wealth was suddenly generated by an isolated mining enclave in response to demands and forces largely extraneous to the country, while at the same time a traditional landed society still set the social tone and controlled politics, had decisive implications. Much of the new wealth was absorbed by agriculture. But this does not necessarily mean that capital was invested to obtain higher yields, but rather that in many cases non-agricultural earnings were simply used to buy land. Although the sources available do not permit close calculations of capital efficiency, they do reveal that improvements were kept to an absolute minimum; and there is no doubting the rush of newly rich miners and merchants to purchase rural estates.[8]

In 1882, the *Mercurio* of Valparaíso published a list of fifty-nine Chilean millionaires as proof of the possibilities 'through order and effort in a free country.' Some writers have used this to show the relative insignificance of agriculture as a generator of individual wealth since less than half of the names are described as landowners. But the interesting point is not that only twenty made their fortune in agriculture but that most of the remaining thirty-nine – designated as miners, bankers, capitalists – subsequently invested their earnings in rural estates. This illustrates as conveniently as anything else the enduring value that land-ownership held in late nineteenth- and early twentieth-century Chile. In such evidence there is the strong suggestion that much of the wealth made in the export enclave instead of creating an industrial 'growth pole,' simply ran out onto the sands of a traditional countryside.[9]

This is a hypothesis and one that is difficult to test. Given the nineteenth-century orthodoxy on tariff policy and the prospect of the internal market for manufactures, much investment in industry probably was not a realistic alternative for local capitalists. Nor is it really possible to determine in any quantitative way how much of the invest-ment in land represented the purchase of status (and thus actually con-sumption), and how much was sound investment from a strictly economic point of view. The problem as it was recently put, is to determine 'the economic cost of the non-economic use of a surplus.'[10] It is clear that a few of the new landowners put a great deal of money and effort into the modernisation of their estates. Irrigation works, dairies, the impressive new vineyards, new varieties of plants and livestock were introduced by a group known by their admirers as *agricultores progresistas*. But many others merely dabbled at 'scientific agriculture' and certainly had no intention of tampering with an obedient work force and a most comfortable way of life. Uncounted others saw a rural estate 'as a spot where delightful vacations are passed,' asked only that their lessee pay on time, or found the shaded gardens of the hacienda house, the horses, and obedient servants a sufficient return on their investment.[11]

In order to understand how this landowning society actually worked, it may be useful to look more closely at a few families. The following are not necessarily typical but each in its way is revealing. The first is a relatively straightforward case. Don Prudencio Lazcano i García Zúñiga came from a distinguished Basque family that had settled in Argentina in the early eighteenth century. He returned to Madrid for his education in law and was sent by Charles IV to Chile in 1805 to assist the Audiencia of Santiago in the unpopular task of collecting funds to back the Crown's issue of Vales Reales. Already wealthy, don Prudencio made a good marriage, and rose in the hierarchy of colonial administration. He remained loyal to the Crown through the vicissi-tudes of the Independence struggle and with the final triumph of the

Republican forces, he was taken captive and murdered in prison by a disgruntled beggar in 1820.[12]

Don Prudencio's first son, Fernando Lazcano Múgica, was born with the republic in 1810 and soon prospered in the new setting. He also studied law – but in Santiago – became secretary to the Santiago Appellate Court and Deputy to the new national Congress for several terms. Manual Montt (President 1851–61) made him Minister of Justice, Religion and Education in the 1850s. An excellent marriage to the daughter of one of the wealthier branches of the Larráin clan enabled don Fernando to purchase the vast but undeveloped hacienda El Guaico which ran for several kilometres from just east of the town of Curicó into the cordillera toward Argentina. El Guaico is listed in the 1854 tax roll as having an annual income of $7000 and it is clear that it was the kind of place we have seen before with uncounted hectares of potentially excellent land within its boundaries but of low value due to its isolation from markets. With his own impressive fortune and the help of the substantial dowry of $123 000 in cash and property brought to the marriage by doña Dolores Echaurren Larraín, Fernando Lazcano bought the hacienda and improved it. Over four thousand hectares were brought under irrigation, and by 1874 the annual income was listed at $20 000. The railroad which reached Curicó in 1870 and the flourishing markets of the early 1870s were producing good yields. Don Fernando apparently then settled back in his Santiago house (on calle Moneda) to enjoy the adequate income drawn from El Guaico. He was elected Senator, sat on the bench of the Supreme Court and helped direct the Santiago charitable foundation. His sons ran the hacienda. When don Fernando died in 1886, the inventory of his property which I have summarised in Table 36 demonstrates the composition of his wealth.

Although the family's principal residence was in Santiago, El Guaico was more comfortably furnished than most haciendas, especially one so deep in the country. There was a billiard table, a piano, a landau and three other carriages, and china service for nine dozen guests. The estate, as many others, had a chapel joined to the main house. This was primarily a livestock hacienda and consequently had little equipment. There was one broken down Pitts thresher, thirty-eight carts, a few rickety tools and crude plows. The total appraised value of all such equipment was $4353. The major investment had been made by don Fernando in irrigation canals which permitted the cultivation of forage crops and some grain. There were 504 work oxen, apparently no draught horses but over 400 for riding and threshing. From May 1886 to May 1887, the year following don Fernando's sudden death, El Guaico was kept intact while the estate was settled. Since the hacianda's income for this period went into the *cuerpo común de bienes*, the accounting records were kept with the inventory and they reveal a gross annual income of about $53 000.[13]

Table 36   Inventory of the total worth (*cuerpo de bienes*) of don Fernando Lazcano in 1886

Description	Appraised value $
Urban property (in Santiago)	
Houses nos. 82 and 84 on calle Moneda	126 200
Houses nos. 15, 16, 17 on calle Gálvez	34 200
Furnishings	12 555
Jewelry of the señora	4000
Rural property (in Curicó)	
Hacienda El Guaico including land, buildings, equipment, and livestock	648 524
Other	
Cash in Bank of Valparaíso	122 777
Cash in Mobiliaro Bank	130 000
Accounts receivable	100 000
Received from sale of stocks and bonds	83 788
Interest on stocks and bonds	12 500
Cash advanced to heirs	99 976
Cash from livestock recently sold	152 000
Total *cuerpo de bienes*	1 594 173

Source: *CJ* (Santiago), leg. 109, no. 11 (1886). Some minor items omitted so the total is not the exact sum of column.

Fernando Lazcano had eight children and since his wife was already dead by 1886 each received an equal share. The total resource of a family is important in determining the distribution of property. When all wealth is concentrated in one estate, multiple heirs demanding their share often meant subdivision of the hacienda; where landowners owned three or four *fundos* each son might receive a farm and other children compensated in other ways. In the example at hand, the Lazcano family had a good deal of cash or assets that could be easily liquified, and one large hacienda. But out of this eight children had to be taken care of. El Guaico was split among three sons: the eldest received the core estate including the main house; the urban property was allotted to other children, and stocks, bonds, livestock were sold off to provide for the remaining heirs. Out of the remains of this one large hacienda, the daughters were well set up and managed to make marriages firmly within the Chilean upper class. Where the original El Guaico had been the landed base behind one important oligarch its resources were now split and underlay the careers of three. All of these – Fernando, Agustín and Prudencio – studied law, were elected to Congress and held important administrative posts. It is instructive to look at each in turn.

The first born, don Fernando Lazcano Echaurren, got his law degree from the University of Chile in 1871, became a Deputy in 1873 and a Liberal Senator in 1894. His marriage to doña Emilia Errázuriz Echaurren, the daughter of one President and the sister of another did nothing to diminish his political fortunes. To cite yet another example of the elaborate interweaving of families, Rosa Lazcano (sister) also married into the Errázuriz clan (to Ladislao Errázuriz a brother of Emilia), one of the truly impressive extended families in the country. Over the century between 1830 and 1930, fifty Errázuriz were Deputies or Senators; three were Presidents; others were Presidential candidates, ministers, and one was an Archbishop. Lazcano Echaurren was a Senator during much of the Parliamentary Republic and the Liberal candidate for President in 1906. The second son, Prudencio (b. 1850), also studied law, was Intendent of Santiago, Minister of Public Works, Ambassador to Bolivia and to the United States. Agustín, the third son who received a section of El Guaico, was a Deputy from 1894 to 1897. The *hijuelas* of El Guaico are listed in the 1902 tax rolls with evaluations of $450 000, $180 000, and $377 000 respectively.[14] By 1923, five fairly large *fundos* (each had about 1200 hectares of irrigated land) had evolved out of the breakup of El Guaico. Family fortunes apparently declined along with the ancestral estate. If social connections and the luster of the name permitted descendants to move in the best social circles, the landed base that supported the first Fernando Lazcano in grand style and three political sons more modestly was now disappearing. The Lazcano no longer figured in national politics and in more recent biographical dictionaries they are listed as professionals, engineers, and doctors.[15]

Although records that might permit an economic analysis of the hacienda are not available, one might speculate on the role played by El Guaico in this story of rising and falling family fortunes. Did this vast sprawling estate act as a sponge that absorbed a fortune accumulated by generations of Crown and Republican office holders? Was the pleasure and prestige implied by ownership of a Santiago mansion and a house in the country where dozens of guests were comfortably entertained too great a drain on a rudimentary productive base? Did the values held by this class, the absentee estate management encouraged by the social system itself, mean that money invested to support an ephemeral status was soaked up by an archaic farming system? Was there not a more economically rational – if socially and aesthetically less tasteful – industry where such men as the Lazcano might have invested their money? This is not to judge the Lazcano harshly for not investing in steel mills or inventing a motorcar; but rather to suggest that the hacienda system not only returned low yields to investment and therefore acted as a brake on economic growth, but also because of the complex of social values implied by such a system absorbed a large part of the investment capital in the country and returned little beyond ephemeral status and, frequently, downward mobility.

From the rather simple and clear-cut example of the Lazcano family, let us turn to the enormous Larraín clan. Of the two main branches, we are concerned here with the one founded by Juan Francisco Larraín de la Cerda, a descendant, like the rest, of Basque immigrants. He was born in Santiago in 1700, a rector of the University of San Felipe (in Santiago), chancellor of the Real Audiencia, Corregidor, Alcalde ordinario of Santiago, and General of Militias.[16] Both of his sons, Augustín Larraín Lecaros and Francisco de Borja Larraín, occupied important governmental and military posts in the eighteenth century, acquired and entailed large blocks of rural property; and as the capstone to this, Augustín's son José Toribio Larraín y Guzmán was awarded the title of Marqués de Larraín in 1787. The Marqués put a great deal of effort into his *mayorazgo* which included a house in Santiago, a *chacra* in Ñuñoa (now a suburb of the capital), the potentially fine estate of Viluco just south of Santiago across the Maipo, and the *estancia* or cattle ranch of Cauquenes in the cordillera behind Rengo. In fact he claimed that transforming the 'sterile fields' of Viluco into what Maria Graham called 'a princely establishment, kept in excellent order,' and the installation of the famous thermal baths on Cauquenes, had so impoverished him that an immediate ex-vinculation of the entail was necessary to survive.[17]

The *mayorazgo* was abolished by the 1828 Constitution but when the Marqués died in 1829, his property was nevertheless all passed to the eldest son, Rafael Larraín Moxó. It was an excellent start. Rich at sixteen, don Rafael studied at the University, toured France, returned to marry the President's daughter (Victoria Prieto), and entered Congress as a Deputy. Don Rafael was not bound by the entail that curbed the ambitions of his titled father. He quickly obtained from the Caja de Crédito Hipotecario $205 000 from mortgage loans on Cauquenes and then sold the entire place to a rich miner for something over $230 000 in 1867. Money and effort were poured into Viluco to make it one of the model haciendas of the central valley. From $7500 in 1854, the annual yield jumped to over $34 000 twenty years later. From this most pleasant and profitable rural base, don Rafael exercised a considerable influence in the country. He held a seat in the Senate throughout the period 1855–82, was one of the founders of the modern National Society of Agriculture and its first President, and the President of the Bank of Chile. From this atmosphere of the 'most refined patrician elegance' his daughters moved naturally in the best circles. Both married distant cousins: doña Ana to José Miguel Irarrázabal Larraín, himself a descendant of another titled and powerful family; and doña Matilde became the wife of Emilio Larraín Urriola.[19]

Viluco, although now not entailed, was again passed to the eldest son, Luis Larraín Prieto, who followed closely in his father's path. Like don Rafael he was a president of the SNA, President of the Club Hípico, director of the Manufacturers Association (Fomento Fabril) and Minister of Agriculture.

By 1923, Viluco was still owned by don Luis but parts had been sold off so that the core hacienda now contained only about 1200 hectares out of the 4700 of the original estate. Surrounding farms such as Santa Victoria de Viluco or Providencia de Viluco, once sections of the hacienda, were now autonomous *fundos*: each still large enough to provide a good income to its owner, but not by itself adequate to support the life-style of such a man as either the Marqués or don Rafael. By the twenties and increasingly thereafter, such 'progressive agriculturalists' as Luis Larraín had widely diversified interests and investments.

The other Larraín Lecaros (Francisco de Borja) also acquired large amounts of rural property in the eighteenth century and like his brother, instituted a *mayorazgo*. There were two sons, Nicolás Larraín Rojas and Juan Francisco Larraín Rojas whose careers we may follow to understand other aspects of rural society. Don Nicolás married his cousin, doña Trinidad, daughter of the Marqués and sister of Rafael Larraín Moxó. When Nicolás died in 1872, Trinidad retained the principal *fundo*, San Javier, a place of 1052 irrigated hectares near Viluco and Aculeo where much of the Larraín's land was. San Javier whose land alone was appraised at $428 000 supported three families. The señora widow received $10 000 a year in rent while her two sons

– to whom it was rented – split the remaining income.[20] Renting such an estate did not of course mean that the renters – in this case the two sons – or the owner lived in the country. In fact, all three lived in Santiago and used their agricultural earnings to pursue mining and business interests. Often the *fundo* was mortgaged to one of the houses that extended long-term credit to obtain cash. San Javier was mortgaged to the Caja de Crédito Hipotecario for $30 000, apparently for non-agricultural purposes.[21]

Land as a base for commercial activities can be seen more clearly in the case of another son, José Luis Larraín Larraín. He also inherited an estate of some 1500 hectares and with the income from this, plus large mortgage loans from the Caja, don José established the 'Tattersall Fair,' the most important wholesale livestock business in Santiago. The *fundo* was rented, and the $90 000 in Caja loans very likely was invested in one of the first *conventillos* (cheap apartments for urban workers), in presumably higher-yielding stocks and bonds (banks, insurance companies), and apparently also in agricultural produce sold on credit that must have yielded more than the six per cent Caja loan cost. The inventory taken on his death in 1898 shows $127 000 in accounts receivable. The same inventory described the mud and straw shacks for horses and *inquilinos* and the primitive quality of improvements on the *fundo* in Colchagua that provided the base for these commercial operations. The total value of all buildings and equipment was only around $15 000.[22]

The more interesting Larraín Rojas was Juan Francisco, *regidor* of Santiago in 1813 and the heir to Aculeo, one of the great haciendas of central Chile. When he died in 1848, the account books for Aculeo show a gross annual income of about $39 000, one-fifth of which came from money lent at interest. The hacienda was operated as a unit by four sons until 1851 when Joaquin, 'a prince of the Church' – lawyer, Deputy, first rector of the Catholic University, and Archbishop of Santiago – sold his share to Francisco de la Borja and Juan sold his quarter to José Patricio. Even then, both halves were operated as a single unit until 1860 when the first got *hijuelas* Nos. 1 and 2 and José Patricio, 3, 4, and 5. By 1888 this first half of Aculeo still contained some 14 000 hectares, over 2000 of them prime irrigated land and together with buildings and equipment was appraised at $421 000. The other section was sold to a rich miner.[23]

Aculeo demonstrates the common difficulty in subdividing old haciendas that over many years had come to form a single large integrated agricultural unit. Canals, roads and fences, buildings, and workers' quarters were arranged in such a way that the one *hijuela* was likely to contain them all and redistribution was extremely costly. In 1888 the appraiser pointed out that it would be possible to *hijuelar* (i.e., create *hijuelas* out of) Aculeo but destroying the integrity of the agricultural unit would cause 'a notable diminution of value.'[24] In fact, only people with the resources to build new buildings and re-route roads and canals could think of taking on the job. In this sense it is no accident that Francisco de Borja Larraín's portion of Aculeo and sections of other large haciendas were bought by wealthy miners such as José Letelier, who made his fortune in the copper mines of Catemu.

For most of the nineteenth century, however, Aculeo was a great estate that formed the social and economic base of one of Chile's patrician families. As noted above one of the Larraín Gandarillas became an Archbishop of Santiago, Francisco de Borja was both Deputy and Senator in the 1860s, and his son José Manuel Larraín Valdés preserved enough of the income (from a fragment of Aculeo) and prestige to remain an important political and social figure into the 1930s. A sister, Trinidad Larraín Gandarillas, married into the powerful Irarrázabal clan. One of their sons was Manual José Irarrázabal Larraín, self-styled heir of the Marqués de la Pica, first President of the Club de la Unión, author of the law of the Comuna Autónoma and the foremost conservative politician of his era; another, Carlos Irarrázabal Larraín, married the principal heiress of the Conde de la Conquista and was the last to inhabit the famous colonial mansion, the Casa Colorada that still stands – now as a shabby and ignored collection of cheap shops – a few blocks from the Plaza de Armas in downtown Santiago. All this may seem excessively repetitious and allusive but it is difficult to explain the unity and cohesiveness of the Chilean oligarchy without pointing out the extraordinary interwoven family ties.[25]

The Larraín family represents better than any other the oligarchy of nineteenth-century Chile. And at that time despite all that has been suggested about overlapping or interlocking economic interests, this was primarily a landed family. The 1888 inventory of Francisco de Borja Larrain's *cuerpo de bienes* yields a total of $1 010 570, and of this amount less than $14 000 (1.5 per cent) was non-agricultural: ten shares of an insurance company; six of the Santiago Gas Company and twenty-one shares in the Bank of Valparaíso.[26]

Perhaps it was this lack of diversity that made survival difficult. Francisco de Borja's wordly goods had seven claimants. The Santiago house was given to one, the hacienda Mostazal to another, parts of Aculeo to a third. Livestock and land were sold off to satisfy the rest and with the proceeds other heirs bought farms elsewhere – smaller to be sure than Aculeo – or married into landed families. This was the way chosen by Patricio Larraín who not only held on to his patrimony but augmented his holdings to launch a numerous family – the Larraín Alcalde – into a wide range of military and important government posts. This way of life reached its apogee in the years of the Parliamentary Republic and was still possible into the 1930s; but after that, if the prestige and status lingered on, the agrarian base, stubbornly resistant to change and eroded by exploitative techniques and numerous heirs who expected the fruits with little labor, was not up to the demands of the new age.[27]

Although the Larraín family and many like it had held rural property at least since the early eighteenth century, many of the better haciendas were formed in the nineteenth century as men who got rich through the exercise of office, in trade, or above all in mining, invested their millions to transform neglected or isolated tracts of land. Ramón and Vicente Subercaseaux invested their huge mining fortunes in haciendas and moved rapidly into the best social circles early in the nineteenth century. Valentín Lambert, called by *El Mercurio* the fourth richest man in the country in 1882, Apolinario Soto, Eduardo Charme, and several others followed the same pattern, as every observer from Gay to McBride noticed.

A number of inventories from the Santiago Judicial archive permit us to examine in some detail another of these families that made the common transition from northern mines to central valley haciendas. It is not clear just when the first Ossa arrived in Chile from the Basque provinces but Francisco Javier de Ossa Palacios apparently was the common generator of both branches that we are concerned with here.[28] Don Francisco occupied minor bureaucratic posts in the colonial government and supervised the tobacco monopoly in Copiapó. Two marriages produced nine prolific heirs, but it is the two brothers, José Ramón Ossa Mercado and Francisco Ignacio Ossa Mercado who interest us here. The first became wealthy mining silver and copper in Copiapó, and he was the principal partner in an early bank (the Bank of Ossa and Cia). Like many of the Ossa he lived a very long time and produced a great many children. Many of these heirs were set up with land in the provinces around Santiago or in comfortable town houses with investments to guarantee a suitable income. One of these was a son, Gregorio Ossa Varas, and the inventory made upon his death in 1885 suggests the cost of improvident management.

Both of his *fundos* were rented (San José for $7000) and heavily mortgaged to obtain cash. The records show that at one time the Caja de Crédito Hipotecario lent $100 000 and in 1879, another loan for $120 000 from a nitrate millionaire, Federico Varela, came due. Both renters were pressed for payment but – 1879 was an especially bad

Table 37 Inventory of the total worth (*cuerpo de bienes*) of don Gregorio Ossa Varas, 1885 (in current pesos)

Description	Appraised value $
Urban property	
House in Santiago on calle Monjitas	40 922
House in Valparaíso	40 050
House in Chañaral	24 103
Rural property	
Fundo, San José de las Claras	135 000
Fundo, Las Nieves	99 335
Other	
Shares of two silver mines	21 150
Stock in Bank of Chile	6780
Total *cuerpo de bienes*	405 002

Source: CJ (Santiago), leg. 69, no. 1 (1885). Some minor items omitted so the total is not the exact sum of column.

agricultural year – neither could produce enough to service the loan. Additional loans from Domingo Matte and the Banco Mobilario were obtained through mortgages on urban property to hold off Varela just as don Gregorio died. His widow managed to hold San José but most of the rest of the property was sold and the heirs forced to cope as best they could.[29]

Francisco Ignacio Ossa Mercado, uncle of the unfortunate Gregorio, also made millions in mining in Copiapó after a brief stint as a customs inspector and provincial politician. Rich by 1830, he moved to the capital, befriended Diego Portales, bought and greatly improved the two fine haciendas of Codao (Rancaugua) and Colleuque (in San Fernando), and built an egregiously vulgar house – that still stands – the Alhambra on Compañía Street in Santiago.[30] Don Francisco left eleven heirs to a vast fortune. One, doña Francisca de Sales Ossa Cerda, remained a spinster for her 100 years, invested and managed wisely her inheritance so that upon her death in 1920 she was able to leave several hundreds of thousands of pesos to the Church and the Catholic University. Another daughter, Candelaria Ossa de Téllez, was also handsomely set up. An 1875 inventory revealed the property listed in Table 38.[31]

Table 38 Inventory of the total worth (*cuerpo de bienes*) of doña Candelaria Ossa de Tellez in 1875 (in current pesos)

Description	Appraised value $
Urban property	
House in Santiago on no. 94 calle Catedral	40 000
Furniture	10 264
Jewels, silver, etc.	11 286
Rural property	
Chacra in suburban Nuñoa	200 000
Other	
5100 shares in Alianza Bank	(not given)
Shares in Banco Nacional de Chile	33 375
Twenty *letras* from mortgage section of Banco Garantizador de Valores	(not given)
Accounts receivable	175 000
Total *cuerpo de bienes*	535 620

Source: *CJ* (Santiago), leg. 35, no. 3 (1875). Total is given in the document.

A large part of her yearly income was in the form of interest from loans judiciously placed, often to the more respectable landowners. Santiago in fact had a good many of these 'widow-bankers' or 'spinster-bankers.' Well set up by wealthy fathers or husbands, they invested their capital and lived from the income of rent and interest. Such an arrangement rarely led to improved agricultural practices on their rented and often distant *fundos*, where the aim too often was to give the señora her share and then squeeze as much as possible beyond that out of land and labor.

The six sons of Francisco Ignacio Ossa Mercado, backed by the mining millions and properly established on some of the more attractive rural estates in Chile, moved quickly into Santiago society and politics. Nicomedes founded the Bank of Ossa and Cia and was elected to Congress, another joined the clergy; Gregorio took over the fine estate of Codao and made it the second most profitable in Chile by 1874. Their piety – don Macario was made a *Caballero de Cristo* for a dramatic prayer on the floor of the Chamber of Deputies for the soul of a Radical opponent – was only exceeded by their landed wealth. On the 1874 tax rolls, the Ossa owned more rural property than any other Chilean family, a general indication of the huge flow of mining wealth into agriculture – or better perhaps, into rural society.

The peak of the Ossa fortunes seems to have been reached in the early decades of the present century and one has the impression that even then many were living on accumulated capital. All of the Ossa Cerda had a great many children to support and judging from Figuroa's frequent praiseful and revealing observations this was no easy task. Gregorio's son Luis Gregorio Ossa Browne, lived 'a most sumptuous [*fastuosa*] social life in Santiago and in recent years, before leaving to live in Europe, gave numerous *banquetes* and receptions.' A nephew, Félix Ossa Vicuña, in 1920 was living in Paris, likewise 'giving *banquetes* and receptions.'[32] Some of the descendants who stayed in Chile continued on the land; Codao for example remained in the family until recent years. But if a hacienda that had supported one owner in wealth and style had to be divided, reducing the lot of each heir, the son accustomed to the amenities of a grander style was little disposed to be a common farmer. The Ossa in this respect seem to bear out the opinion expressed in a 1919 meeting by Francisco Encina and a group of landowners: 'The son of a proprietor of two or three hundred hectares does not want to be a farmer ... he becomes a lawyer, practices medicine, engineering, some other liberal profession, or to his shame, becomes a public employee. . .' Most of don Macario Ossa Cerda's sons became lawyers and petty bureaucrats; and by 1938, the Ossa surnames in the *Who's Who* of Chile are those of two landowners, three ordinary businessmen, two lawyers, two engineers, and a petty bureaucrat.[33]

One other Ossa is worth examining. Although not a member of the more socially distinguished branch we have just seen, José Santos Ossa is one of the legends of Chile, for he is credited with being the first to explore systematically and then exploit the great nitrate fields of the Atacama. The source of his wealth however was not nitrate but the Caracoles mines where an important silver strike was made in 1870. With these earnings – he had shares (*barras*) worth $480 000 in 1877 – he bought a house in Santiago for $35 000 and several rural properties. The maps, telescopes, books, and ledgers of statistics described by the inventory of the thirty-three-room house on Calle Nataniel demonstrate that we are not dealing here with an ordinary, rustic, pious provincial. There is the same 'progressive' air about his hacienda El Porvenir in Parral. There was $6600 in machinery – a $1500 steam engine; a 'Letts' thresher; three reapers, a *turbina* appraised at $1500 and several other examples of the most advanced agricultural technology. The hacienda was rented but stipulated in the contract was a requirement that the renter plant a certain number of trees, acres of alfalfa, and make the appropriate improvements. José Santos moreover extended a credit of $5000 to allow the renter to carry out the improvements while he himself invested in irrigation. All this we may suppose went a long way toward making El Porvenir an up-to-date and productive farm.[34] Few landowners, of course, had the capital or inclination to invest in their estates. Not one of José Santos' fifteen children chose to continue the work in El Porvenir and as far as can be determined only one – of dozens – of grandchildren owned rural property.

Our final example demonstrates the receptivity of the Chilean upper class to new money, the agrarian values of a thoroughly commercial family, and the operation of a foremost *agricultor progresista.* The first Edwards came to Chile at the beginning of the nineteenth century. George Edwards was a doctor on board a British ship operating against French vessels in the Pacific. The ship called at La Serena in 1807 where the young surgeon – then twenty-seven – became so enamored of the landscape and the nubile daughter of a Spanish Basque merchant (Isabel Ossandón Iribarren) that he changed his faith and nationality, married, and stayed forever. By 1835, his first wife had died but he had eight children, a modest stake gained from his medical practice and mining, and, according to Charles Darwin who was his guest for a number of weeks, was 'well-known for his hospitality.'[35] His children married a Tomás Smith; another the American Paul Délano. Agustín business community then forming in the Pacific towns. One daughter married a Tomas Smith; another the American Paul Délano. Augustín Edwards Ossandón who was to grow into Chile's most formidable mid-century capitalist, prospered in the years of the Chañarcillo silver strike (near Copiapó) as a proto-banker advancing the miners equipment and supplies and selling their ore. By 1851 he had moved to Valparaíso, married his niece, Juana Ross, the daughter of one of the more successful local merchants, became a major figure in the new Bank of Valparaíso, and by 1867 had founded his own Bank of A. Edwards and Company. This second generation immigrant although already thoroughly Chilean remained essentially a creature of the commercial port of Valparaíso. If the better families of Santiago society borrowed his money, it does not appear that they enjoyed his company – or he their values. Edwards Ossandón made his home in Valparaíso and although elected to the Senate he rarely, if ever, attended a session of Congress in Santiago. By 1874 he owned two pieces of rural property but they were in the north – Vallenar and Illapel.

It was Juana Ross, who outlived her husband by thirty-five years, and their multimillionaire son, Agustín Edwards Ross, who built on the original wealth and launched their descendants into the best Chilean society. Doña Juana invested a great deal of her inherited wealth in rural property. By 1902 she owned seven large estates from Quillota to Curicó including historic Ucuquer (in Aconcagua) that altogether were worth over $2.5 million. Don Agustín is one of the great economic success stories of the nineteenth century. Born in Valparaíso in 1852, he continued at accelerated pace in the footsteps of his banker father. To a fortune in banking he added the major newspaper, *El Mercurio* of Valparaíso, a great deal of urban property in Santiago and Valparaíso, and four impressive haciendas. When don Agustín died in 1898 the inventory that we will now examine in more detail, appraised his total holdings at $9 124 361; the largest fortune in Chile.[36]

The principal urban property was the neo-classic marble and plaster block that still stands (for a time as the Club de Septiembre) on Catedral. In 1898 this house was worth $450 000 and the furnishings, painting, and various *objets d'art* appraised at another $515 000. There were thirty-five more private and apartment houses, $1 125 000 in bank stock, the *Mercurio* valued at $500 000, a long list of stocks in railroads, utilities, municipal and national bonds. A large part of this immense fortune was given away: $300 000 to the Archbishopric of Santiago; $50 000 to the Firemen of Valparaíso; $310 000 to hospitals and the poor of Santiago and Valparaíso. Beyond this, in a burst of generosity that caused considerable astonishment at the time, article ten of Edwards' will cancelled out the debts due don Agustín – an act that released seventy-eight people, including many of the country's notable citizens but mainly fellow businessmen, of $796 000. Another legacy is more visible: Sr Edwards left $8000 for the statue to Manuel Montt and Antonio Varas that still stands opposite the Chamber of Deputies.[37]

Within the family, the distribution of property is interesting. Don Agustín's widow, Maria Luisa MacClure, got the Catedral Street mansion, other houses in Santiago and cash. The three sons were well set up in business with $1 125 000 in bank stock and the *Mercurio*, while the daughters – there were six – received the rural estates and the leftover urban property. Their husbands – Salas Undurraga, Irarrázabel Correa, Arturo Lyon Peña, Hurtado Concha; Gandarillas Huici; Errázuriz Vergara – reveal to the reader now familiar with these names so redolent of the landowning class, that the Edwards were firmly entrenched in the best society.

But if Agustín Edwards Ross had bought himself into the traditional society, the estates he owned and supervised were among the most modern in the country. La Peña in Quillota had just over 1000 hectares of irrigated land but it contained large investments in machinery, dairy equipment, thoroughbred Durham livestock and – a great rarity in Chilean agriculture – thirty-five Percheron draught horses. Los Nogales and San Isidro were model estates with power-driven irrigation pumps, $25 000 in threshers, reapers, wheeled plows and even two of the first lawn mowers ('maquinitas para segar pasto') used on the hacienda grounds. Here too were draught horses – forty-two Percheron; fifty-six Cleaveland on Los Nogales – steam pumps, refrigerators and an entire range of advanced equipment.[38]

I have gone to some lengths to point out the diversity of landowners and the kinds of rural estates; but as we move into the 1920s, it is appropriate to look again at the entire zone of central Chile to form a general picture of landholding patterns. The Yearbook of Agricultural Statistics is a good place to start because these official data present an impression that must be cleared away if we are to understand the reality of estate ownership. The Yearbook data summarised in Table 39 are

Table 39   Land distribution by property size in central Chile, 1923

Size category (in hectares)	Number of properties	%	Number of hectares	%
Less than 5	26 054	49.5%	38 986	0.3%
5–20	12 848	24.4	130 730	1.6
21–50	5562	10.5	186 123	2.4
51–200	4536	8.6	475 485	6.3
201–1000	2686	5.0	1 226 660	16.3
1001–5000	840	1.5	1 837 032	24.3
5001 and over	243	0.5	3 683 217	48.8
Totals	52 769	100%	7 578 233	100%

Source: *AE* (1923), vol. VII.

misleading because they express only the total acreage in each estate regardless of the quality of land or its yield. Thus, while it may have been true that 243 huge haciendas held over three and a half million hectares (forty-nine per cent of all agricultural land in central Chile), it is also obvious that a list of such estates by acreage would not coincide very well with a list arranged in order of income. Many of the 'great latifundia' that we hear condemned so frequently were actually quite worthless since the Yearbook's data include the dry hills of the coast range and vast stretches of the Andean canyons as well. A hundred hectares of good vineyard were worth more than 10 000 hectares of winter pasture while eight or nine hundred hectares of excellent irrigated land were often enough to support an upper-class way of life. Consequently, the official data by themselves do not really tell how many or which estates were the most important, let alone who their owners were. In 1923, however, Juvenal Valenzuela O. published a detailed and remarkably complete *Albúm de informaciones agrícolas* that described over 1800 of the 'most important *fundos* and haciendas' in central Chile. It is this source that underlies much of the discussion that follows.

Valenzuela claims to have 'personally visited each *agricultor*' in central Chile, gathering from each owner information on the amount and quality of his land, the number of *inquilinos* employed, the name of the owner, the renter, the location, and a wealth of other data. In those cases where it has been possible to compare Valenzuela's figures with independent sources such as inventories or private records of estates, I have invariably found close agreement. There are some omissions: the fine and certainly 'important' hacienda of San José del Carmen in Colchagua, for example, is inexplicably missing and Valenzuela's judgement of what constituted the 'most important' estates may be somewhat arbitrary. Yet, his choice seems at least as justifiable as the notoriously capricious tax records, and since he measures 'importance' by productive capacity the problem in the official data of vast but worthless acreage is avoided.

Although Valenzuela's *Album* describes over 1800 rural properties I have selected from these a more manageable sample of the largest estates through a simple formula designed to compensate for difference in land quality. For each property, the number of *de rulo* (non-irrigated) hectares was divided by a factor of ten and the quotient was added to the number of irrigated hectares. Thus for example, a *fundo* with 1500 hectares of *de rulo* and 400 of irrigated would have an adjusted figure of 550 as would an hacienda of 4500 *de rulo* and 100 of irrigated. A ratio of ten *de rulo* to one irrigated is only a rough measure of value. Lest my manipulation be considered another example of unnecessary originality, it should be emphasised that some factor is needed to reduce the value of unirrigated land. There are many different kinds of this – level, rolling, and mountainous – and, of course, location is also important. The 1965 Agrarian Reform Law recognises this and used a complicated formula to determine the minimum unexpropriable farm, beginning with the 'eighty basic hectares' of irrigated land in the Maipo valley (near Santiago). As one moved out from this region into hill land of the provinces, several hundred hectares would be needed for equivalent value. [39] Since the data we have for 1923 are not accurate enough to bear elaborate calculations, I have chosen the simple factor of ten as a rule of thumb. In more cases than not, the factor should be even greater, further reducing the importance of the hill-country ranches and giving more relative weight to the compact valley *fundos*. In any case, using the adjusted figure of 500 as the minimum to select the most important estates out of Valenzuela's original 1800 'most important haciendas and *fundos*,' we are left with 728 estates in the hands of 563 landowners. Notice carefully that the factor of ten was used only to establish a minimum size in selecting the sample: the acreage within estates in the following discussion of the sample itself is not reduced.

Table 40   Agricultural land contained in the sample as a percentage of all land in central Chile, 1923 (in hectares)

Type of land	Central Chile	Sample of 563 owners	Percentage of central Chile
Total area	8 658 000	—	—
Total agricultural land	7 578 000	3 644 000	48%
De rulo	6 647 000	3 188 000	48%
Irrigated	931 000	455 000	51%

Source: Total area from Instituto Geográfico Militar, *Atlas de la república de Chile*, 2nd ed. (Santiago, 1970), p. 27; other central Chile figures from *AE* (1923), vol. vii; Sample figures from Valenzuela O., *Album*.

The importance of the sample can be judged in Table 40. The 563 landowners controlled over 3.5 million hectares (or forty-eight per cent) of all agricultural land and 455 000 hectares (fifty-one per cent) of all irrigated land in central Chile.

If the total agricultural land of these 563 owners is arranged in the conventional size categories, we see in Table 41 that there are still 195 who have at least 5000 hectares. The difference between 195 here and 243 in the Yearbook can be explained by the fact that we are dealing here with owners and the Yearbook dealt with properties: some owners had more than one 5000 hectare estate. But in the next lowest size category, Valenzuela's criteria apparently eliminated many of the estates in the 1001–5000 category of the Yearbook (see Table 39). Using our factor of ten to shrink the importance of non-irrigated land, there are only 243 owners in the 1001–5000 category (compared with 840 properties in the Yearbook data) and our mental picture of the

Table 41   Distribution of agricultural land contained in the sample of
563 'most important' owners

Size categories (in hectares)	Number of owners	%	Number of hectares	%
Less than 1000	134	24	100 000	3
1001–5000	234	42	554 000	15
5001–10 000	109	19	830 000	23
10 001–25 000	56	10	868 000	24
25 000 and up	30	5	1 292 000	35
Totals	563	100%	3 644 000	100%

Source: Valenzuela O., *Album*.

countryside begins to change: if the estates' resources are described in
more realistic terms, we see a great many compact *fundos* of a few
hundred hectares in the level valley floor, while the 'baronial latifundia'
that one might imagine from the statistics in fact disappear in the
wasteland of the Andes.

In Table 42 our 563 owners are arranged only according to the
amount of irrigated land in their possession and from this we have a

Table 42   Distribution of total irrigated land contained in the sample
of 563 'most important' owners

Size categories (in hectares)	Number of owners	%	Number of hectares	%
Less than 50	40	7	700	less than 1%
51–200	42	7	5000	2
201–500	95	17	40 000	8
501–1000	260	46	184 000	40
1001–5000	122	22	196 000	44
5001 and up	4	1	30 000	6
Totals	563	100%	455 700	100%

Source: Valenzuela O., *Album*.

much closer idea of their real worth. The same Valenzuela data now
show only four owners with over 5000 hectares of irrigated land and 122
with between 1001 and 5000. These are still large and at least potentially
valuable estates and might well be described as latifundia. But there
were not many in this category. The rest of the *fundos* in the sample
and for that matter in the entire zone of central Chile had smaller

quantities of irrigated land. Valenzuela's data show 260 between 501 and 1000; 95 in the 201–500 category, and so on. In the Yearbook data (Table 39) there are 3769 properties of over 200 total hectares while Valenzuela's data, using only irrigated land as the measure, shows only about 670 in these categories. Obviously in some regions in some seasons, non-irrigated land had considerable value – the dry-land vineyards and wheatfields in Talca are good examples – but I have embarked upon this extended exegesis to demonstrate that in central Chile between 30° and 37° south latitude, the amount of irrigated land is a much more accurate measure of value; and if we use that criterion, our picture of landholding patterns is considerably altered.

Who were the main landowners in Chile by 1923? Valenzuela's *Album* describes about 1300 landowners (of the 1800 *fundos* and haciendas we have seen) and they were, first off, almost all private individuals; and except for the Marquis of Bute who owned two large mostly mountain haciendas – one of 10 000 hectares, the other of nearly 80 000 – they were all Chileans.[40] There were very few corporate holdings which contrasts with neighboring Argentina or with other Spanish American countries. The Bank of Chile owned two ordinary *fundos*; the Match Company (Companía Chilena de Fósforos) had 7000 irrigated hectares in wheat and poplar trees; three mining companies owned *fundos*, including Lo Aguirre, the property of the Santiago Mining Company (which in later years was turned into a kind of recreational park for the American colony's Thanksgiving Day celebration). In all, there were thirty-five corporate properties in central Chile with only 20 000 irrigated hectares, or less than three per cent of the total irrigated land in central Chile.

Church lands were also insignificant. There are only four *fundos* totaling 400 irrigated hectares listed for the secular Church and the orders – the Recollect Dominicans; Franciscans; Mercedarians mostly – held only 2000 irrigated hectares in seven *fundos*. This did not represent a decline from a nineteenth-century high, because after the great holdings of the Jesuits were taken over in 1767, the Church in Chile was never an important rural landholder. There were only three middling ecclesiastical properties listed in the 1874 tax rolls. Related to Church activities but supporting a range of hospitals, orphanages, and poor houses, were the properties owned by the Santiago and Concepción Juntas de Beneficencia. There were twelve of these quite large estates with a total of 176 600 hectares (but only 6000 irrigated). They were rented to individuals – a certain Abraham Gatica rented 121 000 hectares – became well-known for their low productivity, and were the first to be taken over by the reform of the 1960s.

If we come back again to the 563 most important landowners in Valenzuela's study, it is clear that the nineteenth-century trend noticed at the beginning of this chapter continued into the 1920s. Among the most important owners are now the Baburizza, Brown, Bruce, Cintolesi, Döll, Espínola, Hages, Mitrovitch, Ghiglioto Salas, Oliva, and Somarriva. Some were nitrate miners, such as Daniel Oliva or Pascual Barburizza; others wealthy businessmen like Brown, or successful engineers such as Enrique Döll. Some of the more familiar names of the nineteenth century, such as Fernando Irrarázabal, owner of Pullalli, or Alfredo Riesco, or the Donoso and Vergara, were still landowners in 1923 but there is no mistaking the change that occurred.

We may conclude by looking again at the twelve surnames whose fortune we followed through the nineteenth century. Although we are dealing with adjusted acreage in the Valenzuela study instead of monetary evaluations as in earlier data, our sample is still roughly comparable. In the 1908 tax rolls, the 504 estates with the highest monetary evaluation represented about thirty-eight per cent of the total appraised value of all rural property in central Chile. In 1923, the 563 'most important owners' in the Valenzuela study held forty-eight per cent of all acreage – fifty-one per cent of all irrigated land – the category that is probably most comparable to the 1908 appraisal value. Out of these samples of 'most valuable' or 'most important' estates, the Ossa, Larraín, Correa, Ovalle, Valdés, Balmaceda, Errázuriz, Vicuña, Echeverría, Subercaseaux, Ruiz-Table, and Garcia-Huidobro in 1908 owned eighty-eight properties whose appraised value was twenty-one per cent of the sample and eight per cent of the total in central Chile. In 1923, the same surnames held eighty-three properties but only thirteen per cent of the irrigated land. Their share of all land in central Chile was seven per cent. The changing fortunes of our twelve surnames can be seen more clearly in Table 43. The twelve owned fewer large properties than before, and the units were now smaller. The principal landowning families of the nineteenth century continued to be replaced by the wealthy buyers from mining and business circles.

The difference between these rural estates owned by a few such wealthy newcomers and the more traditional agrarian families is striking. These men, by and large energetic businessmen, bankers, and miners had the ready cash to invest in the land, to bring in the latest machines, and introduce new varieties of plants and animals. More accustomed to business management, more familiar with accounting, and primarily interested in turning a profit, there is no doubt they brought a different mentality to agriculture. These methods were shared by a few landowners of the more traditional agrarian families especially the few who studied and obtained degrees in agronomy. Yet, the cultural

Table 43   The percentage of agricultural income, appraised value, or acreage held by twelve family surnames: 1854, 1874, 1908, 1923

Categories	1854	1874	1908	1923
Percentage of all income, appraised value, or irrigated land in central Chile contained in the 'larger estates'	27%	40%	38%	51%
The number of 'larger estates' held by twelve family surnames	42	105	88	83
Percentage of income, appraised value, or irrigated land in the 'larger estates' held by twelve family surnames	38%	33%	21%	13%
Percentage of all income, appraised value, or irrigated land in central Chile that was held by twelve family surnames	10%	13%	8%	7%

Source: *Renta agrícola* (1854); *Rol de contribuyentes* (1874); *Indice de propietarios rurales* (1908); Valenzuela O., *Album* (1923).
'Large estates' are defined as follows: in 1854 and 1874: $6000 or more annual income; in 1908: $200 000 or more appraised value; in 1923, I have used the estates owned by the 563 'most important' owners in Valenzuela O., *Album*.

'weight of the night' – the burden of traditional practices – the pervading social values that placed a premium on landownership for non-economic reasons, and above all a degraded, ignorant and exploited mass of rural workers that not even the most 'progressive' of landowners – traditional or modern – attempted to do much about, was a powerful obstacle to a more productive agriculture. Administrators such as C. Hopfenblatt who managed the Edwards estates were forced to bring in from the cities or train locally people to operate and repair exotic equipment. But apart from slightly better houses and the occasional rude school, the age-old system of *inquilinaje* was little altered even on these estates. Neither Raul von Schroeders who owned, nor Hermann Schultz the Munich-trained *ingeniero agrónomo* who managed the hacienda Lo Hermida on the outskits of Santiago, seem to have employed a modern labor force; and in 1923, they were still 'projecting' the construction of a local school. Such an experienced man – *hacendado*, Minister of Agriculture, President of the SNA – as Luis Correa Vergara can only fall back on a historical and racial apology for the plight of rural workers in the 1930s, and his solution for low productivity or the 'social problem' was to relieve the major abuses, to extend and more tightly organise the existing system.[41]

CHAPTER 7

[1] *Renta agrícola* (1854); *Rol de contribuyentes* (1874).

[2] Frederick Pike, 'Aspects of class relations,' pp. 202–19, follows Gene Martin, *La división de la tierra en Chile central* (Santiago, 1960), which deals with a small section of the Maipo plain.

[3] Obviously the tax records are an inexact guide to actual income, but they do have value for the kind of relative statement made here. I am aware that people of common surname may in some cases be only distantly related; but in the nineteenth century the families we are dealing with were more cohesive than now.

[4] E. Espinoza, *Jeografía de Chile*, 5th ed. (Santiago, 1903); quotation on Délano from *BSNA*, vol. VIII (1877), p. 337. Figueroa, *Diccionario histórico*, is an invaluable source. See also, for interpretation, Julio Heise Gonzales, 'La constitución de 1925 y las nuevas tendencias políticos-sociales,' *Anales*, no. 80 (1950), p. 128.

[5] Figueroa, *Diccionario histórico*, II, p. 412; *Indice de propietarios*.

[6] Wright, 'Sociedad nacional de agricultural,' p. 44; Figueroa, *Diccionario histórico*, vols. IV–V, pp. 867, 660–1.

[7] Work now in progress by Marcello Carmagnani, Henry Kirsch, and Robert Oppenheimer should go a long way toward clarifying some of these questions.

[8] It is exceedingly difficult to determine rates of profit, even from the hacienda accounts book, because the Chilean, like the French or Russian estate account books of the eighteenth century, were not designed for cost analysis. See Forster, 'Obstacles to agricultural growth,' p. 1611. Many landowners thought that agriculture yielded some five to six per cent on investment, and Kirsch, 'Industrialization,' p. 129 says that industry produced around fifteen per cent.

[9] *El Mercurio* (Valparaíso), vol. LV, no. 1647 (26 April 1882). See Appendix for list of names. Pike, 'Aspects of class relations,' p. 205, following Heise González, uses the *Mercurio* list to demonstrate the 'rapid transformation' of colonial, landholding society.

[10] Simon Kuznets, quoted in Forster, 'Obstacles to agricultural growth,' p. 1613; see Correa Vergara, *Agricultura chilena*, I, chs. vi and vii; II, ch. xii; and Wright, 'Sociedad nacional de agricultura,' p. 34.

[11] McBride, *Land and Society*, p. 42.

[12] Pedro Pablo Figueroa, *Diccionario biográfico de estranjeros en Chile* (Santiago, 1900), pp. 122–3.

[13] *CJ* (Santiago), leg. 109, no. 11 (1886). Lazcano is identified as an 'old millionaire' in the *Mercurio* list.

[14] Espinoza, *Jeografía*, p. 323.

15 *Diccionario biográfico de Chile*, 13th ed. (Santiago, 1967).
16 Figueroa, *Diccionario histórico*, III, p. 637.
17 Felstiner, 'The Larraín family,' pp. 204–6; Graham, *Journal*, pp. 240, 255.
18 The loans came from several places: the Bank of Chile; an insurance company (Porvenir de las familias); McClure and Co.; Matte and Co., and through a special provision that allowed a part of a Baring Bros. public loan to be lent to individuals. See *CN* (Rengo), vol. 57, nos. 38 and 69; vol. 59, no. 81; vol. 62, no. 16, and vol. 65, no. 36. For sale of Cauquenes, see *CN* (Rengo), vol. 70.
19 Figueroa, *Diccionario histórico*, III, p. 637.
20 *CJ* (Santiago), leg. 107, no. 7.
21 *CJ* (Santiago), leg. 107, no. 7.
22 *CJ* (Santiago), leg. 169, no. 7 (1898). Incidentally, José Luis Larraín Larraín also married an ex-President's daughter, Enriqueta Bulnes.
23 *CJ* (Santiago), leg. 107, no. 4; see also the account books of Aculeo.
24 *CJ* (Santiago), leg. 107, no. 4.
25 Figueroa, *Diccionario histórico*, III, pp. 637–48.
26 *CJ* (Santiago), leg. 107, no 4.
27 Correa Vergara, *Agricultura chilena*, II, pp. 62–4; Figueroa, *Diccionario histórico*, III, pp. 642–7.
28 Figueroa, *Diccionario histórico*, IV–V, pp. 422–33.
29 *CJ* (Santiago), leg. 69, no. 1.
30 Pereira Salas, 'La arquitectura chilena en el siglo XIX,' *Anales* (1956), p. 21; Figueroa, *Diccionario histórico*, IV–V, p. 424.
31 Figueroa, *Diccionario histórico*, IV–V, p. 424; *CJ* (Santiago), leg. 35, no. 3.
32 Figueroa, *Diccionario histórico*, IV–V, pp. 423–6.
33 Quotation from Encina, *et al.*, 'Subdivisión de la propiedad rural,' p. 24; *Diccionario biográfico de Chile*, 2nd ed. (Santiago, 1938).
34 *CJ* (Santiago), leg. 23, no. 4.
35 Figueroa, *Diccionario histórico*, III, pp. 16–32; Darwin, *Voyage of the Beagle*, p. 343.
36 *CJ* (Santiago), leg. 103, no. 1 (1898). The inventory fills some twenty notebooks in the Santiago archive.
37 The outstanding loans include one to the Spanish Governor in the years of the Reconquest (1813–17) and to ex-President Manuel Montt.
38 All from *CJ* (Santiago), leg. 103, no. 1.
39 Or even thousands: a *de rulo* hacienda of some 10 000 hectares in Coquimbo might be barely equivalent to the '80 basic hectares' of the irrigated Maipo valley.
40 I have seen no other information on the Marquis of Bute estates. They were managed by Mr H. C. McGill and Mr Jared Noel Morgan, and were in San Antonio and Curicó Departments.
41 Velenzuela O., *Album*, p. 54; Correa Vergara, *Agricultura chilena*, II, pp. 355–400.

Santiago and the countryside,
ca 1910

> This society constitutes at the
> present time the only aristocracy in
> the world which still has full and
> acknowledged control of the
> economic, political and social forces
> of the State in which they live.
> *Paul S. Reinsch, 1909*

> I am a threat to no one.
> *Chilean President in the
> Parliamentary era*

We do not have to accept completely Virginia Woolf's remark that human society changed in 1910 to agree that even on the outskirts of civilisation, the enormous development wrought by Victorian capitalism was coming to a head. On the periphery of the thriving North Atlantic economy, Chilean export of nitrate reached two and a half million tons a year and the prices were higher than ever. By 1911, there were in the country nearly 6000 'factories' in a light industrial sector that employed some 75 000 workers; the central area of Santiago, at least, was a clean well-lighted place; a dozen prosperous banks were housed in gleaming brass and marble mansions. The centennial celebration of the 1810 Independence brought forth an impressive photographic display and a number of handsome slick-paper volumes as testimony of the marvelous prosperity, and continued progress was considered inevitable if not inexorable in this new world republic whose inhabitants liked to think of themselves as the English or the Prussians of South America. The wealthy classes had few problems and those which might appear, in the words of one cheerfully unobtrusive President, either had no solution or would solve themselves.

Santiago felt the effect of the new prosperity far more than any other place. Already in 1876, Horace Rumbold described its growth and luxury 'out of due proportion with the power and resources of the country of which it is the capital . . . with handsome public buildings, stately dwelling-houses and exceptionally fine promenades.' But what struck the stranger most was the atmosphere of aristocratic ease and exclusiveness.

Long, quiet streets of private houses, mostly built after the fashion of the Parisian *petit hôtel*, with some of far more ambitious style, their drowsiness now and then broken in upon by the clatter of a smart brougham or well-appointed barouche that might figure with credit in the Bois de Boulogne (the models of Chilean élegance are all French); well-dressed, refined looking women gliding along the well-swept pavement . . . all combine to make one ask one's self if this be not the residence of some dreamily-quiet orthodox, luxurious Court sooner than the center of a small, stirring, hard-working Democratic State . . . it is an absorbing place drawing to itself too much of the wealth of the country. The dream of the provincial Chileno is to make enough money to build a house in Santiago and there live at ease.

But Rumbold noticed at this early date the contrast between districts of Santiago which could also be taken as a general symbol of town and country: 'It [Santiago] is termed by its inhabitants "the Paris of South America," but is more like slices of Paris dropped down here and there in the midst of a huge, straggling Indian village.'[1]

The building boom that began modestly in the 1850s gained momentum in Rumbold's years and by 1910 Santiago was a thriving and well-ordered city. The low, adobe colonial city was transformed by brick and timber. The new mansions were of two and three storeys built not only in the *petit hôtel* style but by French and English architects. The Cousiño 'palace' on Diesiocho Street cost $2 000 000 in 1875–8 and it, like the fine house of José Arrieta across from the municipal theatre (and now the French Cultural Institute) was designed by Paul Lathoud. Carpenters and builders from the United States, and often the stone and timber as well, were brought around Cape Horn to help create the new elegance. Potable water had been piped from the Mapocho River since early in the century and by 1910 most houses in the core of the city had adequate interior plumbing. Electric trolleys replaced the earlier *ferrocarril de sangre* (horse-drawn cars) by 1900; electric street lights were increasingly common. The fashionable center moved south from the colonial Plaza de Armas and the new buildings spread across the Alameda – Henry Meiggs, the railway mogul, built at Alameda and Cochrane – and by the turn of the century dozens of new private 'palaces' marched west along the avenues of Diesiocho, Ejército Libertador, and República to the very edge of the elegant Club

Hípico (founded in 1869), which along with the Club de la Unión was the principal social center of the Santiago elite.[2]

Little of the wealth generated in the export sector was applied outside Santiago and Valparaíso. Provincial towns remained dusty and boring, their schools and sanitation inadequate. This melancholy state was the natural consequence of a hacienda-dominated countryside where the estate, not a local market town, was the intermediary between city and country. Of the interior towns, only Talca could claim the semblance of a provincial culture. Few 'respectable' people chose to live in these backwaters, especially as government and bureaucracy became more and more centered on Santiago, and as transportation and the possibility of employment in the few factories or as domestics in the houses of the rich drew people toward the capital.

For the wealthy, Santiago was a small society where everyone who counted was personally acquainted and where it was sufficient for a visitor merely to tell the coachman to drive to the house of 'don Carlos tal y tal' or even just 'don Carlos.' George McBride noted that the small group of influential families was so concentrated in downtown Santiago that the entire country was controlled by four square blocks in the city. This, too, was a 'cosy little status quo,' as L. B. Simpson described the Mexico of Porfirio Diaz, and it had some unusual features. Women occupied a more important position in Chilean society than elsewhere in Latin America where they are usually pictured by Latin Americans and foreigners as well as exotic but vacuous belles behind the inevitable *mantilla*, or as sombre and frumpy politicians' wives. Women in Santiago ran the streetcars, engaged in a wide range of economic and commercial activities and one properly aristocratic lady, doña Inés Echeverría de Larraín, was the first Spanish American woman to obtain a Chair in the University. We may look beyond Maria R. Wright's unrestrained gushing – she dedicated her slick 1904 volume 'to the women of Chile' – to understand that among the upper classes, Chilean women were better off, *más libres* than in neighboring republics.[3]

In all of these accounts of Chile at the turn of the century, and perhaps even more so in present-day works, we must guard against a tendency to divide the upper groups of society into economic categories. In the late colonial years and well into the nineteenth century, there were, it is true, many families whose entire wealth and social standing derived from landownership. The Echenique family that we have already examined in some detail is a good example of a fairly common situation. But practically from the beginning of European settlement the economic interests of the Chilean elite overlapped. Sons of landowners went into trade, miners bought land, bankers owned dairies; and as we move through the nineteenth century, this process of economic intermingling was simply accelerated. Nearly all wealthy Chileans including, of course, absentee landowners, came to be concentrated in Santiago. They met in clubs, in Congress, in innumerable social gatherings – all of which contributed to closely-woven social relationships. In economic matters the new institutions of corporate ownership – the stock market, banks and credit houses – made diversification easy and often invisible. Although recent studies have dealt with certain social groups and more work is in progress, we do not have anything near to a comprehensive historico–quantitative study of the national elite. Yet, it is necessary here to give the reader a sense of the composition of the elite and then, the place of landownership within it.[4]

It is reasonable to begin with the land since Chile developed as an agrarian colony and in the new republic, landownership was clearly the main ingredient in any definition of elite standing. In 1854 there were 145 estates that produced – according to the tax rolls – over $6000 each for their owners. With the growth of markets the prosperity of the agrarian sector increased: in 1874, there were 338 in the comparable largest category and by 1908, over 500. The names of the largest land-owners can be easily obtained from the tax rolls but the kind of in-vestigation that would permit a comprehensive picture of their total economic worth is beyond the scope of this study. Some of these land-owners, even in 1920, owned nothing except the *fundo* and an urban residence; many others, in varying amounts, held shares of mining companies, banks or businesses, and others were only secondarily land-owners. But we can say with assurance that any owner of an important estate, regardless of his other holdings, probably lived in Santiago, was likely a member of the Club de la Unión or the Club Hípico, often in Congress or the public administration, and was considered by others to belong to the national elite or oligarchy.[5] As we have already seen, eighty-eight or over twenty per cent of the largest estates in 1908 were owned by twelve surnames of the traditional 'Castilian–Basque aris-tocracy' and several other undoubtedly derived from families which had been landowners in the colonial era. The rest – and without a close genealogical study the exact percentage is difficult to determine – were wealthy miners and businessmen who had only recently purchased a rural estate.

If one did not have the good fortune to inherit a rural estate, the most common avenues to success were commerce and mining. From the late eighteenth century on a steady flow of immigrants opened shops in the main ports and in Santiago. The Basques were especially prominent in the eighteenth century and after Independence men and women from several countries in western Europe and the United States moved into the vacuum created by the break with Spain. By 1849 sixty per cent of the important Valparaíso import–export houses were listed as foreign-owned. Such a description, however, is somewhat misleading. Nationalities can be changed and in fact many of the post-Independence merchants, like the Basques before them, settled in Chile, married locally, and were economically Chilean. And even while immigrants were moving into the ports, Chileans whose ancestors had come generations before, continued until near the end of the nineteenth century to control over three-fourths of the larger commercial establishments in the inland capital itself and nearly all of the small retail shops. A few of these families, along with the successful nationalised immigrants, became wealthy through trade and banking, and once their fortunes were made, they became pillars of Chilean society. We have no systematic study of this group but such immigrants as the Subercaseaux, Edwards, Lyon, Bunster, and Brown together with the Besa, Salas Bascuñan, and Matte, and Fernández Concha would be appropriate examples. Here again the occupational distinction is partly artificial because several Chilean merchants were in fact sons of landowners or even landowners themselves.

Mining was a more dramatic and also more perilous road to wealth. Before the 1870s silver and copper were the most important minerals and this mining activity was generally in the hands of Chileans or of men economically Chilean. Nitrate, too, was first explored and exploited by Chileans but it is not clear what share of this industry remained in national hands. Most writers have followed Encina in asserting that nitrate passed under British control after the War of the Pacific (1879–83). Encina claimed that by 1901 only fifteen per cent of total investment in the nitrate industry was Chilean, while the British dominated with fifty-five per cent. Julio César Jobet thinks that Chilean nitrate 'interests' were only sixteen per cent in 1879 and Aníbal Pinto Santa Cruz's influential and more recent work essentially follows these figures.[6] As far as one can tell from the official statistics, these estimates of Chilean ownership are low. The Statistical Yearbook puts the value of Chilean nitrate production at around forty per cent of the total throughout the first two decades of the twentieth century and in 1923, when the data are given in tons instead of value of production, the Chilean share is still forty-two per cent. And, of course, things other than nitrate – it represented seventy-two per cent of all mining value in 1916 – were mined. Copper was still largely in Chilean ownership as was all coal. Many of these mining names – the Ossa, Urmeneta, Gallo, Pereira, Cousiño – are well-known in Chile in part because they put their mining fortunes into rural estates (many of these were made into excellent vineyards on the model of French châteaux) and their owners became prominent in Santiago society.[7]

Nor should the industrial sector which steadily expanded after the War of the Pacific be ignored in any discussion of the elite. Until recently, we have been told by authors who based their opinion mainly on a reading of government policy rather than data on industry itself, that Chile began to industrialise only after the 1930 Depression; or – in another version – that a manufacturing sector had begun to emerge between 1840 and 1860 but had then stagnated. But in recent years, Carlos Hurtado noticed the steady increase in raw material imports and inferred from this and other indirect evidence that the country was undergoing a minor industrial boom in the late nineteenth century. Since then Oscar Muñoz has provided evidence of considerable industrial activity after 1914 and a recent study by Henry Kirsch that rests on close research and careful use of statistics has just appeared to put the entire process in perspective and to offer explanation.[8] According to Kirsch, the War of the Pacific marked the beginning of steady growth of manufacturing in Chile and by 1911, the published data that show some 6000 factories employing about 75 000 workmen are probably undernumerated.

Few people of modest origin rose to wealth through industry; rather it was the immigrants, who in Chile unlike in Argentina or in the U.S. were mainly of middle-class background, and already wealthy Chileans. In his analysis of 207 directors of enterprises whose stock was traded on the Santiago Exchange, Kirsch found that by 1922 seventy-three per cent were directors of more than one corporation and that at least forty-six per cent were involved in finance, thirty-four per cent in mining, thirty-eight per cent in agriculture, and seventeen per cent in commerce. This is the first attempt at quantifying the intermingled economic interests among the Chilean elite and the result confirms a common suspicion. Even so, the real connections are probably under-stated because – as Kirsch points out – 'intersectorial links would be considerably higher if the individual's investments rather than his position as an active principal in an industry, bank, trading house, etc., were the criteria employed.'[9]

Just as it makes no sense by the early twentieth century to talk of a 'landed elite' or 'mining elite,' it is also impossible to calculate national product or the share that each economic sector may have produced. A recent attempt, the Ballesteros/Davis study which we have seen before, depends on a series of heroic assumptions and is not convincing for the earlier years of the period it deals with either in terms of output or employment.[10] There are export data but the kind of information that would reveal the number and size of private incomes in mining or business either does not exist or has not yet been put together. The tax records of rural property give an indication of the most important landowners but they certainly cannot be taken as accurate indications of either their gross income or profit.

If most of the new Chilean industrialists came from already established families or from among the middle-class immigrants, this seems to be even more true for the increasing numbers of lawyers, doctors, professors, and writers. Again, we have no study of the social background of public administrators or the liberal professions but one's impression from the names of men in the ministries, the foreign office, in universities as well as those of the most prominent writers and artists up to the 1930s, is that they were drawn from the important landowning or wealthy immigrant families. In fact, this would be the expected thing in a society where few except the wealthy had access to the university or had the money and leisure to travel abroad for education. One or more of a landowner's or wealthy miner's sons often studied law or medicine, frequently as an entry to politics or public administration. This attitude has been condemned by Encina and others as part of the anti-economic mentality of the Chilean elite whose sons sought 'parasitic' positions in law or other liberal professions instead of accepting a modest inheritance and improving a portion of the family *fundo* or business.[11] And Orrego Luco, who knew the Chilean *belle époque* society as well as anyone, tells us that in the early twentieth century, the 'old colonial spirit' was still latent in the Chilean upper class, and because of this, most young men with prestigious and aristocratic names were inclined to enter the university where, 'between parties and cotillion balls' they managed to obtain a degree in medicine or law and with the attendant prestige, but none of the training, felt confident in establishing a family and settling into their rightful place in sociey.[12] As the nitrate revenues were funneled through the expanding bureaucracy into railway and port works, urban modernisation, and public education, there was a vast increase in well-paid posts in public administration and the service sector into which the sons of the *gente bien* could move. The best paid and most influential of these, together with a handful of top ecclesiastics and military officers, round off our sketch of the early twentieth-century Chilean elite.

We may now return to the original aim of discussing the role of landownership within the elite. In fact, landownership and the elite interacted in a reciprocal way. It was not just that landowners invested in urban sectors or that the directors of new industries or mines were recruited from among the traditional families; but also that once men prospered in non-agrarian pursuits, they often invested their earnings in rural estates. Therefore when we see the continued if not growing importance of landownership in Chile, this is not just a reflection of an agriculture that was thriving under the impact of new markets but also the persistent importance that estate ownership had in the value system of the elite. We have already seen the interlocking economic interests of the urban and agricultural sectors but we must not construe this to mean that bankers, miners, or businessmen were either absorbing or brushing aside a 'landed aristocracy.' For although the economics of the industrial West and Chile were linked by new lines of trade and investment, their elites were developing in different directions. Where in western Europe industry led to the creation of a distinct middle-class culture and the political dominance of the city, or where in the USA northern merchants and industrialists destroyed the planter aristocracy, in Chile, the 'South' continued to set the social tone for the entire country and remained politically dominant into the 1920s at least.[13] While British landlords were forced to accept the restrictions imposed by their own bourgeois conquerors, Chilean *hacendados* strolled the Riviera; where in France, Germany, Britain, and the USA, local entrepreneurs rose to the top of the social and political system; Chilean merchants, miners, and businessmen often gave way to the steady pressure of foreign investors in the dynamic sectors of the economy, preferring to copy the style of an already archaic but irresistibly attractive rural way of life.

All this would be incomprehensible without reference to the sudden and distorted developments brought about in late nineteenth-century Chile by the export economy at a time when the social values of a closely knit traditional rural society were still dominant. Although some individual Chileans got rich through nitrates, the ownership of mines progressively came under foreign control. In the case of copper, this was even more true after 1917 as the great mines of El Teniente and Chuquicamata, both developed with American capital, came into operation to dwarf Chilean production.[14] By 1916, the Statistical Yearbook gave the data shown in Table 44 on the value of all mining production in Chile. Several foreigners besides the British and Americans were involved and according to this data, together they accounted for sixty per cent of total production. Even if these figures do not exaggerate the Chilean share (the origin of investment in corporations is unusually difficult to determine) they are still somewhat misleading because the apparatus of commercialisation such as the Nitrate Railways Company, the Bank of Tarapacá and London, the insurance and accounting firms, were generally foreign owned and were perhaps as profitable as the mines themselves.[15]

Table 44   Value of mining production in Chile by nationality, 1916
(in pesos worth 18 pence of the £ sterling)

Nationality Germany	Value $	Percentage	
Chile	197 072 000	40%	
Great Britain	136 870 000	28	
North America	59 000 000	12	
Germany	44 424 000	9	
Various	21 275 000	4	
			all foreign 60%
France	10 014 000	2	
Spain	8 957 000	2	
Belgium	6 650 000	1.5	
Peru	6 218 000	1.5	
Totals	490 480 000	100%	

Source: *AE* (1916), vol. VIII, pp. 5, 7.

After two decades of reflection, Aníbal Pinto finds the peculiar effect of the export economy on Chilean society of 'enormous significance,' one of the keys to understanding the country. Because the mining sector was dominated by foreigners, the economic base of Chilean miners was not directly strengthened (as was, for example, the locally owned 'livestock oligarchy' of Argentina with the export of beef) and a class of powerful miners was not elevated to political power. However, because Chile was a stable and well-organised country with an effective public administration, it was able to impose taxes on mineral exports to raise impressive public revenue. This created a 'structure of demand and employment' considerably different from what would have existed had the income gone to private Chilean mine owners. It expanded public services and the number of social groups dependent in one form or another on

State investment. This led to the creation of a great many bureaucratic and service positions – the best ones largely filled, as we have seen, by relatives of the wealthy families – and the accelerated development of an urban middle class.[16]

The process of denationalisation was also at work in the commercial sector. Although some Chileans had prospered and some immigrant merchants had become rich, nationalised, and prominent during the course of the nineteenth century, it is arguable that by 1916, Chilean merchants were receiving a smaller share of trade than they had in 1850. The Statistical Yearbook for 1916 shows a total of 26 000 'commercial establishments' representing some $366 000 000 pesos. Of these, Chileans owned only ten of the twenty-five largest import–export houses and were being displaced in the Valparaíso and Santiago retail trade by a new and much more imposing foreign commerce represented by such houses as J. W. Hardy and Co., W. R. Grace, the Maison Française, Gath and Chaves, and so on. Foreigners together owned over 6000 retail businesses in Chile in 1916 which were worth over 91 million pesos compared to some 16 000 firms with only 58 million in Chilean hands. These data simply bear out Francisco Encina's observation (made in 1912) that, 'in less than fifty years, the foreign merchant smothered our nascent commerce abroad and even within our own country ['dentro de la propia casa'] ... replaced us in large part, in the retail business.'[17] Among the foreigners, the English, somewhat surprisingly, occupied fifth place. The Spanish, Italian, French, and Germans had more invested in all 'commercial establishments' than the English did, as can be seen in Table 45.

It is the industrial sector that best reveals the Chilean retreat in the face of foreign investment. Into the first decade of the twentieth century, Chilean industrialisation seemed to be under way, but from about 1910 on, the rates of capital investment, industrial employment, and output all appreciably slowed from the pace of previous decades. By 1916, the Yearbook provides an indication of the Chilean investors' involvement in industry and their share seems to slip for the following decade. The problem in these data is to determine the national origin of capital in the corporations. The official statistics are no help but Kirsch's recent work suggests that the large part of this was foreign. It is beyond the scope of this essay to discuss fully the failure of Chilean industry. The explanations range from the 'complicated entrepreneurial problem' alleged by Aníbal Pinto to Marcello Carmagnani's recent analysis of the 'asymmetrical' relationship that grew up between Great Britain and Chile in the nineteenth century. Kirsch's study carries the discussion further with the aid of new information. Whatever the reason, it is clear now that neither the export economy nor the nascent industrial sector served as a 'growth pole.' Chileans were unable to

Table 45   Number and capital value of commercial establishments by nationality in Chile, 1916 (in pesos worth 18 pence of the £ sterling)

Nationality	Number of establishments	Capital $	Percentage
Chile	18 614	144 990 000	39%
Spain	1791	49 067 000	
Italy	2158	39 990 000	
France	420	25 121 000	
Germany	279	24 880 000	
Great Britain	143	14 563 000	61%
'Otoman'	761	10 826 000	
North American	68	9 275 000	
(all others)	1844	47 414 000	
Totals	26 078	366 126 000	100%

Source: *AE* (1916), vol. x, p. 128.

Table 46   Amount of capital invested in industry in Chile by nationality, 1916 (in pesos worth 18 pence of the £ sterling)

Nationality	Amount $	Percentage
Chile	140 702 000	26%
Foreign	148 380 000	27
Mixed	19 783 000	3
Not specified	2 469 000	—
Corporate (Sociedad Anónima)	241 082 000	44
Totals	552 416 000	100%

Source: *AE* (1916), vol. ix, p. 51.

attain a high rate of capital accumulation, did not create a heavy capital goods industry, consumed at high levels, chose to put their money in real estate and banks, and remained content with the crumbs of light industry that fell from the groaning sideboard of the Atlantic economy.[18]

It is easy to imagine a different course of Chilean development. Had the increase in trade after 1860 led to the rise of an influential national merchant class (the case of Boston or Philadelphia in the eighteenth and nineteenth centuries, for example); or had the mines enriched national miners and elevated that sector to political power (the case of France or Belgium); or if those Chileans who in fact did make money through trade, banking or mining, had invested in heavy industry (in place of buying rural estates as so many did); then undoubtedly the place of landownership in society and politics would have been less important than it was. As it was, the Chilean oligarchy remained heavily influenced by the traditional *hacendados* as well as by the new landowners who tended to adopt the policy and values of their esteemed rural neighbors. As we have seen, the disproportionate influence of the countryside was not only because of an absolute increase in agricultural income but also because of the relative weakening economic base of the Chilean urban sectors.

A reflection of the importance of landownership can be seen in the interests of Congressmen. I would not argue that election to Congress is a completely accurate measure of political power; but it is true that Deputies and Senators were, in the Chilean system, an important part of the policy-making machinery throughout the years 1850 and 1920.[19] Nor is Congressional membership a perfect measure of status although there is no doubt that such a position conferred much prestige on its holder. Nor, of course, after what we have seen, is it possible to say that because a person owned a rural estate he was only or even primarily a landowner or that farming provided most of his income. All such questions await a great deal more research. But if we look at the number of Senators and Deputies who owned large rural estates over the period 1850 to 1920, we can gain an impression of the enduring value that men placed on landownership and undoubtedly, also, an indication of their politics.

In 1854, thirty-four (or forty-one per cent) of the eighty-three Congressmen owned large rural estates. As we move through the nineteenth century the number of Senators and Deputies who owned land continually increased: half of them had large *fundos* in 1875, and by 1902, the percentage increased to fifty-seven. As late as 1915–18, nearly half of all Congressmen (forty-six per cent) still included among their interests one of the important estates of central Chile. We must be careful of what this means. It does not mean that these Congressmen were simply *hacendados*; many, already in 1854, had other investments of occupations as well, and as we have seen, the economic interests of the Chilean elite were becoming progressively entangled in the later nineteenth and early twentieth century. But on the other hand, neither do our data mean that simply because a Congressman did not personally

Table 47 Number and percentage of Chilean congressmen who directly own a large rural estate: 1854, 1874, 1902, 1918

	1854		1874		1902		1918	
	Senator	Deputy	Senator	Deputy	Senator	Deputy	Senator	Deputy
Total members of Congress	29	54	30	96	33	94	37	118
Of these, the number who own large estates	14	20	21	42	24	49	25	47
Percentage of Congressmen who own large estates	48%	37%	70%	44%	73%	52%	67%	40%
Total number of Senators and Deputies in Congress	83		126		127		155	
Number of these who own large estates	34		63		73		72	
Percentage of all congressmen who own large estates	41%		50%		57%		46%	

Source: The names of congressmen are from Luis Valencia Avaria, *Anales de la República* (Santiago, 1950), 2 vols.; 'large estates' are defined as having $6000 or more annual income in the 1854 *Renta agrícola* and 1874 *Rol de contribuyentes*; over $200 000 *avalúo* in Espinoza, *Jeografía* and the 1908 *Indice de propietarios*. For 1918, I used the Valenzuela O., *Album*.

own land, that he was not linked by political outlook or familial ties to rural interests. In fact, our simple definition undoubtedly underestimates the true relationship between Congress and landownership. There are several Senators and Deputies throughout these years with the same names as those traditionally associated with landownership which is understandable since frequently one son inherited the estate while others studied law and entered politics. The Correa, Errázuriz, Balmaceda, Echenique are only a few out of many examples of families who used their rural base to launch several sons into law and politics. Often two or three sons from the same family would be together in Congress. None of these, unless they are personally listed in the rural tax rolls, appear in our calculations.

In Congress as in the elite in general, the importance of landowner-ship is a reflection of: (1) the increasing yield of agriculture; (2) the enduring prestige value of land for urban investors; and (3) the relative weakness of the urban sectors of the economy. This is not to say that mining, trade, and industry were not thriving; they clearly were. But because these activities were dominated by foreigners, few individual Chileans directly represented the most dynamic sectors of the country. Chilean nitrates propelled John Thomas North, the famous British 'nitrate king,' to social prominence in England (and very nearly into the House of Commons), but in Chile, the social and political reflection of mining tended to be one step removed from the activity itself; that is, the government obtained the Chilean share through taxation and channeled this revenue through the public administration into transport, education and urban improvement.[20] This then created many well-paid openings for office holders and professionals – as many as thirty-eight per cent of the 1915–18 Congress might be classified as such – but these men and their ideas were more likely to be drawn from the traditional landholding families than anywhere else. As a consequence, it is arguable that the Thirty-first Congress (1915–18) contained fewer direct representatives from the mining and commercial sectors than did the Tenth (1852–5). Thus, even in a period of rapid economic growth, when a great deal of wealth was generated in non-agricultural sectors, when cities and an urban proletariat were rapidly expanding, the main machinery of government was composed of either traditional landowners or men for whom landownership and the life style this implied continued to be a cherished value.

During the first years of the twentieth century, only a few Chileans noticed or seemed to care that the more dynamic sectors of the economy were slipping from their hands. Nitrate exports increased and the flow of public revenue was richer than ever. The paper value of capital invested in new corporations rose from 20 million pesos in 1903 to 342 million in 1905, and the wealthy endulged themselves in an unprecedented burst of spending and display.[21] Viña del Mar, with its racetracks, golf course, and lawn tennis, was just becoming a favorite spot and there is a good account of the rich at play in Marie Wright's admiring book. The railway here too brought a revolution in customs by putting such beach resorts within easy reach of the capital. Interestingly, the train platform itself became a central location for social display where the young and gorgeous gathered some time before departure for rounds of gossip and flirtations. But Santiago offered the best examples of gracious living: the Opera where from June to August 'the Paris gowns, the costliest laces, the richest jewels' could be seen, or at the Club Hípico, or the ostentatious houses. It was during these years – 1891–1910 – that the oligarchy was marked as a *clase derrochadora* (squandering class), an image that appeared along with the emergence of social problems and social critics. 'Civilised consumers but primitive producers' was the apt observation of Enrique Molina, future Rector of the University, which stands as a fitting epitaph for the habits of the *belle époque*.[22]

The increasing charm and lure of Santiago society meant that landowners spent even less time in the countryside. Jaime Eyzaguirre makes this point in his study of the Errázuriz Echaurren administration (1896–1901), and as regular steamship service (via the transisthmian railroad and after 1912 the Panama Canal) provided an alternative to the fearsome Cape Horn passage, many landowners were not only increasingly absent from the *fundo* but from the country as well. In an illuminating examples, the estate of Requínoa (in Caupolicán) was mortgaged to obtain $100 000 for its owner Juan Guillermo Gallo, 'vecino de Paris.' By the end of the century the subject of voluntary exiled Chileans who sought culture and comfort in the Old World was a frequent theme of novels and we are told that in 1891 a large Parisian ballroom was found to be too small to contain the Chilean celebrants of Balmaceda's defeat, most of whose names reveal their descent from traditional landowning families.[23]

The mood and substance of the early twentieth century are caught perfectly by Luis Orrego Luco in *Casa grande* (1907). Before then, the fundamental problem treated by Chilean novelists was that of a humble person hoping to move into the elite through love or money. In *Casa grande* a middle class has arrived, merged with and corrupted the 'sober and responsible' nineteenth-century aristocracy. In Orrego Luco's view, the entire society was carried away by the lust for wealth. The center of speculation and rumor was Bandera Street – the location of the stock exchange and brokers' offices – where shares of the new companies were traded, fortunes made and lost overnight while the aristocratic and moral fabric of the country steadily came undone: 'There was talk of a lawyer who had just sunk 300 000 pesos in a country "chalet"; someone else spent 70 000 pesos on an opera dancer; the wives of the newly rich covered themselves with silk, lace and pearls; accounts were opened in the new luxurious shops and stores of the capital.'[24]

Beneath this froth of getting and spending, Orrego Luco gives us a vivid picture of an elite whose separation from the working classes was widened by economic growth. As mining revenue flowed into the upper reaches of society the Chilean elites that had always looked to Europe were more and more inclined to turn their backs on their less fortunate countrymen and seek culture and manufactures in France and England. Better ocean transport and ready cash encouraged overseas travel and most people able to pay made the trip and returned, affecting French manners and language and ordering wines and furniture to follow. In Chile and several other Latin American countries the gap which from the beginning separated the descendants of the conquerors from the submerged mass was reinforced by racial distinctions and insecurity. As the economic ties of nitrate, credits, and trade brought the Chilean elites into closer touch with Europe and North America, they became steadily alienated from the mass on whose labor the connection depended.[25] Orrego Luco himself is an excellent example of this. His rural scenes are idyllic and unreal; the laboring men are seen from a distance. One is reminded in his writing and that of others in this period of the affecting scene in Fellini's film *La dolce vita* where another estranged elite (the jaded jet set of modern Rome) pauses distractedly on the way to yet another party to wonder what an ordinary local peasant plowing his fields could possibly be doing.

These attitudes are all common in a non-integrated society and we are often reminded of similar features in pre-revolutionary Russia or Bourbon France. But there are some interesting differences. Although sometimes amused and indulgent toward the quaint ways of the popular classes, the Chilean and most other Latin American elites were disinclined to encourage a real nationalist sentiment. Apart from the occasional border squabble there were no national aims to attain, and it certainly needed little wit on the part of the oligarchy to understand that a proper nationalist movement would inevitably turn against a class that was closely allied with – indeed dependent upon – foreign support. The populist champions were not found among the aspirants to the Chilean *belle époque* elite who more than anything sought the acceptance of their social betters. Chilean nationalism found its leaders in the literate and frustrated ranks of society that lay between the working classes and the older elite, who saw in the urban mass their vehicle to power.

The sudden creation of a 'numerous and combative proletariat' was another feature of the peculiar form of Chile's export economy.[26] After 1880 especially, thousands of men and women, leaving behind some of the ignorance and restraints – and also a certain paternalistic welfare – of a traditional rural society, settled in the mining camps and new towns of the desert north, and crowded into the teeming *conventillos* of Santiago. Bare figures cannot convey the desperation, frustration, and hostility that the new conditions bred. In the mining districts conditions were harsh. Workers were exposed to extremes of climate and performed hazardous labor which produced a high rate of injury and death. Waves of unemployment followed brusque oscillations in the world market for nitrate and working families gathered into organisations for survival. At the same time they came into contact with new men and ideas and these were spread along an ideological 'transmission belt' that ran south to the cities. Conditions in Santiago and Valparaíso were not so dramatic as in the nitrate fields but scarcely less desperate. All these – miners, city workers, and marginals – shared the burden of a relentlessly rising cost of living. Under these circumstances the working poor began to organise. The number of organised workers increased from 30 000 in 1900 to 65 000 in 1910 and to 200 000 in 1921. The early 'innocuous mutual aid societies' were superseded by the Chilean Federation of Labor (FOCH) founded in 1909, and the Socialist Labor Party in 1912.[27]

From the turn of the century onward, the urban and mining mass grew rapidly in numbers, appetite, and political clout. The first strikes, in the 1880s, took place among the skilled workers of the city, the construction and dock workers. By 1890, a massive strike in Tarapacá involved some 10 000 workers, in 1903 the major port of Valparaíso was paralysed for weeks, and in 1907 the most violent of all of these early labor conflicts occurred in the nitrate port of Iquique when some 20 000 strikers temporarily took the city and were then brutally routed by army troops pouring machine gun fire into the workers' ranks. Even more ominous was the bloody 'Red Week' in October 1905, when the Santiago urban poor, enraged by soaring food prices and the apparent indifference of the government, took the city for a week. Because the local army garrison was absent, the municipal authorities issued fire-arms to the Club de la Unión and the younger members of this (then) most aristocratic of all Chilean clubs formed an *ad hoc* 'guard of order' to restore order. This led to face-to-face class warfare and the con-frontation of armed aristocrats and the unarmed mob yielded some 300 dead, 1000 wounded, and the enduring enmity of the working classes who were shocked by the zeal and ruthlessness with which a 'young bourgeois horde' opened fire. For its efforts, the president of the Club de la Unión received a note of thanks from the Minister of the Interior.[28]

Until these early years of the twentieth century few people were con-cerned with the plight of the poor, and the agrarian system, supplying adequately as it did a weak market, was rarely questioned. But because of external economic stimuli and consequently the rapid development of a modern urban proletariat, the agrarian structure and an un-responsive government were brought under attack. Two features of the early twentieth century conjuncture made it certain that the rural system was singled out: in the first place, the urban and mining workers, whose purchases were reduced to the bare essentials of life, spent by far the largest part of their wage on food. A Labor Office survey, cited by Thomas Wright in his admirable study of the SNA, revealed that some sixty per cent of working-class income was spent on food, a fact that soon led the champions of the urban mass to focus their discontent on the agricultural sector.[29] At the same time, the landowners were the most visible and easily identifiable element in the oligarchy, and per-haps the most inflexible. The social system was first wrenched by the violent but quickly repressed explosions mentioned above; when strikes failed, the urban intellectuals fell back to write an enormous volume of bitter tracts exposing the 'social question' and singling out the 'landed oligarchy' as the principal villains. When it became clear that the government would not be moved, the frustrated writers and social critics – drawn mainly from the rapidly growing stratum of public administrators, professionals, and professors (the 'intellectual prole-tariat' of Alberto Edwards) – subsided, nurturing a latent *rencor de clase* that has only recently exploded with unexpected fury.

While the nitrate and urban workers organised themselves into co-operatives, unions and political parties, the clamor and strikes of the mines and cities had little echo in the countryside. The absence of rural conflict until very recent years is a stubborn fact that must be acknowledged. Despite the assiduous efforts of several recent writers to uncover a history of peasant revolt, the research so far only serves to confirm the deep conservatism of landlord and *campesino* alike. To say this is not to overlook the desperate plight of hacienda workers or suggest a picture of rural idyl. Landowner, *mayordomo, inquilino,* and peon all behaved like human beings. Even though we are dealing with nearly invisible people about whom the documents and ledgers say little, we can be certain that there was theft, whippings, disdain, protest, oppression. One reads infrequently of *inquilinos* burning property; of peons sacking the hacienda store, of refusals to work, of isolated acts of violence. But this cannot be construed as 'peasant revolt' or 'struggle for justice' in the sense of an organised or self-conscious movement.

Compared with the traditional rural societies of France or Germany, Russia or even Mexico and Peru, the Chilean countryside was remarkably free of conflict. The Labor Office, established in 1906 mainly to deal with urban labor, reported only one rural strike during the otherwise turbulent years of 1911 and 1919, and even though one of the most thoroughly researched of the numerous recent studies refers to 'massive dismissals' and 'waves of rural labor conflict' during the years up to 1933, the author presents little evidence for his assertions.[30] There was a brief flurry of strikes in 1919 and 1920 in a few cases where rural workers were in close touch with organised mine or industrial workers. The National Society of Agriculture complained that attempts were made in the copper mining Catemu region of Aconcagua valley to federate the *inquilinos* with an organisation of miners, and in another case, the FOCH organised a march of 1000 workers from Santiago to a suburban *fundo* to protest what it claimed were illegal acts by the estate management. But these were isolated cases, almost invariably provoked by urban cadres and once they backed off – as they did under force after 1924 – the countryside remained quiet. In fact, only one 'large-scale peasant uprising' was recorded in Chile throughout the entire period between 1909 and 1964, and this took place in a frontier region (the upper Bio-Bio) in 1934.[31] Interestingly enough this was a revolt of a smallholder community, not hacienda workers. And even more significantly, in those few cases where service tenants' complaints are recorded, they demand not the head of the landowner, nor even a new pattern of relations, but rather, the 're-establishment of customary prerogatives' such as food ration and pasturage rights, or some scant amelioration of living conditions. These are by and large conservative demands that seek a return to or a strengthening of the paternalistic hacienda community.[32]

While pressure from the urban working classes gradually began to force changes in Chile's political system, a quiet and cooperative rural mass continued to provide landowners with the votes needed for political survival. Landownership was not just a source of wealth or prestige but also a political base. Where it was becoming increasingly difficult to exclude representatives of the urban working classes from office, landowners used their exclusive prerogatives in the countryside to gain power themselves or insure that their agents were elected to Congress or favored by the public administration. Given their free choice, most rural workers, or at least the service tenantry, would probably have supported their *patrón* against an outside candidate. But even if they did not the landowner had formidable powers of suggestion. The threat of expulsion or fines was undoubtedly a sufficient incentive for workers who, after all, saw little point in making a choice. Although the way rural politics actually worked has not been fully described, there apparently were cases in which the rental contracts of rural estates stipulated that the owner reserved the right to use (*disponer*) the votes of *inquilinos*. Not many votes were needed: around 1920 only five per cent of the total population voted, and in rural provinces less than 2000 votes elected a Deputy to the national Congress.[33] The practice of buying votes (*cohecho*) was widespread in the cities but apparently less so in the countryside. For as Jacques Lambert has pointed out, a vote is for sale only if it is free and selling votes to the highest bidder suggests a competitive, open system which Chile manifestly was not – at least before 1920–5.[34] And if customary authority or coercion were not adequate to gain the support of rural voters, the landowners, who especially after the 'autonomous municipality' was established in 1891 dominated local government and the police force, could simply call upon the local authorities to expel rival politicians or 'troublemakers.' Thus, in 1933, the local *carabineros* hauled Trotskyite Deputy Emilio Zapata, 'biting, kicking, and screaming insults' from a *fundo* near Santiago, and the men who owned rural Chile had more than enough power in national politics to make sure that the transmission belt of new ideas and conflict stopped at the hacienda gate.[35]

CHAPTER 8

1 Rumbold, *Report*, pp. 365–6.
2 Pereira Salas, 'Architectura chilena,' pp. 7–42; Tornero, *Chile ilustrado*, pp. 21–3; Frederick Pike, *Chile and the United States, 1880–1962* (South Bend, 1963), p. 89.

Chilean Rural Society

3 Marie Wright, *The Republic of Chile*, p. 72; McBride, *Land and Society*, p. 207. See the work of Amanda Labarca and the address by Sra Echeverría in *Anales* (1st quarter, 1926), p. 181, and Felícitas Klimpel Alvardo, *La mujer chilena, 1910–1960* (Santiago, 1962).

4 Bauer, 'Hacienda el Huique,' p. 464; Luis Escobar Cerda, *El Mercado de valores* (Santiago, 1959), pp. 44–53, has discussion of the first *sociedades anónimas* in Chile. The law of 1854 made incorporation legal and by 1870 there were a total of fifty-one corporations in Chile, none of an agricultural nature.

5 Paul S. Reinsch, 'Parliamentary government in Chile,' *The American Political Science Review*, vol. III (1909), p. 508; see Guillermo Edwards Matte, *El club de la unión en sus ochenta años, 1864–1944* (Santiago, 1944), which gives the names of presidents and directors of the club, and Wright, 'Sociedad nacional de agricultura.'

6 Encina, *Historia*, vol. 18, p. 314; Jobet, *Ensayo crítico*, p. 117; Aníbal Pinto Santa Cruz, 'Desarrollo económico y relaciones sociales,' pp. 9–18.

7 *AE* (1916) and (1923), vol. VIII; J. R. Brown, 'Nitrate crises, combinations, and the Chilean government in the nitrate age,' *HAHR*, vol. 43, no. 2 (May 1963), p. 234.

8 Kirsch, 'Industrialization of Chile,' Hurtado Ruiz-Tagle, *Concentración de la población*,' pp. 79–101; Oscar Múñoz, *Crecimiento industrial de Chile, 1914–1965* (Santiago, 1968).

9 Kirsch, 'Industrialization of Chile,' pp. 124–30; 152.

10 Múñoz, *Crecimiento*, p. 35. See also Appendix 6.

11 Jaime Eyzaguirre, *Chile durante el gobierno de Errázuriz Echaurren, 1896–1901* (Santiago, 1957), p. 52; Encina et al., 'Subdivisión de la propiedad rural,' p. 24.

12 *Casa grande*, p. 159.

13 Cf. Morse, *Urban development of Latin America*, pp. 6–16.

14 Pierre Vayssiere, 'La division internationale du travail et la dénationalisation du cuivre chilien, 1880–1920,' *CMHLB* (*Caravelle*), no. 20 (1973), pp. 7–30.

15 H. Blakemore, *British Nitrates and Chilean politics 1886–1896: Balmaceda and North* (London, 1974), pp. 45–55.

16 Aníbal Pinto Santa Cruz, 'Desarrollo económico,' pp. 10, 18. Chile's public administration might be compared with Bolivia's which was unable to take advantage of tin exports during the *Patiño* era.

17 *AE* (1916), vol X, pp. 74–6; *Twentieth century impressions* gives abundant description of factories and stores around 1915; see especially pp. 258–315, 340–93. Quotation from Francisco Encina, *Nuestra inferioridad* p. 5.

18 Kirsch, 'Industrialization of Chile,' pp. 150–1; Aníbal Pinto, 'Desarrollo economico,' p. 15; Marcello Carmagnani, *Sviluppo industriale*, pp. 155–63; and Carmagnani, 'Banques étrangères,' pp. 31–52.

19 This 'positional' evidence is corroborated by the 'decisional' approach taken by Wright in 'Sociedad nacional de agricultura.'

20 Blakemore, *British nitrates*, pp. 231, 237.

21 Carl Solberg, *Immigration and Nationalism: Argentina and Chile, 1890–1914* (Austin, 1970), p. 166, notes the 'general apathy' of Chileans toward foreign investors. Some intellectuals such as Pinochet-Le-Brun and Guillermo Subercaseaux were concerned and expressed their discontent in tracts and scholarly articles. On investment, see Kirsch, 'Industrialization of Chile,' p. 30.

22 Wright, *Republic of Chile*, pp. 219–28; see also Samuel Valdés Vicuña, *La solución del gran problema del día* (Santiago, 1895); Marcial González, 'Nuestro enemigo el lujo,' pp. 431–61. Heise González, 'La constitución de 1925,' pp. 163–4.

23 Pike, *Chile and the United States,* p. 34; *CN* (Rengo), vol. 57, no. 69; Alberto Blest Gana, *Los trasplantados* (Paris, 1904) is a well-known novel dealing with wealthy Chileans seeking diversion and marriage with the European aristocracy. Orrego Luco himself provides a marvelous picture of the dandy, recently returned from Paris, affecting the manner of the *boulevardier,* pp. 46, 59.

24 *Casa grande,* pp. 201–4. See also the discussion by Domingo Melfi, 'La novela *casa grande* y la transformación de la sociedad chilena,' *Anales* (1948), pp. 239–57.

25 Jacques Lambert, *Latin America* (trans. from the French by Helen Katel, Berkeley, 1967), pp. 85, 104.

26 Pinto Santa Cruz, 'Desarrollo económico,' pp. 10–12.

27 Wright, 'Sociedad nacional de agricultura,' pp. 172–4; James O. Morris, *Elites, Intellectuals, and Consensus* (Ithaca, New York, 1966), p. 94; see also, Jorge Barría Serón, 'Evolución histórica de Chile de 1910 hasta nuestros dias,' *Anales,* no. 120 (1960), pp. 50–66; and Guillermo Feliú Cruz, 'La evolución política, económica y social de Chile,' *Anales,* no. 119 (1960), pp. 45–85.

28 Morris, *Elites,* pp. 97–9; Wright, 'Sociedad nacional,' p. 157.

29 Wright, 'Sociedad nacional,' pp. 172–5.

30 Loveman, 'Property, politics,' pp. 268, 271, 274.

31 McBride, *Land and Society,* p. 166; Loveman, 'Property, politics and rural labor' rightly acknowledges the uniqueness of the Bío-Bío revolt.

32 Loveman, 'Property and politics,' pp. 283–91; see the recent J. Petras and H. Zemelman, *Peasants in Revolt* (Austin, 1972).

33 Moisés Poblete Troncoso, *El problema de la producción agrícola y la política agraria nacional* (Santiago, 1919), p. 244; *AE* (1923), vol. III, p. 41. Arturo Valenzuela of Duke University has work in progress that should clarify many of these questions.

34 Lambert, *Latin America,* p. 171.

35 Loveman, 'Property, politics and rural labor,' p. 292.

Conclusion and epilogue

In 1930 Dr Karl Brunner, a foreign consultant on urban planning, presented his projection of Chilean population growth. In the 'least favorable case,' he thought, Santiago would not reach a million inhabitants until 1990; at the more likely rate, however, that figure would be reached as early as 1960.[1] In justice to the Viennese expert, few people standing on the far edge of the rift then being formed by the world crisis were able to foresee the tremendous change that 1930 would bring. In 1960 Santiago had, in fact, not one but two million residents – and three million a mere decade later. Reduced mortality rates led to explosive population growth; industry and the concentration of public investment and services drew people into the cities. At first faintly, but then with increasing clarity, politics began to reflect the force of demographic and social change. By 1938 it was clear that political power had shifted decisively to the cities; and from then to the present, the rural system which we have been examining has had to operate within a new array of market forces and politics.

From the perspective of Great Britain or Western Europe, the predominance of the city in Chile seems late – in the industrialised West this was a development of the eighteenth and nineteenth centuries. But even within Latin America, Chile's rapid urbanisation, especially the concentration of people in one major city, is unusual. And, as in the case of so much of its development, the causes were external. The collapse of the world economy in 1930 led to reappraisal of the past and emphasis on national industry. Private capitalists were encouraged and a state corporation (CORFO) was established in 1938 to provide the infrastructure and heavy industry considered necessary to push the country on to economic development. When the export economy – now mainly based on copper – recovered in the 1940s, the economic forces engendered by mining and industry created opportunities – and the illusion of opportunity – in the cities, especially in Santiago. The rural underemployed and a few displaced by a belated mechanisation followed the roads and rails to the capital.[2]

The middle and upper classes spread rapidly outward from the older districts of Santiago, covering the fields of surburban Las Condes and Ñuñoa with their chalets and *búngalows*, while the rural migrants crowded into the squalid downtown *conventillos* or mushrooming shanty towns on the outskirts. *Callampa,* the local term for mushroom, is often applied to these settlements to suggest overnight growth and their close-to-the-earth, somewhat musty quality. This explosive growth of urban Chile created a rapidly growing demand for rural produce, but Chile's agriculture was not up to the task. Industry and urban income in general all increased at a much faster rate than the produce that city people demanded from the country; and from the 1940s on, the ever-increasing gap between domestic demand and supply was filled with imports.[3]

Why did Chilean agriculture not respond to the urban demand? This is not an academic question argued with dry erudition in classroom and conference. It is a vital issue in Chilean politics and the battlefield has spread from the expert offices of FAO and AID to Congress, through armed occupations in the countryside, to tanks in the streets of Santiago. A great many learned and valuable people have devoted themselves to the problem.

Before the most recent conflicts, two main theories, both concerned mainly with economics and each associated with a passionately held political belief, were put forth as explanation. The conservative view emphasised the detrimental effect of governmental intervention, especially the imposition of 'political prices,' that were alleged to cause a reduction in both incentives and investment in agriculture. From the technicians of the international agencies and the Chilean Left has come the 'structuralist' explanation which identified the culprit as *'lati-fundismo,'* psychological and real. In this view – to simplify drastically – a set of quasi-feudal attitudes together with the inherently inefficient large estate explains the low productivity.[4]

There is truth and difficulty in both explanations. Try as some writers do, there is still only scant evidence to support the charge of deteriorating agricultural prices. After 1930, farm prices rose sometimes slower and sometimes faster than the overall price index, but on the whole at about the same rate; the terms of trade between agricultural and industrial prices moved only slightly against agriculture.[5] It seems safe to conclude that, although prices were not permitted to reach a free market level, they were still high enough to provide a great deal of incentive had agriculture been even moderately efficient. There is no denying much of the structuralist argument but it does not go far enough and does not explain very much. The structure of Chilean agriculture was not the outcome of fortuitous circumstances or exceptionally evil motives, but the result of long-term social development and political conflict between urban and rural forces. To say that large units are slovenly farmed or that landowners have non-economic goals is sometimes true, but the explanation offered is often tendentious or distorted by political passion. In any case, neither the haciendas nor their owners can be separated from Chilean society or the historical context in which they arose and functioned.

In the preceding pages I have sought to explain the development of Chile's peculiar rural society in social and historical terms. The pattern was set by the first European settlers. Delighted at the prospect of a 'fertile province' and virtually unrestrained by native resistance or imperial law, they were able to gain a near total control of this patch of the earth's crust and subdue and exploit the racially distinct inhabitants they found. Having little else to do – there was no Potosí or Zacatecas – the new settlers turned to agriculture and made landownership the principal value in their colonial way of life. By the time rail and steam brought Chile more tightly into the orbit of the North Atlantic economy, the social residue of the previous 'agricultural delirium' was still a two-class society, one dominant and the other subjugated, with little hope of integration.[6]

From the 1870s to 1920, the rise of an export economy and the consequent florescence of urban culture did not alter social relations in the countryside and did little to diminish the attraction and political power of landownership. Rather, because of the way the new wealth percolated through this society which was still imbued with older values, the rural system was reinforced; in Santiago, the owners of the countryside absorbed or coopted the new-rich and successful immigrants – much like the *vecindario noble* had absorbed the Bourbon cadres and eager newcomers a century before.

The institutions of banking and credit that came into existence after 1850 served the aims of the landowning class and enabled its members to extend their control of the countryside and diversify their interests in the city. The response of landowners to greater agricultural demand from the mining camps and cities was to extend the existing archaic farming system and more effectively exploit the degraded rural working classes. This was more than anything a passive response, an unwillingness to make the then seemingly Herculean effort of reform. I have gone to some length in this book to demonstrate the social and political context of inaction, and the survival and persistence of habit and structure that were serious obstacles to real improvement. When the massive urban demand came after 1930, it fell on an archaic rural structure already stretched nearly to the limit of its technology and methods.

Timing is very important. This as explanation may seem simple-minded, but the sage advice of Ecclesiastes is well taken. If the hour is not seized, if adjustments are not made when times are propitious, possibilities fade and attitudes once flexible harden into patterns that become ever more resistant to change. We have seen this with race relations in the USA. There was a time when adjustments might have been worked out, a certain harmony established with a minimum of rancor. But the opportunity was not seized and by the end of Reconstruction it was too late. The same seems to me true about the period between the late nineteenth century and 1920 in Chile. During these years the agricultural sector was thriving, credit was abundant, there was social tranquility in the countryside, and landowner interests were absolutely dominant in the government. More than one articulate critic pointed the way; yet no steps were taken to reform the countryside or uplift the recognisedly desperate plight of the rural working classes. More myopic than Louis XV, the men who ran Chile did not even suspect the existence of the coming deluge.[7]

A crucial juncture in Chilean history came in the late nineteenth century when great wealth was suddenly generated by an isolated mining enclave at a time when a traditional landed society still set the social tone and controlled the politics of the country. This had decisive implications. Mining did not serve as a 'growth pole' for economic development; much of the new wealth was spent on rural estates and too often the money was used to buy status or a still coveted way of life rather than invested to obtain higher yields. The way Chileans participated in the mining operation and the attraction that landownership had for the *nouveaux riches* also helps explain why the social forces generated in the northern desert were politically disarmed. First, of course, a large part of the dynamic sector of the Chilean economy was foreign-owned; but, that aside, a great deal of revenue was tapped through export taxes and filtered through the public administration. Thus the mining sector did not directly produce a social class to challenge the landowners, create a middle-class ethos, or recognise its own interests and force rural reform. Rather, Chile's modern development was inorganic and disjointed – one step removed from the source of its wealth. The nitrate fields produced a torrent of wealth but paradoxically this went to fortify an elite whose principal value was still landownership.

The social forces which grew up around the export economy sought alliances not with the rural working classes but with their masters. The *inquilinos* and peons of central Chile remained powerless and neglected until the crisis of the late 1960s. And in the failure of landowners to perceive self-interest or act in a benevolent way, power was the only thing that could have relieved the rural workers' plight and reformed the nature of agriculture. As it was, more produce was wrung from the land but the methods were hopelessly out of date. By 1920, a new set of political circumstances was already emerging that made voluntary or peaceful reform a great deal more difficult.

With the election of Arturo Alessandri to the presidency in 1920, the urban masses began gradually to move onto the stage of Chilean politics, and by 1938, with the election of a Popular Front government, their presence and influence were apparent to everyone. From then on, the interests of the mineworkers, the urban proletariat, and the wage-earning middle classes coincided in the need for low food prices. Their demands could be checked, however, by the still formidable power of the landowning class; so the urban sectors sought the limited aim of controlled food prices rather than a structural reform of the country-side that might have led to a more efficient agriculture.

Food prices had dropped somewhat more sharply than other prices after the 1930 Depression with a consequent reduction in landowner income and investment in agriculture. Yet costs, most notably labor costs, were kept low, and it is likely that the rural laboring classes bore the brunt of this early squeeze on profits. By the late 1930s and into the 1940s, organised labor threatened to extend its influence into the countryside and rural workers began haltingly to develop an 'exacting temperament' and push for better salaries and conditions. As this occurred, the landowners rattled the sabre of higher agricultural prices. It was obvious to urban politicians that if higher food prices were allowed they would cut into the earnings of the flourishing industrial sector and create political problems with the urban mass. Under these circumstances, the industrialists, the proletariat and the landowners struck a mutually beneficial bargain at the expense of the rural workers: the landowners agreed to accept controls on agricultural prices in return for a hands-off policy in the countryside. Rural workers were not permitted to organise; protests were squelched. In this situation where agricultural profits were uncertain and often squeezed and capital was attracted from land to higher-yield investments in the cities, many landowners were reluctant to modernise. Moreover, they had an age-old alternative: they fell back on the large numbers of still power-less and vulnerable rural workers.[8]

What we have seen in the recent Chilean case may be interpreted as another chapter in the modern drama of urban–rural conflict. As the city grows in numbers and political clout, its inhabitants demand a higher standard of living. This demand has come with sudden and brutal force in the twentieth century as the aware and politicised masses see by television and cinema the consumer paradise abroad. They are naturally led to believe by politicians who need their support that the fruits of modernity are rightfully theirs. As the limits to 'development' are reached – in the case of Chile the important economic indicators leveled off in the late 1950s – the urban middle and working classes turned in their quest for surplus to the more vulnerable groups in their own society. These, from Russia through Mexico to Nebraska and Chile, are invariably the peasants, peons, small farmers, and tenants.

The political belief of the government in power actually makes little difference. In Chile, the Popular Front, the Conservatives, the Christian Democrats, the Socialists, and the Communists, and now apparently the Junta, are all prepared to sacrifice the countryside to compete for support in the city. This fact is more striking among the Marxists because their rhetoric is more strident and their motives more self-righteous. Yet as Raymond Williams has recently pointed out in a brilliant study, there is a fundamental ambiguity in Marxism in matters of the country and the city. Although Trotsky condemned the history of capitalism as the victory of town over country, 'he then proceeded, in the critical first years of the Russian Revolution, to outline a programme for just such a victory, on a massive scale, as a way of defeating capitalism and preserving socialism.'[9] There is a pale reflection of this same dilemma in Chile. Although their writers have spent countless pages scourging the 'latifundists,' the Marxists parties, no less than the others, were never reluctant to wring a surplus out of the countryside for the benefit of their own urban constituency. This was done through the mechanism of the annual 'readjustment' of wages to the previous year's inflation and through the insistence on low food prices. Given the fact that rural workers were powerless and denied the right to organise, agricultural profits obviously came out of the hides of rural workers. A clear example of the way urban–rural conflict transcends working-class solidarity can be seen in the crucial years of the Christian Democratic regime. In 1967–8, the Chilean Communist Party withdrew its support of an agrarian reform it had previously supported as soon as its urban constituency was asked to bear part of the (huge) cost.[10]

The story of Chile's rural society has been long, filled with blood and dust and patches of green. It moves inexorably to a melancholy end. In 1965, pressure on the countryside was stepped up as the urban classes broke through a hollow landowner resistance and began to organise the workers and take over estates. After 1970 the process of expropriation was accelerated with less attention to niceties; in late 1973, a military Junta intervened with unparalleled ferocity to smash an ambiguous and occasionally violent reform. By 1975, the rural people of Ercilla's 'fertile province,' the descendants of the Spanish colony most given to agriculture and the Republic most characterised by its rural values, were putting together the pieces of a temporarily shattered life and trying again to wrest their living from an attractive but uncertain countryside.

CHAPTER 9

[1] *Anales* (April–June, 1930), pp. 878–0.

[2] Bruce Herrick, *Urban migration and economic development in Chile* (Cambridge, Mass., 1965). In 1960, over forty-six per cent of all Chileans lived in cities of 20 000 or more; over seventy per cent in towns and cities of 2000 or more. John Friedmann and Tomás Lackington, 'Hyperurbanization and National development in Chile: some hypotheses,' *Urban Affairs Quarterly*, vol. II, no. 4 (June 1967), pp. 3–29.

[3] Markos Mamalakis and Clark Reynolds, *Essays on the Chilean Economy* (Homewood, Ill., 1965), pp. 121–3. Domestic product grew at a rate of 5.3 per cent annually in the 1940s and 3.2 per cent in the 1950s. Agricultural production increased at about 1.5 per cent a year over these two decades. See also CIDA, p. 204. See especially the work of Solon Barraclough.

[4] Mamalakis and Reynolds, *Essays*, summarise the positions in pp. 117–21; see also Osvaldo Sunkel, 'Change and frustration in Chile,' in Véliz, *Obstacles to Change*, pp. 116–44.

[5] Mamalakis and Reynolds, *Essays*, pp. 130–8.

[6] Benjamin Subercaseaux, *Chile, a geographic extravaganza* (translated from the Spanish by Angel Flores, New York, 1943), p. 123.

[7] Edwards Vives, *Fronda aristocrática*, p. 185.

[8] An excellent analysis of Chilean agriculture since 1930 is in Sergio Aranda and Alberto Martínez, 'Estructura económica: algunas características fundamentales,' *Chile Hoy* (Santiago, 1970), pp. 55–172. Brian Loveman, 'Property, politics and rural labor,' pp. 217–352, has a full discussion of political and legal struggles in the countryside.

[9] Raymond Williams, *The Country and the City* (New York, Oxford Press, 1973), p. 302.

[10] Friedman and Lackington, 'Hyperurbanization,' pp. 19–21, has a good discussion of the 'politics of readjustment.' On urban–rural conflict over the agrarian reform, see Robert R. Kaufman, *The Politics of land reform in Chile, 1950–1970* (Cambridge, Mass., 1972), pp. 235–44.

Appendix I

Prices of flour, beans and beef in Santiago for the years 1846–1925 (current pesos)

Year	Flour 46 kg	Beans 100 kg	Cow	Index* (1870=100)
1846	2.25	2.00	10.00	52
1847	1.99	2.00	10.00	50
1848	1.70	2.00	10.00	49
1849	1.75	1.50	10.00	44
1850	2.75	3.82	10.50	72
1851	3.85	3.10	10.50	75
1852	3.40	2.30	12.50	69
1853	3.15	2.75	15.00	76
1854	3.00	3.50	18.25	85
1855	3.00	4.25	21.50	97
1856	3.72	5.08	24.75	116
1857	3.40	4.70	28.00	116
1858	3.23	6.80	23.00	124
1859	2.56	1.75	24.80	79
1860	2.10	2.25	26.50	83
1861	2.12	3.25	23.00	85
1862	3.18	3.75	18.00	89
1863	2.62	2.50	20.00	77
1864	2.50	2.25	21.00	76
1865	2.35	1.75	20.00	69
1866	1.85	2.30	19.00	69
1867	3.03	3.75	21.00	94
1868	3.70	4.25	24.75	109
1869	2.75	3.00	26.00	93
1870	3.32	3.25	25.75	100
1871	2.90	3.22	27.00	98
1872	2.85	4.75	26.00	101
1873	3.00	3.80	32.00	114
1874	3.00	4.00	35.00	120
1875	3.00	5.70	36.00	135
1876	2.90	5.73	34.00	131
1877	4.20	5.75	32.00	138
1878	4.75	6.25	30.00	143
1879	3.82	3.00	27.00	104
1880	3.42	3.00	33.00	111
1881	3.92	3.20	39.00	128
1882	3.20	3.37	41.00	127
1883	3.20	4.00	44.00	139
1884	3.32	8.50	45.00	177
1885	3.85	5.12	48.00	159
1886	3.45	3.65	48.00	144
1887	3.70	5.20	48.00	160
1888	4.18	6.90	51.00	182
1889	5.27	6.95	51.00	191

233

(continues)

Year	Flour 46 kg	Beans 100 kg	Cow	Index* (1870=100)
1890	4.87	6.00	49.00	177
1891	4.69	5.85	52.00	179
1892	4.51	5.70	55.00	182
1893	4.65	7.80	56.00	202
1894	4.82	7.85	56.00	204
1895	4.90	8.00	66.00	224
1896	4.50	8.35	60.00	213
1897	6.30	10.26	63.00	248
1898	7.00	9.75	65.50	254
1899	6.10	6.20	68.00	222
1900	7.07	8.28	68.00	247
1901	7.36	14.00	81.42	321
1902	6.90	11.00	96.76	322
1903	6.44	8.00	103.00	303
1904	5.98	10.00	99.12	309
1905	7.82	18.00	103.84	397
1906	9.66	25.00	115.64	491
1907	10.12	16.00	171.10	521
1908	11.50	17.00	174.64	547
1909	12.88	33.00	175.82	692
1910	12.88	37.00	167.56	707
1911	12.42	28.00	164.02	625
1912	11.50	25.00	188.80	638
1913	11.96	28.00	206.50	698
1914	19.78	46.00	227.74	946
1915	36.68	54.00	248.98	1187
1916	16.10	38.00	244.26	881
1917	18.40	57.00	243.80	1055
1918	19.78	43.00	247.80	958
1919	23.92	47.00	308.00	1153
1920	34.50	50.00	370.00	1356
1921	32.66	43.00	348.00	1244
1922	33.12	49.00	—	—
1923	23.00	60.00	392.00	1383
1924	25.76	60.00	294.00	1230
1925	35.88	85.00	390.00	1688

The commodities were weighted as follows: flour, 45%; beans, 45%; and cow, 10%.

Sources: Figures for this listing and index were taken from *El Mercurio* (Valparaíso), 1846–1900. For the period 1846–55, the *El Mercurio* prices were supplemented with information in Talca papers (*El Alfa*) and Volume 251 of the Archive of Hacienda which gives 'precios corrientes de la plaza' filed by the Intendant every month. The prices that appear here represent an average of the May, September, and December prices of each year.

Prices for flour and beans for 1901 through 1925 were taken from Dirección General de Estadística, *Sinópsis estadístico de Chile*, 1918 and 1925, pp. 118 and 117 respectively.

Prices for cow for the period 1901–18 were calculated from prices cited by Thomas C. Wright in his dissertation 'The Sociedad Nacional de Agricultura in Chilean Politics, 1869–1938' (University of California, History Dept., 1971), Table V-2, p. 150. Prices for 1918–25 were calculated from the *Sinópsis*, 1925.

Appendix II

Mortgage loans in the Department of Talca

Year	Private (1)	Caja (2)	S.A.'s (3)	Totals (4)	$5M-up (5)	1M-$4999 (6)	0-$999 (7)
1838	12 625	—	—	12 625	—	8700	3565
1840	12 762	—	—	12 762	—	8000	4762
1842	16 408	—	—	16 408	—	10 450	5958
1844	24 050	—	—	24 050	—	17 000	7050
1846	36 100	—	3500	39 600	5900	26 200	7500
1848	62 990	—		62 990	20 600	29 500	12 890
1849	42 270	—		42 270	6800	27 100	8370
1850	29 050	—		29 050	6000	15 300	7750
1851	64 500	—		64 500	26 000	30 100	8400
1852	68 570	—	21 000	89 570	51 500	28 800	9270
1853	39 500	—	—	39 500	18 500	12 700	8300
1854	140 900	—	50 000	190 900	163 000	17 600	10 300
1855	131 830	—	5800	137 630	75 700	44 700	17 230
1856	117 300	138 000	140 000	395 300	326 000	55 000	14 300
1857	133 700	109 800	—	243 500	155 800	67 800	19 900
1858	172 800	16 000	206 000	394 800	303 200	74 100	17 500
1859	179 300	204 500	20 000	403 800	314 500	71 900	17 400
1860	197 050	54 700	75 000	326 750	265 700	48 400	12 650
1861	216 550	20 000	44 900	281 450	165 100	100 100	16 250
1862	278 255	29 000	40 000	347 255	242 100	92 200	12 955
1863	222 450	—	39 000	261 450	172 400	74 600	14 450
1864	203 300	9500	15 000	227 800	185 000	29 900	12 900
1865	143 242	5000	10 000	158 242	68 015	77 362	12 865

(continues)

Appendix II (*cont.*) Mortgage loans in the Department of Talca

Year	Private (1)	Caja (2)	S.A.'s (3)	Totals (4)	$5M-up (5)	1M-$4999 (6)	0-$999 (7)
1866	228 428	—	17 640	246 068	172 243	58 665	10 619
1867	310 356	10 800	33 000	354 156	275 24c	57 325	21 591
1868	133 177	6000	65 760	204 937	145 000	38 146	21 791
1869	98 726	30 000	530 000	658 726	580 000	54 340	24 386
1870	203 620	127 200	132 500	463 320	369 420	70 194	23 706
1871	186 612	105 000	177 500	469 112	383 715	64 167	21 230
1872	172 123	—	271 000	443 123	372 000	47 953	23 170
1873	175 694	—	164 500	340 194	239 800	78 880	21 514
1874	215 343	61 000	74 000	350 343	244 142	84 080	22 121
1875	323 873	99 000	96 030	518 903	399 760	98 560	20 583
1876	404 382	89 000	174 482	667 864	525 171	111 458	31 235
1877	471 580	—	270 045	741 625	539 940	158 952	42 733
1878	297 467	—	123 712	421 179	237 617	134 122	59 440
1879	325 436	166 000	82 276	573 712	419 757	132 395	21 560
1880	262 584	534 423	189 900	986 907	857 323	102 258	27 226
1881	324 866	296 000	159 000	759 866	631 000	101 733	27 133
1882	401 337	249 600	196 196	847 133	670 704	151 648	24 781
1883	165 983	127 500	113 446	406 929	279 130	108 200	19 599
1884	249 181	118 000	227 550	594 731	454 544	116 754	23 433
1885	183 351	264 000	303 200	750 551	606 265	120 446	23 840
1886	159 977	30 000	314 831	504 808	375 800	103 858	25 150
1887	112 308	212 000	211 023	535 331	436 237	78 726	20 368
1888	297 429	149 500	587 000	1 034 009	896 203	111 243	26 463
1889	328 556	133 500	593 807	1 055 863	831 650	190 130	34 083
1890	434 108	19 600	520 532	976 532	830 493	116 403	29 636

Source: *Colección Notarial de Talca*, Vols. 40A, 80A, 102, 111, 113, 115, 117, 119, 122, 123, 124, 125, and 126.

Appendix III

Mortgage loans in the Department of Caupolicán

Year	Private (1)	Caja (2)	S.A.'s (3)	Totals (4)	$5M-up (5)	1M-$4999 (6)	0-$999 (7)
1848	400	—	—	400	—	—	400
1849	10 800	—	4000	14 800	9000	4000	1800
1850	28 600	—	—	28 600	21 000	3000	4600
1851	55 030	—	—	55 030	44 500	7200	3230
1852	24 600	—	—	24 600	11 600	11 400	2200
1853	48 490	—	—	48 490	40 000	6600	1890
1854	24 400	—	—	24 400	8000	12 200	4200
1855	44 300	—	—	44 300	18 000	21 700	4600
1856	100 200	44 000	—	144 200	119 000	32 100	3000
1857	154 890	36 000	—	190 890	156 200	27 490	7250
1858	75 000	15 000	—	90 600	61 000	22 200	7400
1859	298 550	4000	30 000	332 550	307 000	22 400	3150
1860	296 500	52 000	237 000	585 500	515 300	68 600	1800
1861	595 980	149 500	—	745 480	687 050	48 506	9924
1862	385 775	—	168 000	553 775	437 380	103 470	12 725
1863	146 090	70 000	33 360	249 450	203 960	31 521	13 969
1864	156 831	—	95 000	251 831	211 000	26 945	13 886
1865	235 769	—	50 000	285 769	222 700	47 415	15 654
1866	157 010	71 000	131 000	359 010	328 110	23 990	6910
1867	233 228	38 000	10 000	281 228	247 000	24 610	9618
1868	155 215	—	—	155 215	102 500	42 050	10 665

(continues)

Appendix III (cont.) Mortgage loans in the Department of Caupolicán

Year	Private (1)	Caja (2)	S.A.'s (3)	Totals (4)	$5M-up (5)	1M-$4999 (6)	0-$999 (7)
1869	141 942	88 500	139 000	369 442	305 950	46 420	17 072
1870	85 480	—	25 000	110 480	46 400	53 144	10 936
1871	332 809	67 000	12 500	412 309	346 500	47 700	18 109
1872	299 452	25 000	72 000	396 452	319 200	55 270	21 982
1873	77 560	55 000	—	132 560	75 000	40 200	17 360
1874	286 797	11 200	130 000	427 997	348 445	55 426	24 126
1875	205 276	186 000	—	391 276	290 200	77 500	23 576
1876	161 089	493 000	57 000	711 089	615 120	72 800	23 169
1877	291 626	133 000	60 000	485 126	384 028	64 252	35 846
1878	277 051	48 000	100 000	425 051	331 390	58 716	34 945
1879	205 961	42 000	49 400	297 361	221 081	46 864	28 517
1880	148 943	715 000	175 000	1 038 943	942 500	67 066	29 377
1881	135 223	173 000	155 000	463 223	365 600	66 730	30 893
1882	211 769	72 000	225 000	508 769	429 300	66 244	13 225
1883	189 749	85 000	14 610	289 359	199 449	65 254	24 656
1884	158 802	394 000	98 150	650 952	551 702	81 150	18 100
1885	108 705	238 000	241 361	588 066	510 861	58 551	18 654
1886	317 769	404 000	192 950	914 719	817 069	73 200	24 450
1887	160 041	162 400	384 000	706 441	638 100	49 909	18 432
1888	254 873	277 500	230 500	762 873	684 470	57 600	20 803
1889	206 255	119 000	347 365	672 620	544 000	103 800	24 820
1890	834 202	651 000	388 500	1 873 702	1 773 170	75 228	25 304

Source: For years 1848–81, Colección Notarial de Rengo, Vols. 37, 49, 51, 54, 57, 59, 62, 65, 67, 70, 76, 80, 84, 90, 94, 97, 102 and 106. For years 1882–90 the vols. marked 'registros de hipotecas' in the Municipal Archive of Rengo.

Appendix IV

Average annual value of the Chilean peso in terms of £ sterling,
1830–1925 (in pence of £, rounded to nearest d)

1830–75	44	1892	19	1909	11
1876	41	1893	15	1910	11
1877	42	1894	13	1911	11
1878	40	1895	17	1912	10
1879	33	1896	18	1913	10
1880	31	1897	18	1914	9
1881	31	1898	16	1915	8
1882	35	1899	15	1916	9
1883	35	1900	17	1917	13
1884	32	1901	16	1918	15
1885	26	1902	15	1919	11
1886	24	1903	17	1920	12
1887	24	1904	16	1921	7
1888	26	1905	16	1922	7
1889	27	1906	14	1923	6
1890	24	1907	13	1924	6
1891	19	1908	10	1925	6

Source: Frank W. Fetter, *Monetary inflation in Chile* (Princeton, 1931), pp.
13–14.

Appendix V

Tienda de Cunaco

Debe		
1847 Nov 19	Por suma del folio 37	$7823.4 5/8
	2pzs mesclilla dobles con 64 yardas a 2 rs	16.
	1 id. id. sencilla con 34 yd a 1 rs	4.2 rs.
	4 pzs Tocuyo arargado con 125 ys al 1	15.
	2 doz. medias finas a 15 rs.	3.6 rs.
	4 doz. id ordinarias a 9	4.4.
	6 lbs hilo blanco a 5–3/4	4.2–1/2
	2 pzs cotin algodón con 5 yds al 1–3/8	9.62.
	4 paquetes fulares a 29	
	1 doz. pañulos algodón en	12.
	1 id. id. en	10.
		——— $94.1–4/8
	3 doz. guinchas blanca a 3–3/4	11.2.
	1 id. pañuelos algodón a 4–1/2	4.4.
	1 saco algodón con 186 lb a $4. qq.	7.3–1/2.
	1 id. yerva mate con 8 a 1 real	11.1.
	10 pzs cintas listón a 7 rs.	8.6.
	12 id id. 1/4 listón a 4–1/2	6.6.
	3 doz. pañuelos algodón de reboza a $5	15.
	20 id. Castilla 11 reales	27.4.
	3 sacos azúcar terciada con 20 a a qq a 18	44.5–1/2.
	6 qq id. de Lima entera a 25–1/2	20.2.
		——— $168.2
	40 Bayetilla en	14.4.
	1 lata agujas con 16 ms a 4 rs.	8.
	6 doz. guinchas itadillo a 2 rs.	1.4.
	1 id. paquete tachuelas a 12 rs.	1.4.
	50 doz. cuchillas—a 3–1/2	21.7.
Dec 28	7 panzs graza con 20 bts, 14 lb que ha llebado	
	en ag⁰ 24, oct 28, nov 24 segun el libro de	
	estancia que neto quedan 19 lb 44	119.2.
1848 en⁰ 4	velas	70.
	1 panza graza con 6 a 15 lb a 6	19.6 256.3
		256.3 $8342.3–2/8
1848 Abril 26	Por suma del folio 42	
	2 fardos tocuyo con 1600 ys a 3/4	150.
	1 id. id. con 800 ancho a 1	100.
	1 id bramante con 864 ys a 3/4	81.
	8 doz id ancho con 328 ys a 7–1/2 8	38.3–1/2.
	2 id. cotin con 82 1/2 ys a 1–1/4	15.4–3/4.

(continues)

Appendix V

75 lb añil a 9–3/4	91.3–1/4.
24 gruzas botones ancha a 2 rs.	6.
2 doz espejitos a 3–1/2	7.
7 a 3 lbs azúcar Pernanbuco a 21	18.5–1/2
21 vazos de bidro a 6–1/2	17.1/2

Source: Account book, hacienda of Cunaco, pp. 42 and 46.

Appendix VI

Reliability of published census data for composition of the labor force

In the absence of good, direct documentation it is tempting to begin with the official census material but in nearly every case where assumptions or definitions are closely examined, one is reluctantly brought to the conclusion that these data have limited value. Some basic trends, of course, are unmistakable: between 1865 and 1930, the total population increased from just under two million to about four and a quarter million. Santiago grew from 115 000 to almost 700 000 while 'urban' population as a whole went from 398 000 to over two million. By 1930 about half the total population lived in towns and cities of over 2000 inhabitants.[1] But as the census takers themselves repeatedly point out, the figures are only the lowest approximations.

In the first complete published census, carried out in April 1854, a seventy-hour rain storm 'came to prejudice to a great extent the hopes regarding the accuracy o fthe census.' Other officials noted that young men often 'fled for fear' that the census would lead to military service. The department of Melipilla counted 29 000 inhabitants but officials 'had the feeling' that 40 000 would be closer to the fact; in Talca and Maule a great number went uncounted because they commonly slept in the fields or were on the move. The 1875 census was hardly more reliable. Santiago Lindsay, head of the Central Office of Statistics for over twenty years, wrote that the census under his direction was full of errors: the city of Talca for example should probably be increased by some forty per cent and 'everyone agreed that the census of Santiago had been very badly taken.' At times more than an insufficient budget or ordinary incompetence lay behind faulty figures. The Department of Lontué, for example, increased from about 20 000 in 1875 to 32 000 in 1885 and then fell to 22 000 in 1895 – a fluctuation that apparently is best explained by the fact that 32 000 inhabitants were needed to permit the election of two Congressmen in 1885. It might seem that all censuses undernumerated the population and that this could be compensated for by adding – as the census people themselves suggested – some ten to fifteen per cent to all categories. But then it is difficult to explain the extraordinary low rate of growth in the 1895 census.[2]

By 1907 there are further admissions of inaccuracy and, in passing, a comment on the quality of the lower bureaucracy. 'We have always preferred,' wrote the president of the census commission, 'that the [1907] census be blamed for incompleteness and lack of scientific method rather than see it fail for having asked more than the country is capable of giving. . . . It is not always possible to obtain here the admirable perfection that reigns in the more advanced nations of Europe; one should not for a moment lose sight of the state of public administration in Chile nor of the general level of culture of its inhabitants.'[3]

If the censuses with their faults do give a general idea of population increase, the closer one looks the more problems there are. The question of rural and urban definitions, in 1954 for example, was 'odious and tiresome' because of the fluidity of population and there is only a half-hearted attempt to make distinctions apart from the obvious cases. In fact, none of the nineteenth-century censuses had any consistent criteria of rural or urban so that often simple hamlets of fifty households might be classified as 'urban' even though their function – as well as that of larger villages – was strictly rural. Even in 1920 and 1930 when definitions were explicit we are faced with a statistical mirage. On the outskirts but within the *limite urbano* of the larger cities were small settlements of smallholders nominally rural but who actually worked in the city; but far more common were rural *pueblos* classified as 'urban' if they contained over 1000 people, although they were usually nothing more than larger *caserios* or *aldeas*, or groups of smallholders. Thus total 'urban' population statistically increased but this did not mean rural depopulation or that the people now called urban ceased to produce as smallholders or to provide labor for rural estates. For these reasons it is exceedingly difficult to relate either total population or rural population to agricultural output in any but the crudest way.[4]

The censuses also provide data on 'occupations' or 'professions' but changing definitions and terminology – to say nothing of the special difficulty of gathering and classifying data in agriculture – make statistical calculation of labor productivity exceedingly difficult if not meaningless. In their widely quoted study on 'The Growth of Output and Employment in Basic Sectors of the Chilean Economy, 1908–1957,' Ballesteros and Davis note that their calculations make sense only 'if the 1907 census is accurate and employed definitions . . . comparable to those of the 1920 and subsequent censuses' and later on they admit that, 'due to ambiguity of certain of these classifications [in the 1907 census] it was necessary to assign, e.g., laborers, to particular sectors, e.g., industry, without any objective criteria for said assignment.' The definitions, however, are by no means comparable as the 1930 census clearly points out and Table 48 shows why arbitrary juggling of figures might be felt necessary.[5] The category *agricultores* was meant to include all proprietors, renters, and presumably *inquilinos* as well. These categories in the 1854 and 1875 censuses agree roughly with the tax roll data but the 1907 figure is patently absurd since there were far more than 37 000 proprietors alone. *Inquilinos* may be included in *labradores* – the census does not distinguish between agricultural or any other kinds of *labradores*. Nor are

Chilean Rural Society

empleados distinguished. Obviously most of the large number in 1907 are outside of agriculture. By 1930, the figure of 53 000 *patrones* inspires little confidence since the tax records for that period show about 100 000 proprietors; but there is now a separate category – for the first time since 1813 – for *inquilinos*. Between these dates there simply is no reliable way of telling how many *inquilinos* existed.

Table 48   Terms and numbers of agricultural population in central Chile: 1854, 1875, 1907, and 1930

Category	1854	1875	1907	1930
Agricultores	70 100	109 700	36 800	53 200 (*patrones*)
Inquilinos	?	?	?	59 300
Gananes	104 100	142 400	151 200	134 000 (*obreros*)
Labradores	no data	7600	82 300	no data
Jornaleros	1900	2300	no data	no data
Empleados	900	8400	60 000	7100
Totals	177 000	270 500	330 300	253 500

Sources: *Censos* for 1854, 1875, 1907, 1930. Numbers are rounded to nearest hundred; totals are from *censos* and are not exact totals of columns.

The data for *gañanes* seem at first glance reasonable but upon examination, reality intrudes here as well. For most of the nineteenth century the term *gañan* (and sometimes *jornalero* or *labrador*) was applied to ordinary agricultural workers but often to anyone else not readily classifiable as well. Moreover, much of this element of rural society formed what contemporaries called a 'floating mass' of seasonal workers who were actually employed only a few months of the year.[6] As agriculture became more diversified and year round labor needs increased, *gañanes* came to augment the service tenantry or settle in the mushrooming towns and hamlets in the central valley. Thus if one is concerned with man-days of labor or some similar measure there is no doubt that labor inputs greatly increased as we come down to 1930. By then the designation had changed to *obrero*, another ambiguous term.

All this may seem to the beleaguered reader like an overly extended labor of the negative; and contrary to appearance the statistics we have seen do have a value: despite their uncertain quality they can serve as a loose check on generalisations; but more importantly, they force us to examine the *quality* of the labor force.

[1] Useful studies of population are Hurtado, *Concentración de población*; and Morse, *et al.*, *Urban Development*, pp. 53–60.

2 *Censo* (1854), pp. 2–9; Rumbold, *Report*, p. 317; Santiago Lindsay, *Noticia preliminar del censo jeneral de la República* (Santiago, 1875), pp. 14–15; *Censo* (1875), pp. xiii–xiv; for the observation on Lontué, Roberto Vergara, *Historia y fines de los censos* (Santiago, 1930), pp. 9–10.

3 *Censo* (1907), pp. v–vi.

4 *Censo* (1854), p. 7; *Censo* (1907), pp. x–xi. The 1930 *censo* established the following definitions: *caserío*=1–200; *aldea*=201–1000; *pueblo*=1001–5000 inhabitants. Any grouping of over 1000 inhabitants was considered 'urban' in 1930. See *Censo* (1930), pp. 10–13.

5 Ballesteros and Davis, 'Growth of output,' pp. 155, 159. The *Censo* (1930), vol. 3, p. vii, says, 'la comparación entre los resultados del censo de 1920 y 1930 no es posible hacerla con mucho detalle pues en 1920 la clasificación de las ocupaciones se hizo con distinto criterio que en 1930.'

6 The *Censo* (1885), vol. I, pp. xiv–xv. On floating population, see Agusto Orrego Luco, 'La cuestion social en Chile,' *Anales* (January–June 1961), p. 50. This article was first published in 1884.

Appendix VII

'Millionaires of old Chile'

Name	Occupation	Residence	Fortune
Juana Ross de Edwards	Benefactora	Valparaíso	16 000 000
Agustín Edwards	Banquero y hacendado	Valparaíso	9 000 000
Arturo Edwards	Estudiante en Europa	—	8 000 000
Carlos Lambert	Minero	Coquimbo	15 000 000
Isidora Goyenechea de Cousiño	Prop. de minas	Lota	14 000 000
Emiterio Goyenechea	Propietario y Capitalista	Santiago	6 000 000
Juan Brown & familia	—	Valparaíso	10 000 000
Senores Matte	Banqueros y Propietarios	Santiago	9 000 000
Manuel Irarrázabal	Hacendado	Santiago	4 000 000
Fco Subercaseaux	Banquero	Santiago	3 000 000
Federico Varela	Capitalista y Minero	Valparaíso	3 000 000
Maximiano Errázuriz	Minero y hacendado	Santiago	3 000 000
Sra Carmen Quiroga de Urmeneta	Propietario	Europa	2 000 000
Adolfo Eastman	Propietario y Capitalista	Europa	1 000 000
Luís Pereira	Propietario y Capitalista	—	2 000 000
Diego Ovalle	Propietario y Capitalista	Santiago	2 000 000
José Agustín Luco	Propietario y Capitalista	Santiago	2 000 000
Francisco Puelma	Minero y Salitrero	Santiago	1 000 000
Carlos Lamarca	Minero y Salitrero	Valparaíso	1 500 000
Fco de Borja Huidobro	Hacendado	Santiago	3 000 000
José Tomás Ramos	Comerciante y Azucarero	Valparaíso	4 000 000
Julio Bernstein	Industrial	Viña del Mar	1 000 000
José Fco. Vergara	Propietario	Viña del Mar	1 000 000
José Diaz Gana	Propietario y Minero	Santiago	1 000 000
Rafael Barazarte	Minero y Industrial	Atacama	3 000 000

Name	Occupation	Residence	Fortune
Candelaria Goyenechea de Gallo	Dueña de Minas	Copiapó	2 000 000
Magdalena Vicuña de Subercaseaux	Propietaria	Santiago	1 500 000
Manuel Valenzuela C.	Hacendado	Santiago	2 000 000
Nicolás Naranjo	Minero	Huasco	2 000 000
Pablo Múñoz	Minero	Coquimbo	1 000 000
Vicente Zorrilla	Minero	Coquimbo	1 000 000
Borja Valdés	Testamentaria	Santiago	1 500 000
J. R. Echeverría	Testamentaria	—	1 000 000
Bruno González	Testamentaria	Talca	1 500 000
Juan Domingo Dávila	Hacendado	Santiago	1 000 000
Antonio Escobar	Comerciante y Minero	Santiago	2 000 000
Rafael Correa	Hacendado	Santiago	3 000 000
Felipe Eujenio Cortés	Hacendado	Paris	2 000 000
Anjel Herquíñigo	Testamentaria	Serena	1 000 000
Carmen Cerda de Ossa	Propietaria	Santiago	3 000 000
Santos Diaz Valdés	Hacendado	Santiago	1 000 000
Eleodoro Gormáz	Banquero y Hacendado	Santiago	1 000 000
Manuel Covarrubias	Hacendado	Santiago	1 000 000
Sra Elena de Buzeta	Hacendado	La Ligua	1 000 000
Carmen Sta María de Lyon	Propietario	Valparaíso	1 000 000
Federico Schwager	Dueño de minas	Coronel	1 500 000
Carlos Anwandter	Cervecero	Valdivia	1 000 000
Miguel Collao	Hacendado	Concepción	1 000 000
Ramón Rosas Mendiburu	Hacendado	Linares	1 500 000
Sra María Ana B. de Ossa	Propietaria	Londres	3 500 000
Antonio Toro	Hacendado	Santiago	1 500 000
Sra Encarnación Fernández de Balmadeda	Propietaria	Santiago	1 000 000
Claudio Vicuña	Hacendado	Santiago	1 500 000
Mozario Elquín	Minero	Santiago	1 500 000
Fernando Lazcano	Hacendado	Curicó	2 000 000
Fco Méndez Urrejola	Hacendado y ganadero	Concepción	1 000 000
Fco Cortéz Monroy	Hacendado	Ovalle	1 000 000
Bernadino Bravo	Industrial y propietario	Santiago	1 000 000
N. Argandoña	—	Concepción	1 000 000
		Total	178 500 000

Source: *El Mercurio* (Valparaíso), LV (No. 1647?), 26 April 1882, p. 2.

SOURCES

I. MANUSCRIPT SOURCES

All collections are held in the Archivo Nacional de Chile, Santiago de Chile, unless otherwise noted.

A. *Archivo del Ministerio de Hacienda*, vols. 111, 152, 250, 304, 306, 318, 362, 403, 412.

B. *Archivo del Ministerio del Interior*, vols. 153, 154, 161, 163, 236, 243, 329, 671.

C. *Colección Judicial*: (Linares) Legajos 81, 88, 97, 98; (Rancagua) Legajos 125, 135, 207; (San Fernando) Legajos 141; (Santiago) Legajos 23, 35, 59, 69, 103, 107, 109, 134, 148, 169, 554; (Talca) Legajos 330, 359, 802.

D. *Colección Notarial*: (Concepción) vol. 49; (Linares) vols. 23, 44; (Rengo) vols. 37, 49, 51, 54, 57, 59, 62, 65, 67, 70, 76, 80, 84, 90, 94, 97, 102, 106, 122, 125; (Santiago) vol. 342; (Talca) vols. 40A, 62, 64, 67, 76, 80A, 83, 88, 90, 96, 97, 98, 102, 111, 113, 115, 117, 119, 122, 123, 124, 125, 126, 313; (Valparaíso) vols. 86, 88.

E. *Contaduría Mayor*, vol. 'Catastro' 1834.

F. *Intendencia de Talca*, vols. 12, 15, 18.

G. *Colección Municipal de Rengo*. In the city of Rengo. Vols. 'Registros de Propiedad' years 1881–90. No volume numbers.

H. *Private records*. Account book of rural estates.
Aculeo: Years 1836–47. In the possession of José Manuel Larraín Echeverría, Santiago.
Cunaco: Years 1842–61. In possession of Manuel Valdés Valdés, Santiago.
El Huique: Years 1853–67. In possession of the González Echenique family in Santiago.
Pichidegua: Fragments for years 1862–80. In possession of Sergio de Toro, Santiago.
Vichiculén: Years 1871–9. In possession of the González Echenique family in Santiago.

II. OFFICIAL PUBLICATIONS

A. *Population censuses, statistics, tax rolls, and agricultural censuses.*

Oficina Central de Estadística. *Censo jeneral de la república de Chile levantado en 1854.* Santiago, 1858.
Cuarto censo jeneral de la población de Chile. (Year 1865) Santiago, 1866.

Sources

Quinto censo jeneral de la población de Chile. (Year 1875) Santiago, 1876.

Sexto censo jeneral de la república. (Year 1885) Santiago, 1885.

Oficina Central de Estadística. *Sétimo censo jeneral de la población de Chile levantado el 28 de noviembre de 1895.* Santiago, 1904.

Dirección general de estadística. *Resultados del X censo de la población efectuado el 27 Noviembre de 1930.* Vol. 1. Santiago, 1931.

Anuario estadístico de Chile. 1861–1926. (To 1915, published by Oficina central de estadística).

Oficina Central de Estadística. *Estadística comercial de Chile.* 1844–1900.

Repertorio nacional. Santiago, 1850.

Estado que manifiesta la renta agrícola de los fundos rústicos que comprende el espresado departamento para duducir el impuesto anual establecido en substitución del diezmo por la lei de 25 oct de 1853. Valparaíso, 1855.

Impuesto agrícola: rol de contribuyentes. Santiago, 1874.

Indice de propietarios rurales i valor de la propiedad rural según los roles de avalúos comunales. Santiago, 1908.

Dirección general de estadística. *Agricultura, 1935-6 censo.* Santiago, 1938.

Servicio nacional de estadística y censo. *III Censo nacional ganadero-april 1955.* 6 vols. Santiago, 195?.

Dirección de estadística y censo. *IV Censo nacional agropecuario, 1964-65.* vols. 6–15. Santiago, 1965.

B. *Congressional and ministerial documents*

Boletín de las leyes y decretos de Chile. I, VII, VIII, XX, XXXIII, XLII.

Sesiones del congreso nacional: cámara de diputados. Years 1857 and 1878.

Sesiones del congreso nacional: cámara de senadores. Years 1852, 1871, and 1882.

Sesiones de los cuerpos lejislativos de la República de Chile 1811 a 1845. (Compiled by Valentín Letelier) Santiago, 1891. Vols. 10, 14.

Memorias Ministerials: 'Hacienda.' 1857–72, 1882.

III. PUBLICATIONS OF
THE NATIONAL SOCIETY OF AGRICULTURE

El Agricultor. 1838–49.

El mensajero de la agricultura. 1856–7.

Boletín de la sociedad nacional de agricultura. 1869–1908.

IV. NEWSPAPERS. All newspapers were consulted in the Biblioteca Nacional, Santiago, Chile.

Correo del Sur (Concepción) 1853.
El Eco (Talca) 1854–60.
El Ferrocarril (Santiago) 1856, 1859.
El Mercurio (Valparaíso) 1828–1910.
El Talquino (Talca) 1850.
La Libertad (Talca) 1880–5.
La Opinión (Santiago) 1875.
La Opinión (Talca) 1872–9.
La República (Santiago) 1877.

Chilean Rural Society

V. BOOKS, ARTICLES, AND PAMPHLETS

Alcaíno, Francisco, 'Estudio de las carnes contagiosas del matadero de Santiago,' *Anales*, vol. LXXV (1889), pp. 455–89.

Amunátegui, Domingo, *Mayorazgos i títulos de Castilla*. 3 vols., Santiago, 1901–4.

Anguita, Ricardo and Quesney, Valerio, *Leyes promulgadas en Chile desde 1810 hasta 1901 inclusive*. 2 vols., Santiago, 1902.

Aranda, Sergio and Martínez, Alberto, 'Estructura económica: algunas características fundamentales,' *Chile hoy*. Santiago (1970), pp. 55–212.

Aránguiz Donoso, Horacio, 'Notas para el estudio de la hacienda de la Calera de Tango,' *Historia* (Catholic University of Chile), no. 6 (1967), pp. 221–62.

Atropos, 'El inquilino en Chile, su vida. un siglo sin variaciones, 1861–1966,' *Mapocho*, vol. 5 (1966), pp. 195–218.

Ballesteros, Marto and Davis, Tom E., 'The growth of output and employment in basic sectors of the Chilean economy, 1908–1957,' *Economic development and social change*, vol. XI, no. 2 (January 1963), pp. 152–76.

Balmaceda, Manuel José, *Manual del hacendado chileno*. Santiago, 1875.

Baraona, Rafael, et al., *Valle de Putaendo*. Santiago, 1960.

Barbier, Jacques, 'Elite and cadres in Bourbon Chile,' *Hispanic American Historical Review*, vol. 52, no. 3 (August 1972), p. 434.

Barría Serón, Jorge, 'Evolucion histórica de Chile de 1910 hasta nuestros dias,' *Anales*, no. 120 (1960), pp. 50–66.

Barros Arana, Diego, *Historia de Chile*. 16 vols., Santiago, 1884–1902.

Barros Arana, Diego, et al., *Cuadro histórico de la administración Montt*. Santiago, 1861.

Barros Grez, Daniel, *Proyecto de división de la Provincia de Colchagua*. Santiago, 1858.

Bauer, Arnold J., 'The Church and Spanish American agrarian structure, 1765–1865,' *The Americas*, vol. XXVIII, no. 1 (July 1971), pp. 78–98.

'The Hacienda el Huique in the agrarian structure of nineteenth-century Chile,' *Agricultural History*, vol. XLVI, no. 4 (October 1972), pp. 455–70.

Bauer, Arnold J. and Johnson, Ann Hagerman, 'Land and labor in rural Chile,' *Patterns of Agrarian Capitalism*. Cambridge, 197?.

Baxley, Henry Willis, *What I saw on the West Coast of South and North America*. New York, 1865.

Bazant, Jan, 'Peones, arrendatarios y aparceros en México, 1851–1853,' *Historia Mexicana*, vol. XXIII, no. 2 (1973), pp. 330–57.

Blakemore, H., *British Nitrates and Chilean politics 1886–1896: Balmaceda and North*. London, 1974.

Blest Gana, Alberto, *Martín Rivas*. (First published in 1862.) Santiago, 1971.

Los trasplantados. Paris, 1904.

Bloch, Marc, *Feudal Society*. (Trans. L. A. Manyon.) 2 vols., Chicago, 1964.

Blum, Jerome, *Noble Landowners and Agriculture in Austria, 1815–1848*. Baltimore, 1943.

Brading, D. A., *Miners and Merchants in Bourbon Mexico 1763–1810*. Cambridge, England, 1971.

Brading, D. A. and Wu, Celia, 'Population growth and crisis in León, 1720–1860,' *Journal of Latin American Studies*, vol. 5, no. 1 (May 1973), pp. 1–36.

Braudel, Fernand, *El Mediterráneo y el mundo mediterráneo en la época de Felipe II*. 2 vols., trans. M. H. Toledo and W. Roces, Mexico City, 1953.

Brown, J. R., 'Nitrate crises, combinations, and the Chilean government in the nitrate age,' *HAHR*, vol. 43, no. 2 (May 1963), pp. 230–46.

Sources

Burkholder, Mark, 'From Creole to *Peninsular*: the transformation of the Audiencia of Lima,' *HAHR*, vol. 52, no. 3 (August 1972), pp. 395–415.

Caldcleugh, Alexander, *Travels in South America During the Years 1819, 1820, 1821.* London, 1825.

Carmagnani, Marcello, 'Banques étrangères et banques nationales au Chile (1900–1920),' *Caravelle*, no. 20 (1973), pp. 31–52.

'Colonial Latin American demography: growth of Chilean population 1700–1830,' *Journal of Social History*, vol. 1, no. 2 (Winter 1967), pp. 179–91.

'Formazione di un mercato coloniale: Cile, 1680–1830,' *Rivista Stórica Italiana* (September 1969), pp. 480–500.

Les mécanismes de la vie économique dans une société coloniale: le Chili, 1680–1830. Paris, 1973.

El salariado minero en Chile colonial. Santiago, 1963.

Sviluppo industriale e sotto-sviluppo económico: il caso cileno (1860–1920). Turin, 1971.

Censo ganadero de la Republica de Chile levantado en el año 1906. Santiago, 1907.

C. G. U., 'Los inquilinos de "El Peumo," ' *BSNA*, vol. vi (1875). *Código Civil de la República de Chile*, ed. revised and corrected. Valparaíso, 1865.

Collier, Simon, *Ideas and Politics of Chilean Independence, 1808–1833.* Cambridge, England, 1967.

Collins, E. J. T., 'Labour supply and demand in European agriculture, 1800–1880', *Agrarian change and economic development.* London, 1969, pp. 61–94.

Comité Interamericano de desarrollo agrícola (CIDA), *Tenencia de la tierra y desarrollo socio-económico del sector agrícola.* Santiago, 1966.

Correa Vergara, Luis, *Agricultura chilena.* 2 vols., Santiago, 1939.

Censo ganadero de la república de Chile levantado en el año 1906. Santiago, 1907.

Cuadra, Pedro Lucía, 'La moneda i los cambios,' *Anales*, vol. 81 (1892), pp. 109–42.

Curtin, Philip, *The Atlantic Slave Trade.* Madison, 1969.

Darwin, Charles, *The Voyage of the Beagle.* Natural History Library ed., Garden City, 1962.

David, Paul, 'The mechanization of reaping in the ante-bellum Midwest,' *Industrialization in two systems.* Ed. Henry Rosovsky. New York, 1966, pp. 3–39.

Davis, Horace, 'California Breadstuffs,' *Journal of Political Economy*, vol. ii (1893–4), pp. 517–35.

Departmento de Agricultura, *Estudio sobre el estado de la agricultura chileno.* Santiago, 1929.

Diccionario biográfico de Chile. 13th ed., Santiago, 1967.

Dominguez, Ramón, *Nuestro sistemo de inquilinaje.* Santiago, 1867.

Donoso, Ricardo, *Las ideas políticas en Chile.* 2nd ed., Santiago, 1967.

Dovring, Folke, 'The transformation of European Agriculture,' *Cambridge Economic History of Europe*, vol. vi, part ii. Cambridge (1965), pp. 604–72.

Drouilly, M., and Cuadra, Pedro Lucío, 'Ensayo sobre el estado económico de la agricultura en Chile,' *BSNA*, vol. x (1878).

Dunsdorfs, Edgars, *The Australian Wheat-Growing Economy 1788–1948.* New York, 1956.

Echeverría, Felix, 'Las máquinas y el trabajador agrícola,' *BSNA*, vol. ii (1870).

Edgar, William C., *The Story of a Grain of Wheat.* New York, 1903.

Edwards Matte, Guillermo, *El club de la unión en sus ochenta años, 1864–1944.* Santiago, 1944.

Edwards Vives, Alberto, *La fronda aristocrática*, 6th ed., Santiago, 1966.

Encina, Francisco, *Historia de Chile*. 4th ed., 20 vols., Santiago, 1955.

Nuestra inferioridad económica. 2nd ed., Santiago, 1955.

Encina, Francisco, *et al.*, 'La subdivisión de la propiedad rural en Chile en 1919,' *Mapocho*, vol. 13, no. 1 (1966), pp. 20–9.

Erasmus, Charles, 'Reciprocal Labor: A study of its Occurrence and Disappearance among Farming People in Latin America' (Ph.D. diss., University of California, Berkeley, 1955).

Escobar Cerda, Luis, *El Mercado de valores*. Santiago, 1959.

Espinoza, E., *Jeografía de Chile*. 5th ed., Santiago, 1903.

'Estatutos del banco de Valparaiso,' Valparaíso, 1854.

Eyzaguirre, Jaime, *Chile durante el gobierno de Errázuriz Echáurren: 1896–1901*. Santiago, 1957.

El conde de la conquista. Santiago, 1966.

Faron, Louis, *The Mapuche Indians of Chile*. New York, 1968.

Feliu Cruz, Guillermo, 'Un esquema de la evolución social de Chile en el siglo hasta 1891,' *Chile visto a través de Agustín Ross*. Santiago, 1950, pp. 19–40.

'La evolución política, económica y social de Chile,' *Anales*, no. 119 (1960), pp. 45–85.

Imágenes de Chile, Santiago, 1937.

Notas para una bibliografía sobre viajeros relativos a Chile. Santiago, 1965.

Santiago a comienzos del siglo XIX: crónicas de los viajeros. Santiago, 1970.

Feliu Cruz, Guillermo and Stuardo Ortiz, Carlos, *Correspondencia de Claudio Gay*. Trans. Villablanca, Luis. Santiago, 1962.

Feliú Silva, Guillermo, 'Medio siglo de la industria chilena,' *Anales*, no. 120 (September–December 1960), pp. 111–25.

Felstiner, Mary Lowenthal, 'The Larraín family in the independence of Chile, 1780–1830,' Unpublished Ph.D. diss. in History, Stanford, 1970.

Ferns, H. S., *Britain and Argentina in the Nineteenth Century*. Oxford, 1960.

Fetter, Frank W., *Monetary Inflation in Chile*. Princeton, 1931.

Figueroa, Pedro Pablo, *Diccionario biográfico de estranjeros en Chile*. Santiago, 1900.

Figueroa, Virgilio, *Diccionario histórico y biográfico de Chile*. 5 vols. in 4, Santiago, 1925–31.

Forster, Robert, 'Obstacles to Agricultural Growth in eighteenth-century France,' *American Historical Review*, vol. LXXV, no. 6 (October 1970), pp. 1600–15.

Frank, Andrew Gunder, *Capitalism and Underdevelopment in Latin America*. New York, 1967.

Friedmann, John and Lackington, Tomás, 'Hyperurbanization and national development in Chile: some hypotheses,' *Urban Affairs Quarterly*, vol. II, no. 4 (June 1967), pp. 3–29.

Galdames, Luis. *A History of Chile*. Trans. and ed. I. J. Cox. Chapel Hill, N.C., 1941.

Jeografía económica de Chile. Santiago, 1911. Gay, Claudio. *Historia físca y política de Chile: Agricultura*. 2 vols., Paris, 1862–5.

Gilliss, Lieut. J. M. *The U.S. Naval Astronomical Expedition to the Southern Hemisphere during the Years 1849–'50–'51–'52*. Washington, 1855. vol. I (Chile).

Góngora, Mario. *Encomenderos y estancieros*. Santiago. 1970.

El estado en el derecho indiano. Santiago, 1951.

Origen de los 'inquilinos' de Chile central. Santiago, 1960.

'Vagabundaje y sociedad fronteriza en Chile (siglos XVII a XIX),' *Cuadernos del Centro de Estudios Socioeconómicos*, no. 2. Santiago, 1966.

Sources

Góngora, Mario and Borde, Jean. *Evolución de la propiedad rural en el valle del Puangue.* 2 vols., Santiago, 1956.

González, Marcial. 'Nuestro enemigo el lujo,' *Estudios económicos,* Santiago (1889), pp. 429–62.

González Pomés, Maria Isabel. 'La economienda indígena en Chile durante el siglo XVIII,' *Historia* (Catholic University of Chile), no. 5 (1966), pp. 5–103.

Gosselman, Carl August. *Informes sobre los estados sudamericanos en los años 1837–1938.* Intro. by Magnus Morner, trans. from the Swedish by Ernesto Dethorey. Stockholm, 1962.

Graham, Maria. *Journal of a residence in Chile during the year 1822.* London, 1824.

Greve, Ernesto. 'Mensuras de Ginés de Lillo,' Colección de Historiadores de *Chile,* vol. 48, Santiago, 1941, pp. ix-xi.

Guevara, Tomás. *Historia de Curicó.* Santiago, 1890.

Halperin Donghi, Tulio. *Historia Contempóranea de América Latina.* Madrid, 1969.

Head, Francis. *Rough Notes Taken During Some Rapid Journeys Across the Pampas and Among the Andes 1825–6.* London, 1826.

Heise González, Julio. 'La constitución de 1925 y las nuevas tendencias políticos-sociales,' *Anales,* no. 80 (1950), pp. 95–234.

Hernández, Silva. 'Transformaciones technológicas en la agricultura de Chile central. Siglo XIX,' *Cuadernos del centro de estudios socioeconómicos.* Santiago (1966), no. 3, pp. 1–31.

Herrera, Rafael, 'Memoria sobre la hacienda "Las Condes" en 1895,' Intro. Gonzales Izquierdo, *Boletin de la Academia Chilena de la Historia,* no. 79 (1968), pp. 121–205.

Herrick, Bruce. *Urban migration and economic development in Chile.* Cambridge, Mass., 1965.

Hirschman, Albert O. *Journeys toward progress.* New York, 1963.

Horvitz, Maria Eugenia. 'Ensayo sobre el crédito en Chile colonial,' (Unpublished *Memoria* in the Faculty of Philosophy and Letters, University of Chile, 1966).

Hurley, Edward N. *Banking and Credit in Argentina, Brazil, Chile, and Peru.* Washington, 1914.

Hurtado Ruiz-Tagle, Carlos. *Concentración de la población y desarrollo económico: el caso chileno.* Santiago, 1966.

Illanes Adaro, Graciela. 'Sentimiento estético de la literatura chilena,' *Anales* (1939), pp. 201–41.

Instituto geográfico militar. *Atlas de la república de Chile.* 2nd. ed., Santiago, 1970.

Izquierdo, Gonzalo. *Un estudio de las ideologias chilenas: la sociedad de agricultura en el siglo XIX.* Santiago, 1968.

Jara, Alvaro. *Guerre et société au Chili: essai de sociologie coloniale.* Paris, 1961.

   'Importaciones de trabajadores indígenas en el siglo XVII,' *Revista Chilena de Historia y Geografía,* no. 124, pp. 177–212.

   'Lazos de dependencia personal y adscripción de los indios a la tierre en la American española: el caso de Chile,' *Cahiers du monde hispanique et luso-brésilien, Caravelle,* no. 20 (1973), pp. 51–67.

   'Salario en una economía caracterizada por las relaciones de dependencia personal,' *Revista Chilena de Historia y Geografía,* no. 133 (1965), pp. 40–60.

Jobet, Julio César. *Ensayo crítico del desarrollo económico y social de Chile.* Santiago, 1955.

Kahan, Arcadius. 'Notes on Serfdom in Western and Eastern Europe,' *Journal of Economic History*, vol. XXXIII, no. 1 (March 1973), pp. 86–99.

Kaufman, Robert R. *The politics of land reform in Chile, 1950–1970*. Cambridge, Mass., 1972.

Kay, Cristóbal, 'Comparative development of the European manorial system and the Latin American hacienda system: an approach to a theory of agrarian change for Chile,' (unpublished Ph.D. diss., University of Sussex, England, 1971).

'The development of the Chilean hacienda system, 1850–1972,' to appear in *Patterns of Agrarian Capitalism*. Cambridge (1975).

Keller, Carlos. *Una revolución en la agricultura*. Santiago, 1956.

Kieniewicz, Stefan. *The emancipation of the Polish peasantry*. Chicago, 1969.

Kirkland, John. *Three centuries of prices of wheat, bread and flour*. London, 1917.

Kirsch, Henry. 'The industrialization of Chile, 1880–1930,' (unpublished Ph.D. diss., University of Florida, 1973).

Klimpel Alvarado, Felicitas. *La mujer Chilena El aporte feminino al progreso de Chile, 1910–1960*. Santiago, 1962.

Laclau, Ernesto. 'Modos de producción, sistemas económicos y Población excedente: aproximación histórica a los casos argentinos y chileno,' *Revista Latinoamericana de Sociología*, vol. V, no. 2, Santiago (July 1969), pp. 276–342.

Ladin, Jay. 'Mortgage credit in Tippecanoe County, Indiana, 1865–1880,' *Agricultural History*, vol. XLI, no. 1 (January 1967), pp. 37–44.

Lafond de Lurcy, Gabriel. *Viaje a Chile* (first pub. 1844). Santiago, 1970.

Lambert, Jacques. *Latin America*. Trans. Helen Katel, Berkeley, 1967.

Larraín, Carlos J. *El Huique*. Buenos Aires, 1944.

Las Condes. Santiago, 1952.

Latcham, Ricardo. 'Ethnology of the Araucanos,' *Journal of the Royal Anthropological Institute*, vol. 39 (1909), pp. 334–70.

Latorre Subercaseaux, Adolfo. 'Relación entre el circulante y los precios en Chile,' *Memoria* in the Catholic University of Chile, Santiago, 1958.

León, Victor. *Uvas y vinos de Chile*. Santiago, 1947.

Letelier, Valentín, comp. *Sesiones de los cuerpos lejislativos de la República de Chile 1811–1845*. Santiago, 1891.

Levin, Jonathan. *The export economies*. Cambridge, Mass., 1960.

Lindsay, Santiago. *Noticia preliminar del censo jeneral de la Republica*. Santiago, 1875.

Lipsey, Robert E. *Price and Quantity Trends in the Foreign Trade of the United States*. Princeton, N.J., 1965.

Lockhart, James, 'Economienda and Hacienda; the Evolution of the Great Estate in the Spanish Indies,' *Hispanic American Historical Review*, vol. 49, no. 3 (August 1969), pp. 411–29.

Loveman, Brian. 'Property, politics and rural labor: agrarian reform in Chile, 1919–1972,' (unpublished Ph.D. diss. in Political Science, University of Indiana, 1973).

Malenbaum, Wilfred. *The World Wheat Economy: 1855–1939*. Cambridge, Mass., 1953.

Mamalakis, Markos and Reynolds, Clark. *Essays on the Chilean Economy*. Homewood, Ill., 1965.

Manual o instucción para los subdelegados e inspectores en Chile. Santiago, 1860.

Marten, E. E. 'The Development of Wheat Culture in the San Joaquín Valley 1846–1900,' (unpublished Master's thesis in History, University of California at Berkeley).

Sources

Martin, Gene. *La división de la tierra en Chile central.* Santiago, 1960.

Maury, M. F. *Explanations and Sailing Directions to Accompany the Wind and Current Charts.* 1850.

Medina, José Toribio. *Las monedas chilenas.* Santiago, 1902.

Melfi, Domingo. 'La novela casa grande y la transformación de la sociedad chilena,' *Anales* (1948), pp. 239–57.

Mellafe, Rolando. *La introducción de la esclavitud negra en Chile.* Santiago, 1959.

'Memoria . . . del banco de Valparaiso,' Valparaíso, 1858.

'Memoria que la sociedad de fomento fabril presenta sobre el concurso de molinería,' Santiago, 1892.

Menandier, Julio. 'Aforismos sobre la molinería nacional,' *BSNA,* vol. XVII (1885).

'La hacienda de Viluco,' *BSNA,* vol. III (1872).

'El porvenir de nuestro cultivo i comercio de trigo,' *BSNA,* vol. XII (1880).

Miers, John. 'La agricultura en Chile en 1825,' *Mensajero,* 2 (1856).

Travels in Chile and La Plata (1819–35). 2 vols., London, 1826.

Moltoni, Paola. 'Il passaggio dalla conduzione diretta all' affittanza capitalista nell, economia agraria cilena: il caso dell' hacienda "El melón" nel Cile centrale (1890–1898),' (thesis in History, University of Turin, 1972).

Moore, Barrington, Jr. *Social Origins of Dictatorship and Democracy: Lord and Peasant in the Making of the Modern World.* Boston, 1967.

Mörner, Magnus. 'A Comparative Study of Tenent Labor in Parts of Europe, Africa, and Latin America 1700–1900: A Preliminary Report of a Research Project in Social History,' *Latin American Research Review,* 5, no. 2 (1970), 3–15.

'The Spanish American hacienda: a critical survey of recent research and debate,' *Hispanic American Historical Review,* vol. 53, no. 2 (May 1973), pp. 183–216.

Morris, James O. *Elites, Intellectuals, and Consensus.* Ithaca, N.Y., 1966.

Morse, Richard (ed.)., *The Urban Development of Latin America 1750–1920.* Stanford, 1971.

Muñoz, Oscar. *Crecimiento industrial de Chile, 1914–1965.* Santiago, 1968.

McBride, George. *Chile: Land and Society.* Baltimore, 1936.

Opazo, Gustavo M. *Historia de Talca 1742–1942.* Santiago, 1942.

Opazo, Roberto. *Ha disminuido la fertilidad de los suelos en nuestro pais?* Santiago, 1934.

'Opinión del comercio de Valparaíso sobre bancos de emisión,' Valparaíso, 1855.

Orrego Luco, Agusto. 'La cuestion social en Chile,' *Anales* (January–June 1961), pp. 43–55.

Ortúzar, Adolfo. *Chile of Today.* New York, 1907.

Ots Capdequí, José Maria. *El estado Español en las Indias.* Mexico, 1957.

Manual de historia del derecho español en las Indias y el derecho propiamente indiano. 2 vols., Buenos Aires, 1943.

Palma, Alejo. *Historia de la hipoteca especial en Chile.* Santiago, 1866.

Perez Rosales, Vicente. *Recuerdos del pasado.* 6th ed., Santiago, 1958.

Periera Salas, Eugenio. 'Architectura chilena,' *Anales* (1956), Santiago, pp. 7–42.

'El desenvolvimiento histórico–étnico de la población,' *Geografia economica de Chile.* Santiago, 1967, pp. 337–56.

Petras, J. and Zemelman, H. *Peasants in Revolt.* Austin, 1972.

Pike, Frederick. 'Aspects of class relations in Chile, 1850–1960,' *Latin America: Reform and Revolution.* Ed. by James Petras and Maurice Zeitlin. New York, 1968, pp. 202–19.

Chile and the United States 1880–1962. University of Notre Dame, 1963.

255

Pinochet Le-Brun, Tancredo. 'Inquilinos en la hacienda de su Excelencia,' *Antolgia Chilena de la Tierra*, Santiago, 1970, pp. 81–112.

Pinto Santa Cruz, Aníbal. *Chile, un caso de desarrollo frustrado.* 2nd ed., Santiago, 1962.

'Desarrollo económico y relaciones socials,' *Chile hoy*, pp. 9–18.

Platt, D. C. M. *Latin America and the British Trade 1806–1914.* London, 1972.

Poblete Troncoso, Moisés. *El problema de la producción agrícola y la politica agraria nacional.* Santiago, 1919.

Pöeppig, Eduard. *Un testigo en la alborada de Chile 1826–29.* Trans. Carlos Keller, Santiago, 1960.

Poirier, Eduardo. *Chile in 1910.* Santiago, 1910.

Polanyi, Karl. *The Great Transformation.* Boston, 1968.

Prado, Santiago. 'El Inquilinaje en el departamento de Caupolicán,' *BSNA*, vol. II (1871).

Primer censo de la República Argentina verificado en los dias 15, 16, 17 setiembre, 1869. Buenos Aires, 1872.

'Proyecto de un ferrocarril a vapor entre la ciudad de Talca y el puerto de Constitución,' Valparaíso, 1879.

Ramírez Necochea, Hernán. *Historia del movimiento obrero.* Santiago, 1957.

Ramos, Demetrio. *Trigo chileno, navieros del Callao y hacendados limeños entre la crisis agrícola del siglo XVII y la comercial de la primera mitad del XVIII.* Madrid, 1967.

Rasmussen, Wayne D. 'The impact of technological change on American agriculture,' *Journal of Economic History*, vol. XXII (1962), pp. 578–91.

Reinsch, Paul S. 'Parliamentary government in Chile,' *The American Political Science Review*, vol. III (1909), pp. 507–38.

'Representación al Supremo Gobierno sobre la reforma de la lejislación,' Valparaíso, 1851, pp. 1–17.

Resúmen de la hacienda publica de Chile desde 1833 hasta 1914. London, 1914.

Rogin, Leo. *The introduction of farm machinery . . . during the nineteenth century.* Berkeley, 1931.

Román, Manuel. *Diccionario de Chilenismos.* Santiago, 1913.

Romano, Ruggiero. *Una economía colonial: Chile en el siglo XVIII.* Buenos Aires, 1965.

'La "tesis" de Frank,' *Desarrollo económico.*

Rosales, Francisco Javier. *Progresos de la agricultura Europea y mejoras practicables en la de Chile.* Paris, 1855.

Ross, Agustín. *Chile, 1851–1910. Sesenta años de cuestiones monetarias y financieras.* Santiago, 1911.

Rumbold, Horace. *Reports by Her Majesty's Secretaries . . . on the Manufactures, Commerce, Etc.* London, 1876.

Ruschenberger, Wm S. W. *Three Years in the Pacific (1831–34).* Philadelphia, 1834.

Rutter, W. P. *Wheat growing in Canada, the United States, and the Argentine.* London, 1911.

Safford, Frank. 'Social aspects of politics in nineteenth-century Spanish America,' *Journal of Social History* (1972), pp. 344–70.

Santa Maria, Domingo. *Memoria del intendente de Colchagua.* Santiago, 1848.

Santelices, Ramón. *Apuntes para una memoria sobre los bancos Chilenos.* Santiago, 1889.

Los banco Chilenos. Santiago, 1893.

Los bancos de emisión. Santiago, 1900.

Sources

Saunders, M. H. 'California Wheat 1867–1910; Influences of Transportation on the Export Trade and the Location of the Producing Areas,' (unpublished Master's thesis in Geography, University of California at Berkeley, 1960).

Schneider, Teodoro. *La agricultura en Chile durante los últimos cincuenta años*. Santiago, 1904.

Scobie, James R. *Revolution on the Pampas: A social history of Argentine Wheat 1860–1910*. Austin, 1964.

Segall, Marcelo. *Desarrollo del capitalismo en Chile*. Santiago, 1953.

Sepúlveda, Sergio. *El trigo chileno en el mercado mundial*. Santiago, 1956.

Seura Salvo, Carlos. 'Tipos chilenos en la novela y en el cuerto naccional,' *Anales*, 3rd series (1937), pp. 5–85.

Severson, Robert *et al.* 'Mortgage borrowing as a frontier developed; a study of mortgages in Champaign County, Illinois, 1836–1895,' *Journal of Economic History*, vol. XXVI, no. 2 (June 1966), 147–68.

Silva Castro, Raul (ed). *Artículos de costumbres*. Santiago, 195?.

Silva Vargas, Fernando. *Tierras y pueblos de indios en el Reino del Chile*. Santiago, 1962.

Slicher Van Bath, B. H. *The Agrarian History of Western Europe A.D. 500–1850*. Trans. from Dutch by Olive Ordish. London, 1963.

Solberg, Carl. *Immigration and nationalism: Argentina and Chile 1890–1914*. University of Texas Press, 1970.

Statistical History of the United States from colonial times to the present. Stanford, 1965.

Stewart, Watt. *El trabajador Chileno y los ferro-carriles del Perú*. Santiago, 1939.

Stone, Lawrence. 'News from everywhere' (review of Barrington Moore, Jr, *Social Origins of Dictatorship and Democracy*), *The New York Review of Books*, vol. 9, no. 31 (24 August 1967).

Storck, John and Teague, Walter. *Flour for Man's Bread*. Minneapolis, 1952.

Subercaseaux, Benjamin. *Chile, a geographic extravaganza*. Trans. from the Spanish by Angel Flores, New York, 1943.

Subercaseaux, Guillermo. *El sistema monetario i la organización bancaria en Chile*. Santiago, 1921.

Subercaseaux, Ramon. *Memorias de ochenta años*. 2nd ed., 2 vols., Santiago, 1936.

Sunkel, Osvaldo. 'Change and frustration in Chile,' in Véliz, *Obstacles to Change*, pp. 116–44.

Thayer Ojeda, Luis. *Elementos etnicos que han intervenido e nla población de Chile*. Santiago, 1919.

Navarros and vascongados en Chile. Santiago, 1904.

Tocornal, Enrique. *Análisis comparado de nuestra legislación hipotecaria*. Santiago, 1859.

Tornero, Recaredo S. *Chile ilustrado, guía descriptivo*. Valparaíso, 1872.

Tracy, Michael. *Agriculture in Western Europe*. New York, 1964.

Twentieth Century Impressions of Chile. London, 1915.

Urízar Garfias, Fernando, *Estadística de la República de Chile: provincia de Maule*. Santiago, 1845.

Repertio Chileno. Santiago, 1835.

Valdes Vicuña, Samuel. *La solución del gran problema del dia*. Santiago, 1895.

Valdivia, Pedro de. *Cartas*. Intro. by Jaime Eyzaguirre. Santiago, 1955.

Valencia Avaria, Luis. *Anales de la república*. 2 vols. Santiago, 1951.

Valenzuela, Juvenal O. *Album de informacion agrícolas; zona central de Chile*. Santiago, 1923.

Vayssiere, Pierre. 'La division internationale du travail et la denationalisation du cuivre chilien, 1880–1920. *Caravelle*, no. 20 (1973), pp. 7–30.

Véliz, Claudio. *Historia de la marina mercante de Chile.* Santiago, 1961.

'La mesa de tres patas,' *Desarrollo económico*, vol. 3, nos. 1–2 (April–September 1963), pp. 231–47.

Véliz, Claudio (ed.). *Obstacles to Change in Latin America.* Oxford, 1965.

Vergara, Roberto, *Historia y fines de los censos.* Santiago, 1930.

Vicuña, Pedro Félix. *Cartas sobre bancos.* Valparaíso, 1945.

Vicuña Mackenna, Benjamin. *Paginas de ni diario durante tres años de viaje 1853–1855.* Santiago, 1856.

Villalobos, Sergio. *Comercio y Contrabando en el Rio de la Plata y Chile.* Buenos Aires, 1965.

El comercio y la crisis colonial. Santiago, 1968.

Vitale, Luis. *Interpretación marxista de la historia de Chile.* 2nd ed., 3 vols., Santiago, 1967–71.

von Hagen, Victor (ed.), *The Incas of Pedro Cieza de León.* Trans. Harriet de Onís. Norman. Okla., 1959.

Weber, Max. *General Economic History.* New York, 1961.

Williams, Raymond. *The Country and the City.* Oxford, 1973.

Wilson, Henry Lane. *Diplomatic Episodes in Mexico, Belgium, and Chile.* New York, 1927.

Wolf, Eric. *Sons of the Shaking Earth.* Chicago, 1959.

Wright, Marie. *The Republic of Chile.* Philadelphia, 1904.

Wright, Thomas C. 'Origins of the politics of inflation in Chile, 1888–1918.' *HAHR*, vol. 53, no. 2 (May 1973), pp. 239–59.

'The Sociedad Nacional de Agricultura in Chilean politics, 1869–1938,' (unpublished Ph.D. diss., University of California, Berkeley, 1971).

Zapiola José. *Recuerdos de treinta años, 1810–1840.* 8th ed., Santiago, 1945.

INDEX

Index

export economy, 174, 180–1, 228–30; concept of, 78–80 (figure); impact on social systems, 77–8, 174, 211, 215, 217, compared with Argentina, 212, compared with U.S.A. and Europe, 214–5; relationship with agriculture, 77–82; *see also* mining

Eyzaguirre, Jaime, 21n, 25n, 224n

Felstiner, Mary, 22n, 24n

Fetter, Frank W., 107

feudal system, 8; debate over, 10–12

flour milling, 64–7; American technicians in, 83n; compared with Budapest and Minneapolis, 66–7; *see also* wheat (and flour) export trade

Frank, Andrew G., 23–4n

freight rates, *see* transportation; railways

fundos, see estates, large; haciendas

Gay, Claudio, xiv, 51–2, 54, 60n, 74, 147, 162

gañanes, *see* laborers, agricultural

Gibbs, Anthony, company of, 87

Gilliss, Lt J. M., 27, 46, 53

Góngora, Mario, 6, 8, 10, 13, 22n

Graham, Maria Dundas, 14, 30, 47, 117, 185

hacienda(s), in central Chile; Aculeo 19, 35, 89, 101, 121, 187–8; Bucalemu, 21; Calera de Tango, 18; Cauquenes, 21, 185; La Compañía, 19, 56, 121, 131; Cunaco, 19, 88; El Guaico, 182–3; El Huique, 35, 138, 139, 177; Las Condes, 127, 167; Rio Colorado, 127, 130; Vichiculén, 153–4; Viluco, 122, 161, 185–6; *see also* estates, large

hacienda community, 134–5, 138, 165–6, 170

hacienda houses, furnishings of, 177; in colonial epoch, 12; in El Guaico, 182; sparseness of, 35, 49

hacienda store (*pulpería*): importance of, 96 (inventory, Appendix V); rôle in rural drinking

horticulture, 10, 99; grants for, 4–5; Indian practice, 13; in San Felipe, 127; and sharecroppers, 80

Hurtado Ruiz-Tagle, Carlos, 209

Indian lands, usurpation of, 4

Indians, assimilation of, 14, 46–7; ethnic groups, 2 (map); Huarpe group, 7; insurrection (1599), 6; low status of, 7–8; pre-Hispanic settlement of 5, 47

industry and industrialists, 204, 210; artisan, 42–3; cottage, 40, 53–4; impact of imports on, 54; investment in, 214 (table); listed on stock exchange, 209; State encouragement of, 226–7

inflation: landowner culpability in, 106–7; and mortgage credit, 106

inheritance practice, 130, 176; in Edwards family, 194; on El Guaico, 183–4; of *mayorazgos*, 20–1; *see also* estates, large, subdivision of

inquilinos, see service tenants

interest rates, 93, 96, 98–9 (tables)

Irarrázabal Larraín, Manuel José, 188

irrigation, 105–6; on La Compañía, 19; compared with dry land, 196; importance of, 120–1; related to miners, 106

Izquierdo, Gonzalo, 171n

Jara, Alvaro, 11, 22n

Kay, Cristóbal, 114n

Keller, Carlos, xiv

Kirsch, Henry, 209, 213

laborers, agricultural; habits and customs, 148; in conjunction with service tenants, 159–60, 168; migration of peons, 146, 151–2; need in wheat harvest, 150; peons, 135, 145–59; resistance to labor discipline, 148; shortage of hands, 149–51 (table); *see also* population, 'floating'; service tenants; slavery; wages

laborers, industrial, 174, 220–2; Marxism, attraction to, 81, 220; political organisation, 220; rural origins of, 146; strikes, 220–1

La Ligua, Department of, 124 (table)

Index